Fantastic Four 4

Point of Origin

Ben and Alicia's honeymoon didn't go quite as planned, but they have returned to their quiet life on Yancy Street. But when it comes to the Fantastic Four family, things never stay quiet for long...not if Reed Richards can help it!

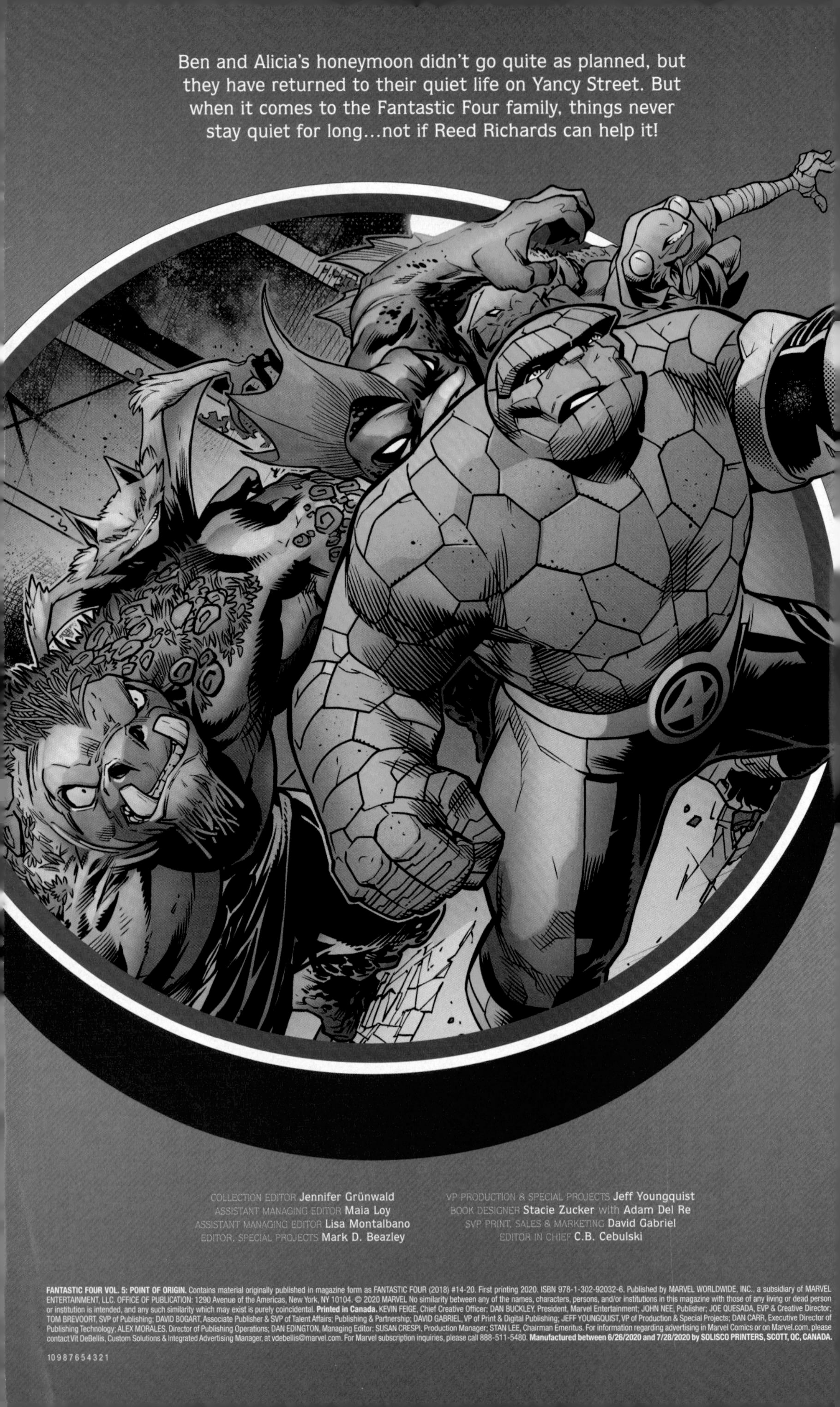

COLLECTION EDITOR Jennifer Grünwald
ASSISTANT MANAGING EDITOR Maia Loy
ASSISTANT MANAGING EDITOR Lisa Montalbano
EDITOR, SPECIAL PROJECTS Mark D. Beazley
VP PRODUCTION & SPECIAL PROJECTS Jeff Youngquist
BOOK DESIGNER Stacie Zucker with Adam Del Re
SVP PRINT, SALES & MARKETING David Gabriel
EDITOR IN CHIEF C.B. Cebulski

FANTASTIC FOUR VOL. 5: POINT OF ORIGIN. Contains material originally published in magazine form as FANTASTIC FOUR (2018) #14-20. First printing 2020. ISBN 978-1-302-92032-6. Published by MARVEL WORLDWIDE, INC., a subsidiary of MARVEL ENTERTAINMENT, LLC. OFFICE OF PUBLICATION: 1290 Avenue of the Americas, New York, NY 10104. © 2020 MARVEL No similarity between any of the names, characters, persons, and/or institutions in this magazine with those of any living or dead person or institution is intended, and any such similarity which may exist is purely coincidental. **Printed in Canada.** KEVIN FEIGE, Chief Creative Officer; DAN BUCKLEY, President, Marvel Entertainment; JOHN NEE, Publisher; JOE QUESADA, EVP & Creative Director; TOM BREVOORT, SVP of Publishing; DAVID BOGART, Associate Publisher & SVP of Talent Affairs; Publishing & Partnership; DAVID GABRIEL, VP of Print & Digital Publishing; JEFF YOUNGQUIST, VP of Production & Special Projects; DAN CARR, Executive Director of Publishing Technology; ALEX MORALES, Director of Publishing Operations; DAN EDINGTON, Managing Editor; SUSAN CRESPI, Production Manager; STAN LEE, Chairman Emeritus. For information regarding advertising in Marvel Comics or on Marvel.com, please contact Vit DeBellis, Custom Solutions & Integrated Advertising Manager, at vdebellis@marvel.com. For Marvel subscription inquiries, please call 888-511-5480. **Manufactured between 6/26/2020 and 7/28/2020 by SOLISCO PRINTERS, SCOTT, QC, CANADA.**

10 9 8 7 6 5 4 3 2 1

A brilliant scientist — his best friend — the woman he loved — and her
fiery-tempered kid brother! Together, they braved the unknown terrors of outer space
and were changed by cosmic rays into something more than merely human! They became the...

FANTASTIC FOUR

Point of Origin

Dan Slott
WRITER

Paco Medina (#14-15, #18, #20), **Sean Izaakse** (#16-17, #19),
Bob Quinn (#15, #17), **Luciano Vecchio** (#17),
Carlos Magno (#17-18) & **Francesco Manna** (#18)
ARTISTS

Jesus Aburtov (#14-15, #20), **Marcio Menyz** (#16, #19) &
Erick Arciniega (#17-19)
COLOR ARTISTS

VC's Joe Caramagna (#14-16, #20) & **Travis Lanham** (#17-18)
LETTERERS

Mike Deodato Jr. & **Romulo Fajardo Jr.** (#14) and
Nick Bradshaw & **John Rauch** (#15-20)
COVER ART

Shannon Andrews Ballesteros
ASSISTANT EDITOR

Martin Biro
ASSISTANT EDITOR

Alanna Smith
ASSOCIATE EDITOR

Tom Brevoort
EDITOR

The Fantastic Four created by Stan Lee & Jack Kirby

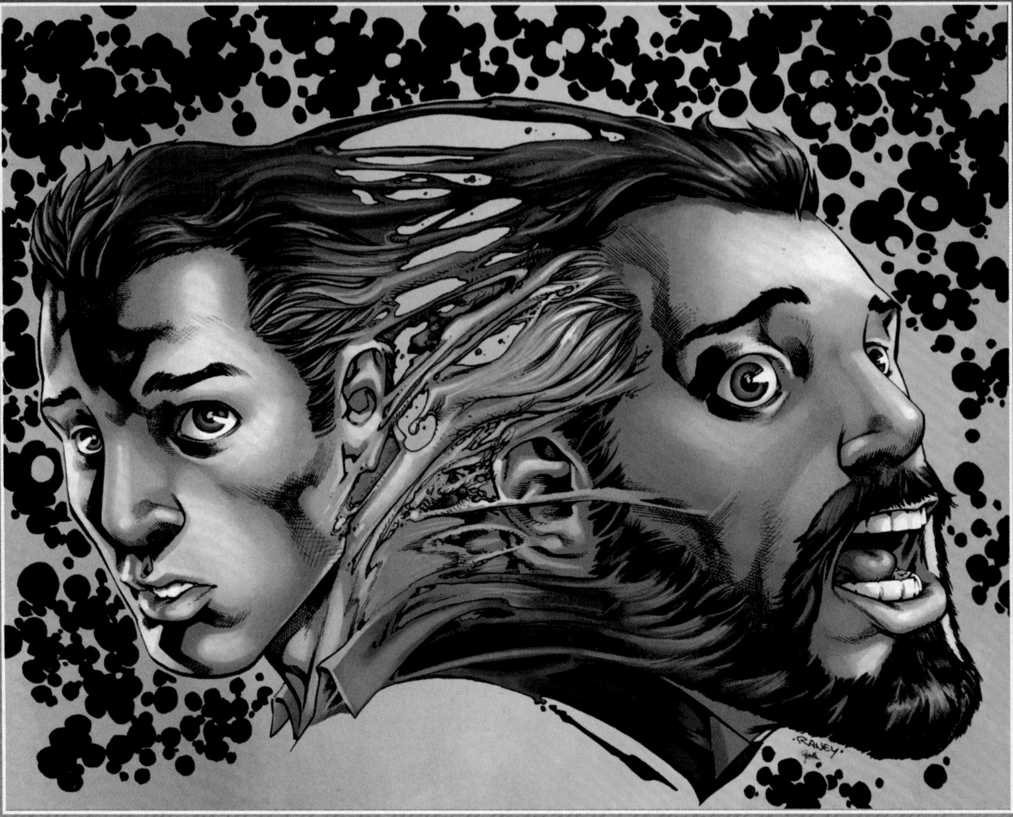

#14 Immortal variant by
Tom Raney & **Rachelle Rosenberg**

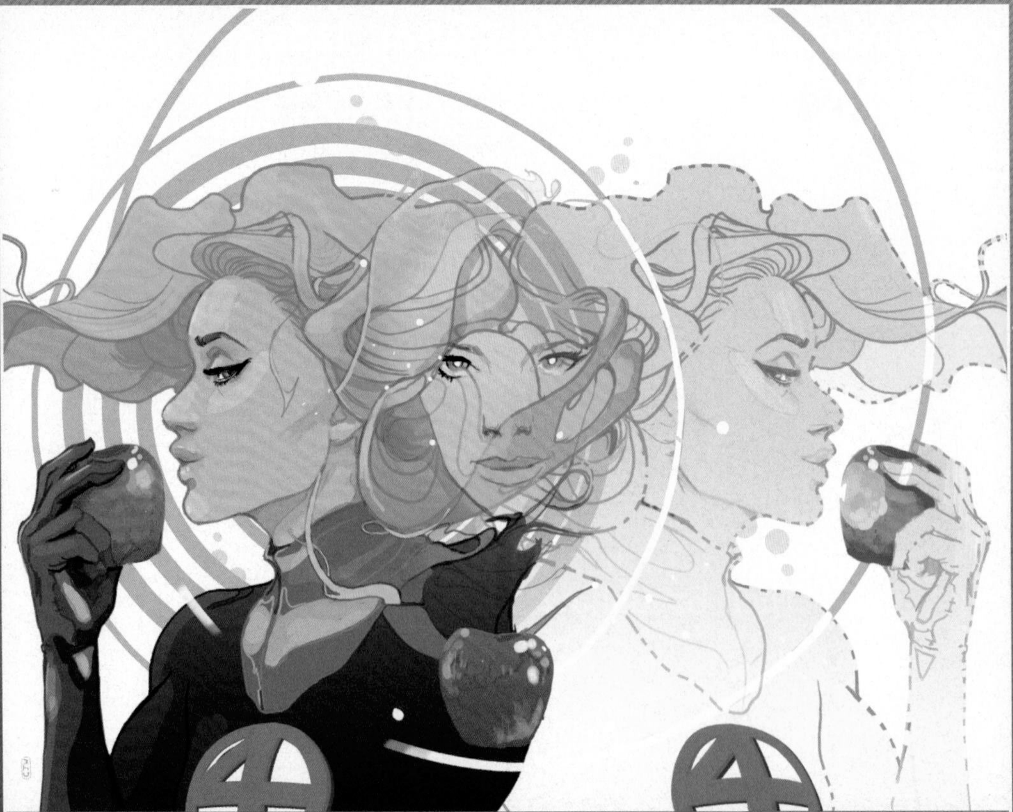

#14 Immortal variant by
Christian Ward

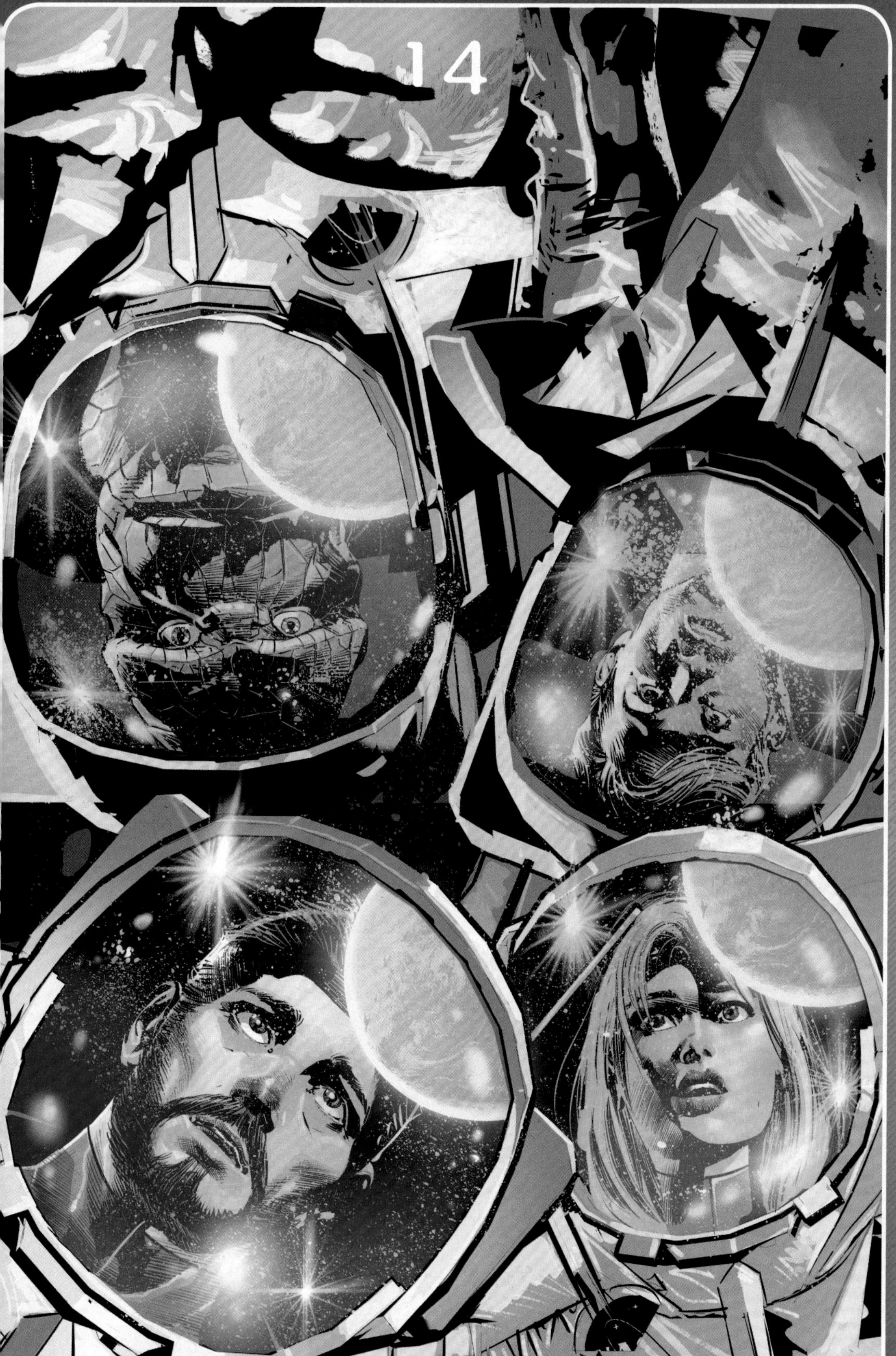
14

"Wanderlust"

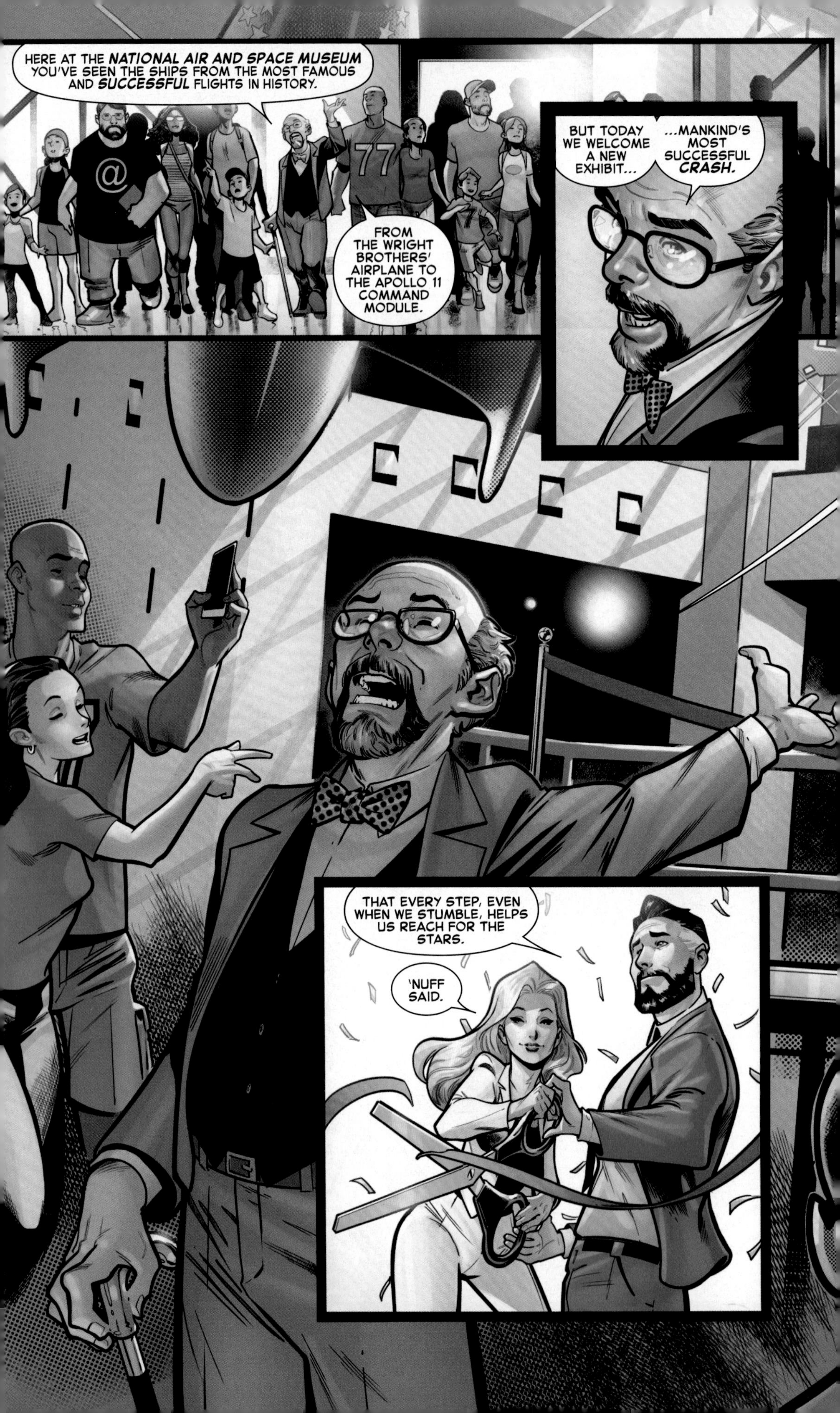
HERE AT THE NATIONAL AIR AND SPACE MUSEUM YOU'VE SEEN THE SHIPS FROM THE MOST FAMOUS AND SUCCESSFUL FLIGHTS IN HISTORY.
FROM THE WRIGHT BROTHERS' AIRPLANE TO THE APOLLO 11 COMMAND MODULE.
BUT TODAY WE WELCOME A NEW EXHIBIT...
...MANKIND'S MOST SUCCESSFUL CRASH.
THAT EVERY STEP, EVEN WHEN WE STUMBLE, HELPS US REACH FOR THE STARS.
'NUFF SAID.

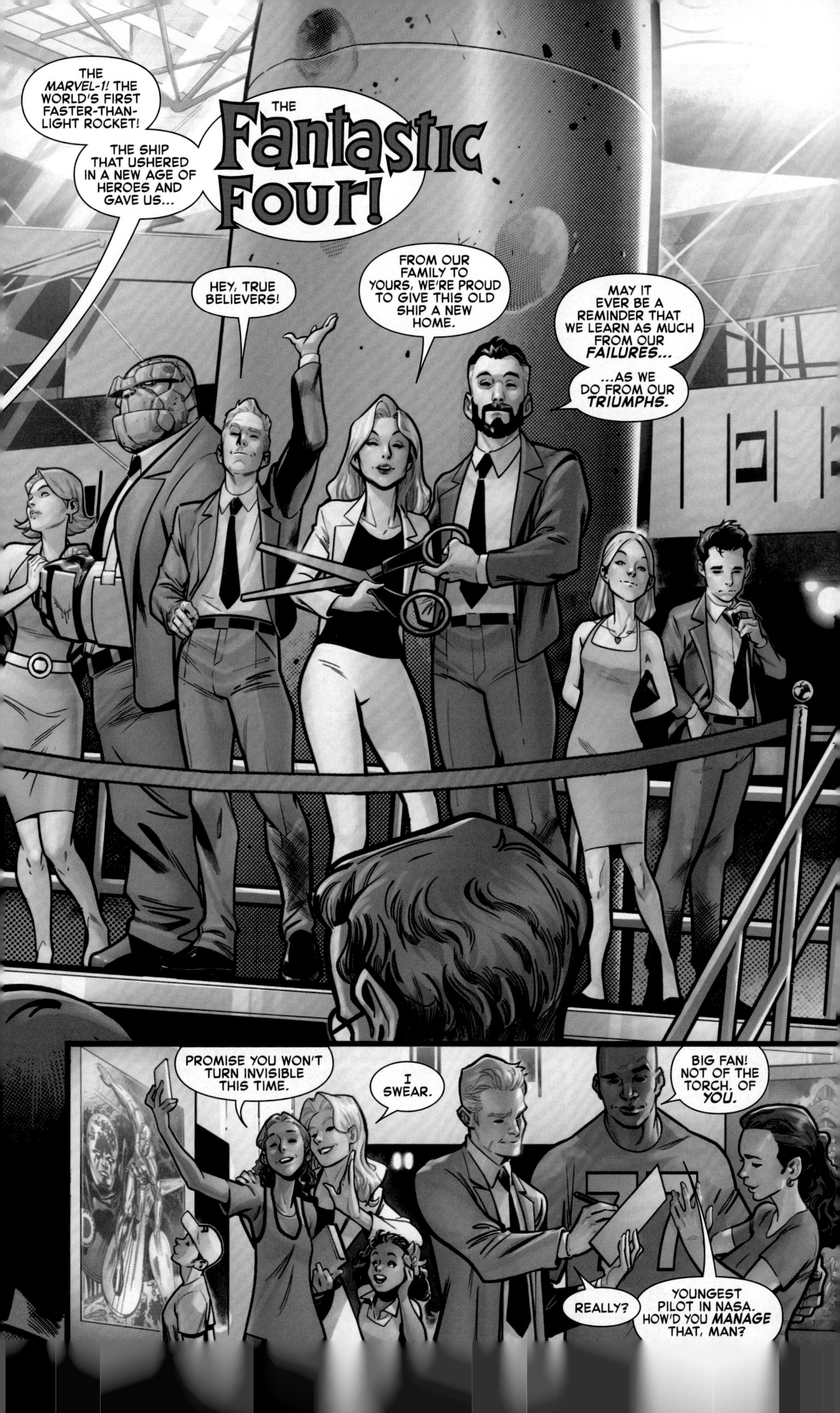
THE MARVEL-1! THE WORLD'S FIRST FASTER-THAN-LIGHT ROCKET!
THE SHIP THAT USHERED IN A NEW AGE OF HEROES AND GAVE US...
THE Fantastic Four!
HEY, TRUE BELIEVERS!
FROM OUR FAMILY TO YOURS, WE'RE PROUD TO GIVE THIS OLD SHIP A NEW HOME.
MAY IT EVER BE A REMINDER THAT WE LEARN AS MUCH FROM OUR FAILURES...
...AS WE DO FROM OUR TRIUMPHS.
PROMISE YOU WON'T TURN INVISIBLE THIS TIME.
I SWEAR.
BIG FAN! NOT OF THE TORCH. OF YOU.
REALLY?
YOUNGEST PILOT IN NASA. HOW'D YOU MANAGE THAT, MAN?

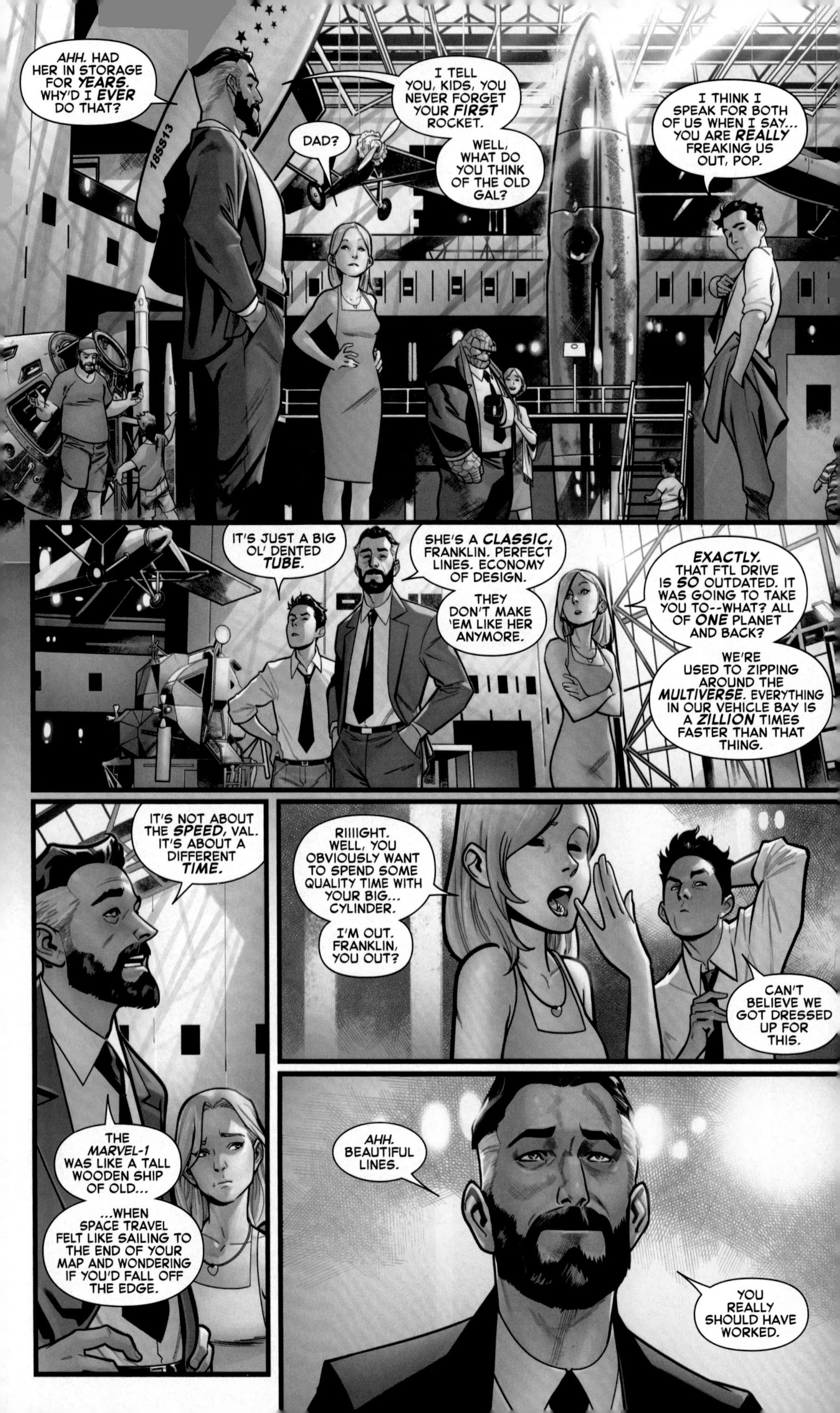
AHH. HAD HER IN STORAGE FOR YEARS. WHY'D I EVER DO THAT?
18SS13
I TELL YOU, KIDS, YOU NEVER FORGET YOUR FIRST ROCKET.
DAD?
WELL, WHAT DO YOU THINK OF THE OLD GAL?
I THINK I SPEAK FOR BOTH OF US WHEN I SAY... YOU ARE REALLY FREAKING US OUT, POP.
IT'S JUST A BIG OL' DENTED TUBE.
SHE'S A CLASSIC, FRANKLIN. PERFECT LINES. ECONOMY OF DESIGN.
THEY DON'T MAKE 'EM LIKE HER ANYMORE.
EXACTLY. THAT FTL DRIVE IS SO OUTDATED. IT WAS GOING TO TAKE YOU TO--WHAT? ALL OF ONE PLANET AND BACK?
WE'RE USED TO ZIPPING AROUND THE MULTIVERSE. EVERYTHING IN OUR VEHICLE BAY IS A ZILLION TIMES FASTER THAN THAT THING.
IT'S NOT ABOUT THE SPEED, VAL. IT'S ABOUT A DIFFERENT TIME.
THE MARVEL-1 WAS LIKE A TALL WOODEN SHIP OF OLD...
...WHEN SPACE TRAVEL FELT LIKE SAILING TO THE END OF YOUR MAP AND WONDERING IF YOU'D FALL OFF THE EDGE.
RIIIIGHT. WELL, YOU OBVIOUSLY WANT TO SPEND SOME QUALITY TIME WITH YOUR BIG... CYLINDER.
I'M OUT. FRANKLIN, YOU OUT?
CAN'T BELIEVE WE GOT DRESSED UP FOR THIS.
AHH. BEAUTIFUL LINES.
YOU REALLY SHOULD HAVE WORKED.

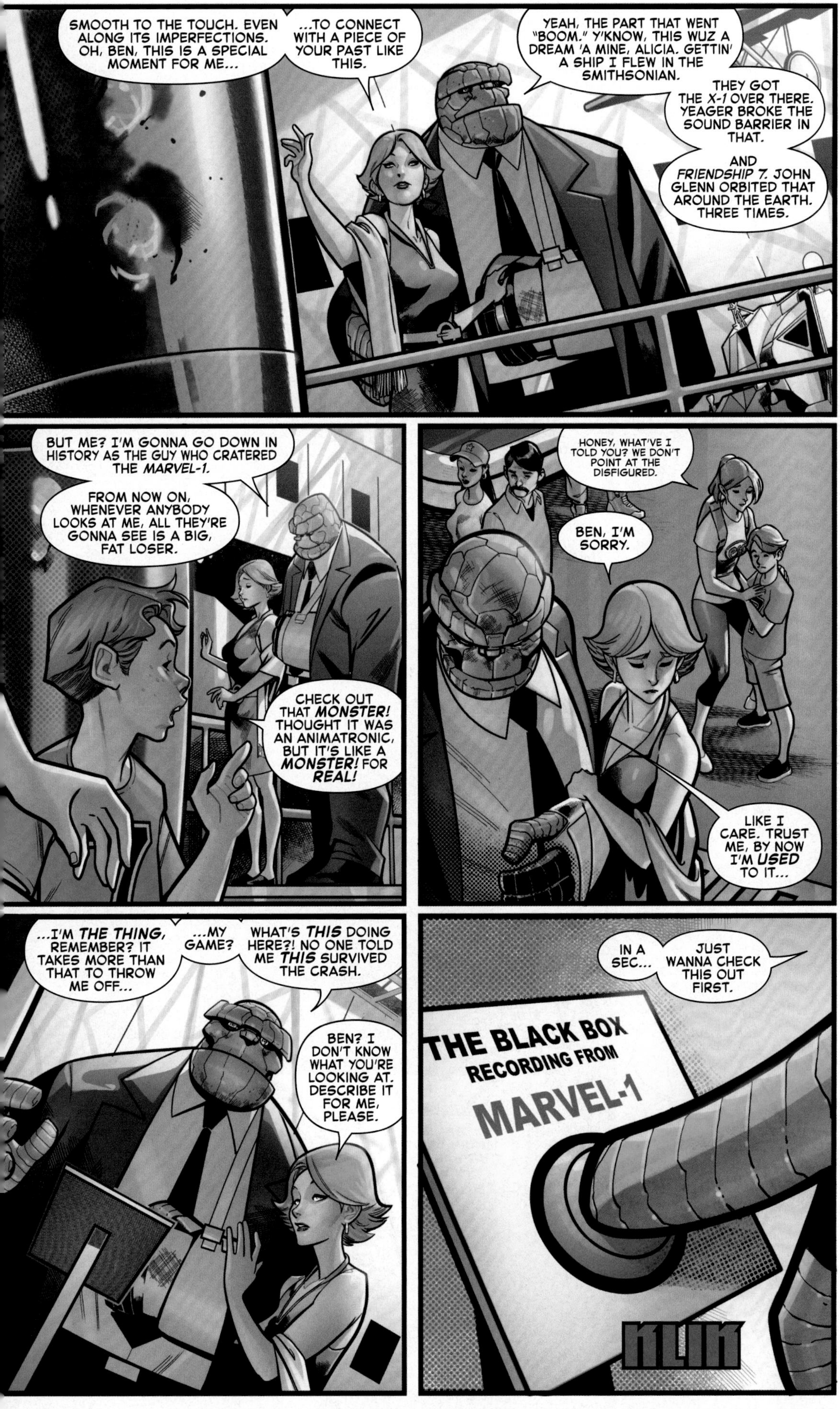
SMOOTH TO THE TOUCH. EVEN ALONG ITS IMPERFECTIONS. OH, BEN, THIS IS A SPECIAL MOMENT FOR ME...
...TO CONNECT WITH A PIECE OF YOUR PAST LIKE THIS.
YEAH, THE PART THAT WENT "BOOM." Y'KNOW, THIS WUZ A DREAM 'A MINE, ALICIA. GETTIN' A SHIP I FLEW IN THE SMITHSONIAN.
THEY GOT THE X-1 OVER THERE. YEAGER BROKE THE SOUND BARRIER IN THAT.
AND FRIENDSHIP 7. JOHN GLENN ORBITED THAT AROUND THE EARTH. THREE TIMES.
BUT ME? I'M GONNA GO DOWN IN HISTORY AS THE GUY WHO CRATERED THE MARVEL-1.
FROM NOW ON, WHENEVER ANYBODY LOOKS AT ME, ALL THEY'RE GONNA SEE IS A BIG, FAT LOSER.
CHECK OUT THAT MONSTER! THOUGHT IT WAS AN ANIMATRONIC, BUT IT'S LIKE A MONSTER! FOR REAL!
HONEY, WHAT'VE I TOLD YOU? WE DON'T POINT AT THE DISFIGURED.
BEN, I'M SORRY.
LIKE I CARE. TRUST ME, BY NOW I'M USED TO IT...
...I'M THE THING, REMEMBER? IT TAKES MORE THAN THAT TO THROW ME OFF...
...MY GAME?
WHAT'S THIS DOING HERE?! NO ONE TOLD ME THIS SURVIVED THE CRASH.
BEN? I DON'T KNOW WHAT YOU'RE LOOKING AT. DESCRIBE IT FOR ME, PLEASE.
IN A SEC...
JUST WANNA CHECK THIS OUT FIRST.
THE BLACK BOX RECORDING FROM MARVEL-1
KLIK

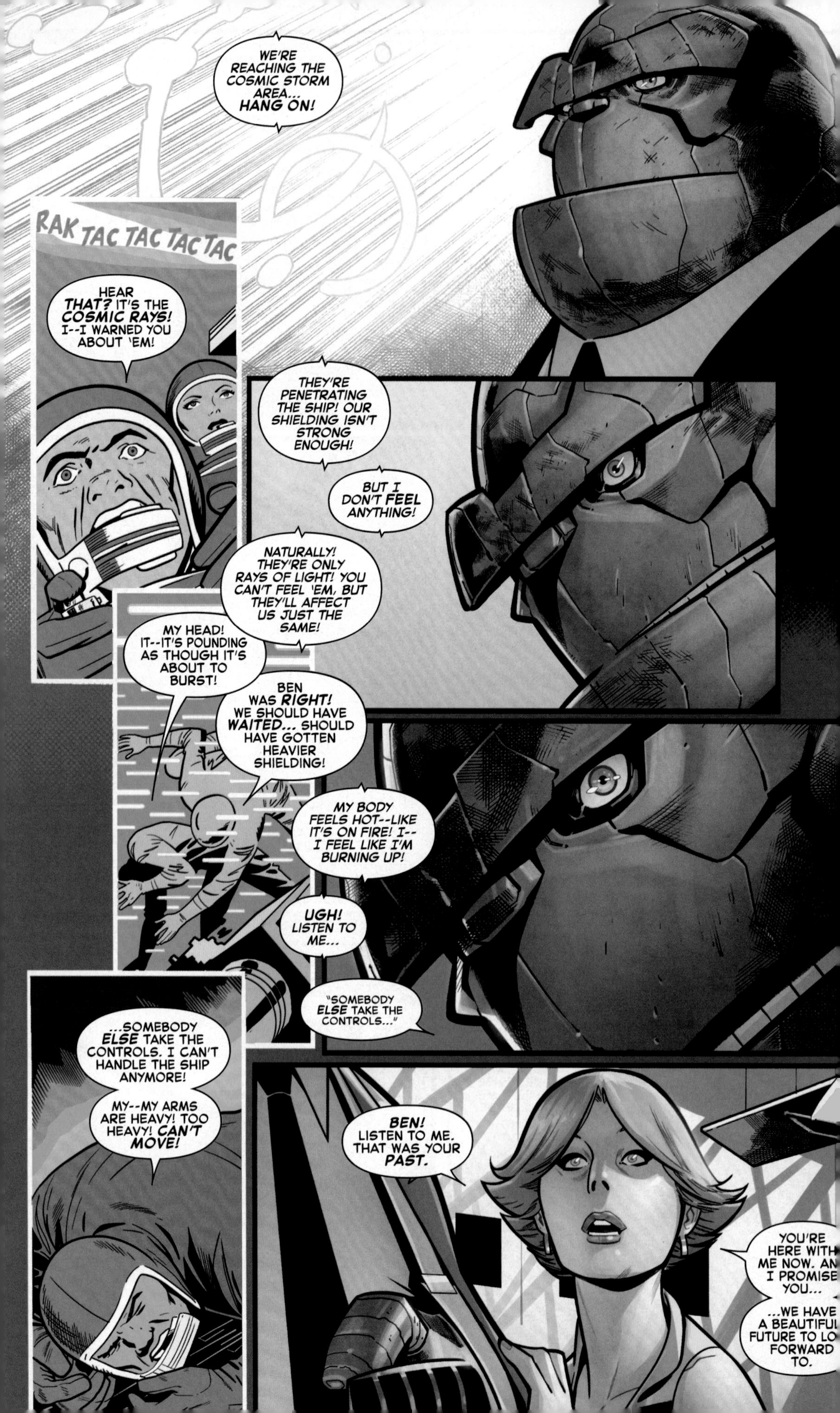

WE'RE REACHING THE COSMIC STORM AREA... HANG ON!
RAK TAC TAC TAC TAC
HEAR THAT? IT'S THE COSMIC RAYS! I--I WARNED YOU ABOUT 'EM!
THEY'RE PENETRATING THE SHIP! OUR SHIELDING ISN'T STRONG ENOUGH!
BUT I DON'T FEEL ANYTHING!
NATURALLY! THEY'RE ONLY RAYS OF LIGHT! YOU CAN'T FEEL 'EM, BUT THEY'LL AFFECT US JUST THE SAME!
MY HEAD! IT--IT'S POUNDING AS THOUGH IT'S ABOUT TO BURST!
BEN WAS RIGHT! WE SHOULD HAVE WAITED... SHOULD HAVE GOTTEN HEAVIER SHIELDING!
MY BODY FEELS HOT--LIKE IT'S ON FIRE! I--I FEEL LIKE I'M BURNING UP!
UGH! LISTEN TO ME...
"SOMEBODY ELSE TAKE THE CONTROLS..."
...SOMEBODY ELSE TAKE THE CONTROLS. I CAN'T HANDLE THE SHIP ANYMORE!
MY--MY ARMS ARE HEAVY! TOO HEAVY! CAN'T MOVE!
BEN! LISTEN TO ME. THAT WAS YOUR PAST.
YOU'RE HERE WITH ME NOW. AN I PROMISE YOU...
...WE HAVE A BEAUTIFU FUTURE TO LO FORWARD TO.

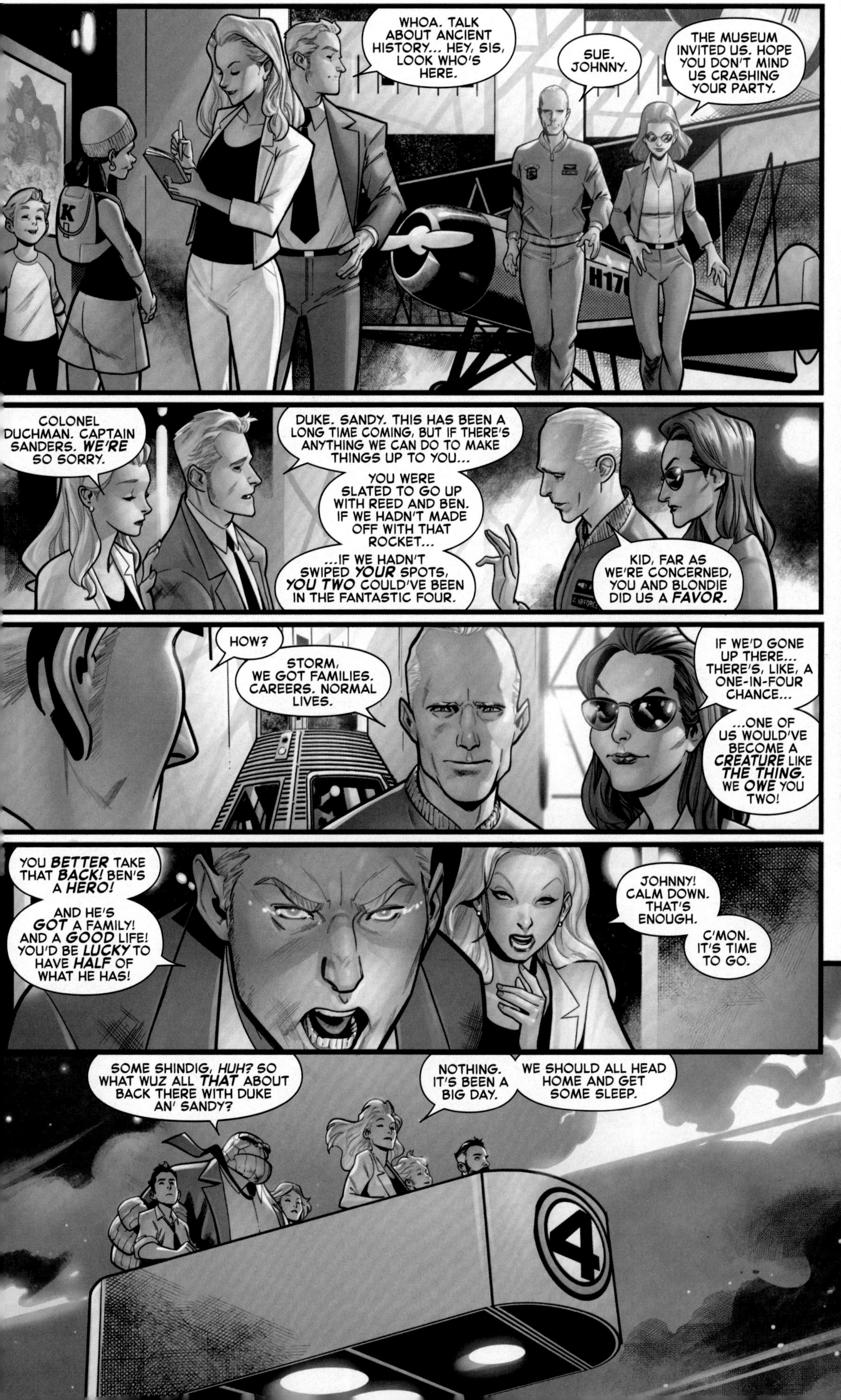
WHOA. TALK ABOUT ANCIENT HISTORY... HEY, SIS, LOOK WHO'S HERE.
SUE. JOHNNY.
THE MUSEUM INVITED US. HOPE YOU DON'T MIND US CRASHING YOUR PARTY.
COLONEL DUCHMAN. CAPTAIN SANDERS. WE'RE SO SORRY.
DUKE. SANDY. THIS HAS BEEN A LONG TIME COMING, BUT IF THERE'S ANYTHING WE CAN DO TO MAKE THINGS UP TO YOU...
YOU WERE SLATED TO GO UP WITH REED AND BEN. IF WE HADN'T MADE OFF WITH THAT ROCKET...
...IF WE HADN'T SWIPED YOUR SPOTS, YOU TWO COULD'VE BEEN IN THE FANTASTIC FOUR.
KID, FAR AS WE'RE CONCERNED, YOU AND BLONDIE DID US A FAVOR.
HOW?
STORM, WE GOT FAMILIES. CAREERS. NORMAL LIVES.
IF WE'D GONE UP THERE... THERE'S, LIKE, A ONE-IN-FOUR CHANCE...
...ONE OF US WOULD'VE BECOME A CREATURE LIKE THE THING. WE OWE YOU TWO!
YOU BETTER TAKE THAT BACK! BEN'S A HERO!
AND HE'S GOT A FAMILY! AND A GOOD LIFE! YOU'D BE LUCKY TO HAVE HALF OF WHAT HE HAS!
JOHNNY! CALM DOWN. THAT'S ENOUGH.
C'MON. IT'S TIME TO GO.
SOME SHINDIG, HUH? SO WHAT WUZ ALL THAT ABOUT BACK THERE WITH DUKE AN' SANDY?
NOTHING. IT'S BEEN A BIG DAY.
WE SHOULD ALL HEAD HOME AND GET SOME SLEEP.

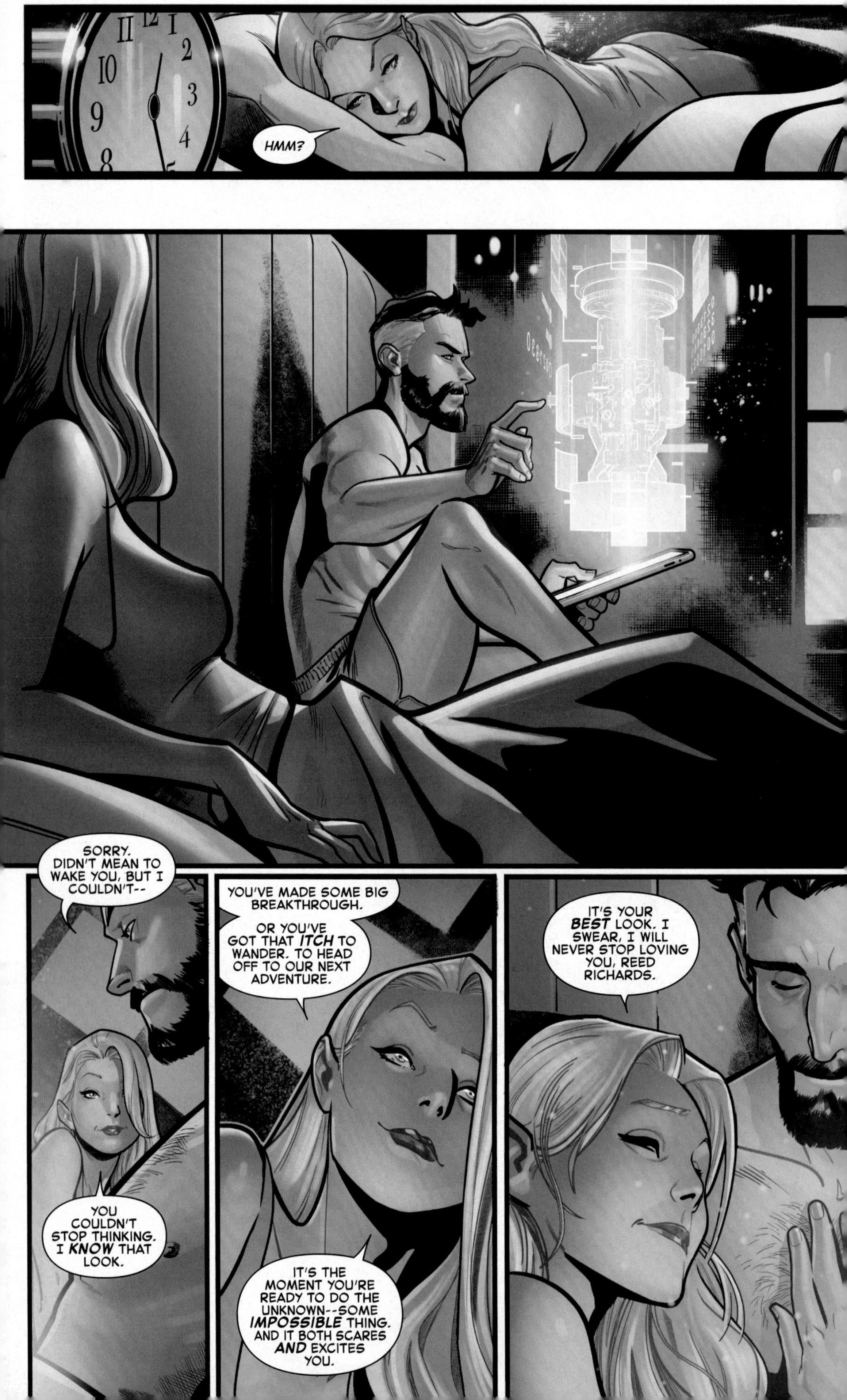
HMM?
SORRY. DIDN'T MEAN TO WAKE YOU, BUT I COULDN'T--
YOU COULDN'T STOP THINKING. I KNOW THAT LOOK.
YOU'VE MADE SOME BIG BREAKTHROUGH.
OR YOU'VE GOT THAT ITCH TO WANDER. TO HEAD OFF TO OUR NEXT ADVENTURE.
IT'S THE MOMENT YOU'RE READY TO DO THE UNKNOWN--SOME IMPOSSIBLE THING. AND IT BOTH SCARES AND EXCITES YOU.
IT'S YOUR BEST LOOK. I SWEAR, I WILL NEVER STOP LOVING YOU, REED RICHARDS.

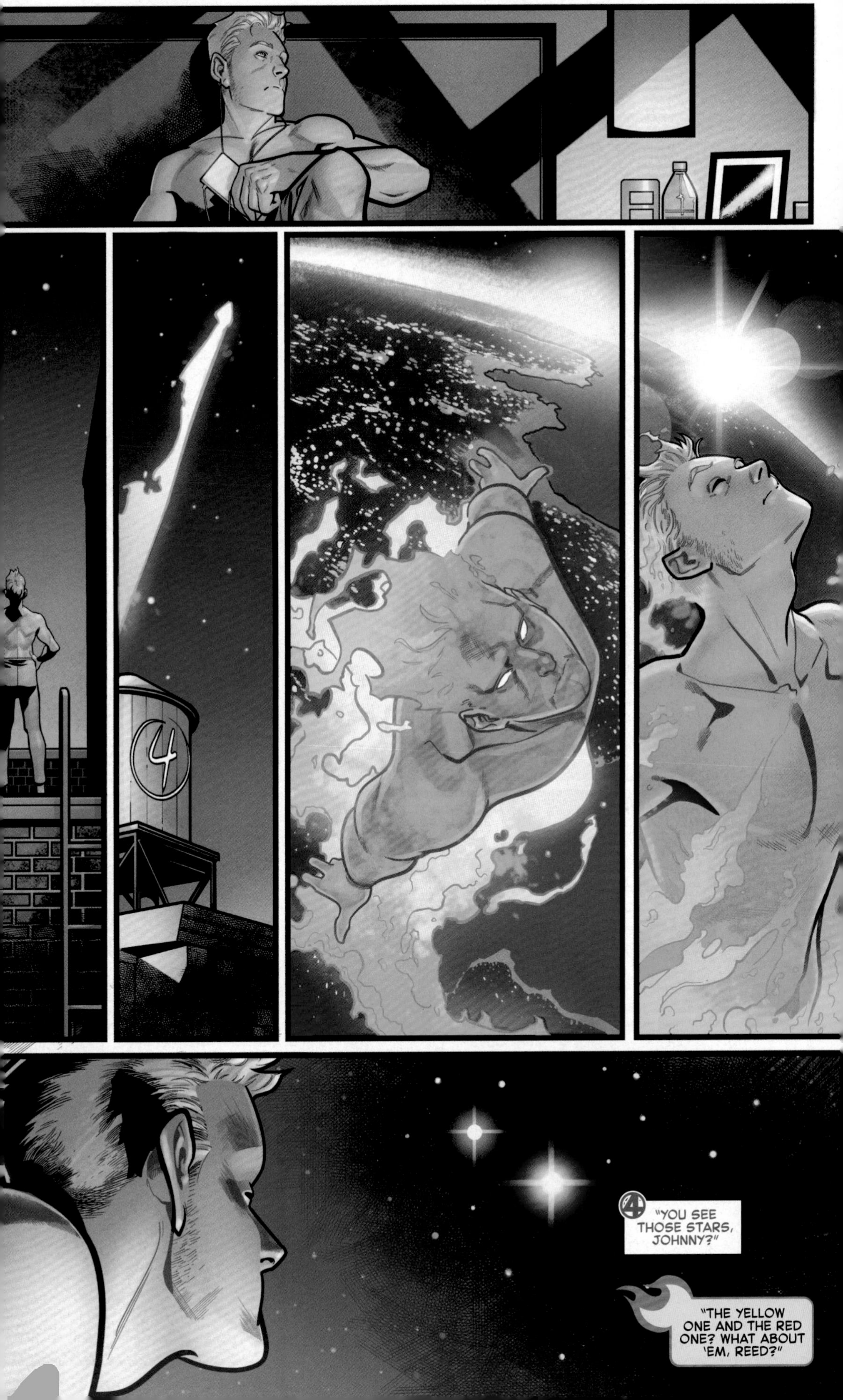
"YOU SEE THOSE STARS, JOHNNY?"
"THE YELLOW ONE AND THE RED ONE? WHAT ABOUT 'EM, REED?"

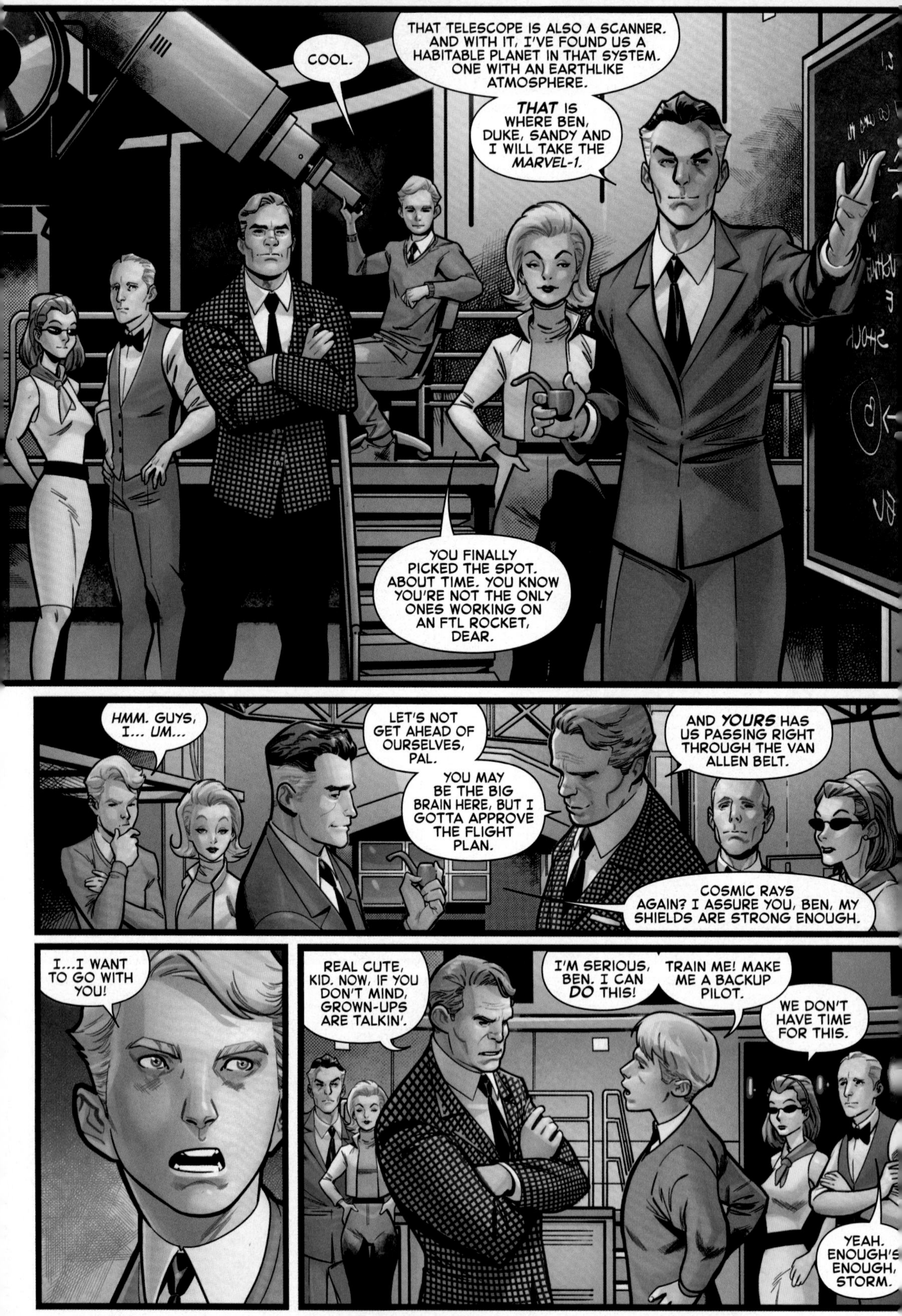
COOL.
THAT TELESCOPE IS ALSO A SCANNER. AND WITH IT, I'VE FOUND US A HABITABLE PLANET IN THAT SYSTEM. ONE WITH AN EARTHLIKE ATMOSPHERE.
THAT IS WHERE BEN, DUKE, SANDY AND I WILL TAKE THE *MARVEL-1*.
YOU FINALLY PICKED THE SPOT. ABOUT TIME. YOU KNOW YOU'RE NOT THE ONLY ONES WORKING ON AN FTL ROCKET, DEAR.
HMM. GUYS, I... UM...
LET'S NOT GET AHEAD OF OURSELVES, PAL.
YOU MAY BE THE BIG BRAIN HERE, BUT I GOTTA APPROVE THE FLIGHT PLAN.
AND *YOURS* HAS US PASSING RIGHT THROUGH THE VAN ALLEN BELT.
COSMIC RAYS AGAIN? I ASSURE YOU, BEN, MY SHIELDS ARE STRONG ENOUGH.
I...I WANT TO GO WITH YOU!
REAL CUTE, KID. NOW, IF YOU DON'T MIND, GROWN-UPS ARE TALKIN'.
I'M SERIOUS, BEN. I CAN *DO* THIS!
TRAIN ME! MAKE ME A BACKUP PILOT.
WE DON'T HAVE TIME FOR THIS.
YEAH. ENOUGH'S ENOUGH, STORM.

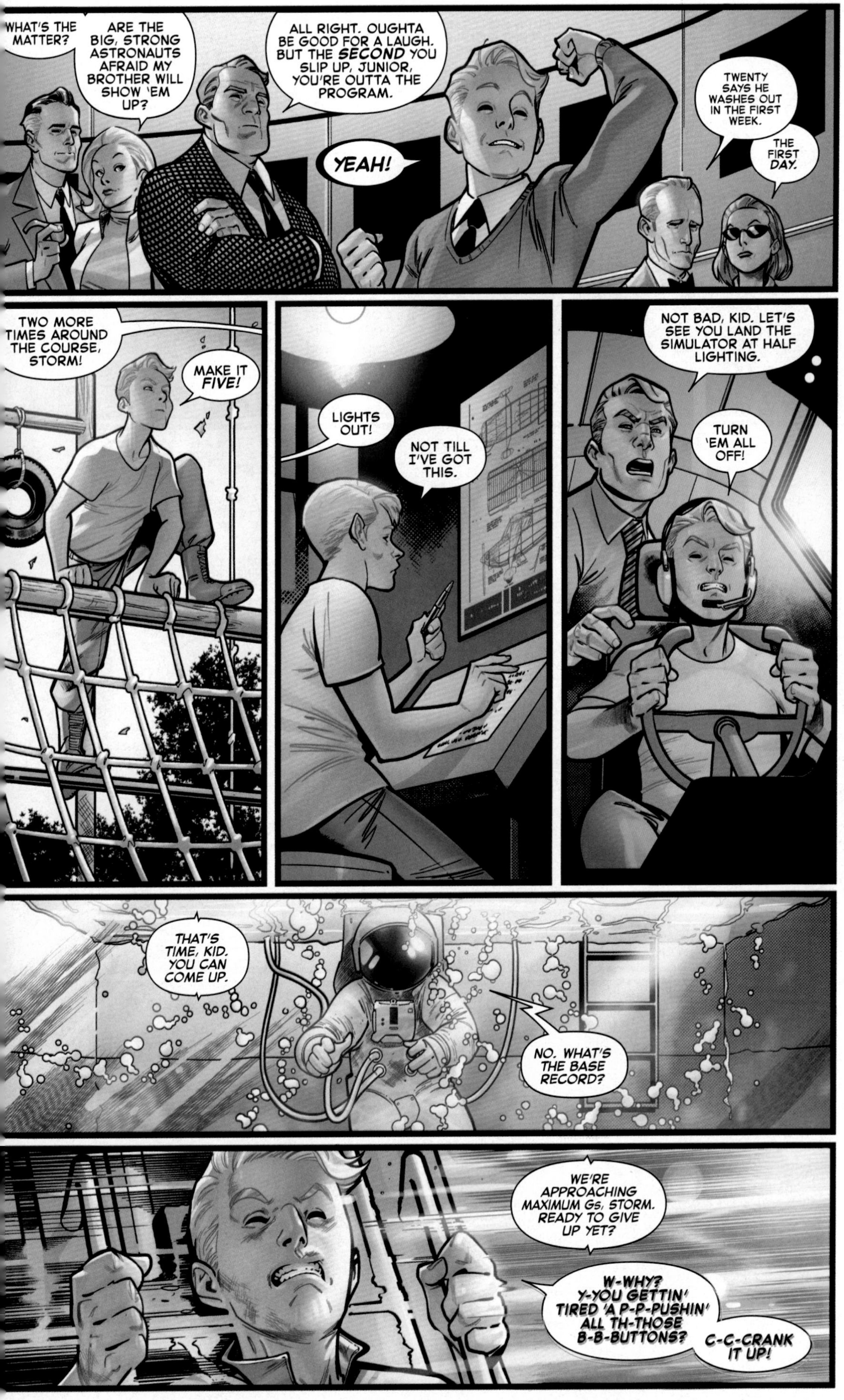
WHAT'S THE MATTER?
ARE THE BIG, STRONG ASTRONAUTS AFRAID MY BROTHER WILL SHOW 'EM UP?
ALL RIGHT. OUGHTA BE GOOD FOR A LAUGH. BUT THE SECOND YOU SLIP UP, JUNIOR, YOU'RE OUTTA THE PROGRAM.
YEAH!
TWENTY SAYS HE WASHES OUT IN THE FIRST WEEK.
THE FIRST DAY.
TWO MORE TIMES AROUND THE COURSE, STORM!
MAKE IT FIVE!
LIGHTS OUT!
NOT TILL I'VE GOT THIS.
NOT BAD, KID. LET'S SEE YOU LAND THE SIMULATOR AT HALF LIGHTING.
TURN 'EM ALL OFF!
THAT'S TIME, KID. YOU CAN COME UP.
NO. WHAT'S THE BASE RECORD?
WE'RE APPROACHING MAXIMUM Gs, STORM. READY TO GIVE UP YET?
W-WHY? Y-YOU GETTIN' TIRED 'A P-P-PUSHIN' ALL TH-THOSE B-B-BUTTONS?
C-C-CRANK IT UP!

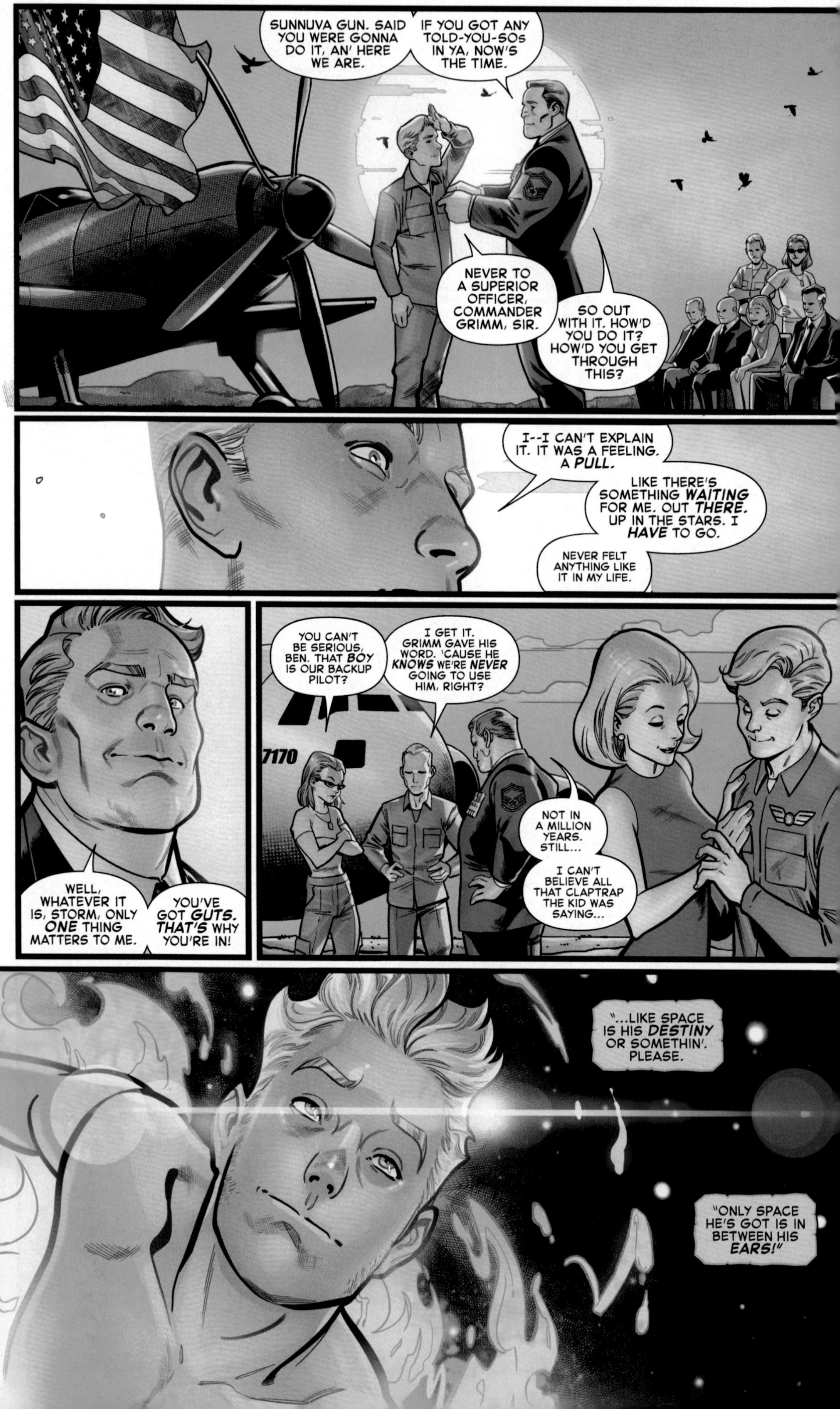

SUNNUVA GUN. SAID YOU WERE GONNA DO IT, AN' HERE WE ARE.
IF YOU GOT ANY TOLD-YOU-SOs IN YA, NOW'S THE TIME.
NEVER TO A SUPERIOR OFFICER, COMMANDER GRIMM, SIR.
SO OUT WITH IT. HOW'D YOU DO IT? HOW'D YOU GET THROUGH THIS?
I--I CAN'T EXPLAIN IT. IT WAS A FEELING. A PULL.
LIKE THERE'S SOMETHING WAITING FOR ME. OUT THERE. UP IN THE STARS. I HAVE TO GO.
NEVER FELT ANYTHING LIKE IT IN MY LIFE.
WELL, WHATEVER IT IS, STORM, ONLY ONE THING MATTERS TO ME.
YOU'VE GOT GUTS. THAT'S WHY YOU'RE IN!
YOU CAN'T BE SERIOUS, BEN. THAT BOY IS OUR BACKUP PILOT?
I GET IT. GRIMM GAVE HIS WORD. 'CAUSE HE KNOWS WE'RE NEVER GOING TO USE HIM, RIGHT?
7170
NOT IN A MILLION YEARS. STILL...
I CAN'T BELIEVE ALL THAT CLAPTRAP THE KID WAS SAYING...
"...LIKE SPACE IS HIS DESTINY OR SOMETHIN'. PLEASE.
"ONLY SPACE HE'S GOT IS IN BETWEEN HIS EARS!"

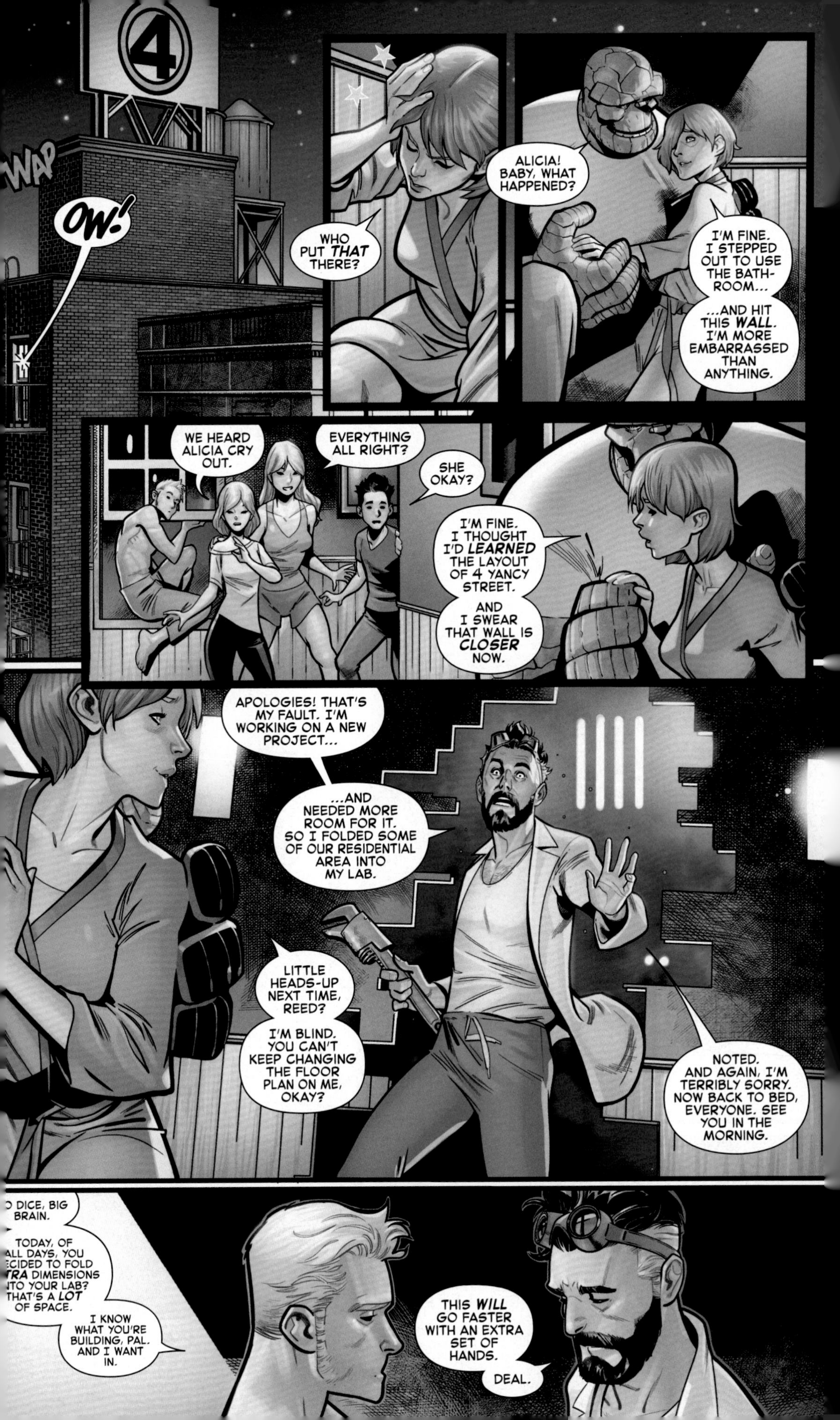

WAP
OW!
WHO PUT THAT THERE?
ALICIA! BABY, WHAT HAPPENED?
I'M FINE. I STEPPED OUT TO USE THE BATH-ROOM...
...AND HIT THIS WALL. I'M MORE EMBARRASSED THAN ANYTHING.
WE HEARD ALICIA CRY OUT.
EVERYTHING ALL RIGHT?
SHE OKAY?
I'M FINE. I THOUGHT I'D LEARNED THE LAYOUT OF 4 YANCY STREET.
AND I SWEAR THAT WALL IS CLOSER NOW.
APOLOGIES! THAT'S MY FAULT. I'M WORKING ON A NEW PROJECT...
...AND NEEDED MORE ROOM FOR IT. SO I FOLDED SOME OF OUR RESIDENTIAL AREA INTO MY LAB.
LITTLE HEADS-UP NEXT TIME, REED?
I'M BLIND. YOU CAN'T KEEP CHANGING THE FLOOR PLAN ON ME, OKAY?
NOTED. AND AGAIN, I'M TERRIBLY SORRY. NOW BACK TO BED, EVERYONE. SEE YOU IN THE MORNING.
BRAIN.
TODAY, OF ALL DAYS, YOU
DIMENSIONS
YOUR LAB?
THAT'S A LOT OF SPACE.
I KNOW WHAT YOU'RE BUILDING, PAL. AND I WANT IN.
THIS WILL GO FASTER WITH AN EXTRA SET OF HANDS.
DEAL.

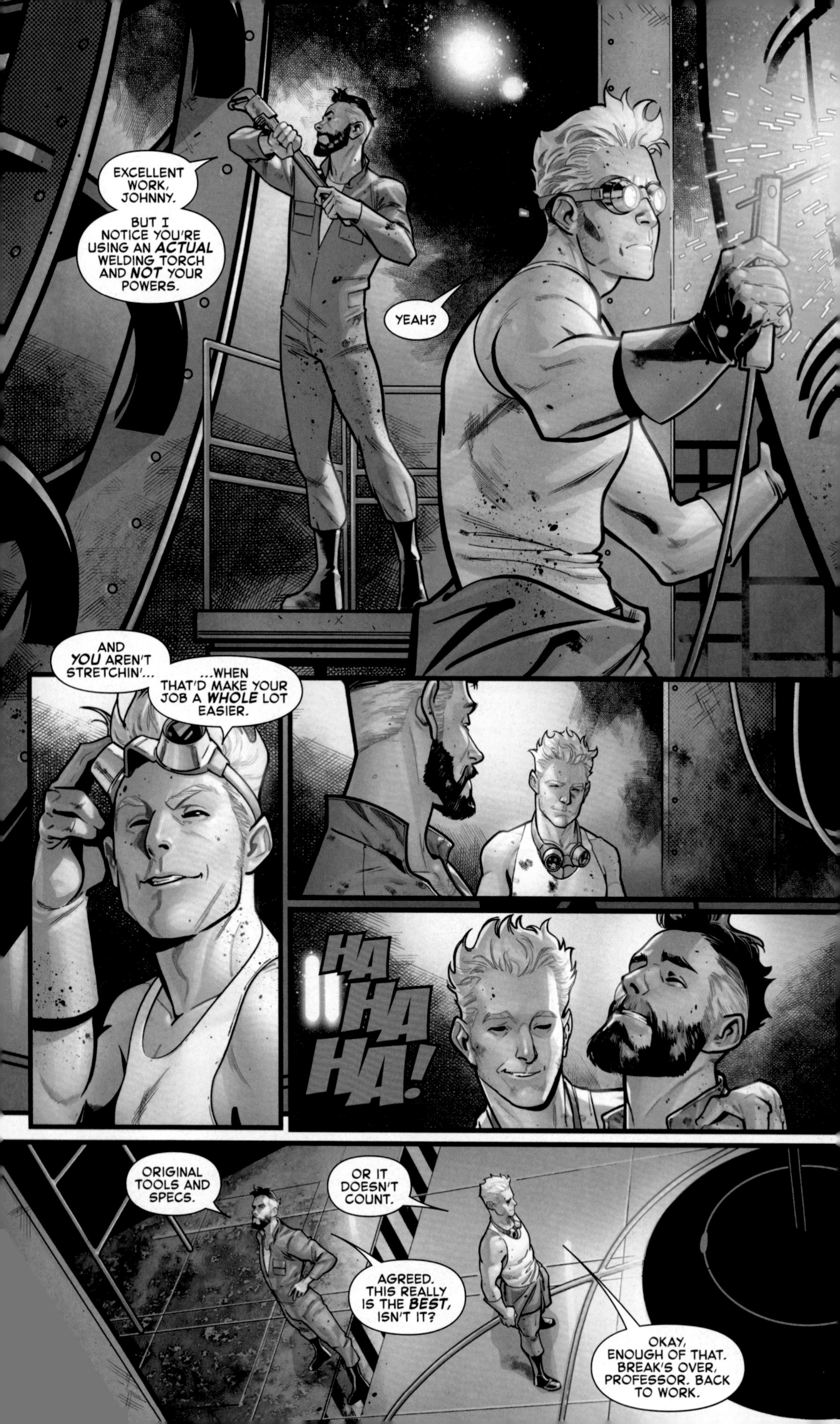
EXCELLENT WORK, JOHNNY.
BUT I NOTICE YOU'RE USING AN ACTUAL WELDING TORCH AND NOT YOUR POWERS.
YEAH?
AND YOU AREN'T STRETCHIN'...
...WHEN THAT'D MAKE YOUR JOB A WHOLE LOT EASIER.
HA HA HA!
ORIGINAL TOOLS AND SPECS.
OR IT DOESN'T COUNT.
AGREED. THIS REALLY IS THE BEST, ISN'T IT?
OKAY, ENOUGH OF THAT. BREAK'S OVER, PROFESSOR. BACK TO WORK.

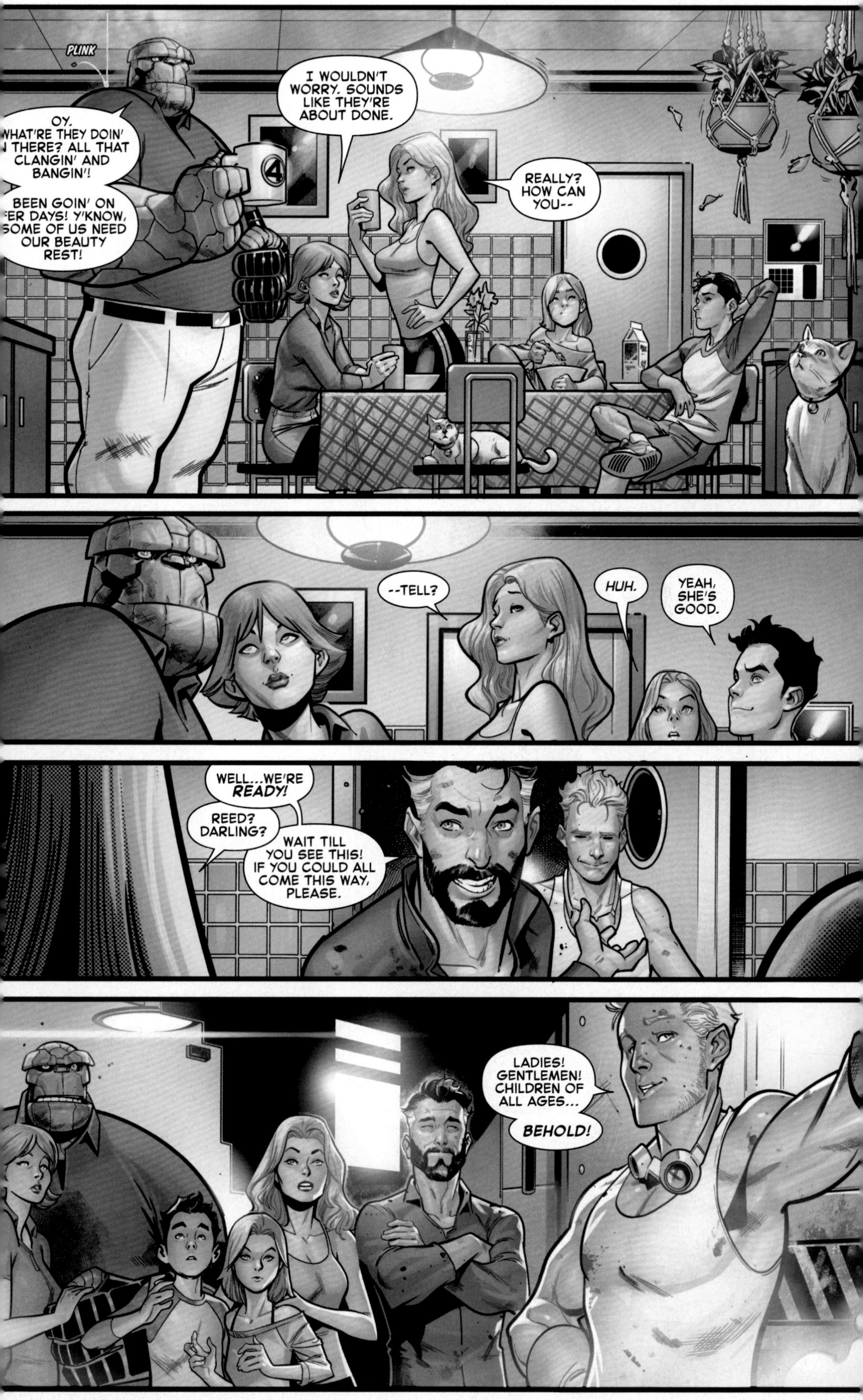
PLINK
OY. WHAT'RE THEY DOIN' IN THERE? ALL THAT CLANGIN' AND BANGIN'!
BEEN GOIN' ON FER DAYS! Y'KNOW, SOME OF US NEED OUR BEAUTY REST!
I WOULDN'T WORRY. SOUNDS LIKE THEY'RE ABOUT DONE.
REALLY? HOW CAN YOU--
--TELL?
HUH.
YEAH, SHE'S GOOD.
WELL...WE'RE READY!
REED? DARLING?
WAIT TILL YOU SEE THIS! IF YOU COULD ALL COME THIS WAY, PLEASE.
LADIES! GENTLEMEN! CHILDREN OF ALL AGES...
BEHOLD!

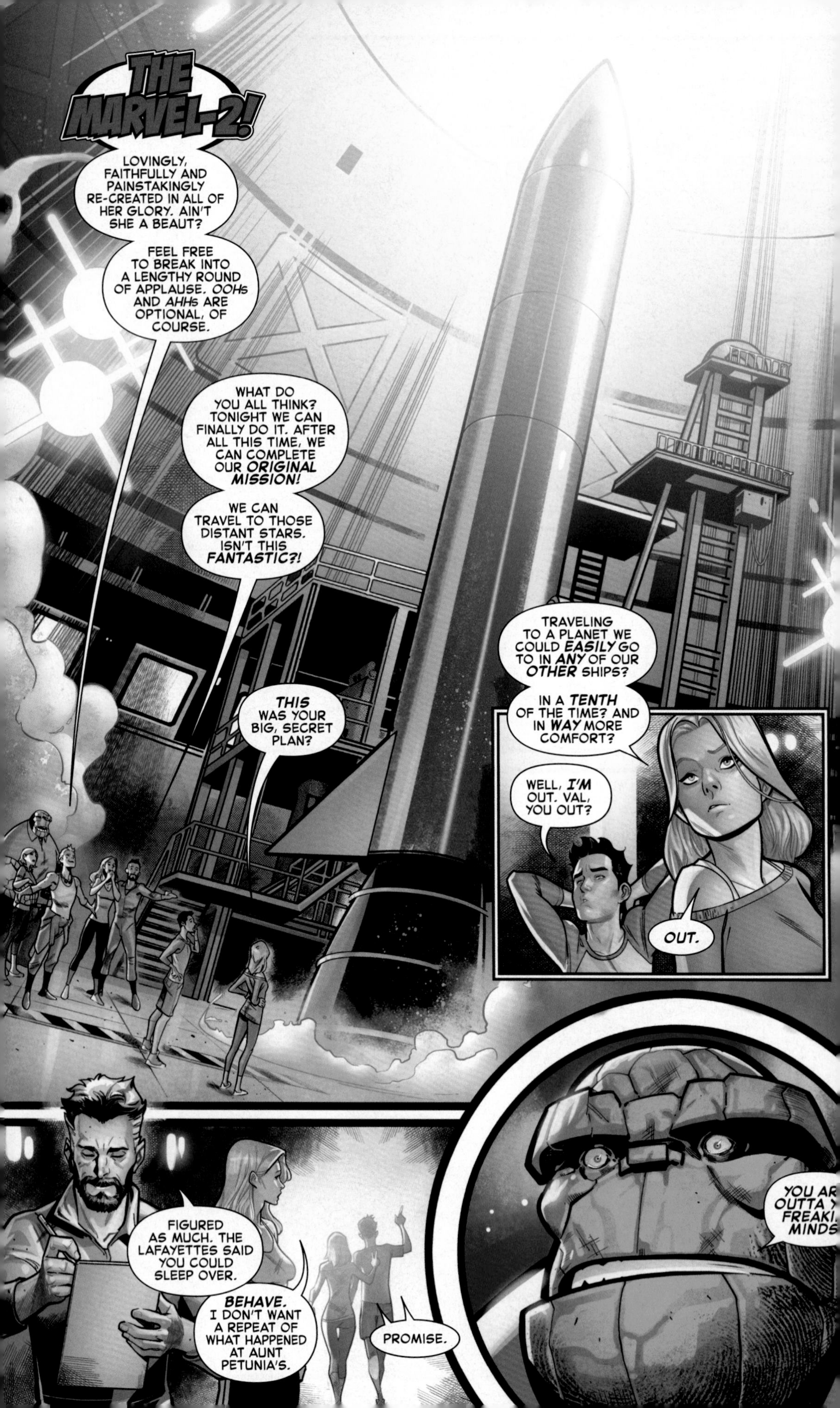
THE MARVEL-2!
LOVINGLY, FAITHFULLY AND PAINSTAKINGLY RE-CREATED IN ALL OF HER GLORY. AIN'T SHE A BEAUT?
FEEL FREE TO BREAK INTO A LENGTHY ROUND OF APPLAUSE. OOHs AND AHHs ARE OPTIONAL, OF COURSE.
WHAT DO YOU ALL THINK? TONIGHT WE CAN FINALLY DO IT. AFTER ALL THIS TIME, WE CAN COMPLETE OUR ORIGINAL MISSION!
WE CAN TRAVEL TO THOSE DISTANT STARS. ISN'T THIS FANTASTIC?!
THIS WAS YOUR BIG, SECRET PLAN?
TRAVELING TO A PLANET WE COULD EASILY GO TO IN ANY OF OUR OTHER SHIPS?
IN A TENTH OF THE TIME? AND IN WAY MORE COMFORT?
WELL, I'M OUT. VAL, YOU OUT?
OUT.
FIGURED AS MUCH. THE LAFAYETTES SAID YOU COULD SLEEP OVER.
BEHAVE. I DON'T WANT A REPEAT OF WHAT HAPPENED AT AUNT PETUNIA'S.
PROMISE.

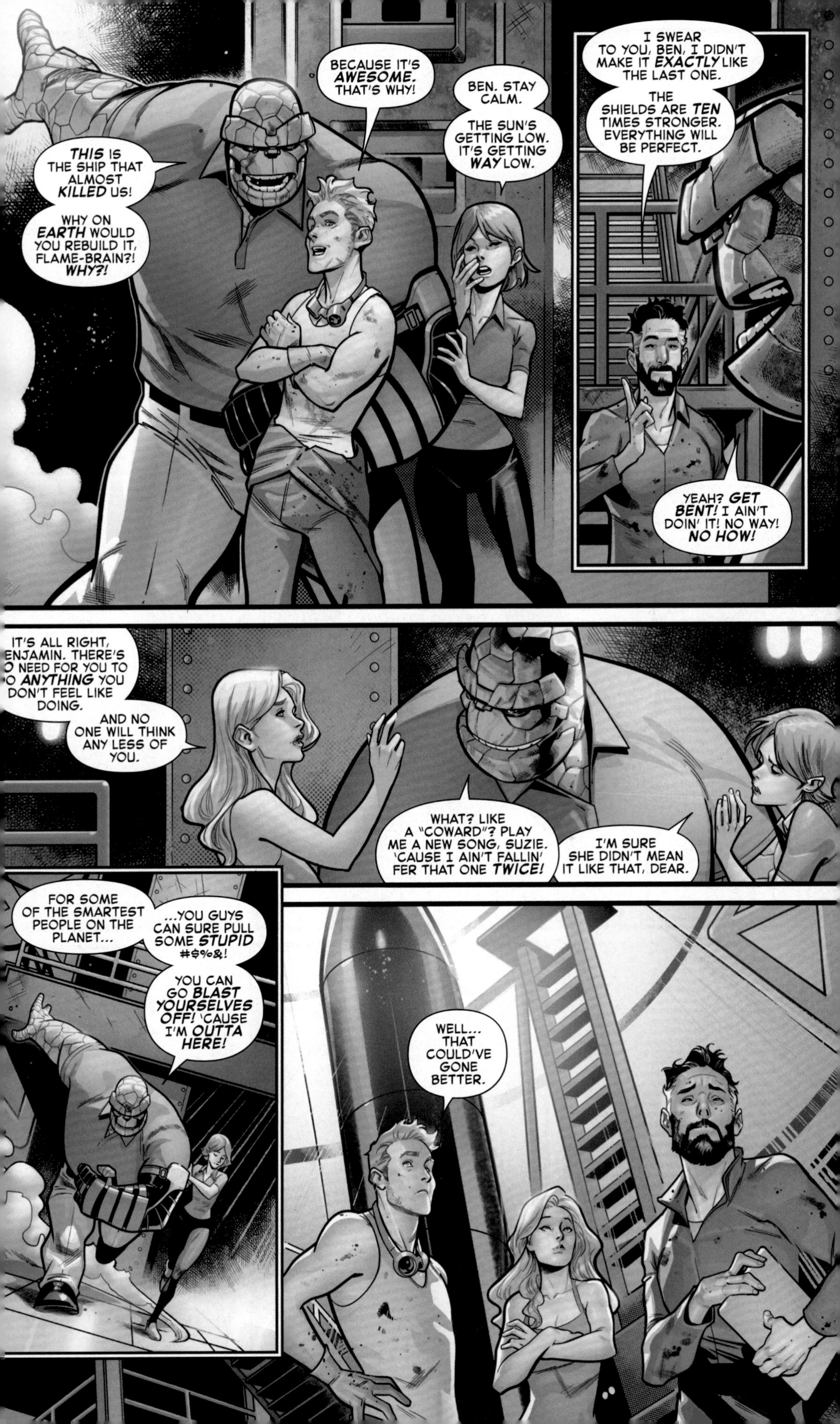
THIS IS THE SHIP THAT ALMOST KILLED US!
WHY ON EARTH WOULD YOU REBUILD IT, FLAME-BRAIN?! WHY?!
BECAUSE IT'S AWESOME. THAT'S WHY!
BEN. STAY CALM.
THE SUN'S GETTING LOW. IT'S GETTING WAY LOW.
I SWEAR TO YOU, BEN, I DIDN'T MAKE IT EXACTLY LIKE THE LAST ONE.
THE SHIELDS ARE TEN TIMES STRONGER. EVERYTHING WILL BE PERFECT.
YEAH? GET BENT! I AIN'T DOIN' IT! NO WAY! NO HOW!
IT'S ALL RIGHT, ENJAMIN. THERE'S O NEED FOR YOU TO O ANYTHING YOU DON'T FEEL LIKE DOING.
AND NO ONE WILL THINK ANY LESS OF YOU.
WHAT? LIKE A "COWARD"? PLAY ME A NEW SONG, SUZIE. 'CAUSE I AIN'T FALLIN' FER THAT ONE TWICE!
I'M SURE SHE DIDN'T MEAN IT LIKE THAT, DEAR.
FOR SOME OF THE SMARTEST PEOPLE ON THE PLANET...
...YOU GUYS CAN SURE PULL SOME STUPID #$%&!
YOU CAN GO BLAST YOURSELVES OFF! 'CAUSE I'M OUTTA HERE!
WELL... THAT COULD'VE GONE BETTER.

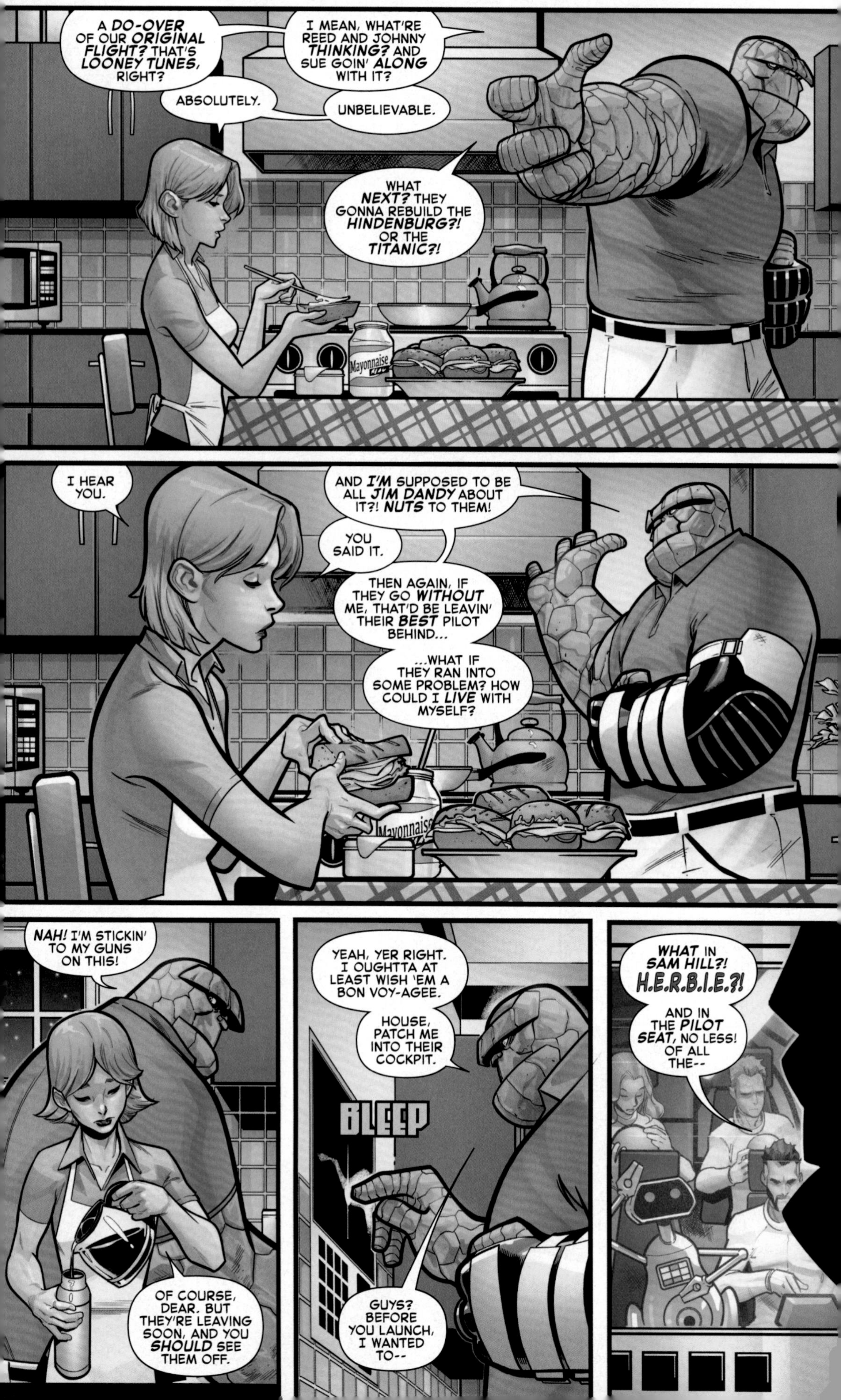
A DO-OVER OF OUR ORIGINAL FLIGHT? THAT'S LOONEY TUNES, RIGHT?
ABSOLUTELY.
I MEAN, WHAT'RE REED AND JOHNNY THINKING? AND SUE GOIN' ALONG WITH IT?
UNBELIEVABLE.
WHAT NEXT? THEY GONNA REBUILD THE HINDENBURG?! OR THE TITANIC?!
Mayonnaise
I HEAR YOU.
AND I'M SUPPOSED TO BE ALL JIM DANDY ABOUT IT?! NUTS TO THEM!
YOU SAID IT.
THEN AGAIN, IF THEY GO WITHOUT ME, THAT'D BE LEAVIN' THEIR BEST PILOT BEHIND...
...WHAT IF THEY RAN INTO SOME PROBLEM? HOW COULD I LIVE WITH MYSELF?
Mayonnaise
NAH! I'M STICKIN' TO MY GUNS ON THIS!
OF COURSE, DEAR. BUT THEY'RE LEAVING SOON, AND YOU SHOULD SEE THEM OFF.
YEAH, YER RIGHT. I OUGHTTA AT LEAST WISH 'EM A BON VOY-AGEE.
HOUSE, PATCH ME INTO THEIR COCKPIT.
BLEEP
GUYS? BEFORE YOU LAUNCH, I WANTED TO--
WHAT IN SAM HILL?! H.E.R.B.I.E.?!
AND IN THE PILOT SEAT, NO LESS! OF ALL THE--

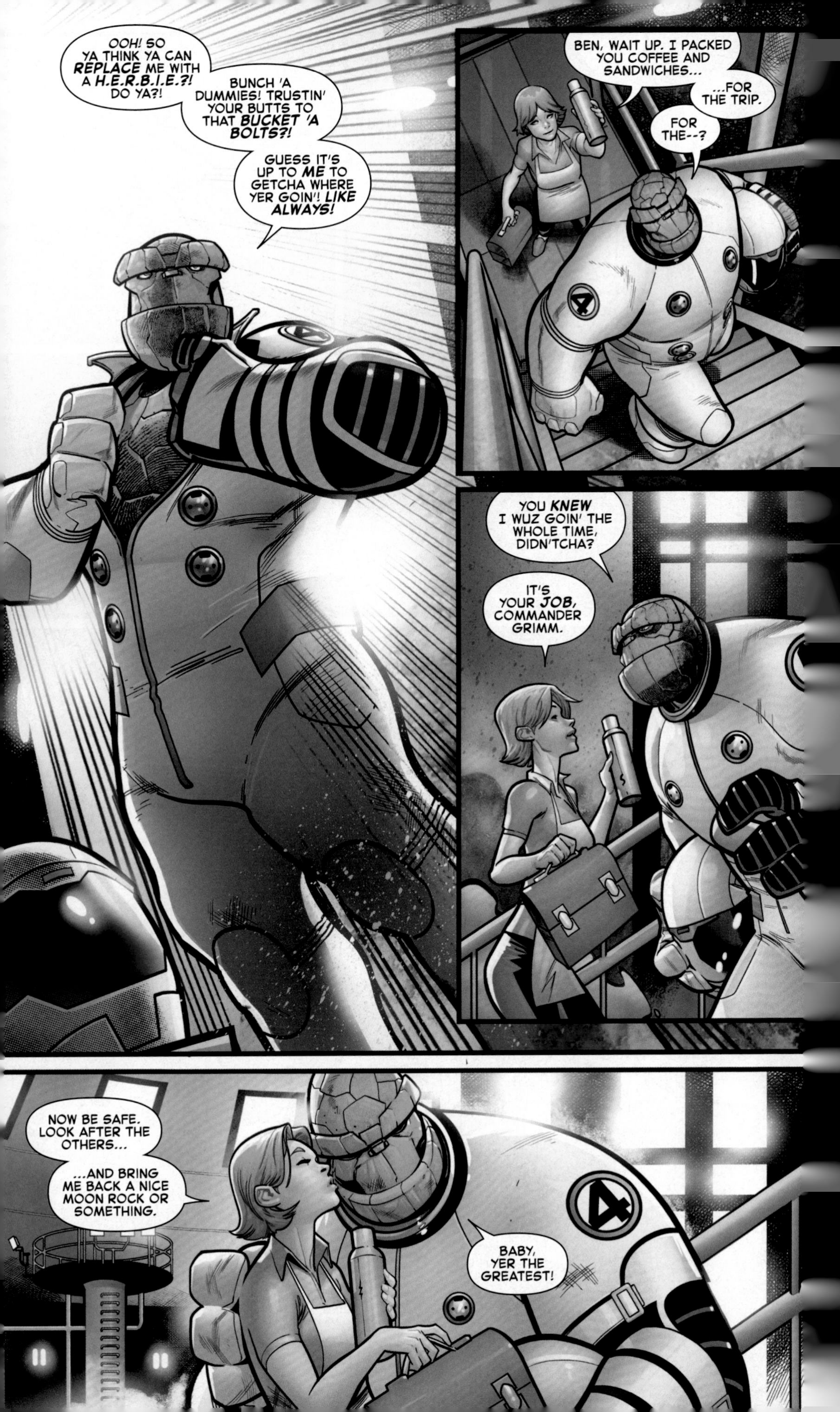

OOH! SO YA THINK YA CAN REPLACE ME WITH A H.E.R.B.I.E.?! DO YA?!
BUNCH 'A DUMMIES! TRUSTIN' YOUR BUTTS TO THAT BUCKET 'A BOLTS?!
GUESS IT'S UP TO ME TO GETCHA WHERE YER GOIN'! LIKE ALWAYS!
BEN, WAIT UP. I PACKED YOU COFFEE AND SANDWICHES...
...FOR THE TRIP.
FOR THE--?
YOU KNEW I WUZ GOIN' THE WHOLE TIME, DIDN'TCHA?
IT'S YOUR JOB, COMMANDER GRIMM.
NOW BE SAFE. LOOK AFTER THE OTHERS...
...AND BRING ME BACK A NICE MOON ROCK OR SOMETHING.
BABY, YER THE GREATEST!

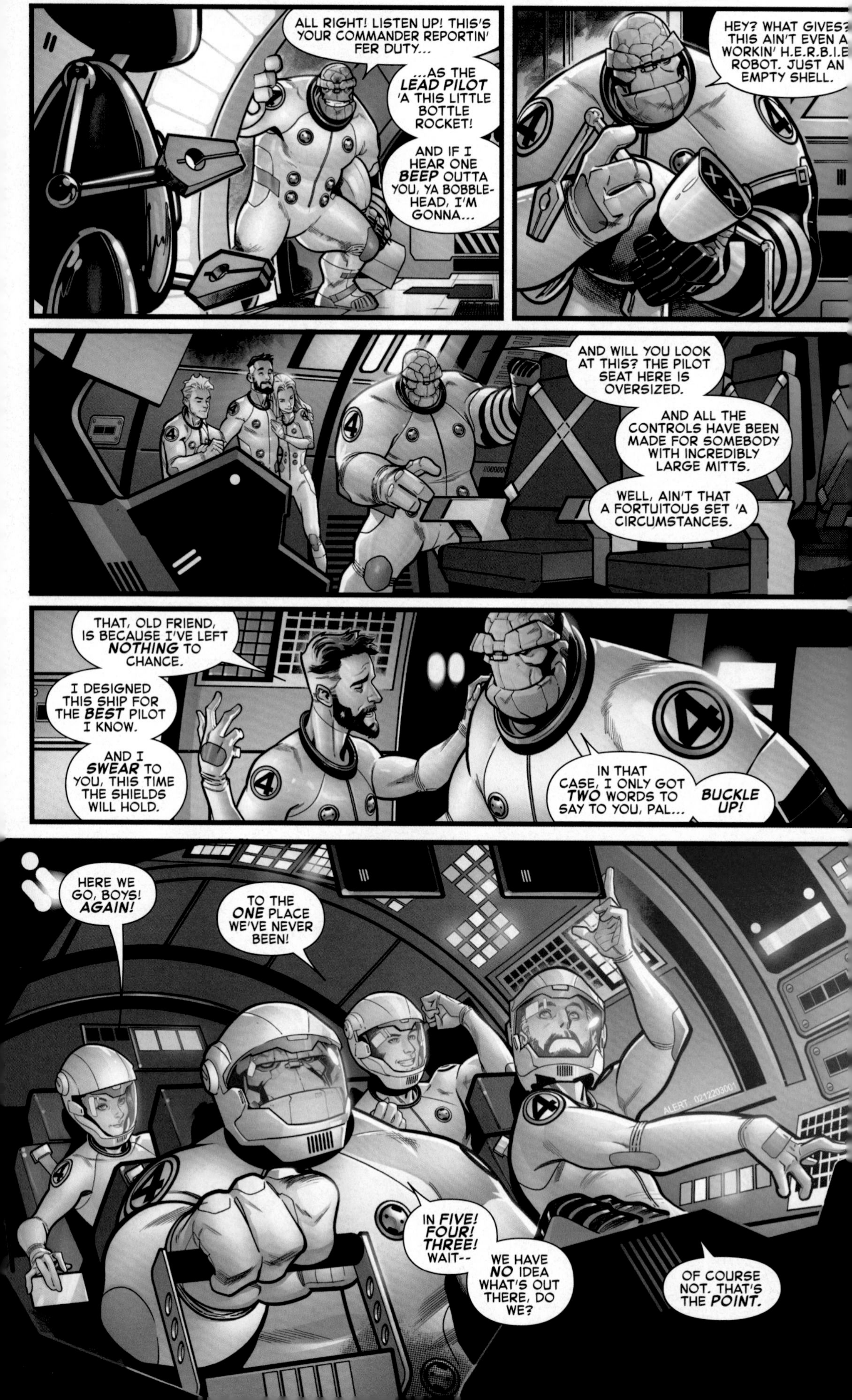
ALL RIGHT! LISTEN UP! THIS'S YOUR COMMANDER REPORTIN' FER DUTY...
...AS THE LEAD PILOT 'A THIS LITTLE BOTTLE ROCKET!
AND IF I HEAR ONE BEEP OUTTA YOU, YA BOBBLE-HEAD, I'M GONNA...
HEY? WHAT GIVES? THIS AIN'T EVEN A WORKIN' H.E.R.B.I.E. ROBOT. JUST AN EMPTY SHELL.
AND WILL YOU LOOK AT THIS? THE PILOT SEAT HERE IS OVERSIZED.
AND ALL THE CONTROLS HAVE BEEN MADE FOR SOMEBODY WITH INCREDIBLY LARGE MITTS.
WELL, AIN'T THAT A FORTUITOUS SET 'A CIRCUMSTANCES.
THAT, OLD FRIEND, IS BECAUSE I'VE LEFT NOTHING TO CHANCE.
I DESIGNED THIS SHIP FOR THE BEST PILOT I KNOW.
AND I SWEAR TO YOU, THIS TIME THE SHIELDS WILL HOLD.
IN THAT CASE, I ONLY GOT TWO WORDS TO SAY TO YOU, PAL...
BUCKLE UP!
HERE WE GO, BOYS! AGAIN!
TO THE ONE PLACE WE'VE NEVER BEEN!
IN FIVE! FOUR! THREE! WAIT--
WE HAVE NO IDEA WHAT'S OUT THERE, DO WE?
OF COURSE NOT. THAT'S THE POINT.

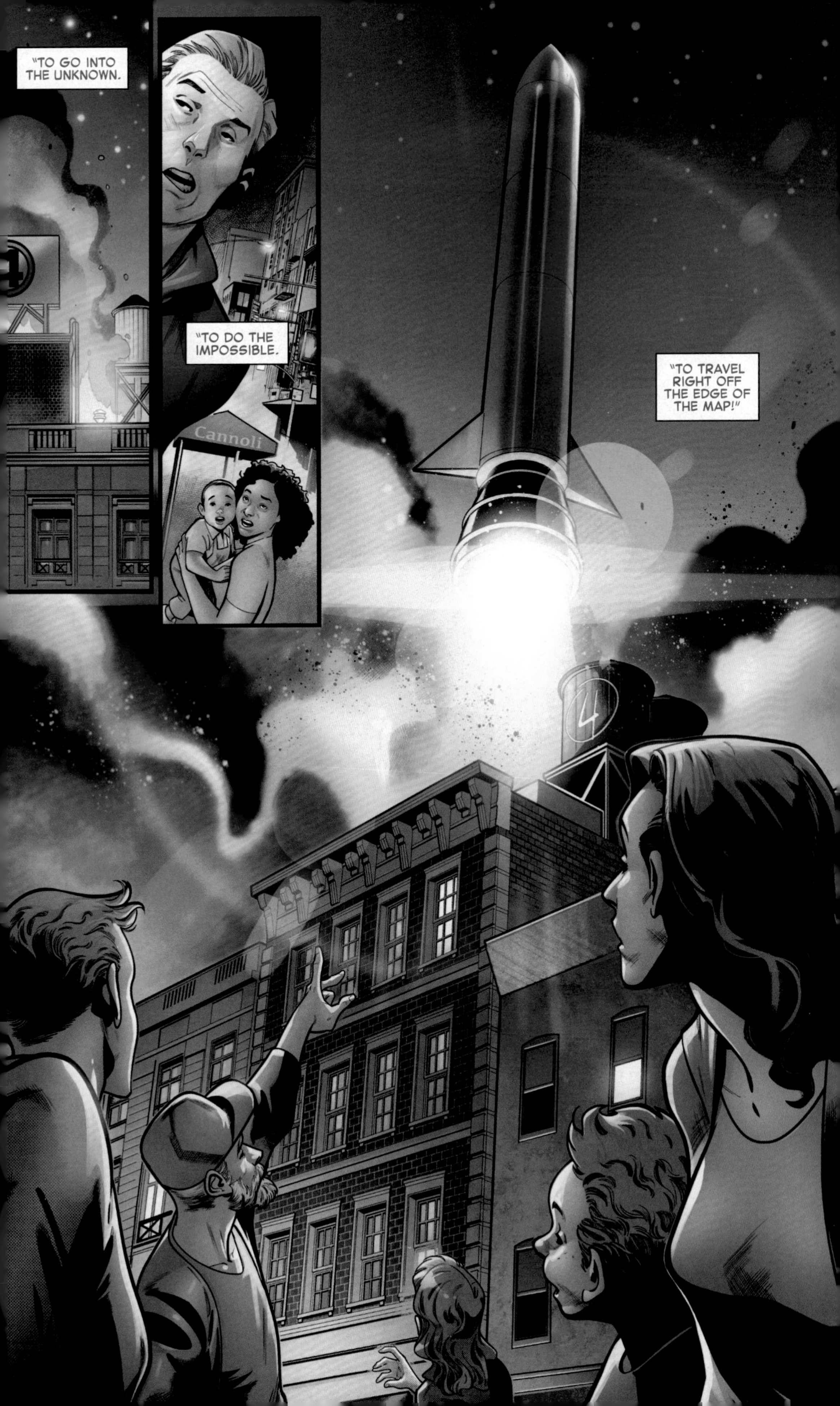
"TO GO INTO THE UNKNOWN.
"TO DO THE IMPOSSIBLE.
Cannoli
"TO TRAVEL RIGHT OFF THE EDGE OF THE MAP!"

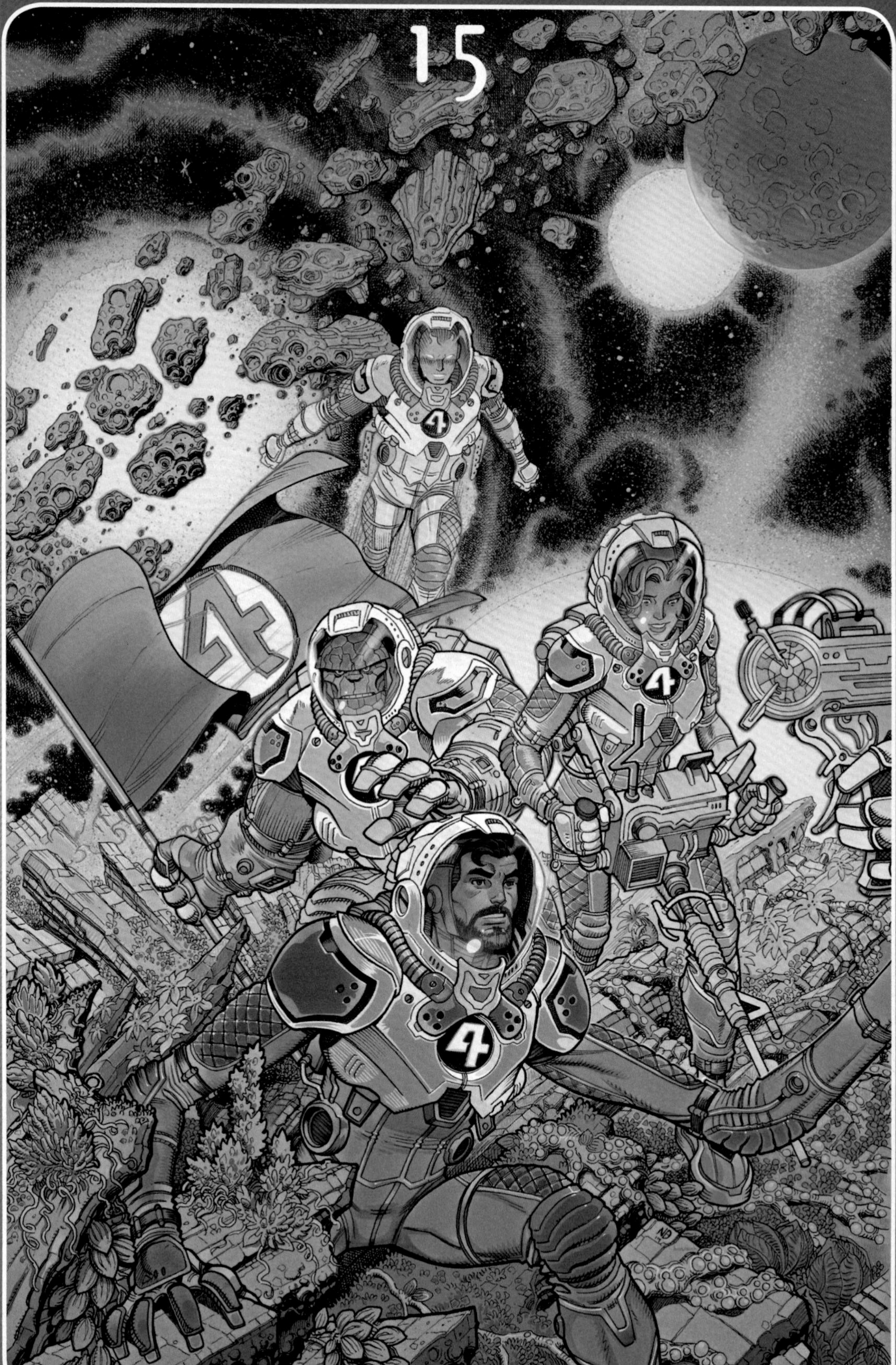
15

"The Invasion"

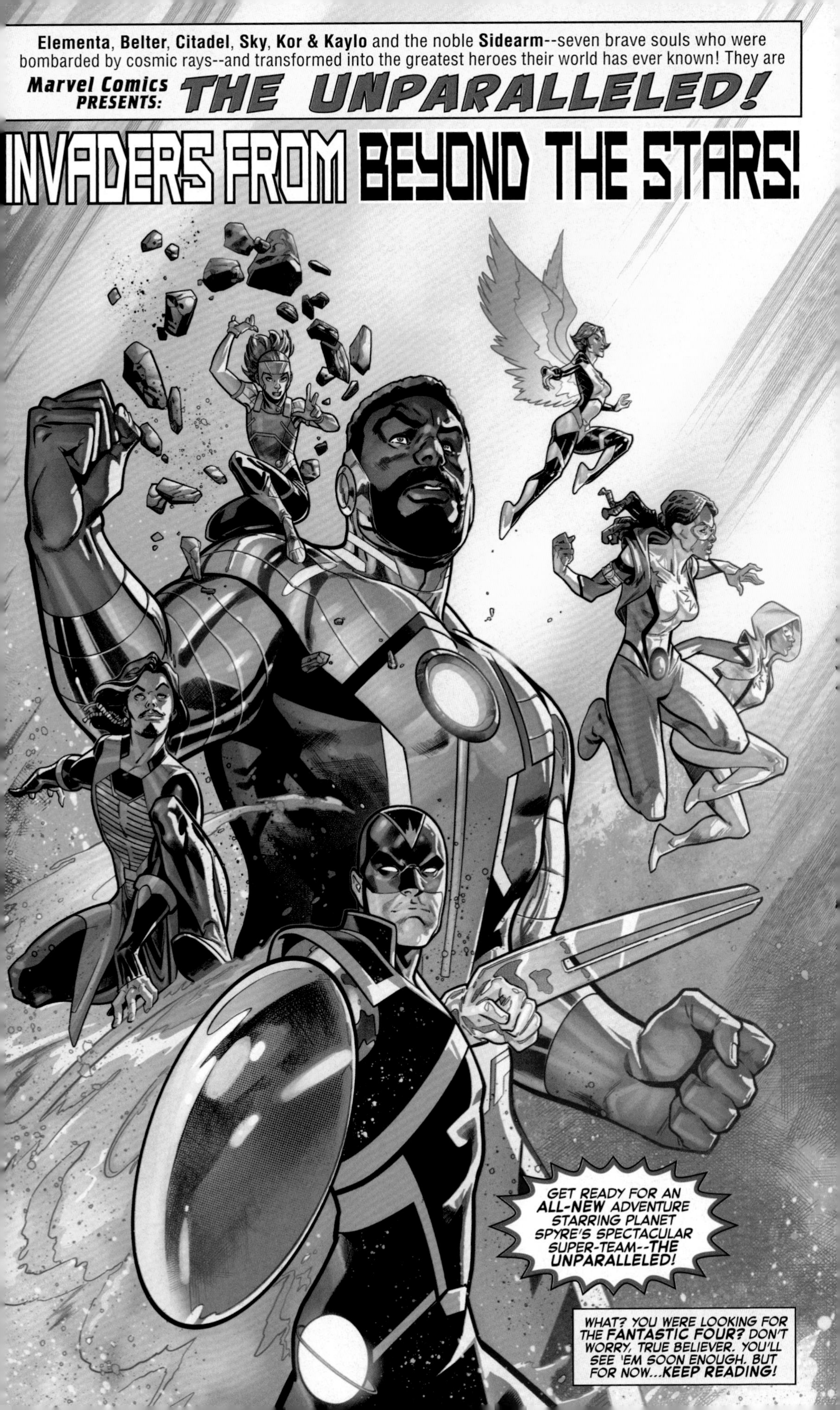
Elementa, Belter, Citadel, Sky, Kor & Kaylo and the noble Sidearm--seven brave souls who were bombarded by cosmic rays--and transformed into the greatest heroes their world has ever known! They are
Marvel Comics PRESENTS: THE UNPARALLELED!
INVADERS FROM BEYOND THE STARS!
GET READY FOR AN ALL-NEW ADVENTURE STARRING PLANET SPYRE'S SPECTACULAR SUPER-TEAM--THE UNPARALLELED!
WHAT? YOU WERE LOOKING FOR THE FANTASTIC FOUR? DON'T WORRY, TRUE BELIEVER. YOU'LL SEE 'EM SOON ENOUGH. BUT FOR NOW...KEEP READING!

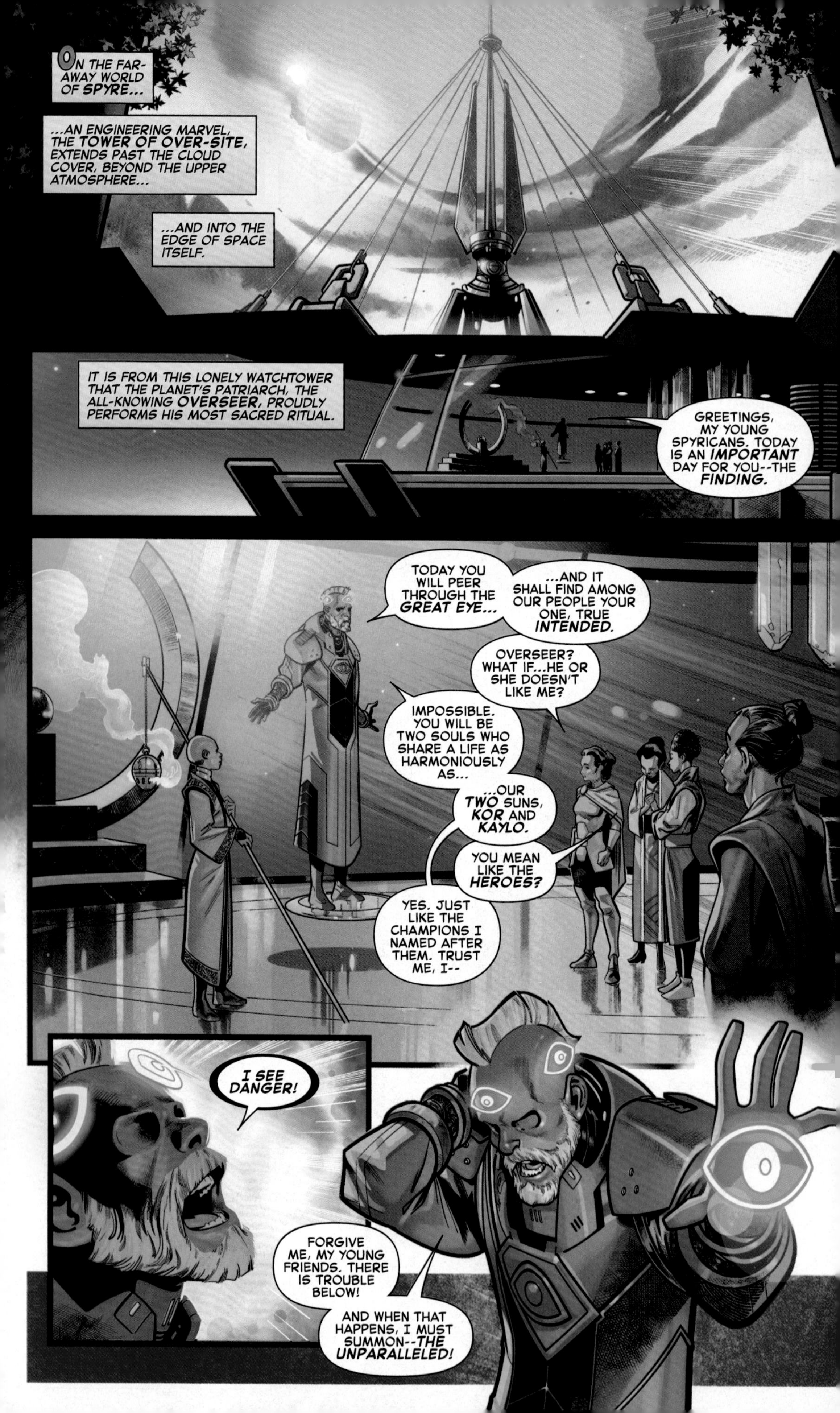
ON THE FAR-AWAY WORLD OF SPYRE...
...AN ENGINEERING MARVEL, THE TOWER OF OVER-SITE, EXTENDS PAST THE CLOUD COVER, BEYOND THE UPPER ATMOSPHERE...
...AND INTO THE EDGE OF SPACE ITSELF.
IT IS FROM THIS LONELY WATCHTOWER THAT THE PLANET'S PATRIARCH, THE ALL-KNOWING OVERSEER, PROUDLY PERFORMS HIS MOST SACRED RITUAL.
GREETINGS, MY YOUNG SPYRICANS. TODAY IS AN IMPORTANT DAY FOR YOU--THE FINDING.
TODAY YOU WILL PEER THROUGH THE GREAT EYE...
...AND IT SHALL FIND AMONG OUR PEOPLE YOUR ONE, TRUE INTENDED.
OVERSEER? WHAT IF...HE OR SHE DOESN'T LIKE ME?
IMPOSSIBLE. YOU WILL BE TWO SOULS WHO SHARE A LIFE AS HARMONIOUSLY AS...
...OUR TWO SUNS, KOR AND KAYLO.
YOU MEAN LIKE THE HEROES?
YES. JUST LIKE THE CHAMPIONS I NAMED AFTER THEM. TRUST ME, I--
I SEE DANGER!
FORGIVE ME, MY YOUNG FRIENDS. THERE IS TROUBLE BELOW!
AND WHEN THAT HAPPENS, I MUST SUMMON--THE UNPARALLELED!

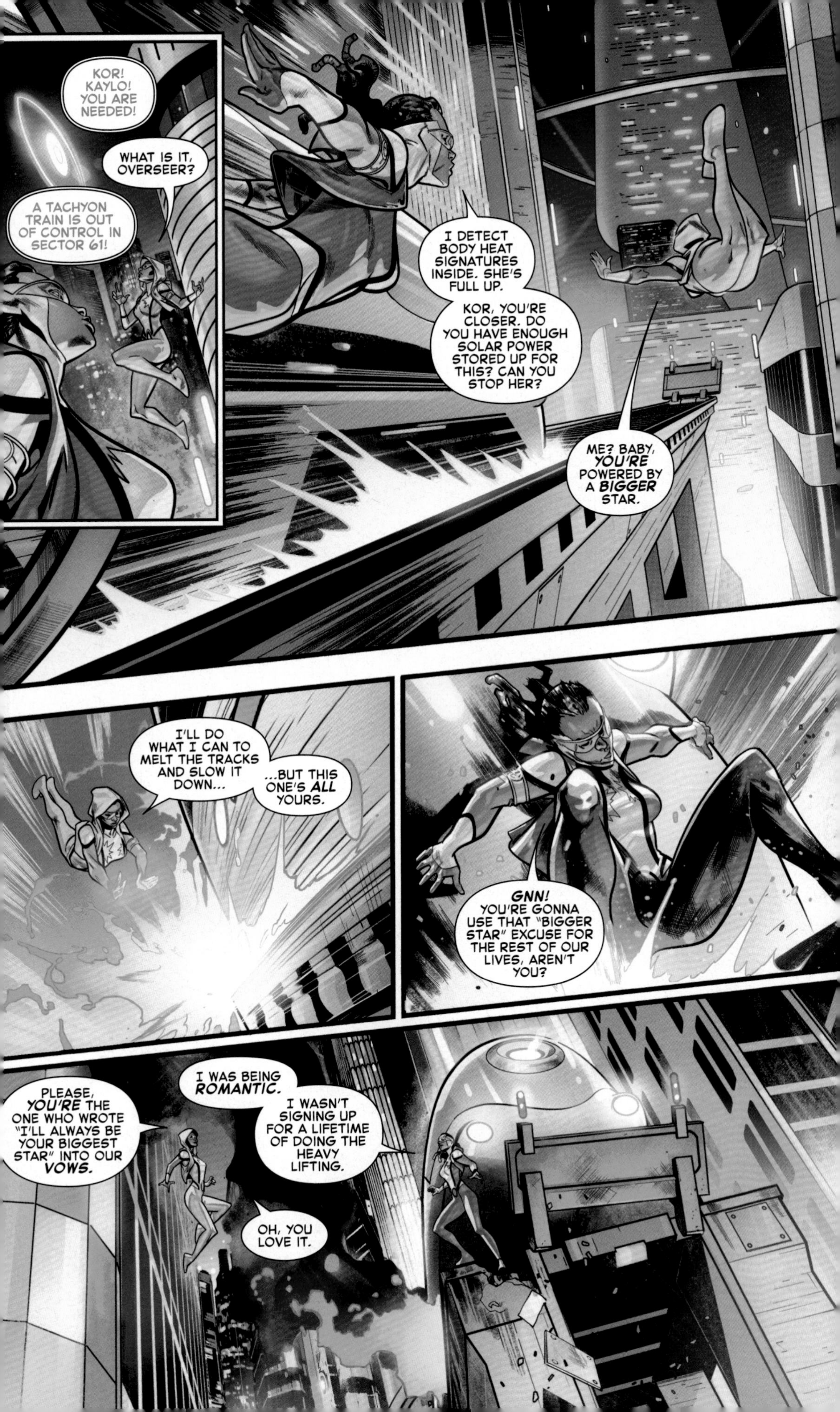
KOR! KAYLO! YOU ARE NEEDED!
WHAT IS IT, OVERSEER?
A TACHYON TRAIN IS OUT OF CONTROL IN SECTOR 61!
I DETECT BODY HEAT SIGNATURES INSIDE. SHE'S FULL UP.
KOR, YOU'RE CLOSER. DO YOU HAVE ENOUGH SOLAR POWER STORED UP FOR THIS? CAN YOU STOP HER?
ME? BABY, *YOU'RE* POWERED BY A **BIGGER** STAR.
I'LL DO WHAT I CAN TO MELT THE TRACKS AND SLOW IT DOWN...
...BUT THIS ONE'S **ALL** YOURS.
GNN! YOU'RE GONNA USE THAT "BIGGER STAR" EXCUSE FOR THE REST OF OUR LIVES, AREN'T YOU?
PLEASE, ***YOU'RE*** THE ONE WHO WROTE "I'LL ALWAYS BE YOUR BIGGEST STAR" INTO OUR ***VOWS.***
I WAS BEING ***ROMANTIC.***
I WASN'T SIGNING UP FOR A LIFETIME OF DOING THE HEAVY LIFTING.
OH, YOU LOVE IT.

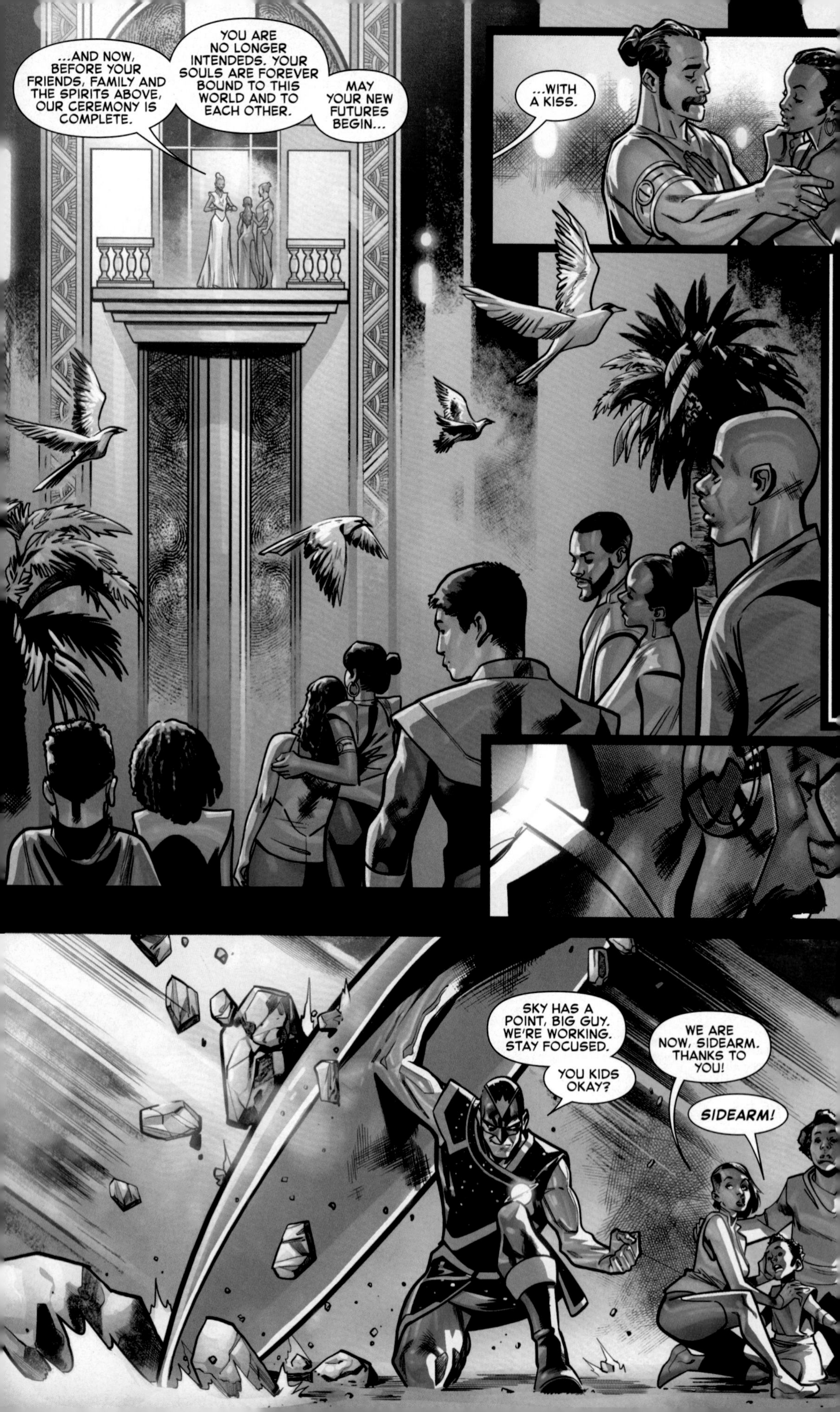
...AND NOW, BEFORE YOUR FRIENDS, FAMILY AND THE SPIRITS ABOVE, OUR CEREMONY IS COMPLETE.
YOU ARE NO LONGER INTENDEDS. YOUR SOULS ARE FOREVER BOUND TO THIS WORLD AND TO EACH OTHER.
MAY YOUR NEW FUTURES BEGIN...
...WITH A KISS.
SKY HAS A POINT, BIG GUY. WE'RE WORKING. STAY FOCUSED.
YOU KIDS OKAY?
WE ARE NOW, SIDEARM. THANKS TO YOU!
SIDEARM!

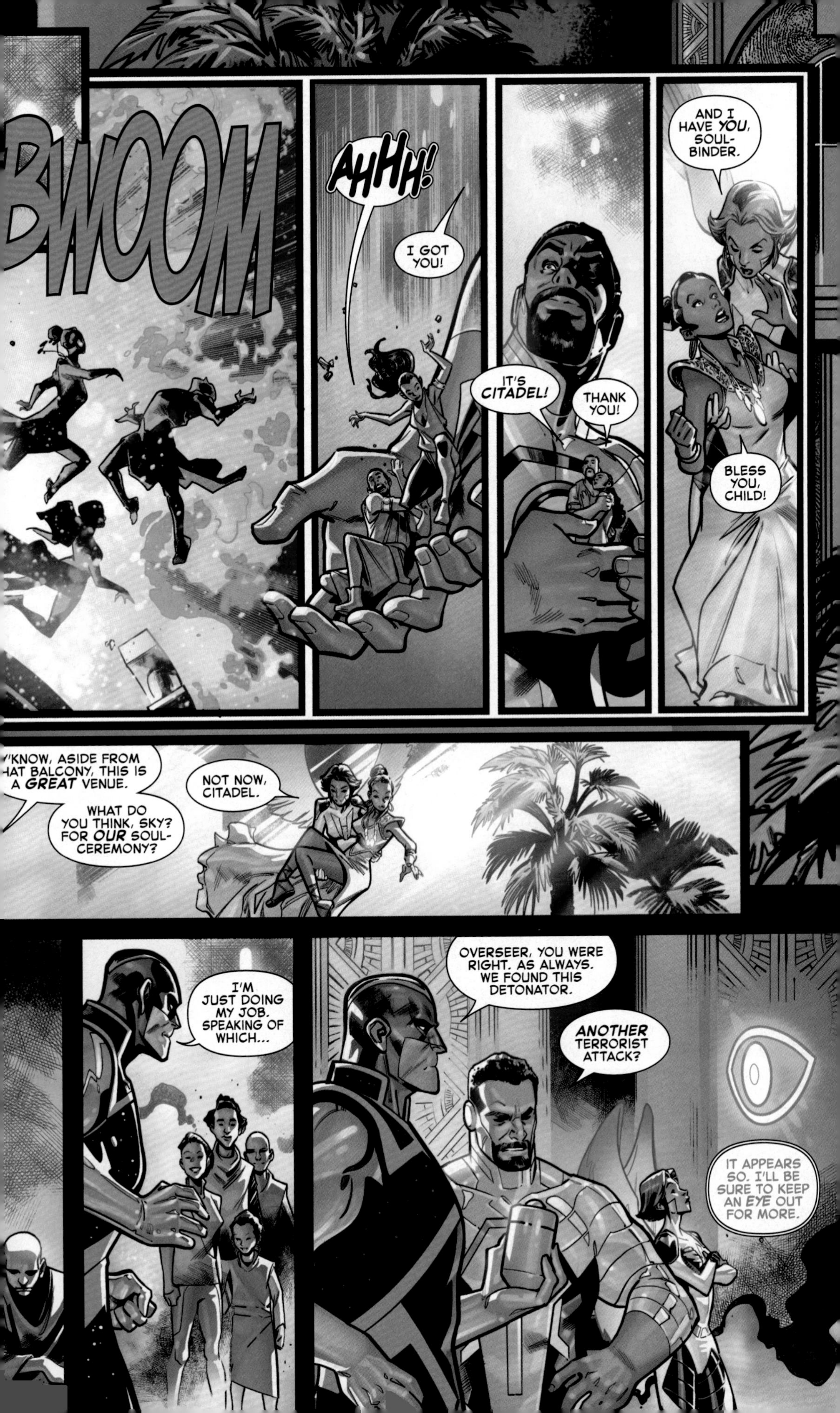
BWOOM
AHHH!
I GOT YOU!
IT'S CITADEL!
THANK YOU!
AND I HAVE YOU, SOUL-BINDER.
BLESS YOU, CHILD!
Y'KNOW, ASIDE FROM THAT BALCONY, THIS IS A GREAT VENUE.
WHAT DO YOU THINK, SKY? FOR OUR SOUL-CEREMONY?
NOT NOW, CITADEL.
I'M JUST DOING MY JOB. SPEAKING OF WHICH...
OVERSEER, YOU WERE RIGHT. AS ALWAYS. WE FOUND THIS DETONATOR.
ANOTHER TERRORIST ATTACK?
IT APPEARS SO. I'LL BE SURE TO KEEP AN EYE OUT FOR MORE.

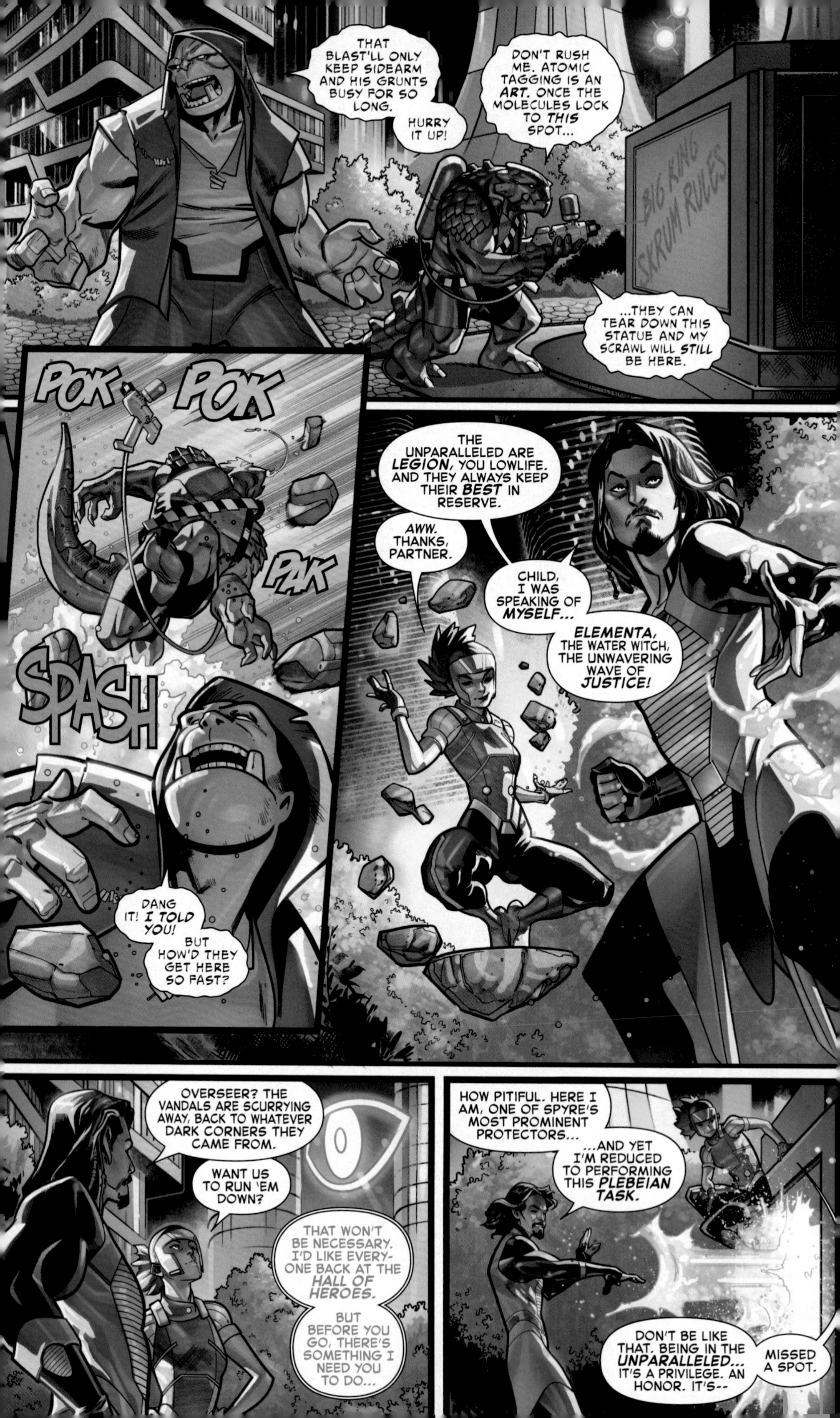
THAT BLAST'LL ONLY KEEP SIDEARM AND HIS GRUNTS BUSY FOR SO LONG.
HURRY IT UP!
DON'T RUSH ME. ATOMIC TAGGING IS AN ART. ONCE THE MOLECULES LOCK TO THIS SPOT...
BIG KING SKRUM RULES
...THEY CAN TEAR DOWN THIS STATUE AND MY SCRAWL WILL STILL BE HERE.
POK POK
PAK
SPASH
DANG IT! I TOLD YOU!
BUT HOW'D THEY GET HERE SO FAST?
THE UNPARALLELED ARE LEGION, YOU LOWLIFE. AND THEY ALWAYS KEEP THEIR BEST IN RESERVE.
AWW. THANKS, PARTNER.
CHILD, I WAS SPEAKING OF MYSELF...
ELEMENTA, THE WATER WITCH, THE UNWAVERING WAVE OF JUSTICE!
OVERSEER? THE VANDALS ARE SCURRYING AWAY, BACK TO WHATEVER DARK CORNERS THEY CAME FROM.
WANT US TO RUN 'EM DOWN?
THAT WON'T BE NECESSARY. I'D LIKE EVERY-ONE BACK AT THE HALL OF HEROES.
BUT BEFORE YOU GO, THERE'S SOMETHING I NEED YOU TO DO...
HOW PITIFUL. HERE I AM, ONE OF SPYRE'S MOST PROMINENT PROTECTORS...
...AND YET I'M REDUCED TO PERFORMING THIS PLEBEIAN TASK.
DON'T BE LIKE THAT. BEING IN THE UNPARALLELED... IT'S A PRIVILEGE. AN HONOR. IT'S--
MISSED A SPOT.

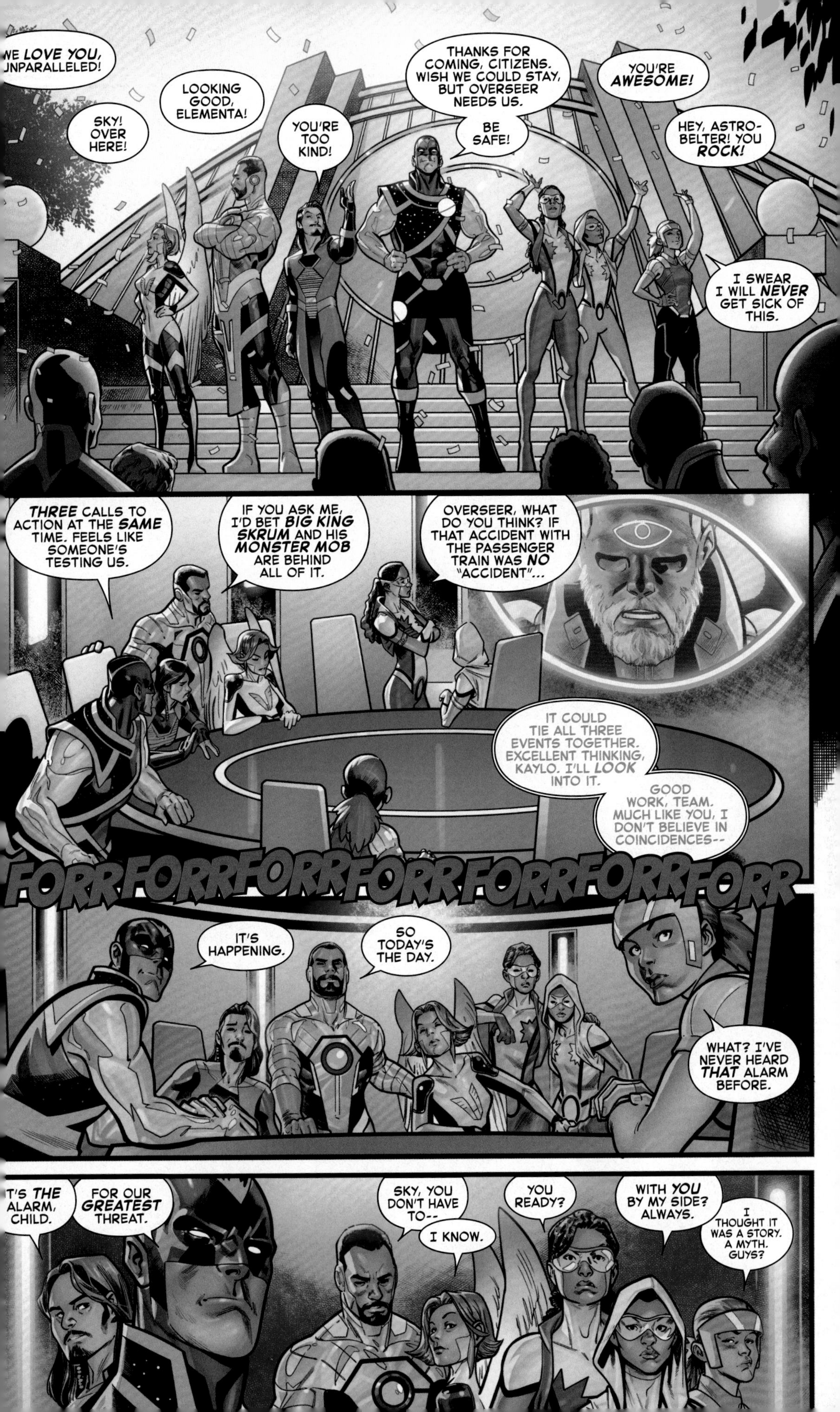
WE LOVE YOU, UNPARALLELED!
SKY! OVER HERE!
LOOKING GOOD, ELEMENTA!
YOU'RE TOO KIND!
THANKS FOR COMING, CITIZENS. WISH WE COULD STAY, BUT OVERSEER NEEDS US.
BE SAFE!
YOU'RE AWESOME!
HEY, ASTRO-BELTER! YOU ROCK!
I SWEAR I WILL NEVER GET SICK OF THIS.
THREE CALLS TO ACTION AT THE SAME TIME. FEELS LIKE SOMEONE'S TESTING US.
IF YOU ASK ME, I'D BET BIG KING SKRUM AND HIS MONSTER MOB ARE BEHIND ALL OF IT.
OVERSEER, WHAT DO YOU THINK? IF THAT ACCIDENT WITH THE PASSENGER TRAIN WAS NO "ACCIDENT"...
IT COULD TIE ALL THREE EVENTS TOGETHER. EXCELLENT THINKING, KAYLO. I'LL LOOK INTO IT.
GOOD WORK, TEAM. MUCH LIKE YOU, I DON'T BELIEVE IN COINCIDENCES--
FORRFORRFORRFORRFORRFORRFORRFORR
IT'S HAPPENING.
SO TODAY'S THE DAY.
WHAT? I'VE NEVER HEARD THAT ALARM BEFORE.
IT'S THE ALARM, CHILD.
FOR OUR GREATEST THREAT.
SKY, YOU DON'T HAVE TO--
I KNOW.
YOU READY?
WITH YOU BY MY SIDE? ALWAYS.
I THOUGHT IT WAS A STORY. A MYTH. GUYS?

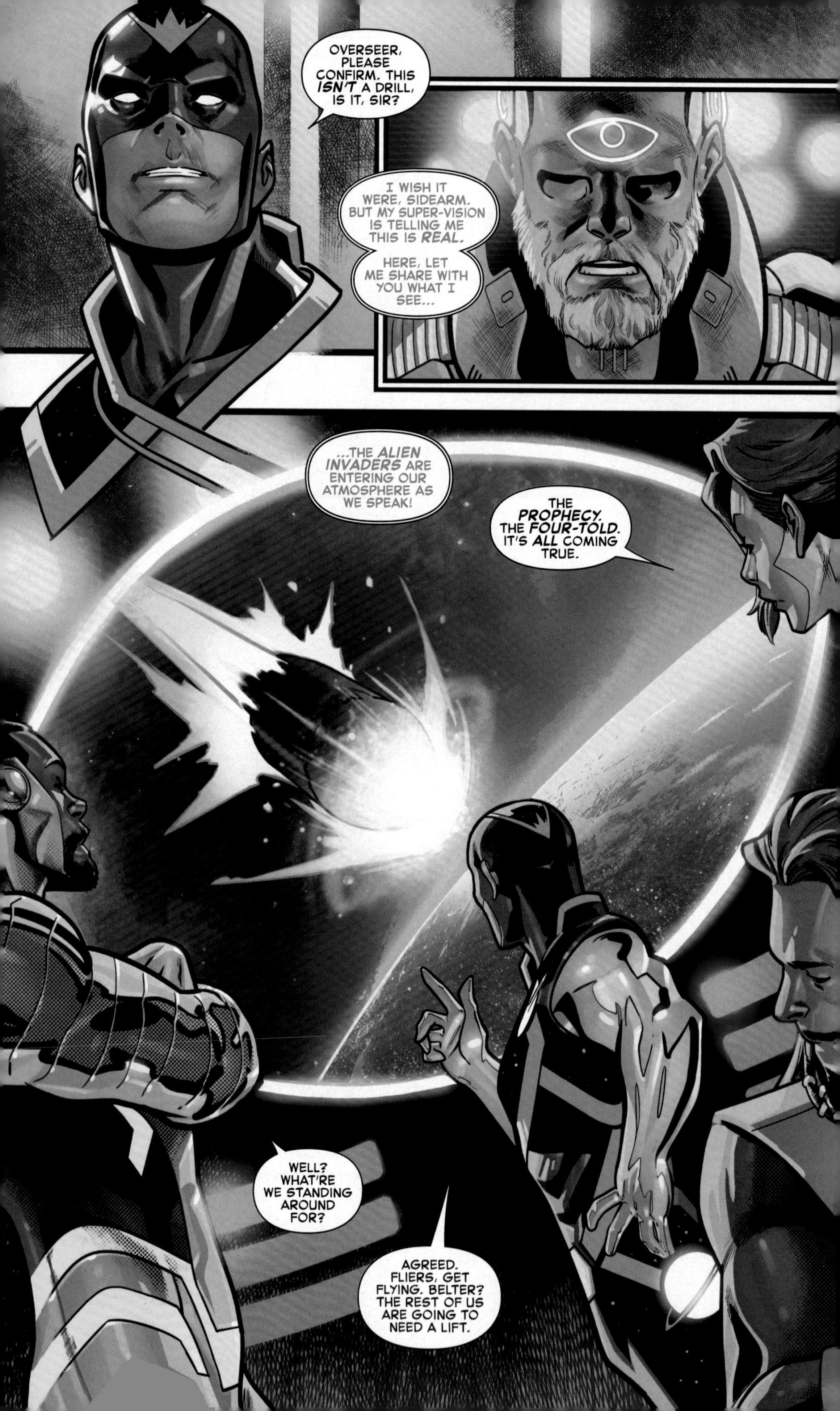
OVERSEER, PLEASE CONFIRM. THIS ISN'T A DRILL, IS IT, SIR?
I WISH IT WERE, SIDEARM. BUT MY SUPER-VISION IS TELLING ME THIS IS REAL.
HERE, LET ME SHARE WITH YOU WHAT I SEE...
...THE ALIEN INVADERS ARE ENTERING OUR ATMOSPHERE AS WE SPEAK!
THE PROPHECY. THE FOUR-TOLD. IT'S ALL COMING TRUE.
WELL? WHAT'RE WE STANDING AROUND FOR?
AGREED. FLIERS, GET FLYING. BELTER? THE REST OF US ARE GOING TO NEED A LIFT.

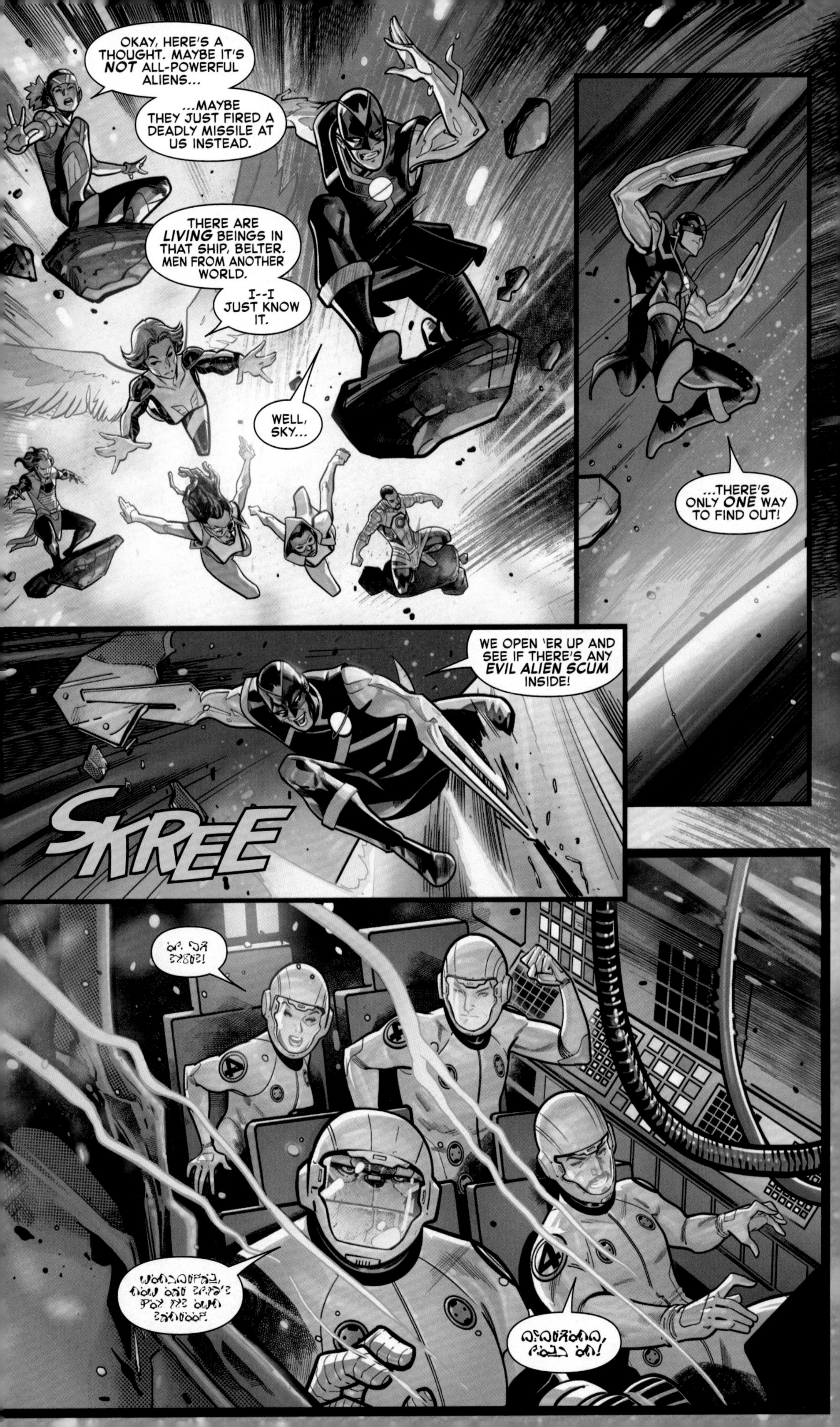
OKAY, HERE'S A THOUGHT. MAYBE IT'S NOT ALL-POWERFUL ALIENS...
...MAYBE THEY JUST FIRED A DEADLY MISSILE AT US INSTEAD.
THERE ARE LIVING BEINGS IN THAT SHIP, BELTER. MEN FROM ANOTHER WORLD.
I--I JUST KNOW IT.
WELL, SKY...
...THERE'S ONLY ONE WAY TO FIND OUT!
WE OPEN 'ER UP AND SEE IF THERE'S ANY EVIL ALIEN SCUM INSIDE!
SKREE

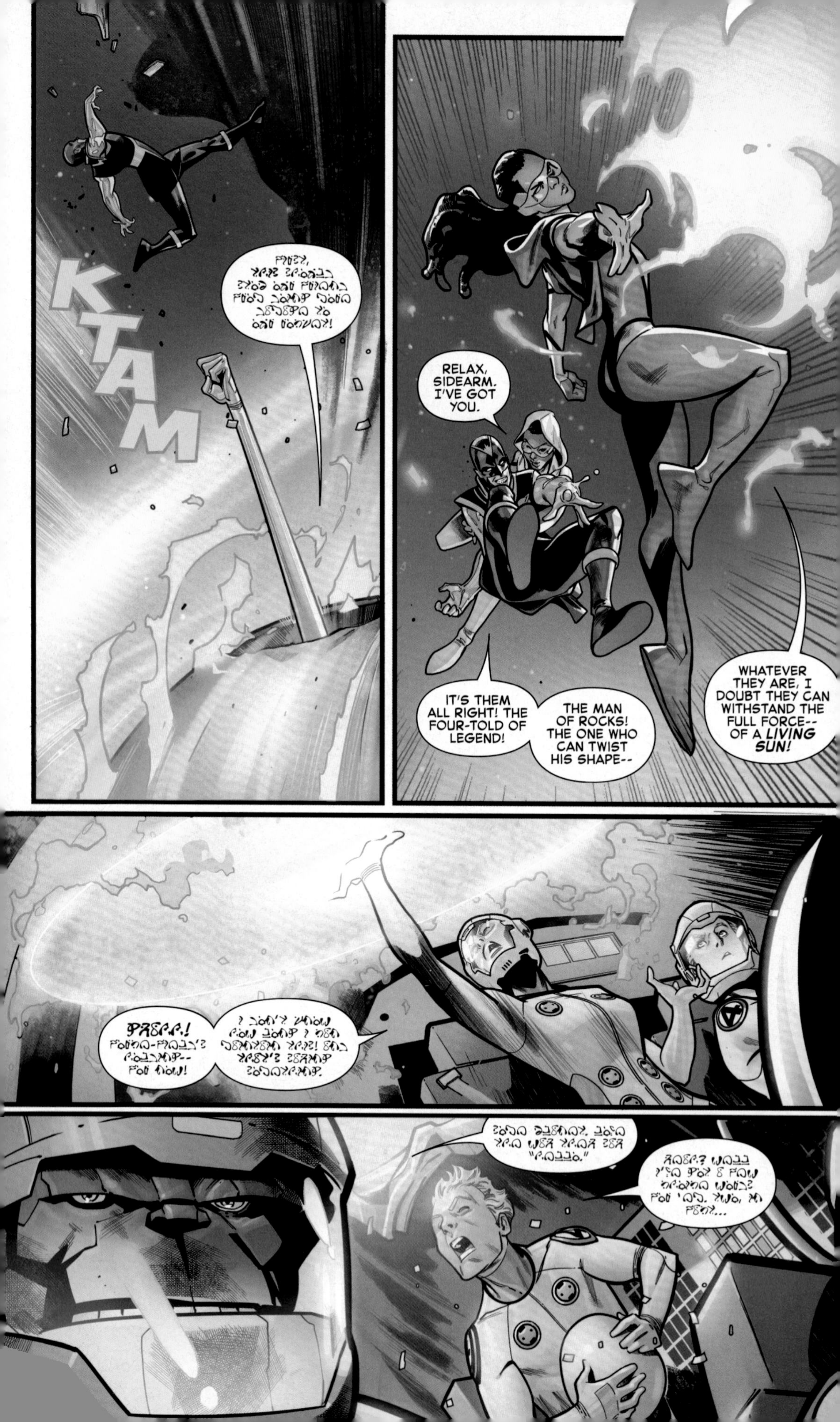
KTAM
RELAX, SIDEARM. I'VE GOT YOU.
IT'S THEM ALL RIGHT! THE FOUR-TOLD OF LEGEND!
THE MAN OF ROCKS! THE ONE WHO CAN TWIST HIS SHAPE--
WHATEVER THEY ARE, I DOUBT THEY CAN WITHSTAND THE FULL FORCE-- OF A *LIVING SUN!*

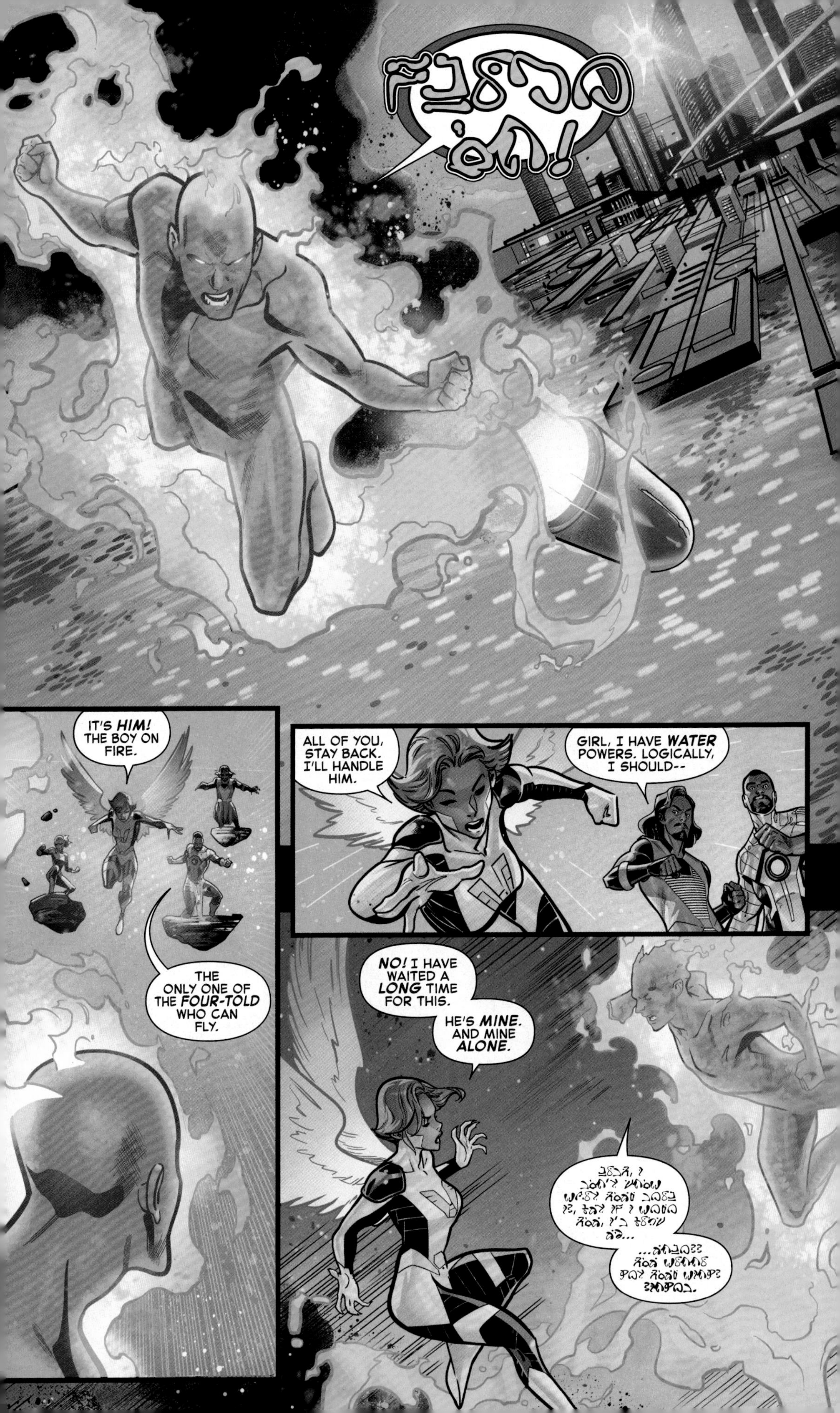
IT'S **HIM!** THE BOY ON FIRE.
THE ONLY ONE OF THE **FOUR-TOLD** WHO CAN FLY.
ALL OF YOU, STAY BACK. I'LL HANDLE HIM.
GIRL, I HAVE **WATER** POWERS. LOGICALLY, I SHOULD--
NO! I HAVE WAITED A **LONG** TIME FOR THIS.
HE'S **MINE.** AND MINE **ALONE.**

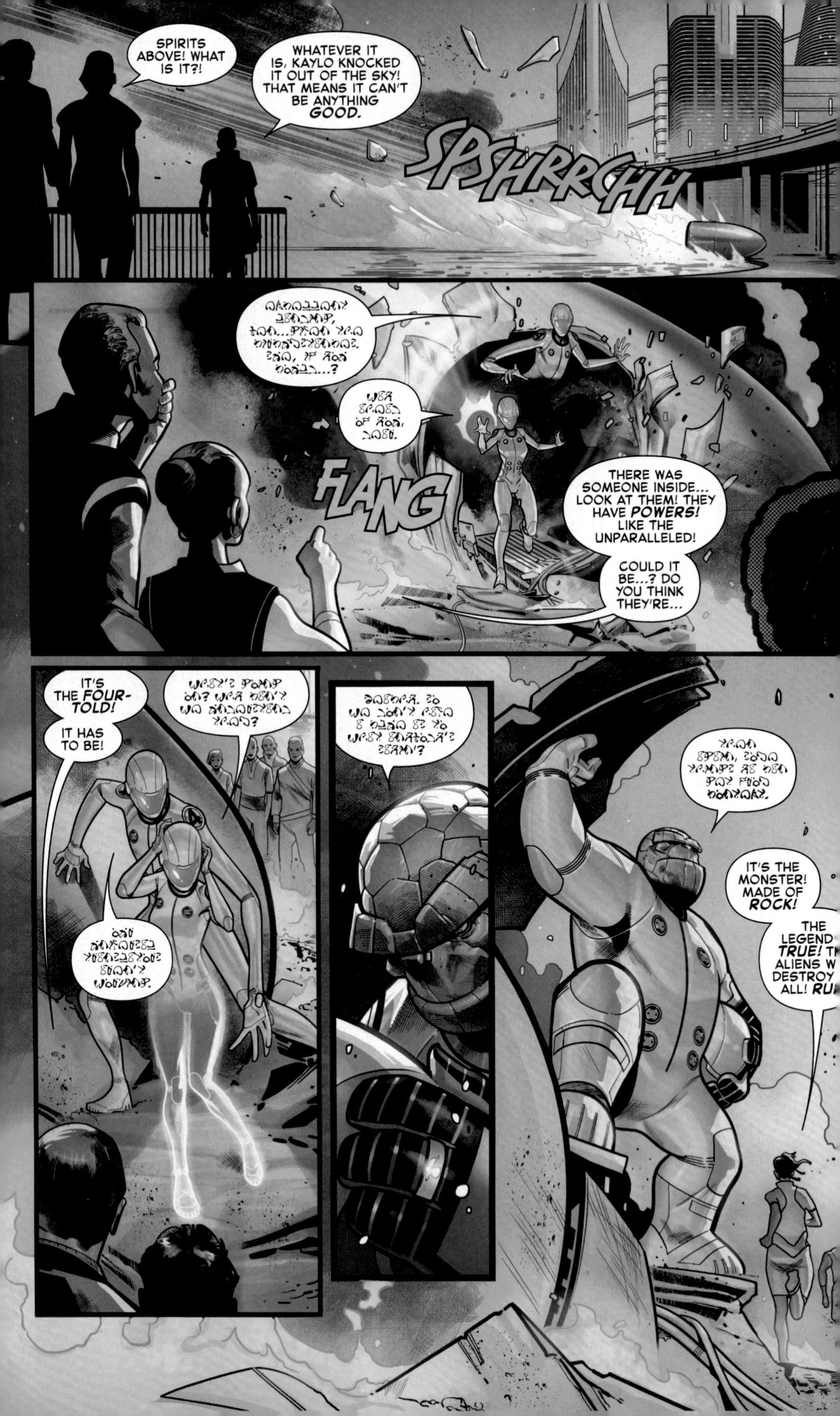
SPIRITS ABOVE! WHAT IS IT?!
WHATEVER IT IS, KAYLO KNOCKED IT OUT OF THE SKY! THAT MEANS IT CAN'T BE ANYTHING GOOD.
SPSHRRCHH
FLANG
THERE WAS SOMEONE INSIDE... LOOK AT THEM! THEY HAVE POWERS! LIKE THE UNPARALLELED!
COULD IT BE...? DO YOU THINK THEY'RE...
IT'S THE FOUR-TOLD!
IT HAS TO BE!
IT'S THE MONSTER! MADE OF ROCK!
THE LEGEND TRUE! T ALIENS W DESTROY ALL! RU

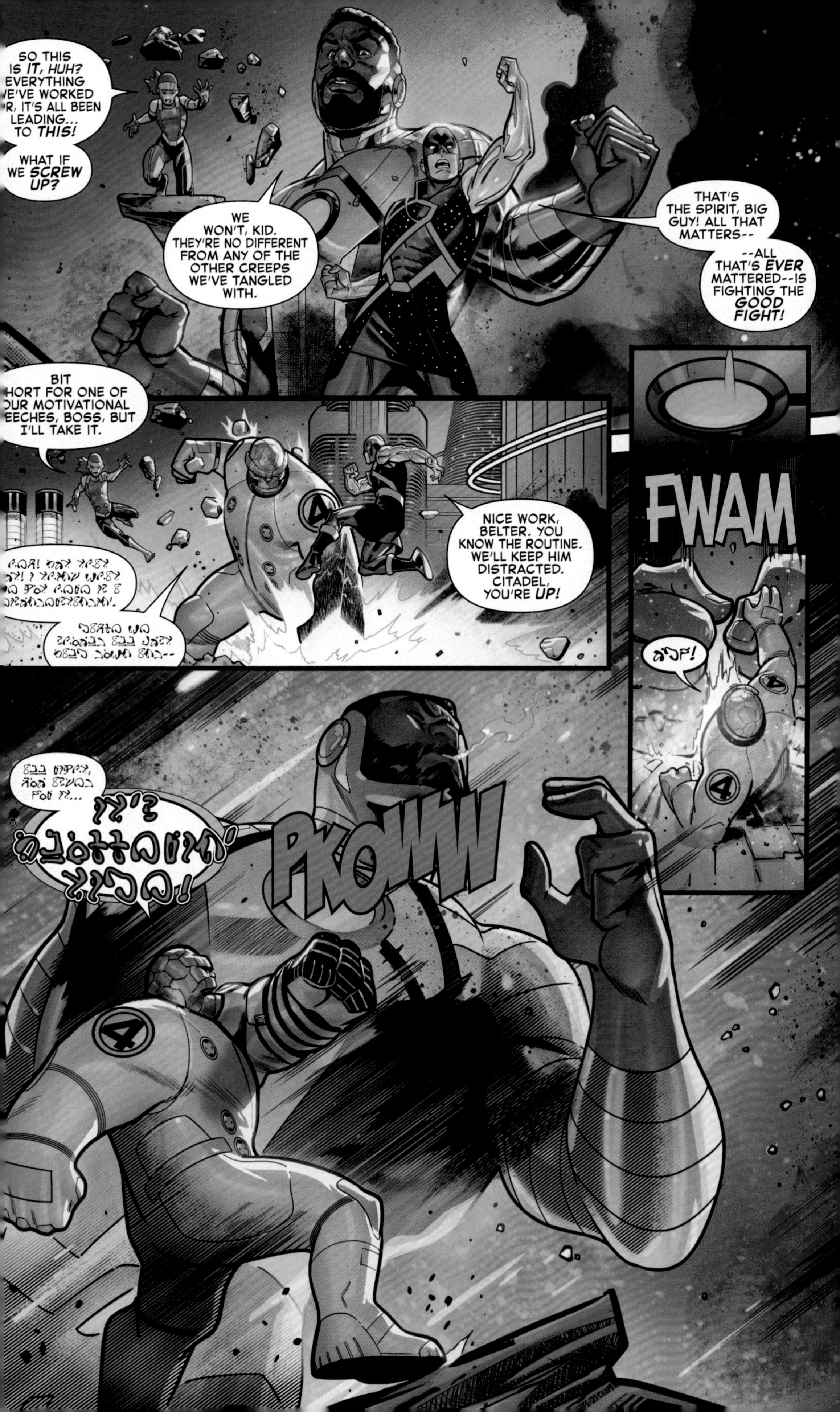
SO THIS IS IT, HUH? EVERYTHING VE'VE WORKED R, IT'S ALL BEEN LEADING... TO THIS!
WHAT IF WE SCREW UP?
WE WON'T, KID. THEY'RE NO DIFFERENT FROM ANY OF THE OTHER CREEPS WE'VE TANGLED WITH.
THAT'S THE SPIRIT, BIG GUY! ALL THAT MATTERS--
--ALL THAT'S EVER MATTERED--IS FIGHTING THE GOOD FIGHT!
BIT HORT FOR ONE OF OUR MOTIVATIONAL EECHES, BOSS, BUT I'LL TAKE IT.
NICE WORK, BELTER. YOU KNOW THE ROUTINE. WE'LL KEEP HIM DISTRACTED. CITADEL, YOU'RE UP!
FWAM
PKOWW

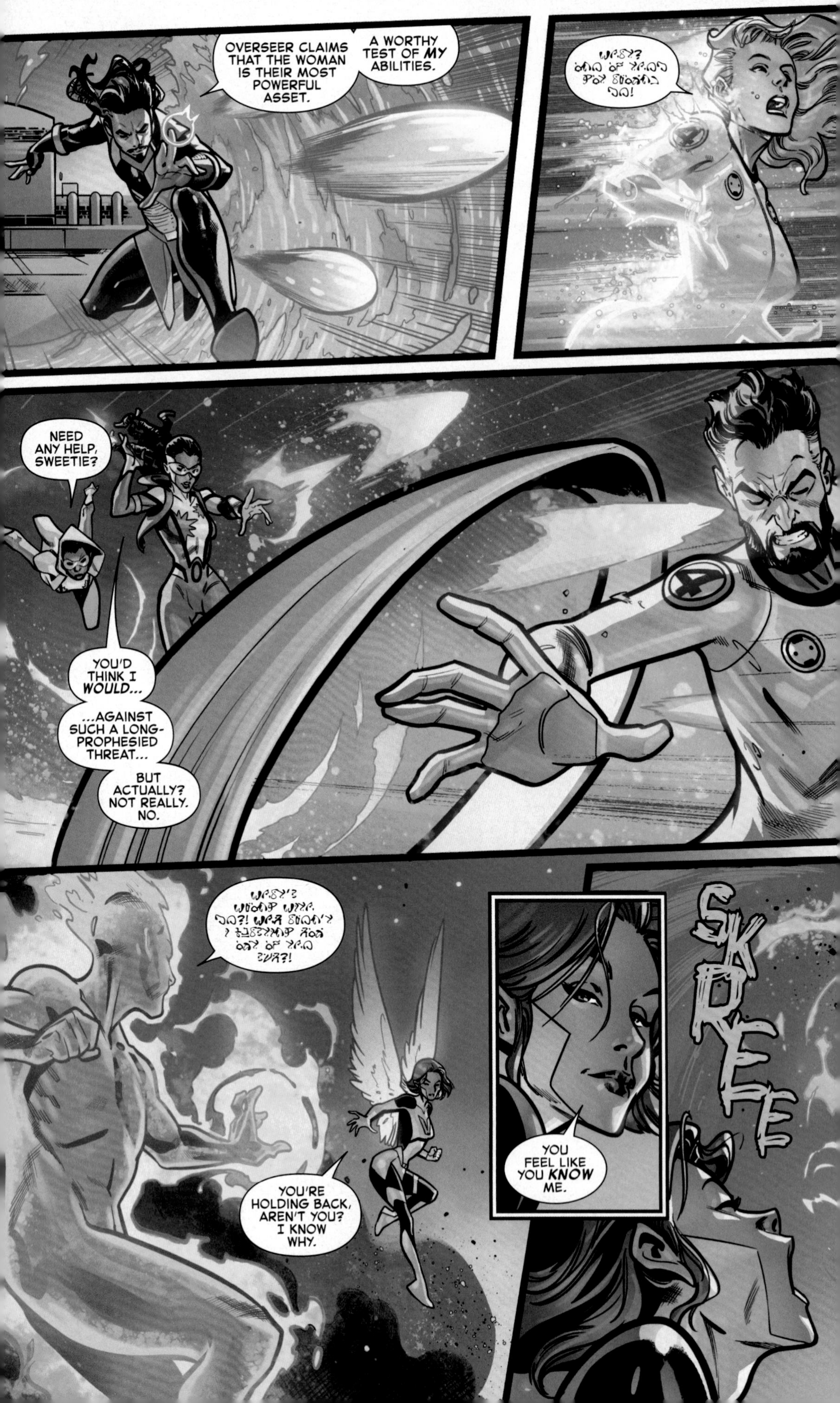
OVERSEER CLAIMS THAT THE WOMAN IS THEIR MOST POWERFUL ASSET.
A WORTHY TEST OF **MY** ABILITIES.
NEED ANY HELP, SWEETIE?
YOU'D THINK I **WOULD...**
...AGAINST SUCH A LONG-PROPHESIED THREAT...
BUT ACTUALLY? NOT REALLY. NO.
YOU'RE HOLDING BACK, AREN'T YOU? I KNOW WHY.
YOU FEEL LIKE YOU **KNOW** ME.
SKREEE

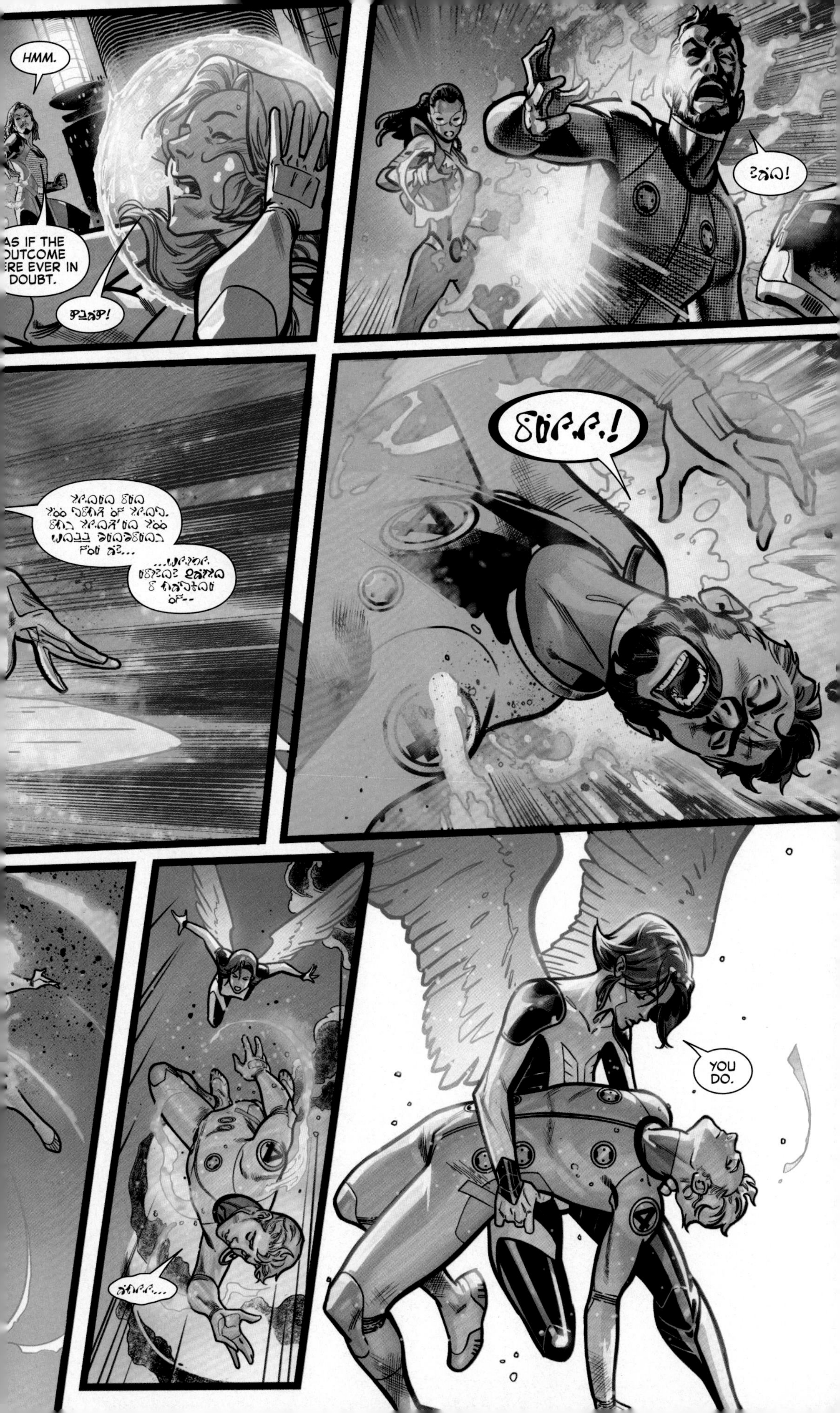
HMM.
AS IF THE
OUTCOME
ERE EVER IN
DOUBT.
YOU
DO.

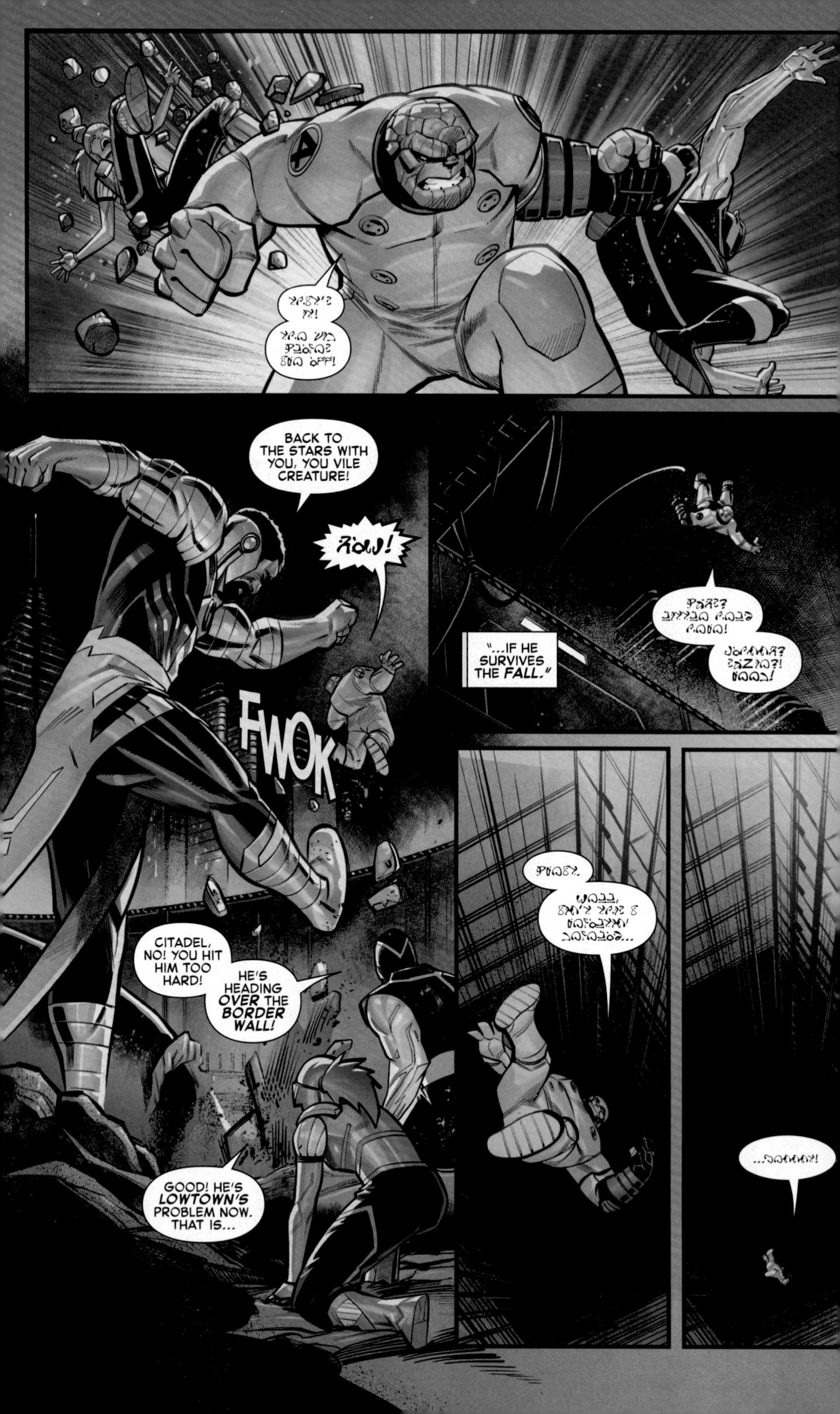
BACK TO THE STARS WITH YOU, YOU VILE CREATURE!
FWOK
CITADEL, NO! YOU HIT HIM TOO HARD!
HE'S HEADING OVER THE BORDER WALL!
GOOD! HE'S LOWTOWN'S PROBLEM NOW. THAT IS...
"...IF HE SURVIVES THE FALL."

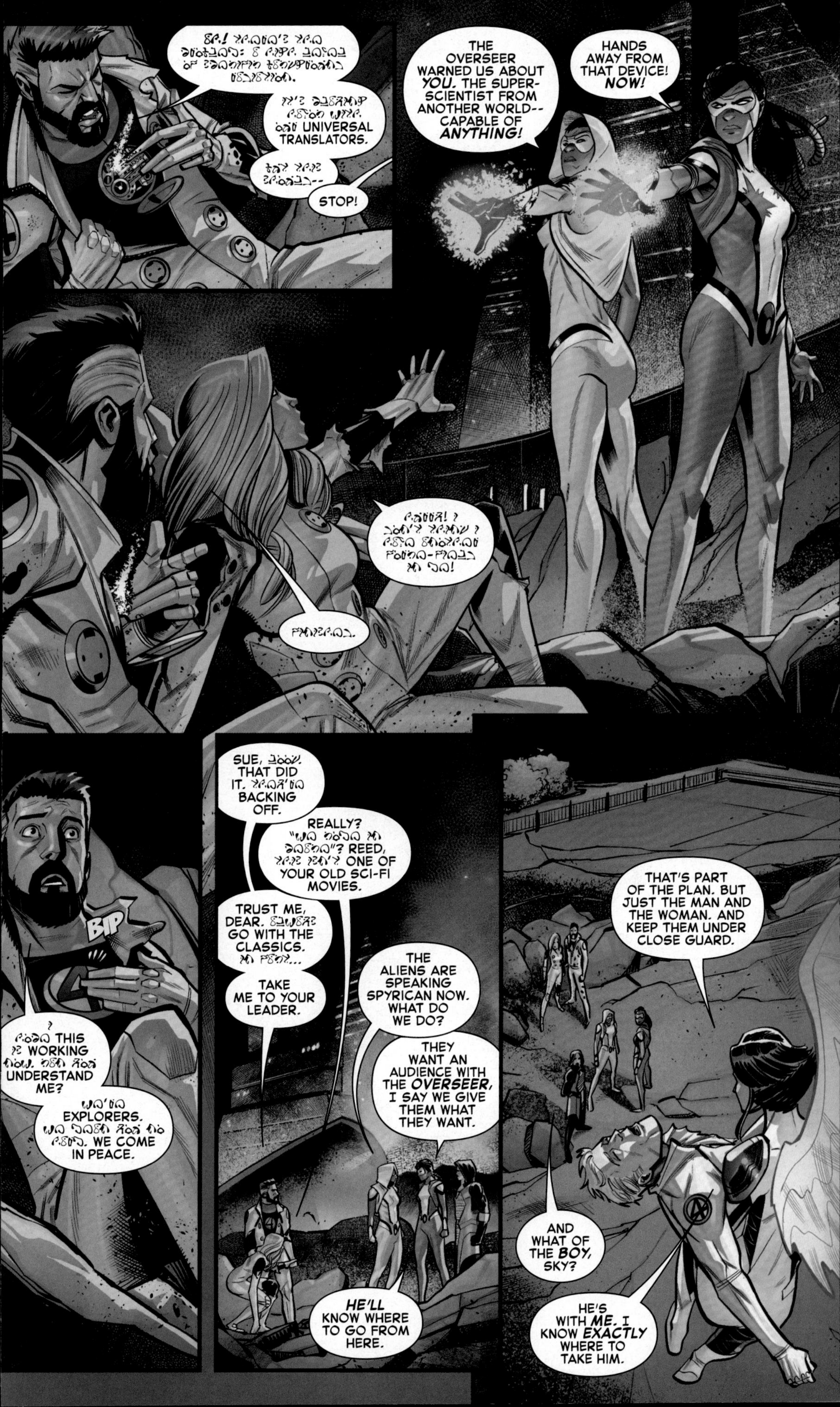
UNIVERSAL TRANSLATORS.
STOP!
THE OVERSEER WARNED US ABOUT YOU. THE SUPER-SCIENTIST FROM ANOTHER WORLD-- CAPABLE OF ANYTHING!
HANDS AWAY FROM THAT DEVICE! NOW!
BIP
THIS WORKING UNDERSTAND ME?
EXPLORERS. WE COME IN PEACE.
SUE, THAT DID IT. BACKING OFF.
REALLY? REED, ONE OF YOUR OLD SCI-FI MOVIES.
TRUST ME, DEAR. GO WITH THE CLASSICS.
TAKE ME TO YOUR LEADER.
THE ALIENS ARE SPEAKING SPYRICAN NOW. WHAT DO WE DO?
THEY WANT AN AUDIENCE WITH THE OVERSEER, I SAY WE GIVE THEM WHAT THEY WANT.
HE'LL KNOW WHERE TO GO FROM HERE.
THAT'S PART OF THE PLAN. BUT JUST THE MAN AND THE WOMAN. AND KEEP THEM UNDER CLOSE GUARD.
AND WHAT OF THE BOY, SKY?
HE'S WITH ME. I KNOW EXACTLY WHERE TO TAKE HIM.

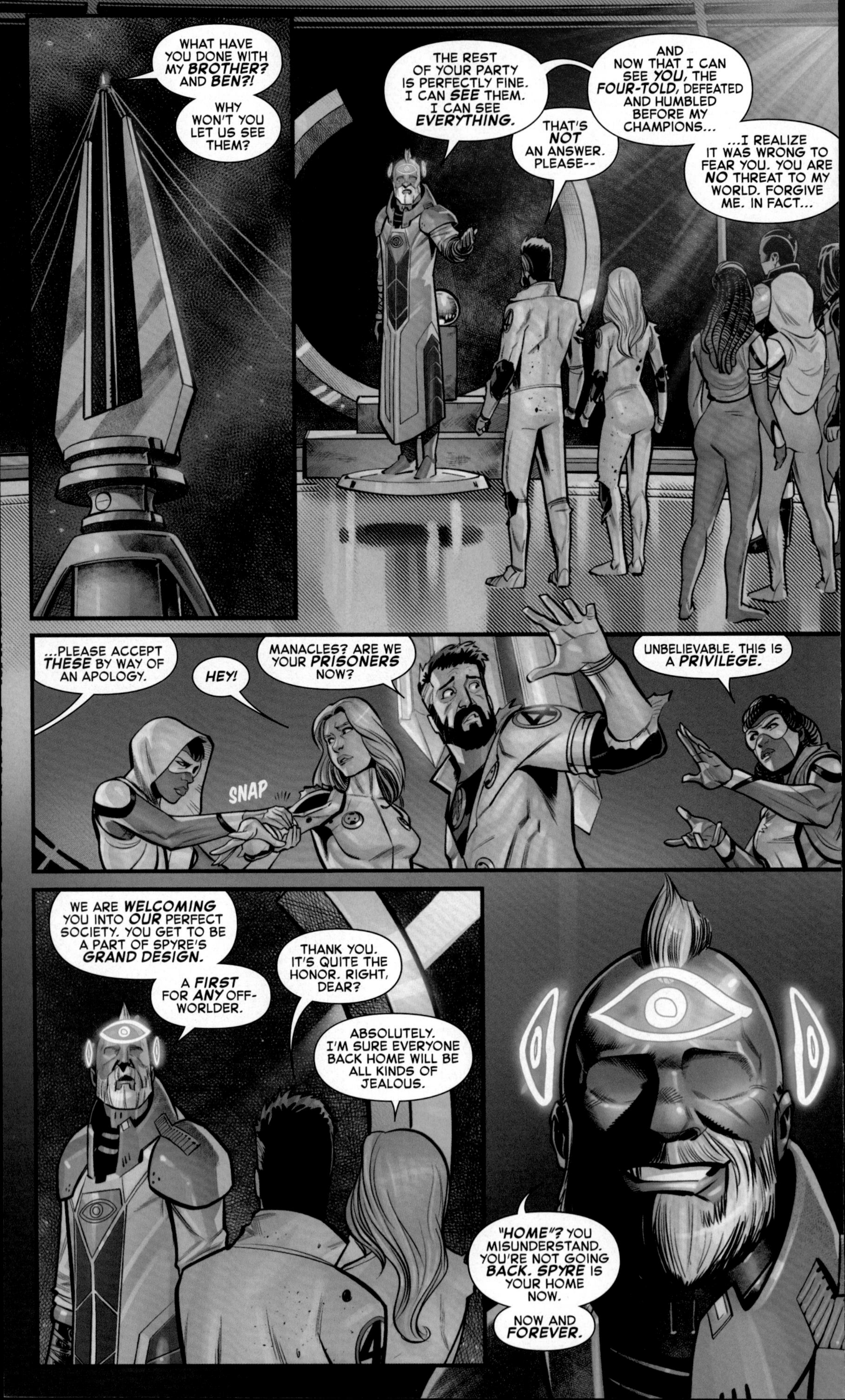

WHAT HAVE YOU DONE WITH MY BROTHER? AND BEN?!
WHY WON'T YOU LET US SEE THEM?
THE REST OF YOUR PARTY IS PERFECTLY FINE. I CAN SEE THEM. I CAN SEE EVERYTHING.
THAT'S NOT AN ANSWER. PLEASE--
AND NOW THAT I CAN SEE YOU, THE FOUR-TOLD, DEFEATED AND HUMBLED BEFORE MY CHAMPIONS...
...I REALIZE IT WAS WRONG TO FEAR YOU. YOU ARE NO THREAT TO MY WORLD. FORGIVE ME. IN FACT...
...PLEASE ACCEPT THESE BY WAY OF AN APOLOGY.
HEY!
SNAP
MANACLES? ARE WE YOUR PRISONERS NOW?
UNBELIEVABLE. THIS IS A PRIVILEGE.
WE ARE WELCOMING YOU INTO OUR PERFECT SOCIETY. YOU GET TO BE A PART OF SPYRE'S GRAND DESIGN.
A FIRST FOR ANY OFF-WORLDER.
THANK YOU. IT'S QUITE THE HONOR. RIGHT, DEAR?
ABSOLUTELY. I'M SURE EVERYONE BACK HOME WILL BE ALL KINDS OF JEALOUS.
"HOME"? YOU MISUNDERSTAND. YOU'RE NOT GOING BACK. SPYRE IS YOUR HOME NOW.
NOW AND FOREVER.

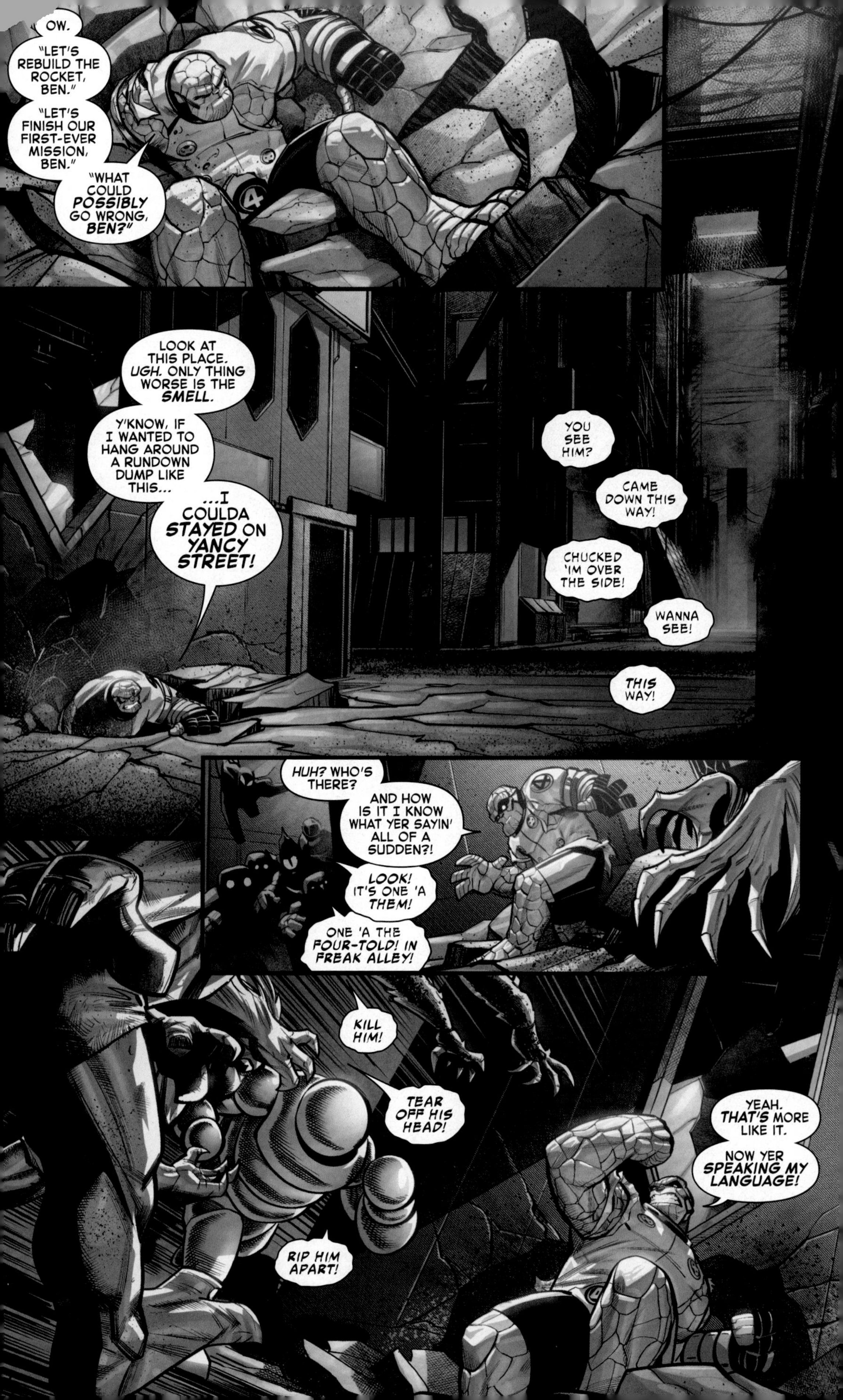
OW.
"LET'S REBUILD THE ROCKET, BEN."
"LET'S FINISH OUR FIRST-EVER MISSION, BEN."
"WHAT COULD POSSIBLY GO WRONG, BEN?"
LOOK AT THIS PLACE. UGH. ONLY THING WORSE IS THE SMELL.
Y'KNOW, IF I WANTED TO HANG AROUND A RUNDOWN DUMP LIKE THIS...
...I COULDA STAYED ON YANCY STREET!
YOU SEE HIM?
CAME DOWN THIS WAY!
CHUCKED 'IM OVER THE SIDE!
WANNA SEE!
THIS WAY!
HUH? WHO'S THERE?
AND HOW IS IT I KNOW WHAT YER SAYIN' ALL OF A SUDDEN?!
LOOK! IT'S ONE 'A THEM!
ONE 'A THE FOUR-TOLD! IN FREAK ALLEY!
KILL HIM!
TEAR OFF HIS HEAD!
RIP HIM APART!
YEAH. THAT'S MORE LIKE IT.
NOW YER SPEAKING MY LANGUAGE!

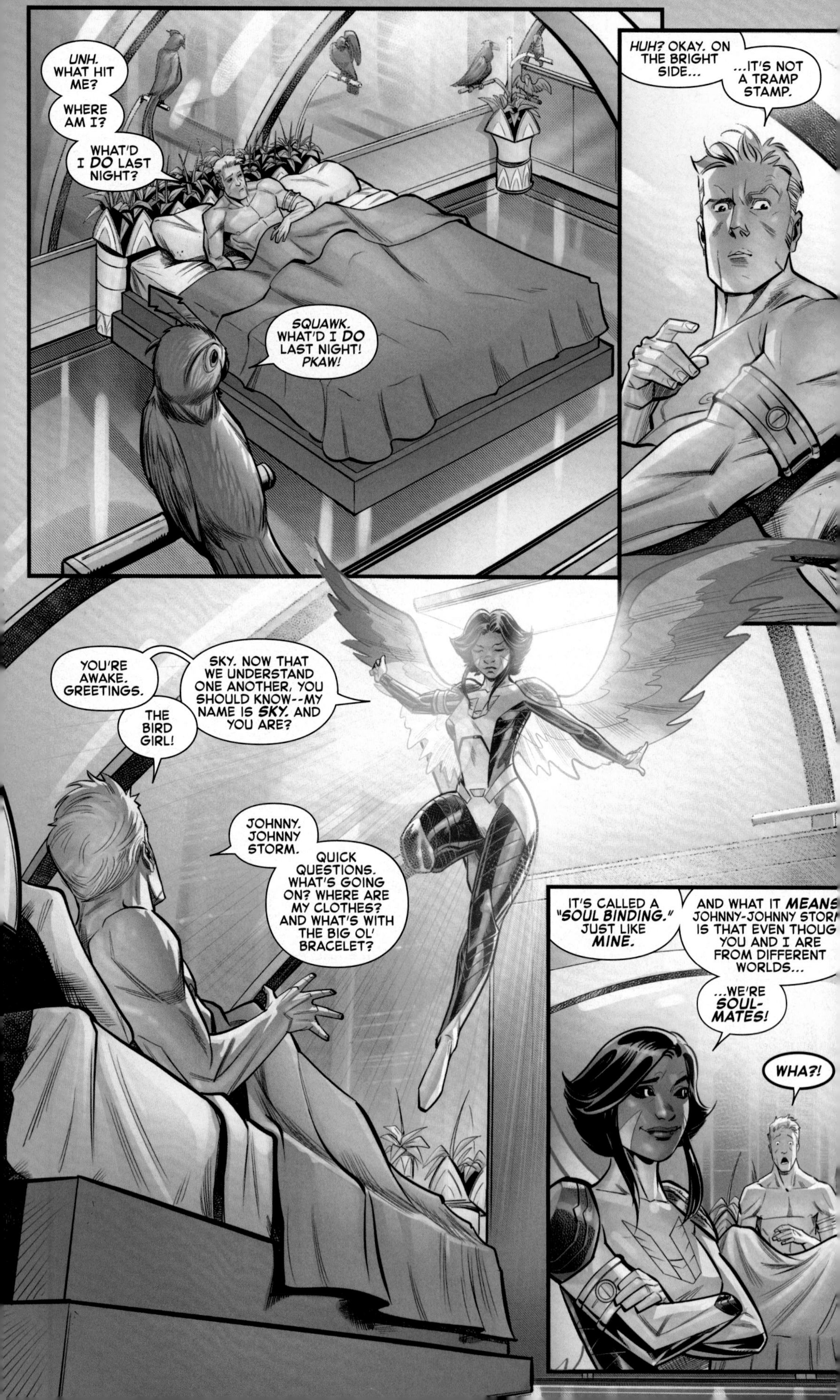

UNH. WHAT HIT ME?
WHERE AM I?
WHAT'D I DO LAST NIGHT?
SQUAWK. WHAT'D I DO LAST NIGHT! PKAW!
HUH? OKAY. ON THE BRIGHT SIDE...
...IT'S NOT A TRAMP STAMP.
YOU'RE AWAKE. GREETINGS.
THE BIRD GIRL!
SKY. NOW THAT WE UNDERSTAND ONE ANOTHER, YOU SHOULD KNOW--MY NAME IS SKY. AND YOU ARE?
JOHNNY. JOHNNY STORM.
QUICK QUESTIONS. WHAT'S GOING ON? WHERE ARE MY CLOTHES? AND WHAT'S WITH THE BIG OL' BRACELET?
IT'S CALLED A "SOUL BINDING." JUST LIKE MINE.
AND WHAT IT MEANS JOHNNY-JOHNNY STOR IS THAT EVEN THOUG YOU AND I ARE FROM DIFFERENT WORLDS...
...WE'RE SOUL-MATES!
WHA?!

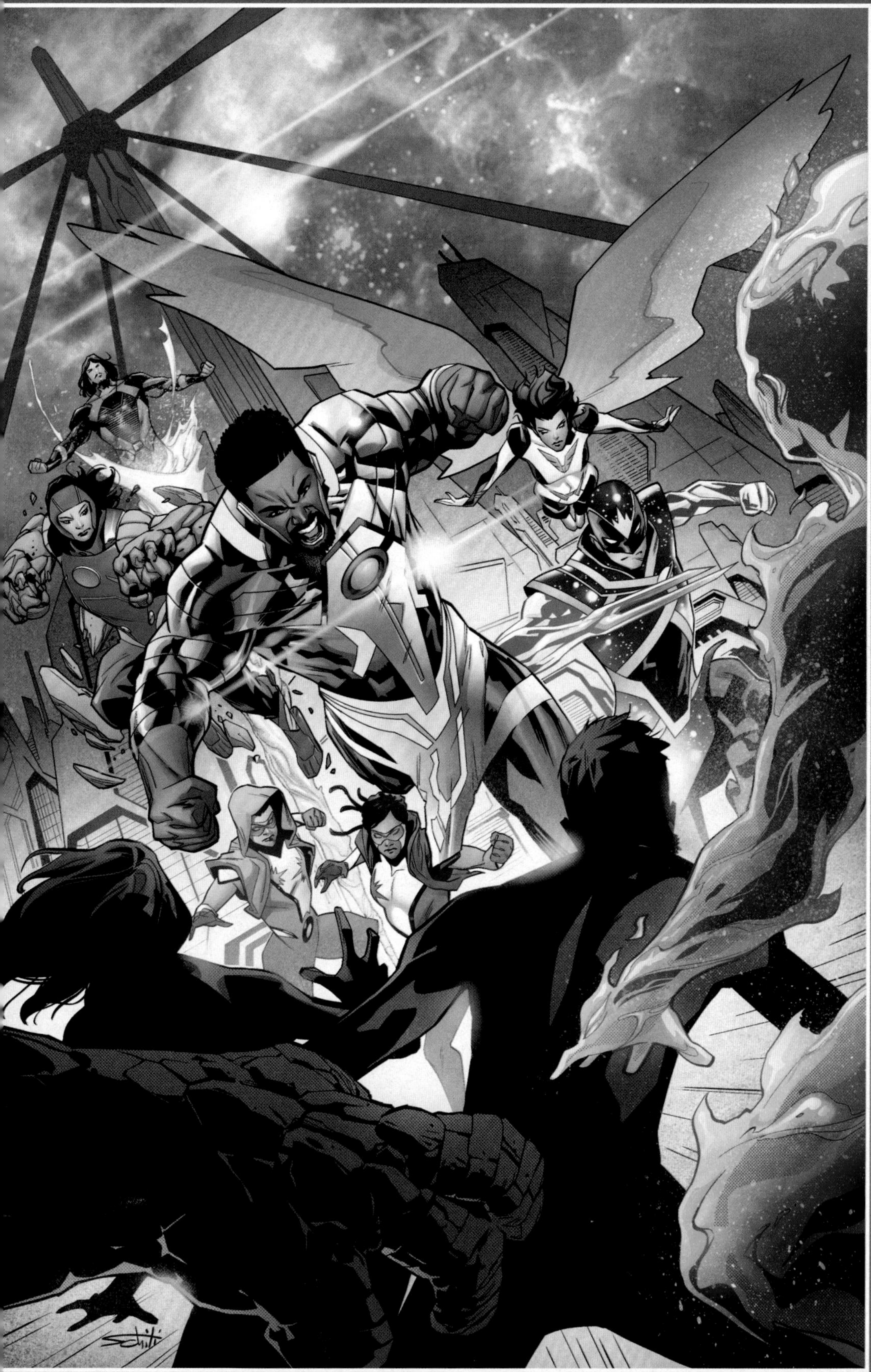

SCHITI

#15 variant by **Valerio Schiti** & **Richard Isanove**

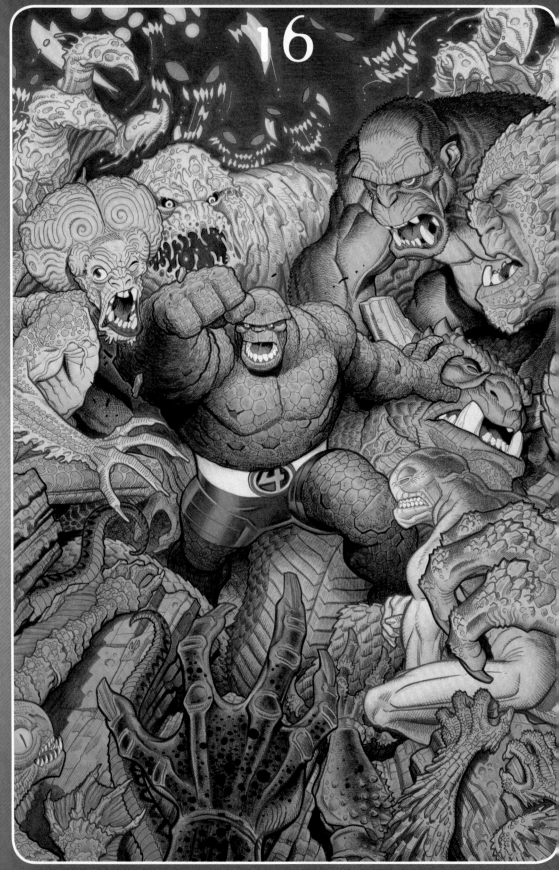

"Fantastic Planet"

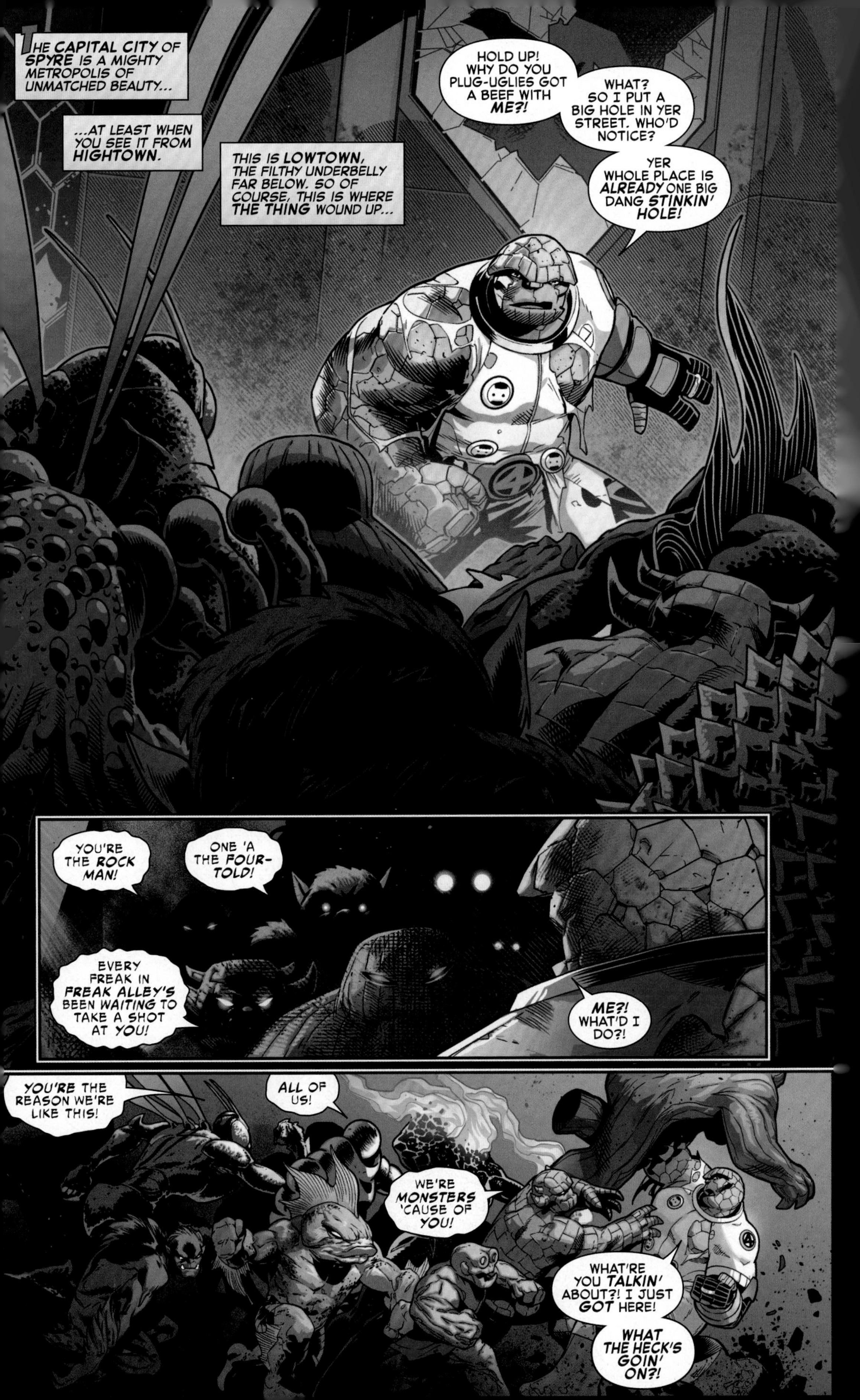
THE CAPITAL CITY OF SPYRE IS A MIGHTY METROPOLIS OF UNMATCHED BEAUTY...
...AT LEAST WHEN YOU SEE IT FROM HIGHTOWN.
THIS IS LOWTOWN, THE FILTHY UNDERBELLY FAR BELOW. SO OF COURSE, THIS IS WHERE THE THING WOUND UP...
HOLD UP! WHY DO YOU PLUG-UGLIES GOT A BEEF WITH ME?!
WHAT? SO I PUT A BIG HOLE IN YER STREET. WHO'D NOTICE?
YER WHOLE PLACE IS ALREADY ONE BIG DANG STINKIN' HOLE!
YOU'RE THE ROCK MAN!
ONE 'A THE FOUR-TOLD!
EVERY FREAK IN FREAK ALLEY'S BEEN WAITING TO TAKE A SHOT AT YOU!
ME?! WHAT'D I DO?!
YOU'RE THE REASON WE'RE LIKE THIS!
ALL OF US!
WE'RE MONSTERS 'CAUSE OF YOU!
WHAT'RE YOU TALKIN' ABOUT?! I JUST GOT HERE!
WHAT THE HECK'S GOIN' ON?!

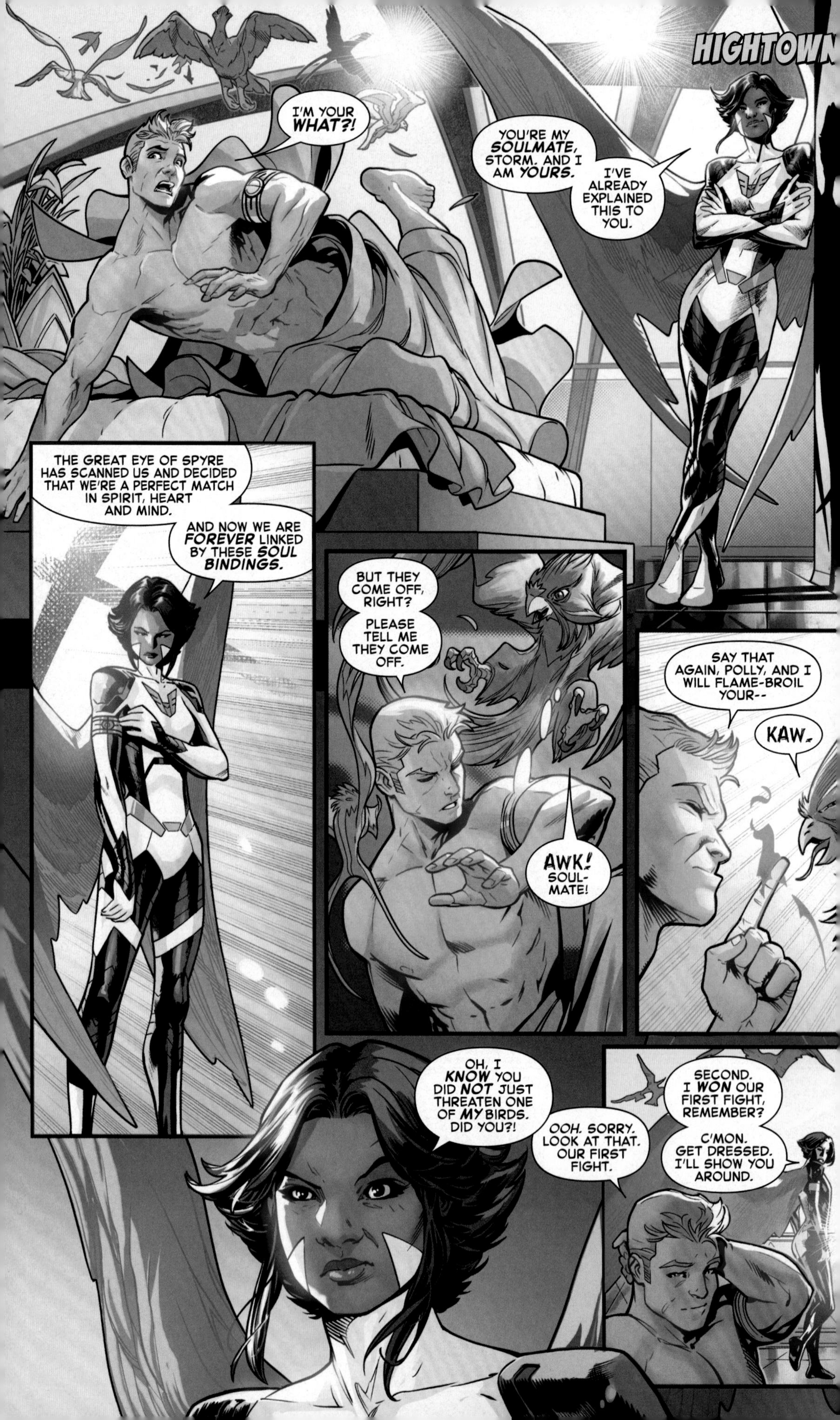
HIGHTOWN
I'M YOUR WHAT?!
YOU'RE MY SOULMATE, STORM. AND I AM YOURS.
I'VE ALREADY EXPLAINED THIS TO YOU.
THE GREAT EYE OF SPYRE HAS SCANNED US AND DECIDED THAT WE'RE A PERFECT MATCH IN SPIRIT, HEART AND MIND.
AND NOW WE ARE FOREVER LINKED BY THESE SOUL BINDINGS.
BUT THEY COME OFF, RIGHT?
PLEASE TELL ME THEY COME OFF.
AWK! SOUL-MATE!
SAY THAT AGAIN, POLLY, AND I WILL FLAME-BROIL YOUR--
KAW.
OH, I KNOW YOU DID NOT JUST THREATEN ONE OF MY BIRDS. DID YOU?!
OOH. SORRY. LOOK AT THAT. OUR FIRST FIGHT.
SECOND. I WON OUR FIRST FIGHT, REMEMBER?
C'MON. GET DRESSED. I'LL SHOW YOU AROUND.

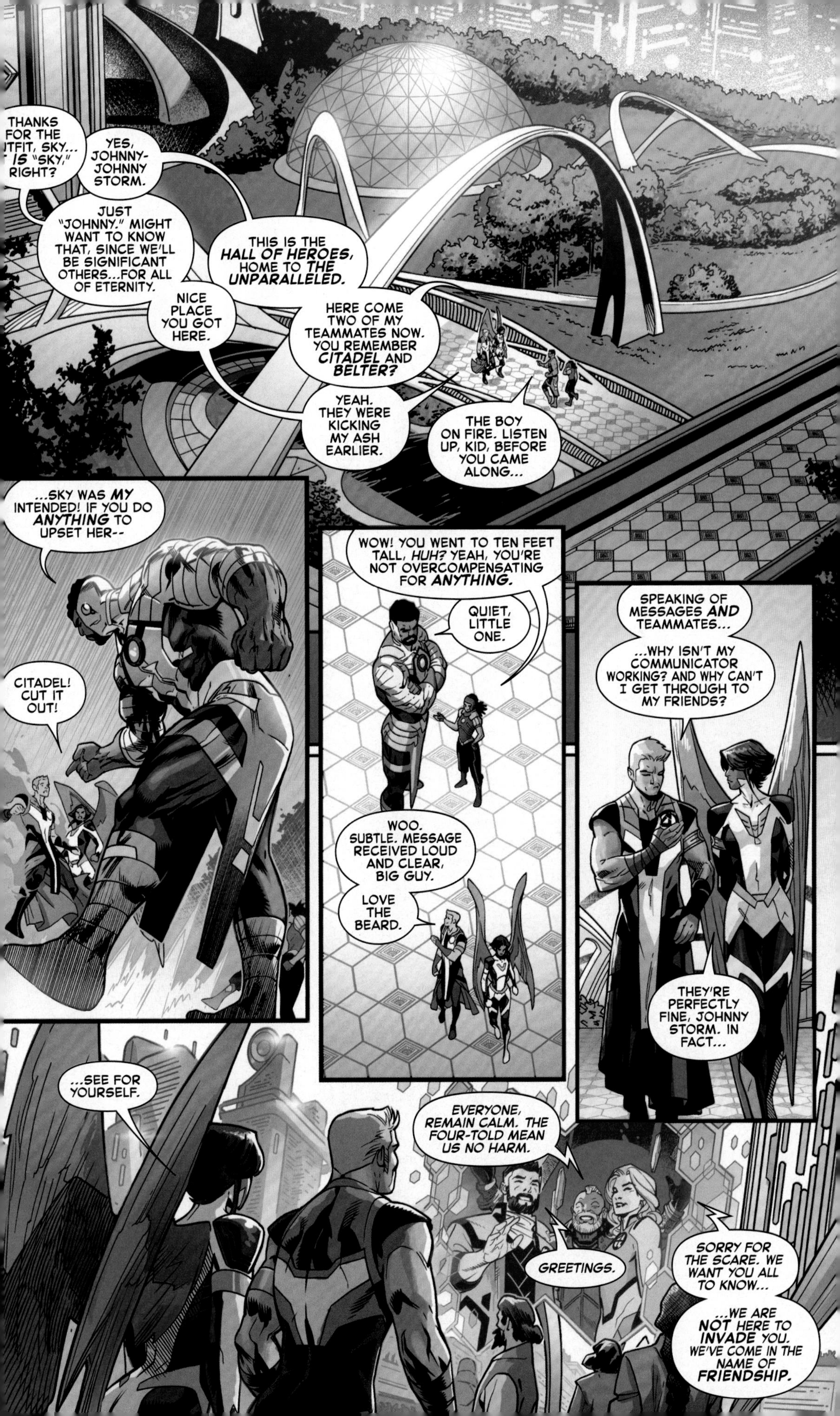

THANKS FOR THE ...TFIT, SKY... ...T IS "SKY," RIGHT?
YES, JOHNNY- JOHNNY STORM.
JUST "JOHNNY." MIGHT WANT TO KNOW THAT, SINCE WE'LL BE SIGNIFICANT OTHERS...FOR ALL OF ETERNITY.
THIS IS THE HALL OF HEROES, HOME TO THE UNPARALLELED.
NICE PLACE YOU GOT HERE.
HERE COME TWO OF MY TEAMMATES NOW. YOU REMEMBER CITADEL AND BELTER?
YEAH. THEY WERE KICKING MY ASH EARLIER.
THE BOY ON FIRE. LISTEN UP, KID, BEFORE YOU CAME ALONG...
...SKY WAS MY INTENDED! IF YOU DO ANYTHING TO UPSET HER--
CITADEL! CUT IT OUT!
WOW! YOU WENT TO TEN FEET TALL, HUH? YEAH, YOU'RE NOT OVERCOMPENSATING FOR ANYTHING.
QUIET, LITTLE ONE.
WOO. SUBTLE. MESSAGE RECEIVED LOUD AND CLEAR, BIG GUY.
LOVE THE BEARD.
SPEAKING OF MESSAGES AND TEAMMATES...
...WHY ISN'T MY COMMUNICATOR WORKING? AND WHY CAN'T I GET THROUGH TO MY FRIENDS?
THEY'RE PERFECTLY FINE, JOHNNY STORM. IN FACT...
...SEE FOR YOURSELF.
EVERYONE, REMAIN CALM. THE FOUR-TOLD MEAN US NO HARM.
GREETINGS.
SORRY FOR THE SCARE. WE WANT YOU ALL TO KNOW...
...WE ARE NOT HERE TO INVADE YOU. WE'VE COME IN THE NAME OF FRIENDSHIP.

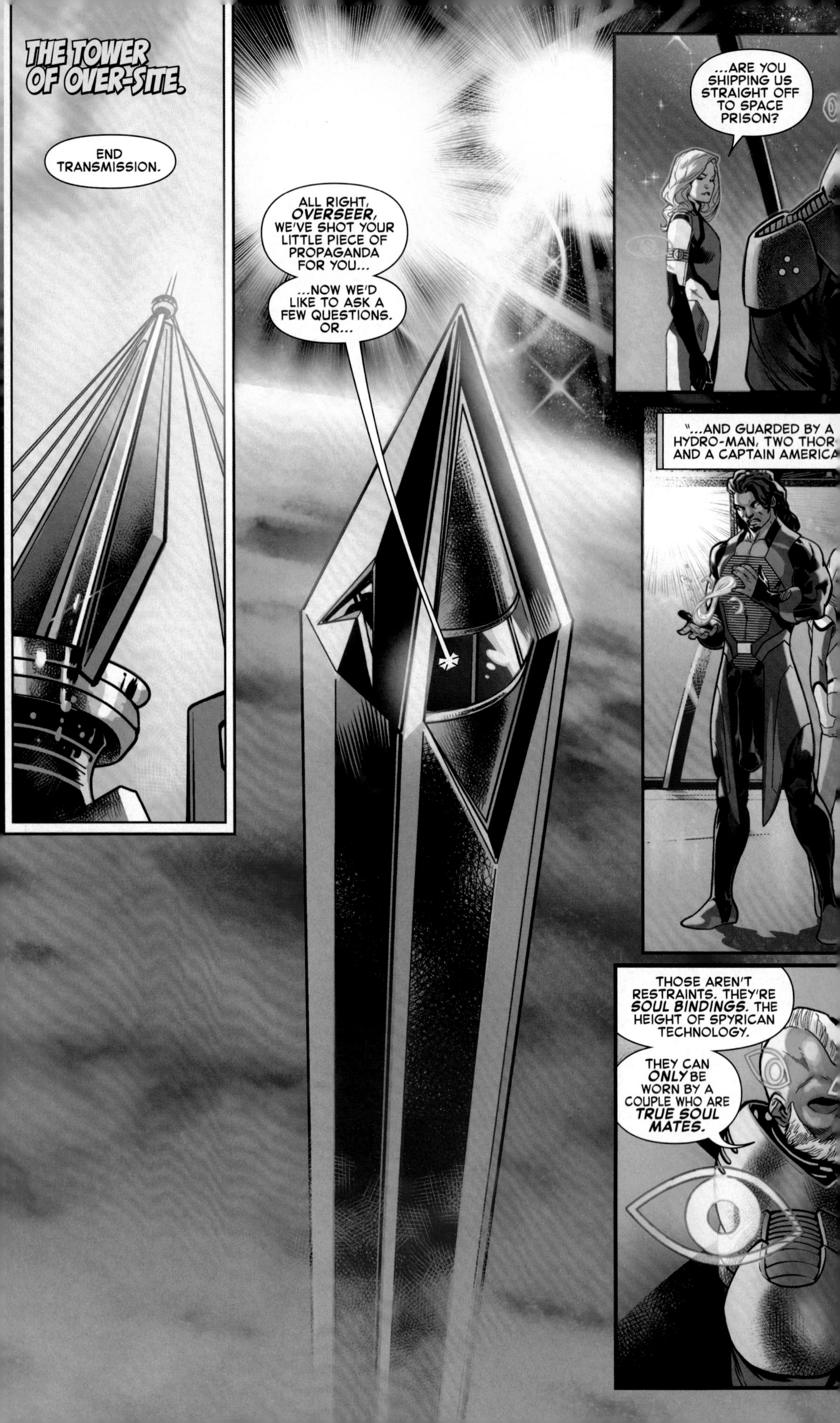

THE TOWER OF OVER-SITE.
END TRANSMISSION.
ALL RIGHT, OVERSEER, WE'VE SHOT YOUR LITTLE PIECE OF PROPAGANDA FOR YOU...
...NOW WE'D LIKE TO ASK A FEW QUESTIONS. OR...
...ARE YOU SHIPPING US STRAIGHT OFF TO SPACE PRISON?
"...AND GUARDED BY A HYDRO-MAN, TWO THOR AND A CAPTAIN AMERICA
THOSE AREN'T RESTRAINTS. THEY'RE SOUL BINDINGS. THE HEIGHT OF SPYRICAN TECHNOLOGY.
THEY CAN ONLY BE WORN BY A COUPLE WHO ARE TRUE SOUL MATES.

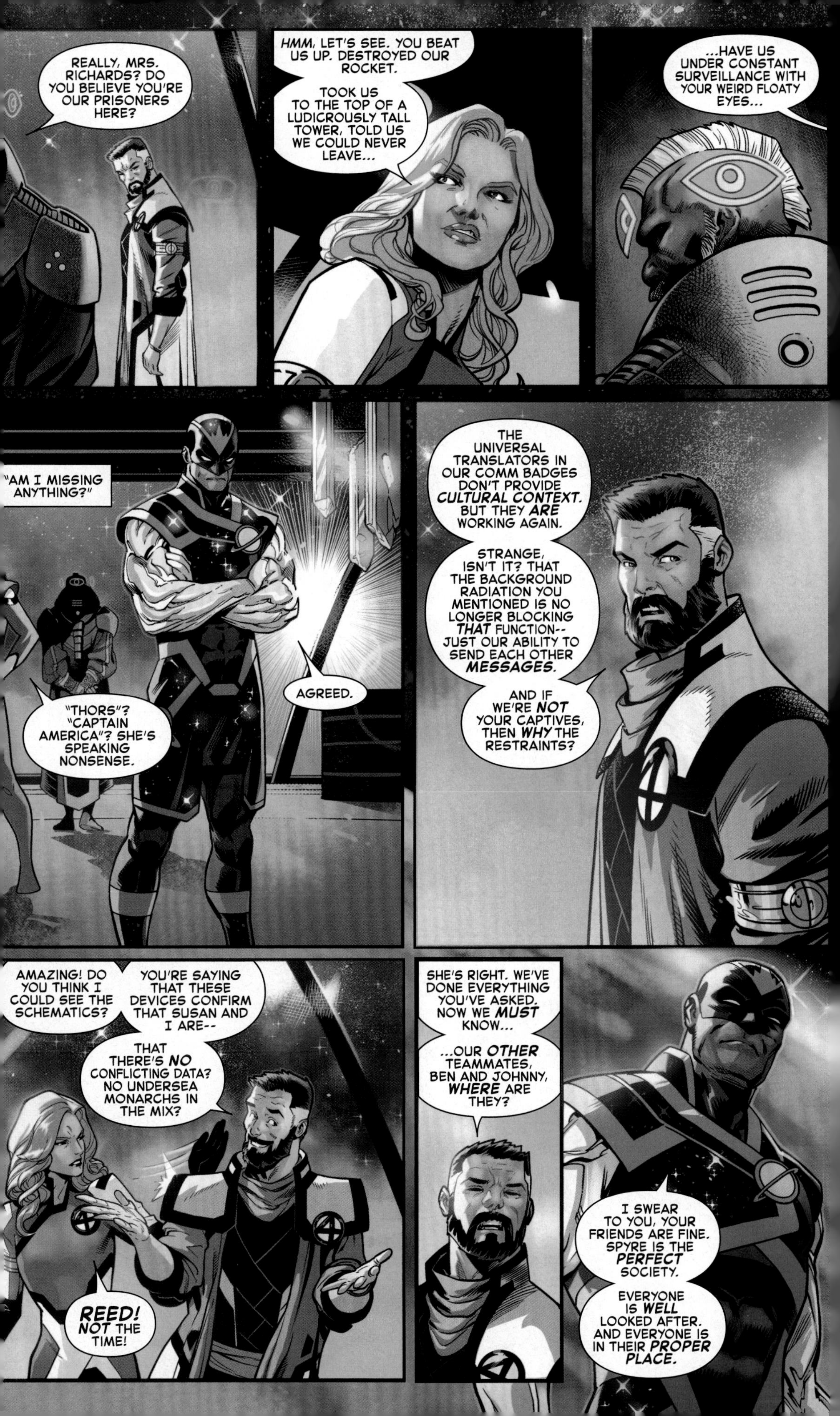

REALLY, MRS. RICHARDS? DO YOU BELIEVE YOU'RE OUR PRISONERS HERE?
HMM, LET'S SEE. YOU BEAT US UP. DESTROYED OUR ROCKET.
TOOK US TO THE TOP OF A LUDICROUSLY TALL TOWER, TOLD US WE COULD NEVER LEAVE...
...HAVE US UNDER CONSTANT SURVEILLANCE WITH YOUR WEIRD FLOATY EYES...
"AM I MISSING ANYTHING?"
"THORS"? "CAPTAIN AMERICA"? SHE'S SPEAKING NONSENSE.
AGREED.
THE UNIVERSAL TRANSLATORS IN OUR COMM BADGES DON'T PROVIDE CULTURAL CONTEXT. BUT THEY ARE WORKING AGAIN.
STRANGE, ISN'T IT? THAT THE BACKGROUND RADIATION YOU MENTIONED IS NO LONGER BLOCKING THAT FUNCTION-- JUST OUR ABILITY TO SEND EACH OTHER MESSAGES.
AND IF WE'RE NOT YOUR CAPTIVES, THEN WHY THE RESTRAINTS?
AMAZING! DO YOU THINK I COULD SEE THE SCHEMATICS?
YOU'RE SAYING THAT THESE DEVICES CONFIRM THAT SUSAN AND I ARE--
THAT THERE'S NO CONFLICTING DATA? NO UNDERSEA MONARCHS IN THE MIX?
REED! NOT THE TIME!
SHE'S RIGHT. WE'VE DONE EVERYTHING YOU'VE ASKED. NOW WE MUST KNOW...
...OUR OTHER TEAMMATES, BEN AND JOHNNY, WHERE ARE THEY?
I SWEAR TO YOU, YOUR FRIENDS ARE FINE. SPYRE IS THE PERFECT SOCIETY.
EVERYONE IS WELL LOOKED AFTER. AND EVERYONE IS IN THEIR PROPER PLACE.

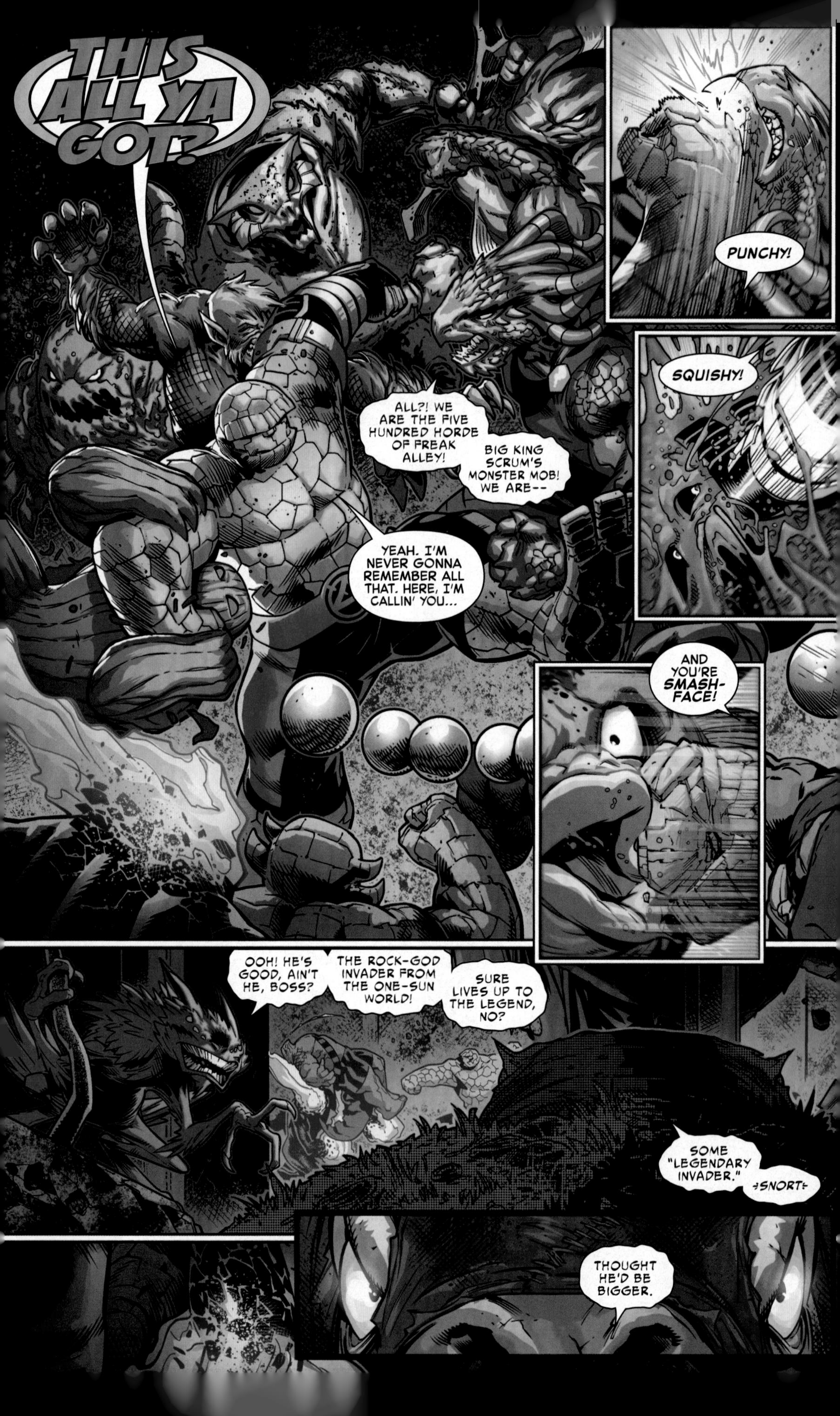
THIS ALL YA GOT?!
PUNCHY!
ALL?! WE ARE THE FIVE HUNDRED HORDE OF FREAK ALLEY!
BIG KING SCRUM'S MONSTER MOB! WE ARE--
SQUISHY!
YEAH. I'M NEVER GONNA REMEMBER ALL THAT. HERE, I'M CALLIN' YOU...
AND YOU'RE SMASH-FACE!
OOH! HE'S GOOD, AIN'T HE, BOSS?
THE ROCK-GOD INVADER FROM THE ONE-SUN WORLD!
SURE LIVES UP TO THE LEGEND, NO?
SOME "LEGENDARY INVADER."
=SNORT=
THOUGHT HE'D BE BIGGER.

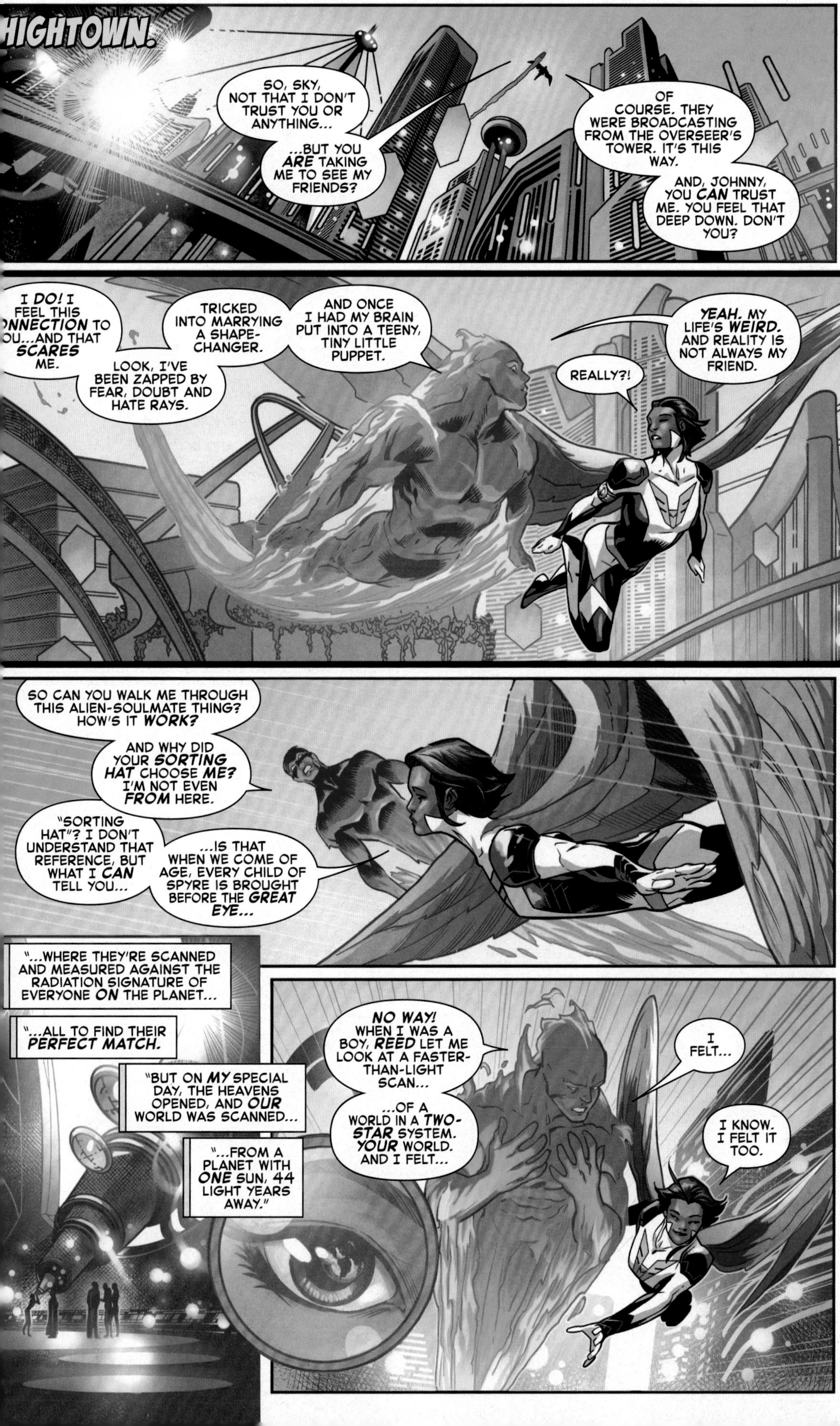
HIGHTOWN.
SO, SKY, NOT THAT I DON'T TRUST YOU OR ANYTHING...
...BUT YOU ARE TAKING ME TO SEE MY FRIENDS?
OF COURSE. THEY WERE BROADCASTING FROM THE OVERSEER'S TOWER. IT'S THIS WAY.
AND, JOHNNY, YOU CAN TRUST ME. YOU FEEL THAT DEEP DOWN. DON'T YOU?
I DO! I FEEL THIS NNECTION TO OU...AND THAT SCARES ME.
LOOK, I'VE BEEN ZAPPED BY FEAR, DOUBT AND HATE RAYS.
TRICKED INTO MARRYING A SHAPE-CHANGER.
AND ONCE I HAD MY BRAIN PUT INTO A TEENY, TINY LITTLE PUPPET.
REALLY?!
YEAH. MY LIFE'S WEIRD. AND REALITY IS NOT ALWAYS MY FRIEND.
SO CAN YOU WALK ME THROUGH THIS ALIEN-SOULMATE THING? HOW'S IT WORK?
AND WHY DID YOUR SORTING HAT CHOOSE ME? I'M NOT EVEN FROM HERE.
"SORTING HAT"? I DON'T UNDERSTAND THAT REFERENCE, BUT WHAT I CAN TELL YOU...
...IS THAT WHEN WE COME OF AGE, EVERY CHILD OF SPYRE IS BROUGHT BEFORE THE GREAT EYE...
"...WHERE THEY'RE SCANNED AND MEASURED AGAINST THE RADIATION SIGNATURE OF EVERYONE ON THE PLANET...
"...ALL TO FIND THEIR PERFECT MATCH.
"BUT ON MY SPECIAL DAY, THE HEAVENS OPENED, AND OUR WORLD WAS SCANNED...
"...FROM A PLANET WITH ONE SUN, 44 LIGHT YEARS AWAY."
NO WAY! WHEN I WAS A BOY, REED LET ME LOOK AT A FASTER-THAN-LIGHT SCAN...
...OF A WORLD IN A TWO-STAR SYSTEM. YOUR WORLD. AND I FELT...
I FELT...
I KNOW. I FELT IT TOO.

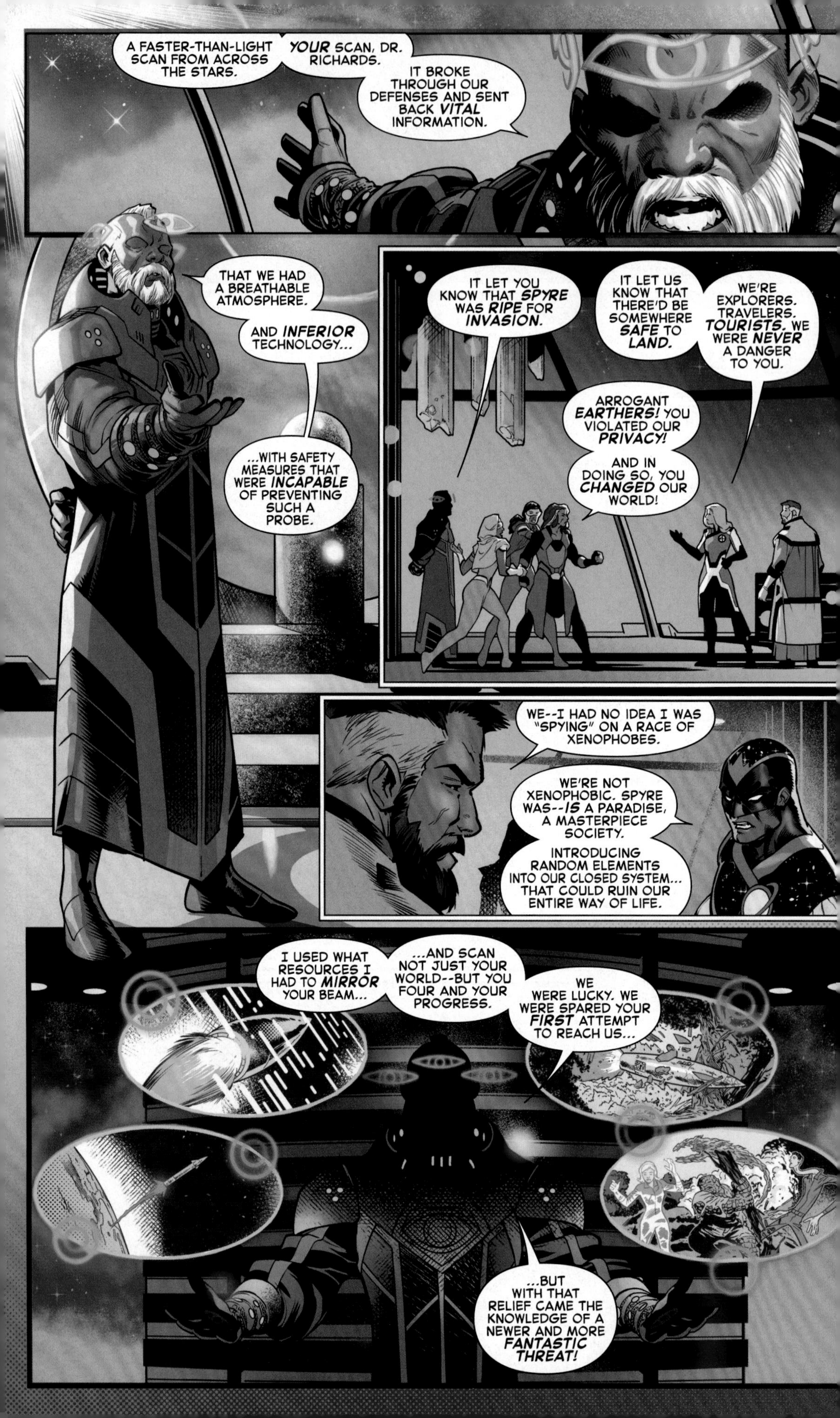
A FASTER-THAN-LIGHT SCAN FROM ACROSS THE STARS.
YOUR SCAN, DR. RICHARDS.
IT BROKE THROUGH OUR DEFENSES AND SENT BACK VITAL INFORMATION.
THAT WE HAD A BREATHABLE ATMOSPHERE.
AND INFERIOR TECHNOLOGY...
...WITH SAFETY MEASURES THAT WERE INCAPABLE OF PREVENTING SUCH A PROBE.
IT LET YOU KNOW THAT SPYRE WAS RIPE FOR INVASION.
IT LET US KNOW THAT THERE'D BE SOMEWHERE SAFE TO LAND.
WE'RE EXPLORERS. TRAVELERS. TOURISTS. WE WERE NEVER A DANGER TO YOU.
ARROGANT EARTHERS! YOU VIOLATED OUR PRIVACY!
AND IN DOING SO, YOU CHANGED OUR WORLD!
WE--I HAD NO IDEA I WAS "SPYING" ON A RACE OF XENOPHOBES.
WE'RE NOT XENOPHOBIC. SPYRE WAS--IS A PARADISE, A MASTERPIECE SOCIETY.
INTRODUCING RANDOM ELEMENTS INTO OUR CLOSED SYSTEM... THAT COULD RUIN OUR ENTIRE WAY OF LIFE.
I USED WHAT RESOURCES I HAD TO MIRROR YOUR BEAM...
...AND SCAN NOT JUST YOUR WORLD--BUT YOU FOUR AND YOUR PROGRESS.
WE WERE LUCKY. WE WERE SPARED YOUR FIRST ATTEMPT TO REACH US...
...BUT WITH THAT RELIEF CAME THE KNOWLEDGE OF A NEWER AND MORE FANTASTIC THREAT!

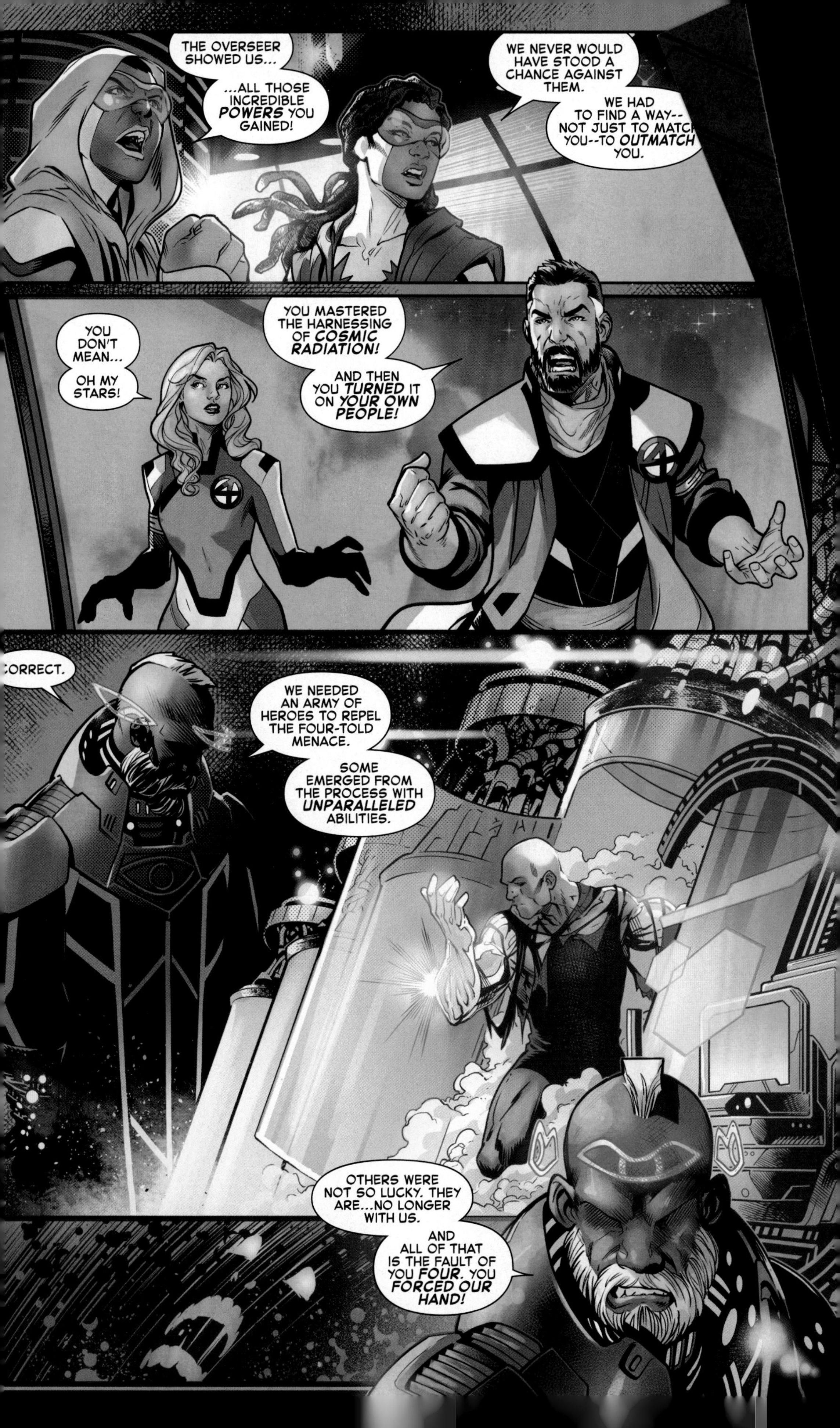
THE OVERSEER SHOWED US...
...ALL THOSE INCREDIBLE POWERS YOU GAINED!
WE NEVER WOULD HAVE STOOD A CHANCE AGAINST THEM.
WE HAD TO FIND A WAY-- NOT JUST TO MATCH YOU--TO OUTMATCH YOU.
YOU DON'T MEAN...
OH MY STARS!
YOU MASTERED THE HARNESSING OF COSMIC RADIATION!
AND THEN YOU TURNED IT ON YOUR OWN PEOPLE!
CORRECT.
WE NEEDED AN ARMY OF HEROES TO REPEL THE FOUR-TOLD MENACE.
SOME EMERGED FROM THE PROCESS WITH UNPARALLELED ABILITIES.
OTHERS WERE NOT SO LUCKY. THEY ARE...NO LONGER WITH US.
AND ALL OF THAT IS THE FAULT OF YOU FOUR. YOU FORCED OUR HAND!

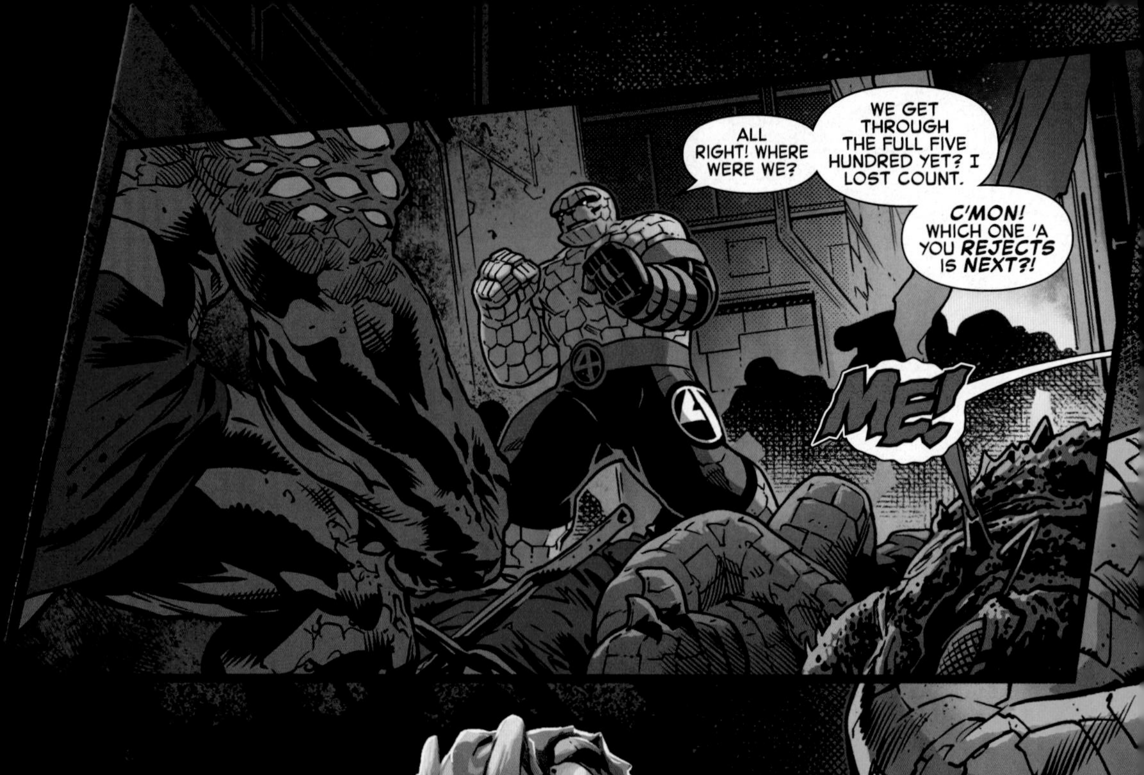
ALL RIGHT! WHERE WERE WE?
WE GET THROUGH THE FULL FIVE HUNDRED YET? I LOST COUNT.
C'MON! WHICH ONE 'A YOU REJECTS IS NEXT?!
ME!

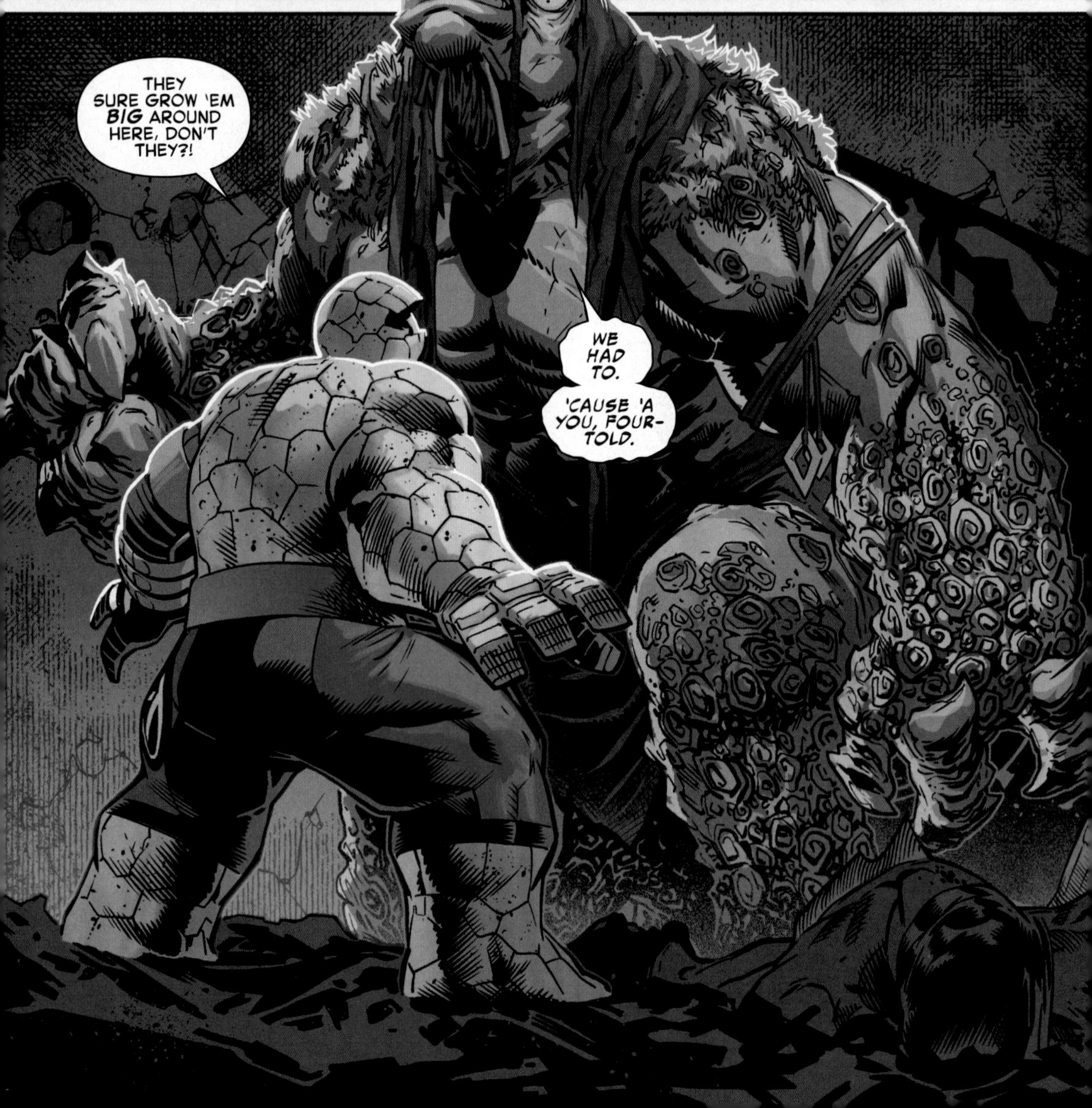
THEY SURE GROW 'EM BIG AROUND HERE, DON'T THEY?!
WE HAD TO.
'CAUSE 'A YOU, FOUR-TOLD.

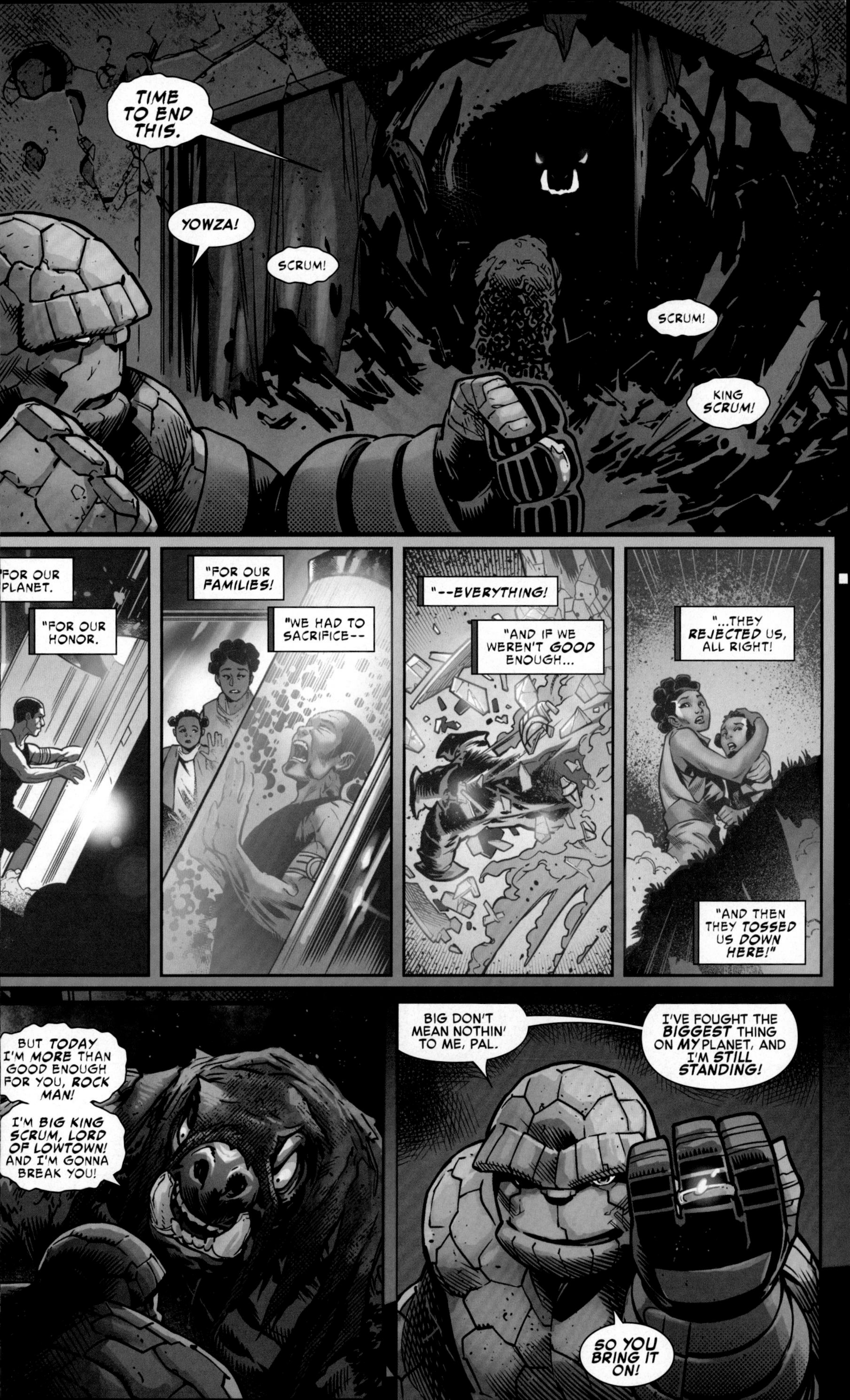
TIME TO END THIS.
YOWZA!
SCRUM!
SCRUM!
KING SCRUM!
"FOR OUR PLANET.
"FOR OUR HONOR.
"FOR OUR FAMILIES!
"WE HAD TO SACRIFICE--
"--EVERYTHING!
"AND IF WE WEREN'T GOOD ENOUGH...
"...THEY REJECTED US, ALL RIGHT!
"AND THEN THEY TOSSED US DOWN HERE!"
BUT TODAY I'M MORE THAN GOOD ENOUGH FOR YOU, ROCK MAN!
I'M BIG KING SCRUM, LORD OF LOWTOWN! AND I'M GONNA BREAK YOU!
BIG DON'T MEAN NOTHIN' TO ME, PAL.
I'VE FOUGHT THE BIGGEST THING ON MY PLANET, AND I'M STILL STANDING!
SO YOU BRING IT ON!

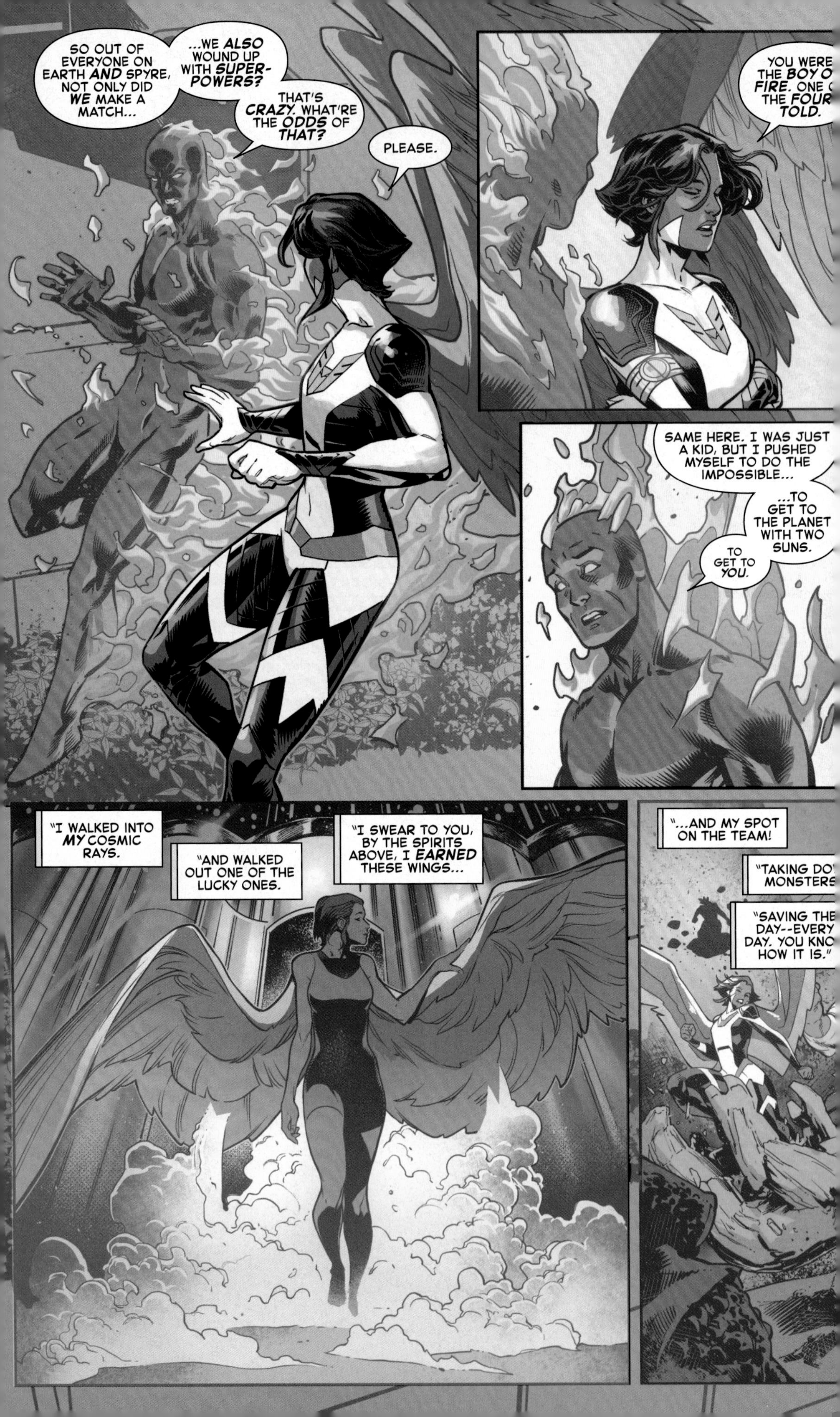
SO OUT OF EVERYONE ON EARTH AND SPYRE, NOT ONLY DID WE MAKE A MATCH...
...WE ALSO WOUND UP WITH SUPER-POWERS?
THAT'S CRAZY. WHAT'RE THE ODDS OF THAT?
PLEASE.
YOU WERE THE BOY O FIRE. ONE THE FOUR TOLD.
SAME HERE. I WAS JUST A KID, BUT I PUSHED MYSELF TO DO THE IMPOSSIBLE...
...TO GET TO THE PLANET WITH TWO SUNS.
TO GET TO YOU.
"I WALKED INTO MY COSMIC RAYS.
"AND WALKED OUT ONE OF THE LUCKY ONES.
"I SWEAR TO YOU, BY THE SPIRITS ABOVE, I EARNED THESE WINGS...
"...AND MY SPOT ON THE TEAM!
"TAKING DO MONSTERS
"SAVING THE DAY--EVERY DAY. YOU KNO HOW IT IS."

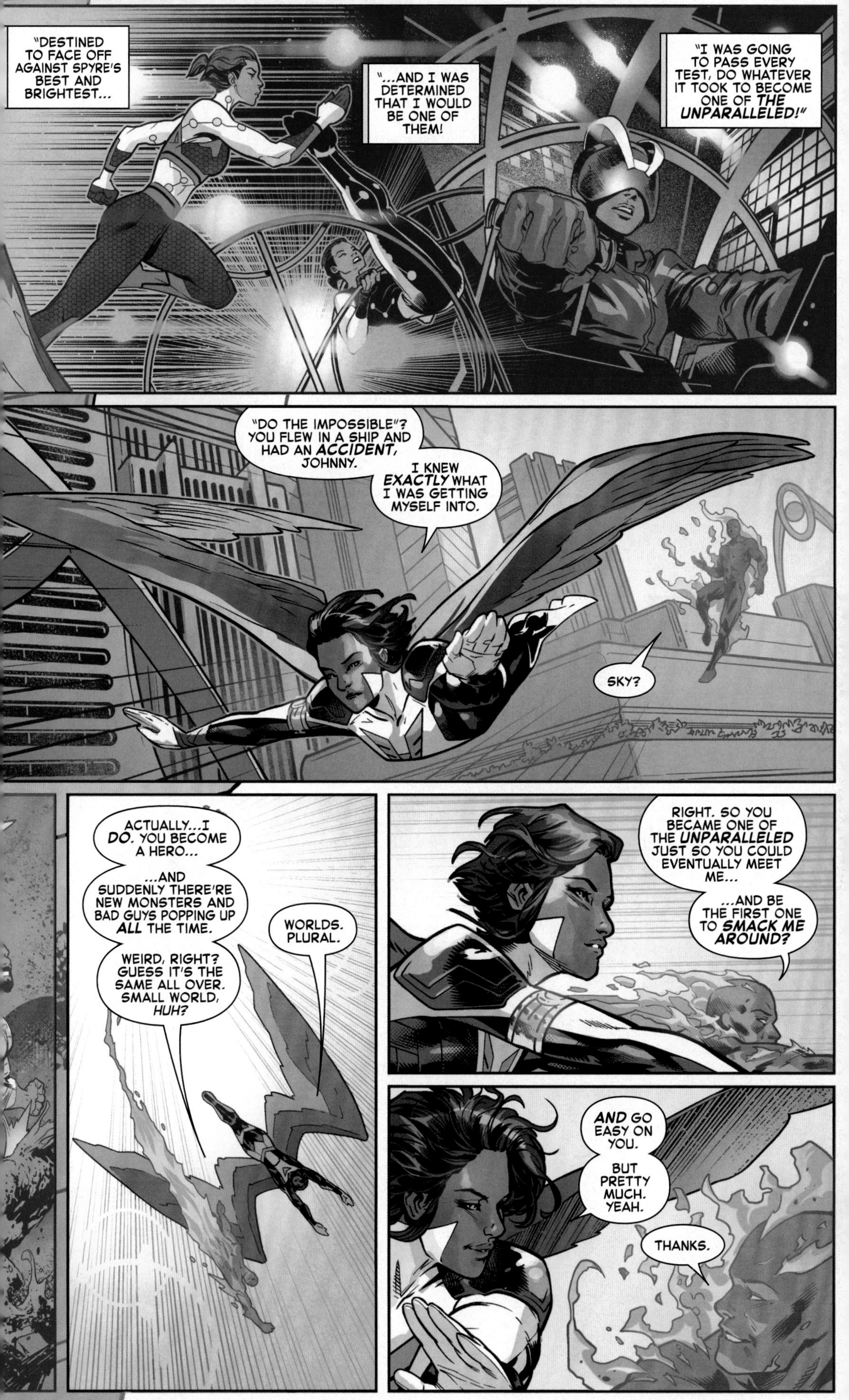
"DESTINED TO FACE OFF AGAINST SPYRE'S BEST AND BRIGHTEST...
"...AND I WAS DETERMINED THAT I WOULD BE ONE OF THEM!
"I WAS GOING TO PASS EVERY TEST, DO WHATEVER IT TOOK TO BECOME ONE OF THE UNPARALLELED!"
"DO THE IMPOSSIBLE"? YOU FLEW IN A SHIP AND HAD AN ACCIDENT, JOHNNY.
I KNEW EXACTLY WHAT I WAS GETTING MYSELF INTO.
SKY?
ACTUALLY...I DO. YOU BECOME A HERO...
...AND SUDDENLY THERE'RE NEW MONSTERS AND BAD GUYS POPPING UP ALL THE TIME.
WEIRD, RIGHT? GUESS IT'S THE SAME ALL OVER. SMALL WORLD, HUH?
WORLDS. PLURAL.
RIGHT. SO YOU BECAME ONE OF THE UNPARALLELED JUST SO YOU COULD EVENTUALLY MEET ME...
...AND BE THE FIRST ONE TO SMACK ME AROUND?
AND GO EASY ON YOU.
BUT PRETTY MUCH. YEAH.
THANKS.

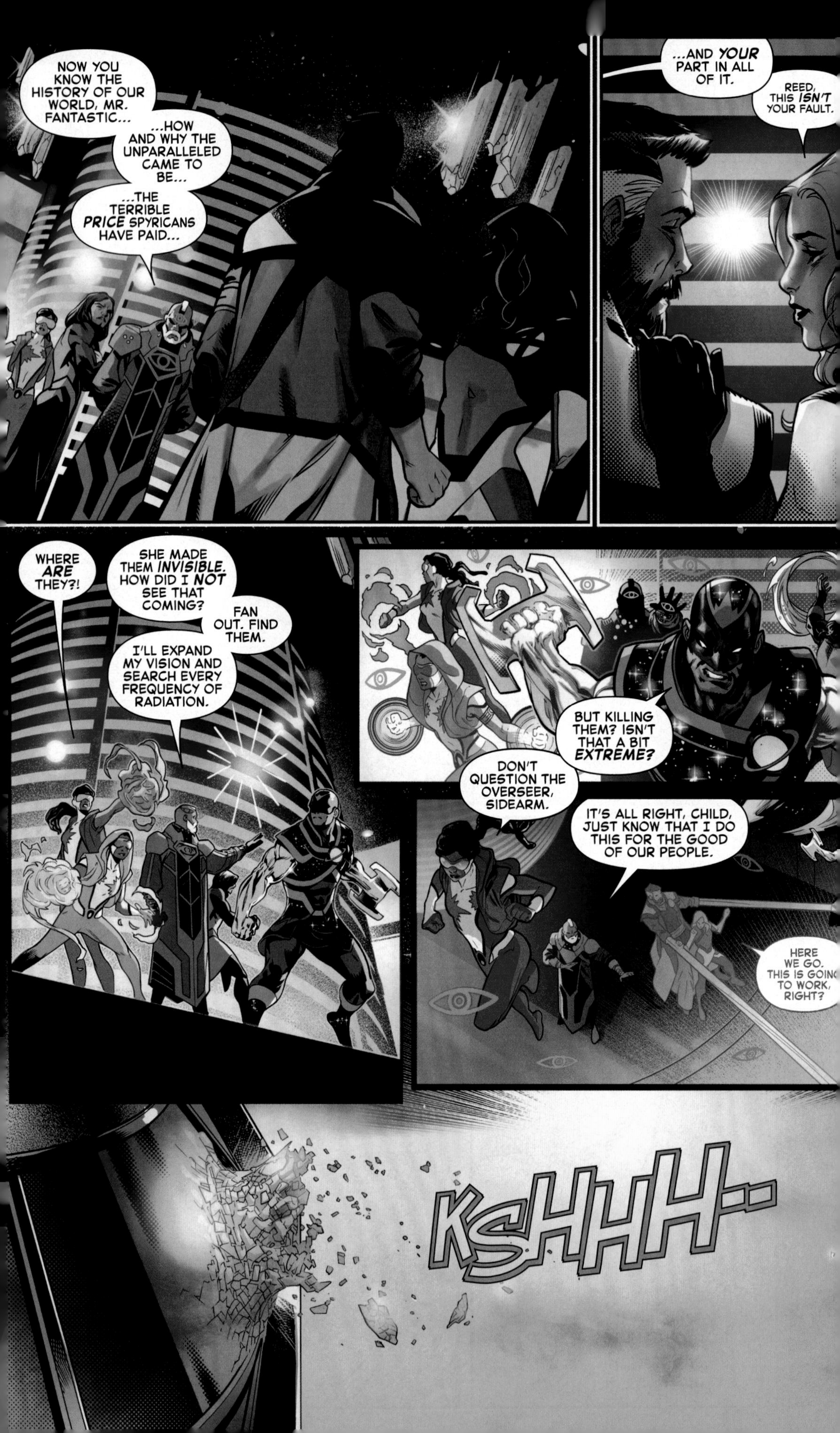
NOW YOU KNOW THE HISTORY OF OUR WORLD, MR. FANTASTIC...
...HOW AND WHY THE UNPARALLELED CAME TO BE...
...THE TERRIBLE PRICE SPYRICANS HAVE PAID...
...AND YOUR PART IN ALL OF IT.
REED, THIS ISN'T YOUR FAULT.
WHERE ARE THEY?!
SHE MADE THEM INVISIBLE. HOW DID I NOT SEE THAT COMING?
FAN OUT. FIND THEM.
I'LL EXPAND MY VISION AND SEARCH EVERY FREQUENCY OF RADIATION.
BUT KILLING THEM? ISN'T THAT A BIT EXTREME?
DON'T QUESTION THE OVERSEER, SIDEARM.
IT'S ALL RIGHT, CHILD, JUST KNOW THAT I DO THIS FOR THE GOOD OF OUR PEOPLE.
HERE WE GO. THIS IS GOING TO WORK, RIGHT?
KSHHHH--

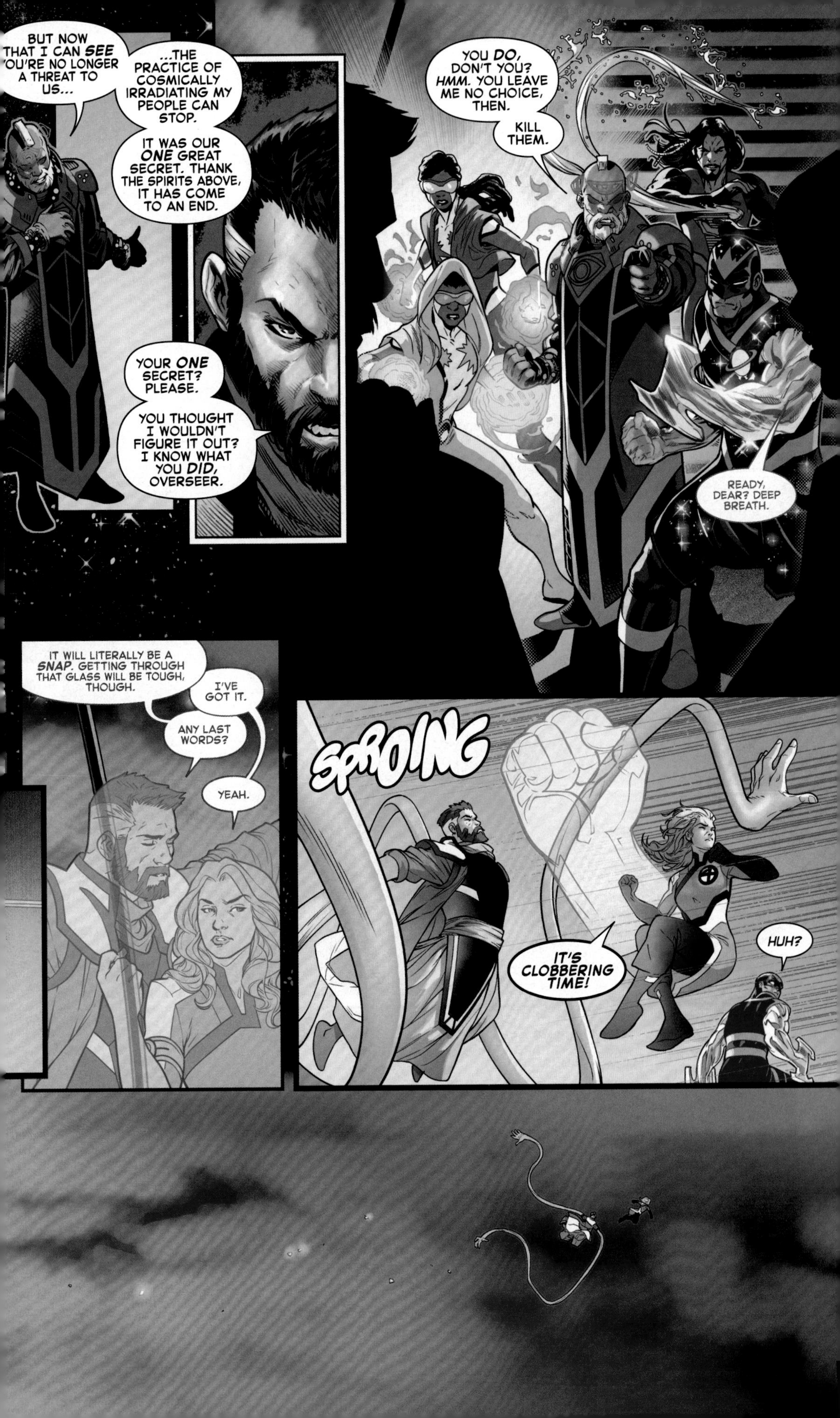
BUT NOW THAT I CAN SEE YOU'RE NO LONGER A THREAT TO US...
...THE PRACTICE OF COSMICALLY IRRADIATING MY PEOPLE CAN STOP.
IT WAS OUR ONE GREAT SECRET. THANK THE SPIRITS ABOVE, IT HAS COME TO AN END.
YOUR ONE SECRET? PLEASE.
YOU THOUGHT I WOULDN'T FIGURE IT OUT? I KNOW WHAT YOU DID, OVERSEER.
YOU DO, DON'T YOU? HMM. YOU LEAVE ME NO CHOICE, THEN.
KILL THEM.
READY, DEAR? DEEP BREATH.
IT WILL LITERALLY BE A SNAP. GETTING THROUGH THAT GLASS WILL BE TOUGH, THOUGH.
I'VE GOT IT.
ANY LAST WORDS?
YEAH.
SPROING
IT'S CLOBBERING TIME!
HUH?

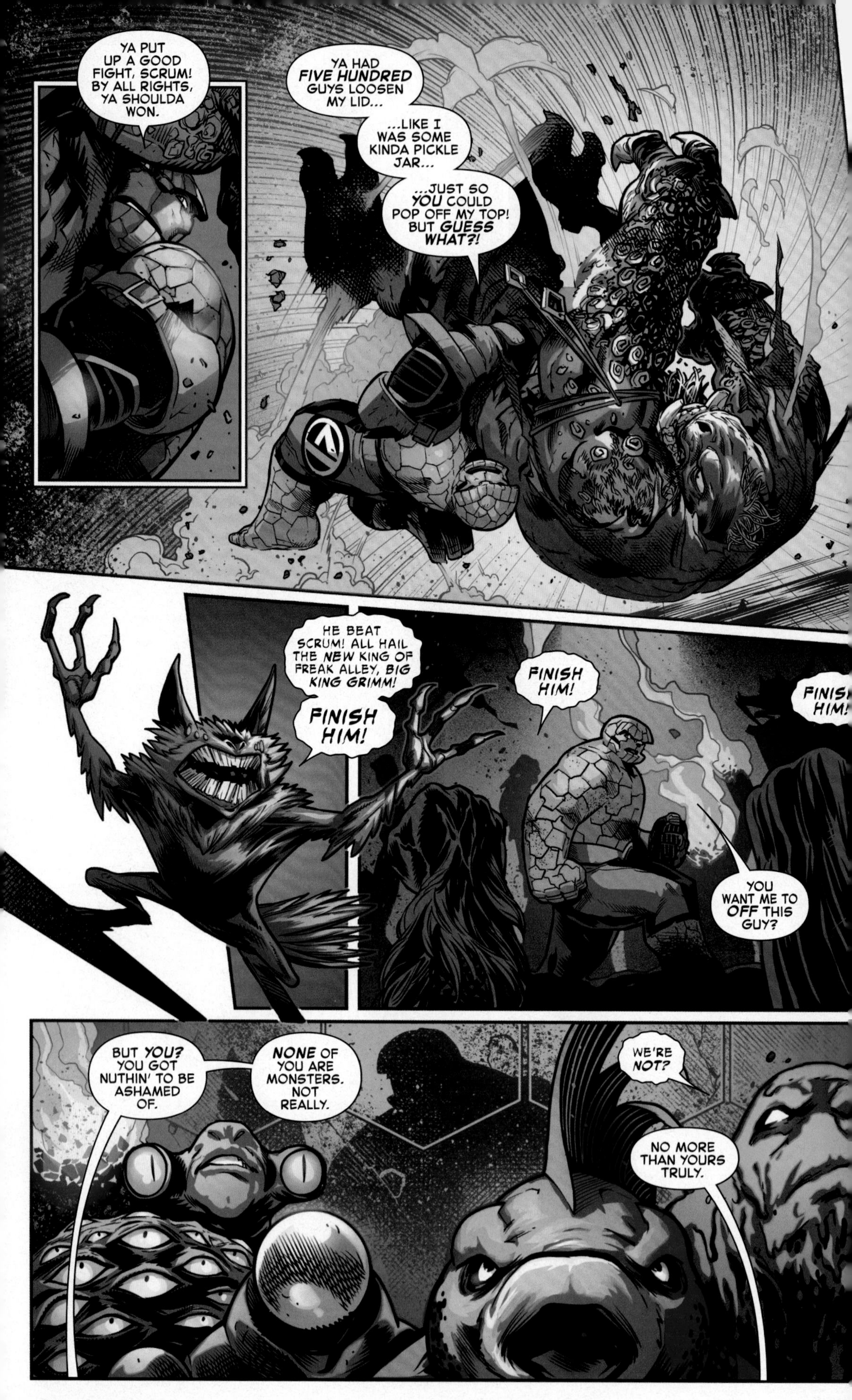
YA PUT UP A GOOD FIGHT, SCRUM! BY ALL RIGHTS, YA SHOULDA WON.
YA HAD FIVE HUNDRED GUYS LOOSEN MY LID...
...LIKE I WAS SOME KINDA PICKLE JAR...
...JUST SO YOU COULD POP OFF MY TOP! BUT GUESS WHAT?!
HE BEAT SCRUM! ALL HAIL THE NEW KING OF FREAK ALLEY, BIG KING GRIMM!
FINISH HIM!
FINISH HIM!
FINISH HIM!
YOU WANT ME TO OFF THIS GUY?
NONE OF YOU ARE MONSTERS. NOT REALLY.
WE'RE NOT?
NO MORE THAN YOURS TRULY.
BUT YOU? YOU GOT NUTHIN' TO BE ASHAMED OF.

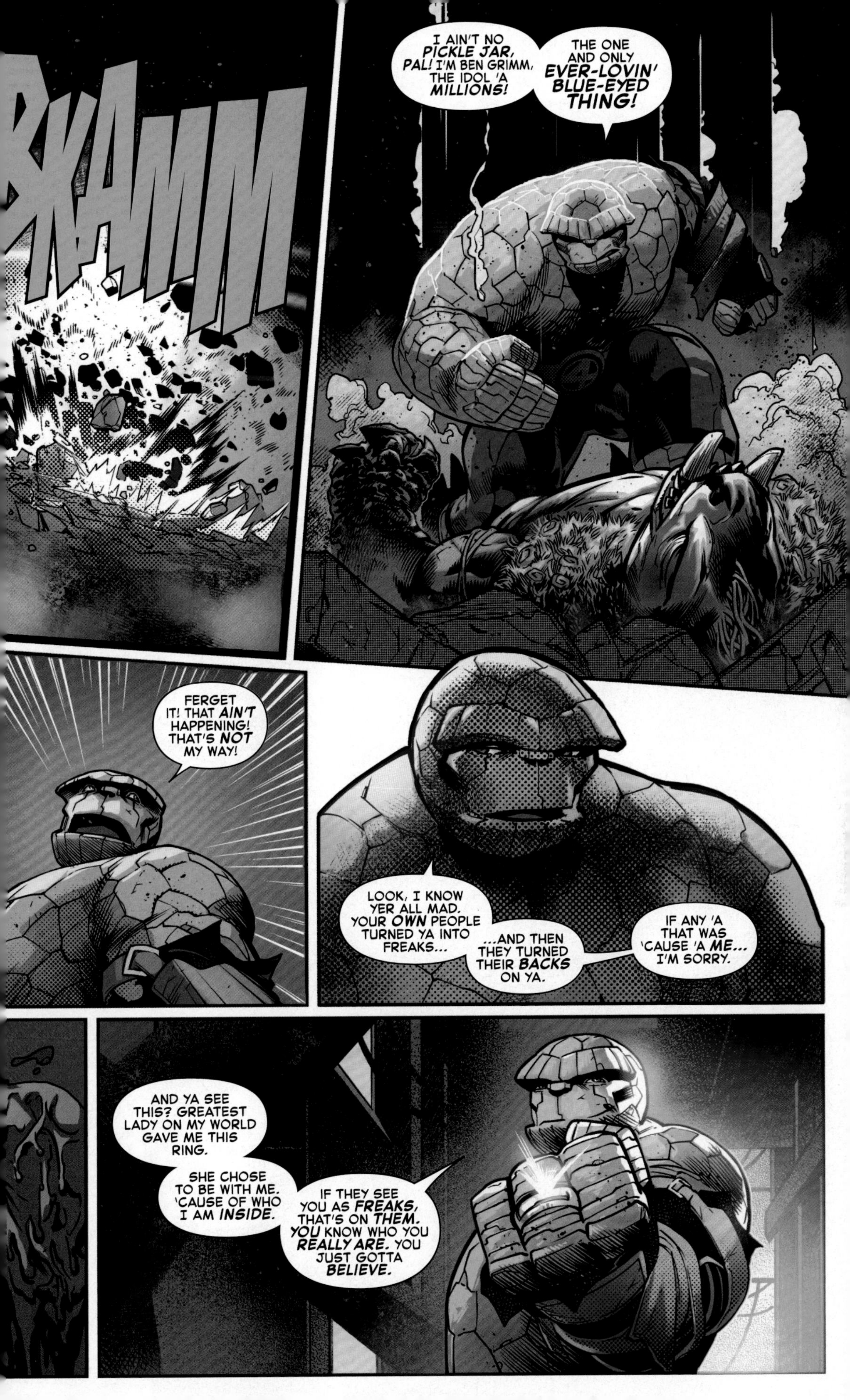
BKAMM
I AIN'T NO PICKLE JAR, PAL! I'M BEN GRIMM, THE IDOL 'A MILLIONS!
THE ONE AND ONLY EVER-LOVIN' BLUE-EYED THING!
FERGET IT! THAT AIN'T HAPPENING! THAT'S NOT MY WAY!
LOOK, I KNOW YER ALL MAD. YOUR OWN PEOPLE TURNED YA INTO FREAKS...
...AND THEN THEY TURNED THEIR BACKS ON YA.
IF ANY 'A THAT WAS 'CAUSE 'A ME... I'M SORRY.
AND YA SEE THIS? GREATEST LADY ON MY WORLD GAVE ME THIS RING.
SHE CHOSE TO BE WITH ME. 'CAUSE OF WHO I AM INSIDE.
IF THEY SEE YOU AS FREAKS, THAT'S ON THEM. YOU KNOW WHO YOU REALLY ARE. YOU JUST GOTTA BELIEVE.

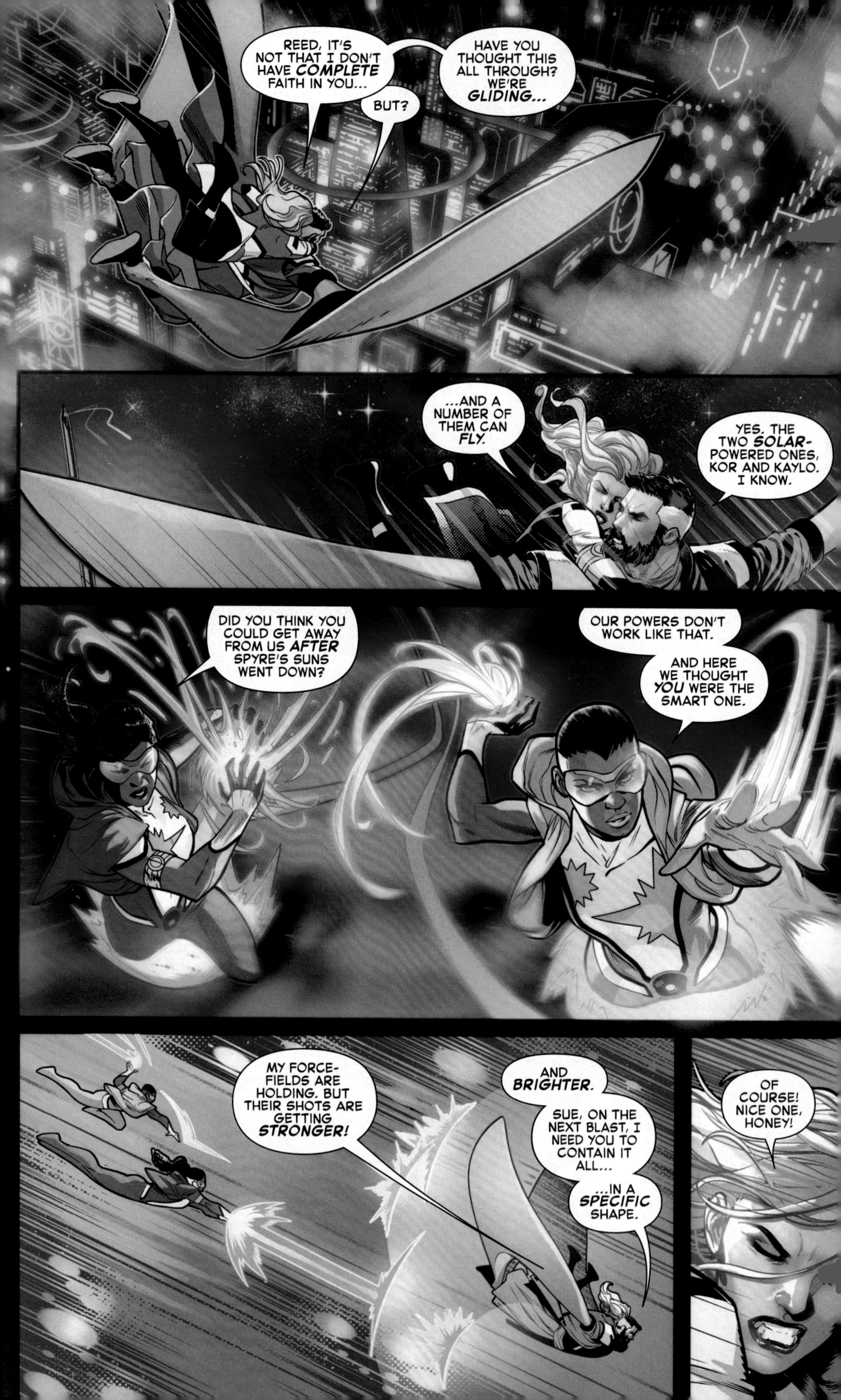
REED, IT'S NOT THAT I DON'T HAVE COMPLETE FAITH IN YOU...
BUT?
HAVE YOU THOUGHT THIS ALL THROUGH? WE'RE GLIDING...
...AND A NUMBER OF THEM CAN FLY.
YES. THE TWO SOLAR-POWERED ONES, KOR AND KAYLO. I KNOW.
DID YOU THINK YOU COULD GET AWAY FROM US AFTER SPYRE'S SUNS WENT DOWN?
OUR POWERS DON'T WORK LIKE THAT.
AND HERE WE THOUGHT YOU WERE THE SMART ONE.
MY FORCE-FIELDS ARE HOLDING. BUT THEIR SHOTS ARE GETTING STRONGER!
AND BRIGHTER.
SUE, ON THE NEXT BLAST, I NEED YOU TO CONTAIN IT ALL...
...IN A SPECIFIC SHAPE.
OF COURSE! NICE ONE, HONEY!

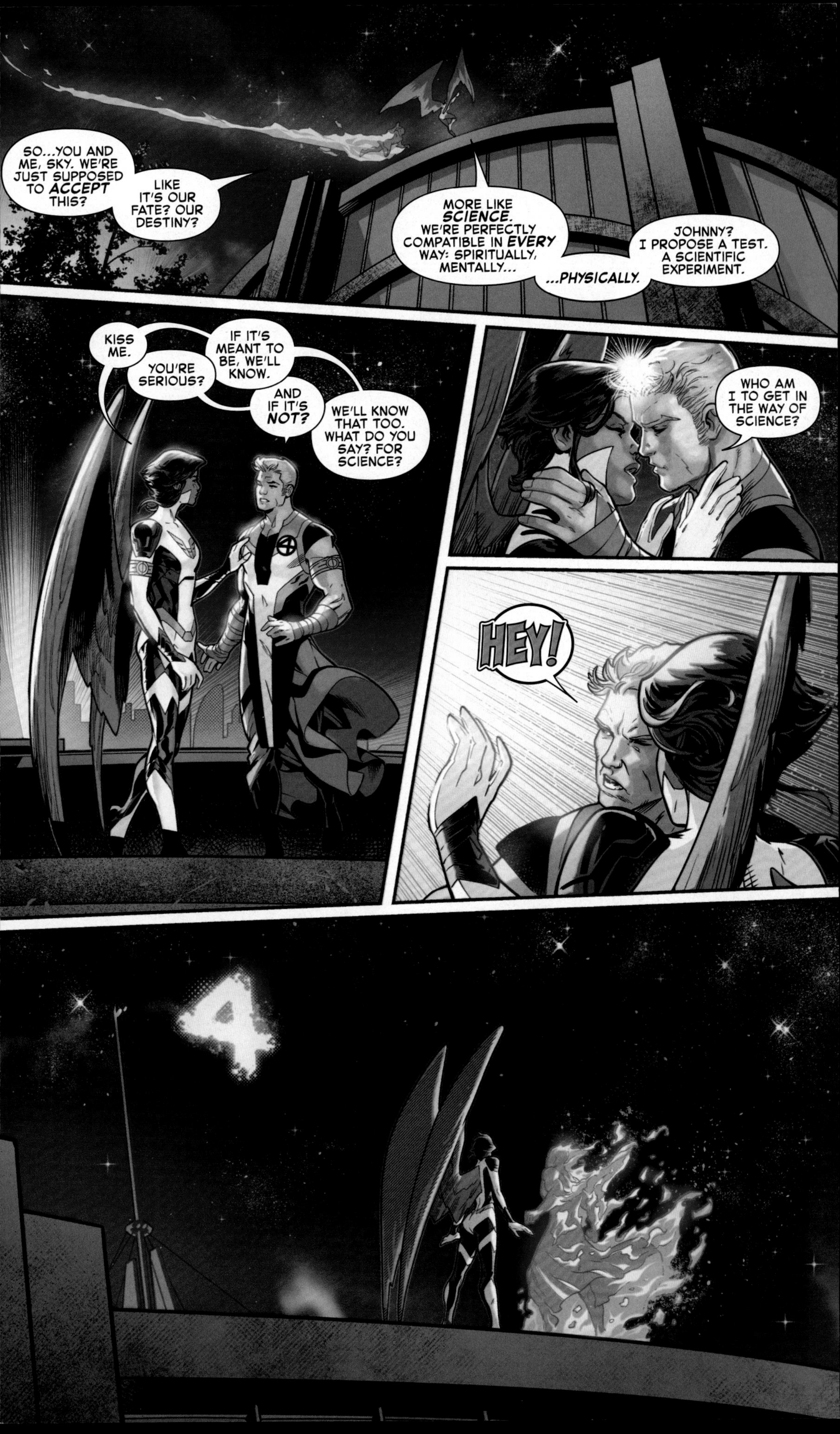
SO...YOU AND ME, SKY. WE'RE JUST SUPPOSED TO ACCEPT THIS?
LIKE IT'S OUR FATE? OUR DESTINY?
MORE LIKE SCIENCE. WE'RE PERFECTLY COMPATIBLE IN EVERY WAY: SPIRITUALLY, MENTALLY...
...PHYSICALLY.
JOHNNY? I PROPOSE A TEST. A SCIENTIFIC EXPERIMENT.
KISS ME.
YOU'RE SERIOUS?
IF IT'S MEANT TO BE, WE'LL KNOW.
AND IF IT'S NOT?
WE'LL KNOW THAT TOO. WHAT DO YOU SAY? FOR SCIENCE?
WHO AM I TO GET IN THE WAY OF SCIENCE?
HEY!

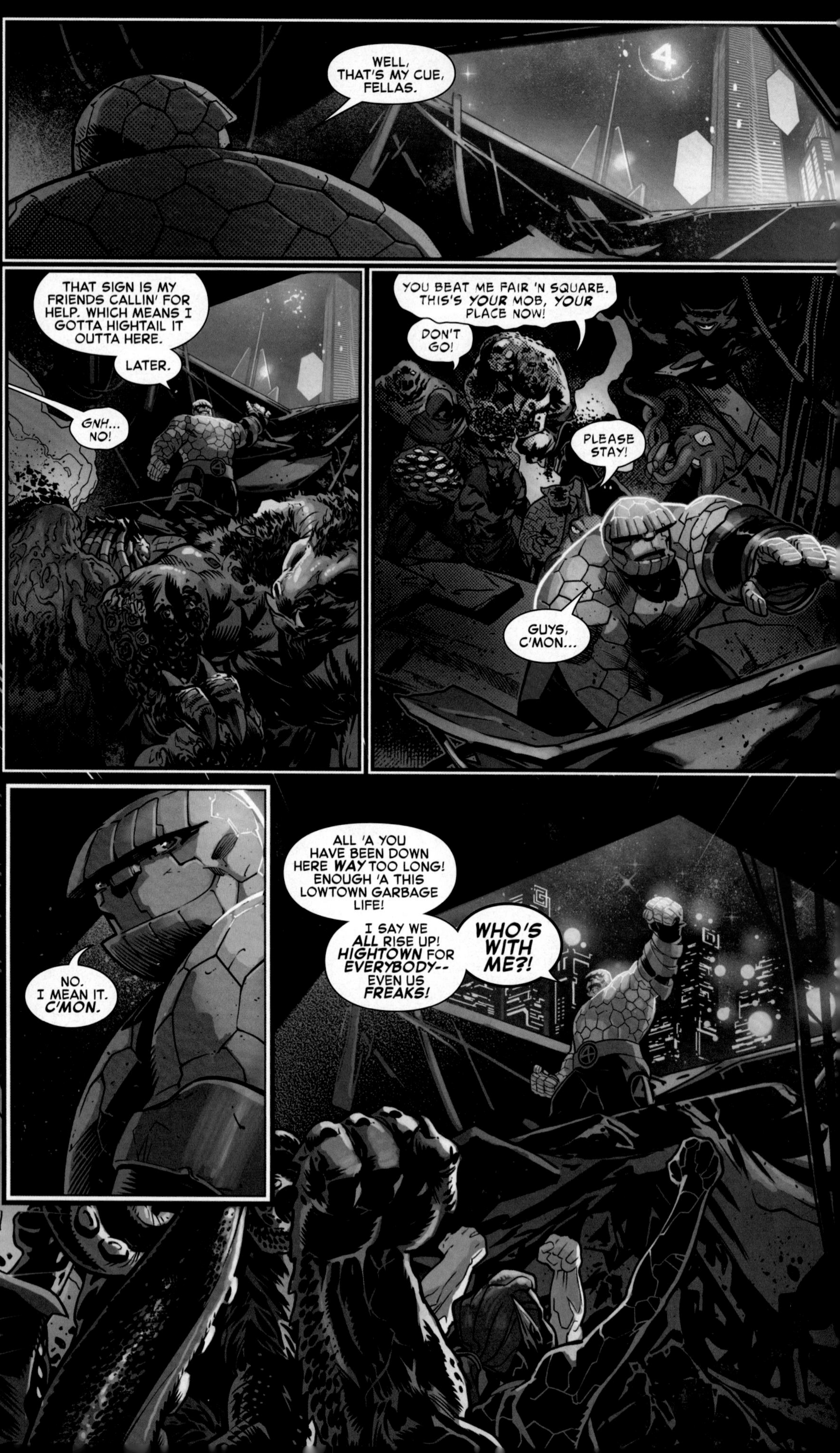
WELL, THAT'S MY CUE, FELLAS.
THAT SIGN IS MY FRIENDS CALLIN' FOR HELP. WHICH MEANS I GOTTA HIGHTAIL IT OUTTA HERE.
LATER.
GNH... NO!
YOU BEAT ME FAIR 'N SQUARE. THIS'S YOUR MOB, YOUR PLACE NOW!
DON'T GO!
PLEASE STAY!
GUYS, C'MON...
NO. I MEAN IT. C'MON.
ALL 'A YOU HAVE BEEN DOWN HERE WAY TOO LONG! ENOUGH 'A THIS LOWTOWN GARBAGE LIFE!
I SAY WE ALL RISE UP! HIGHTOWN FOR EVERYBODY-- EVEN US FREAKS!
WHO'S WITH ME?!

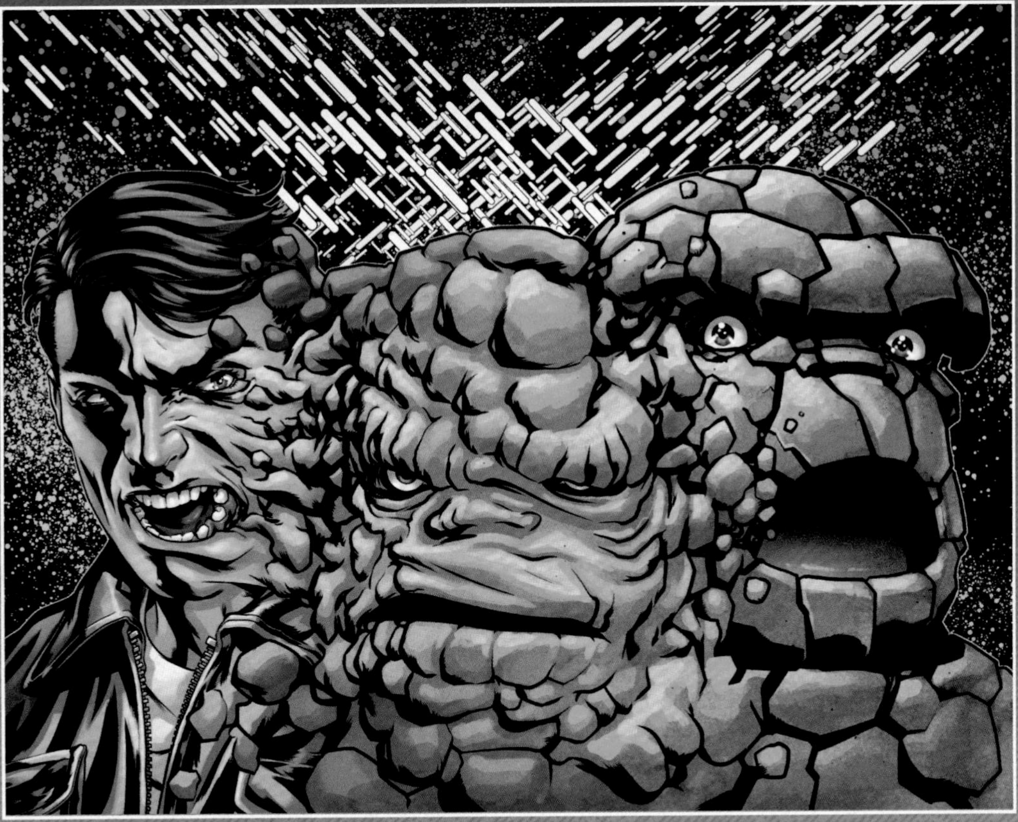

#14 Immortal variant by
Mike McKone & **Rachelle Rosenberg**

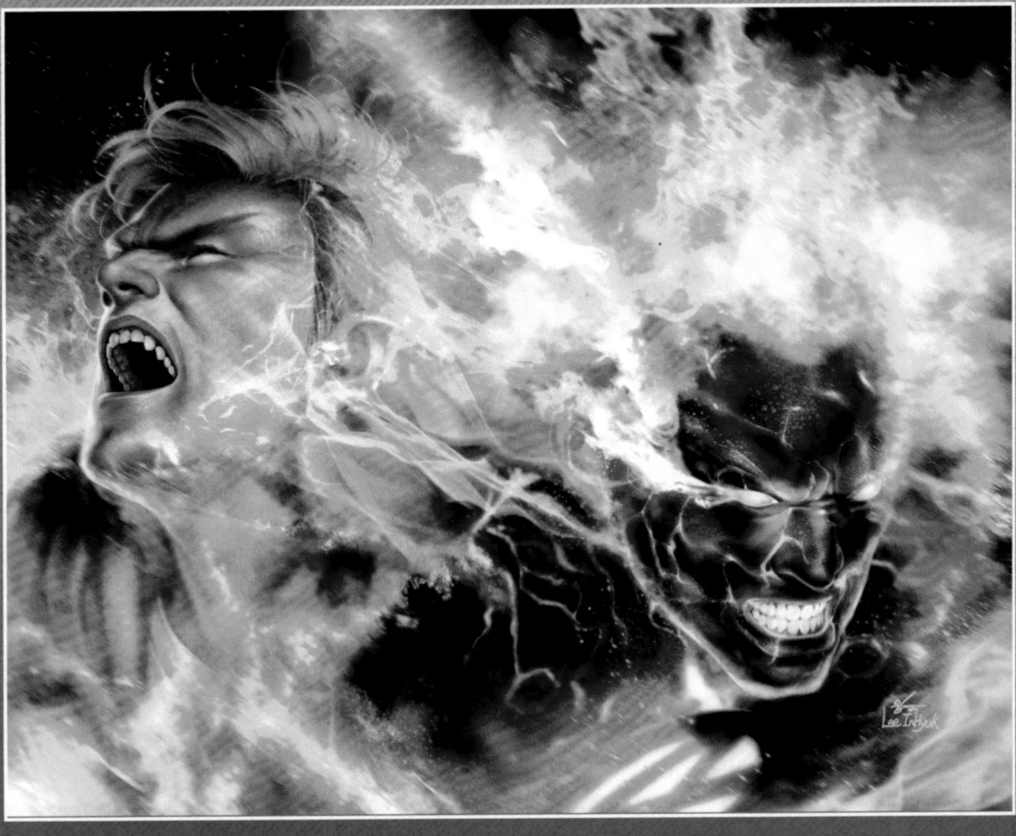
Lee InHyuk

#14 Immortal variant by
InHyuk Lee

17

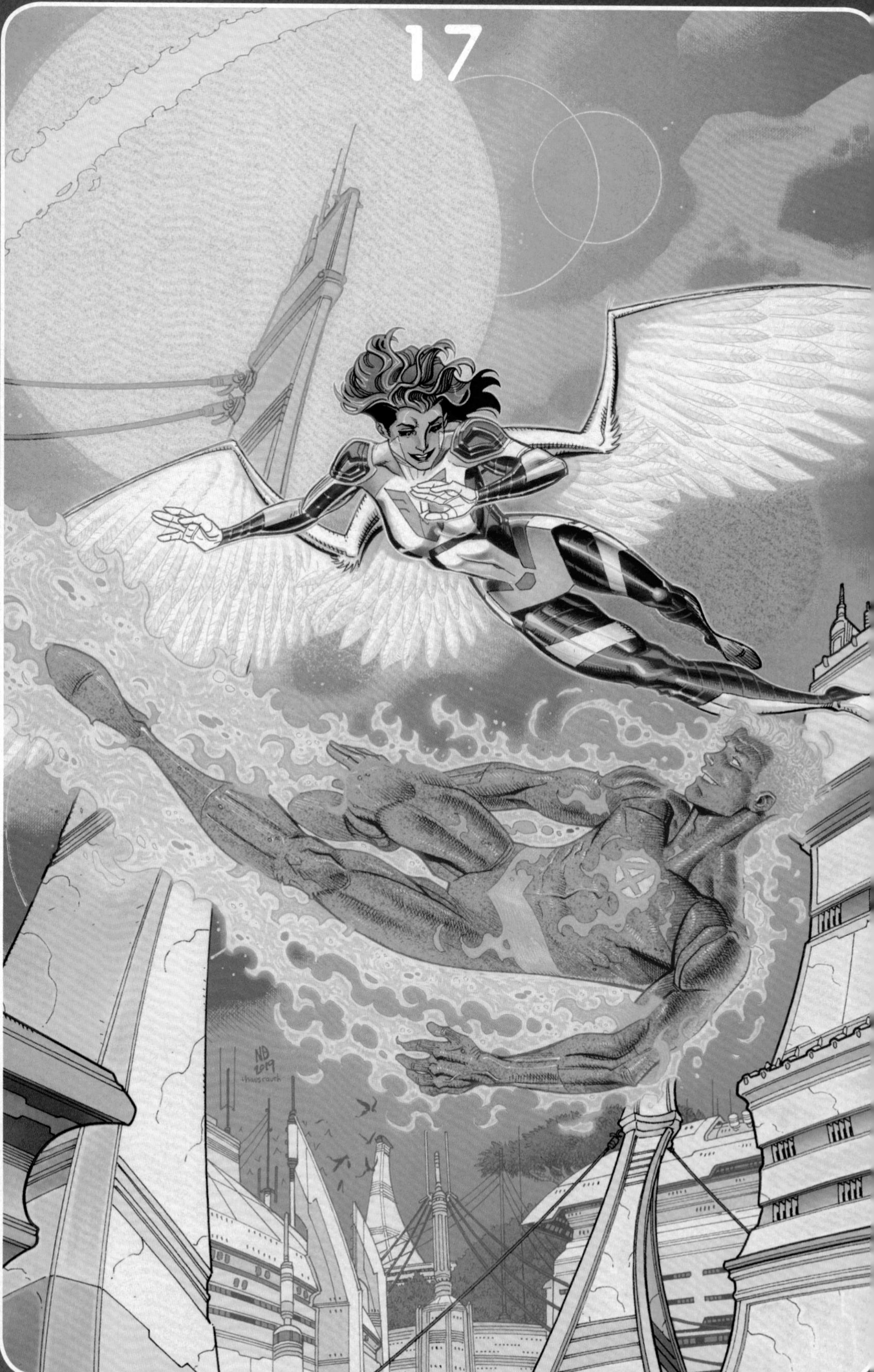

"Secret Agenda"

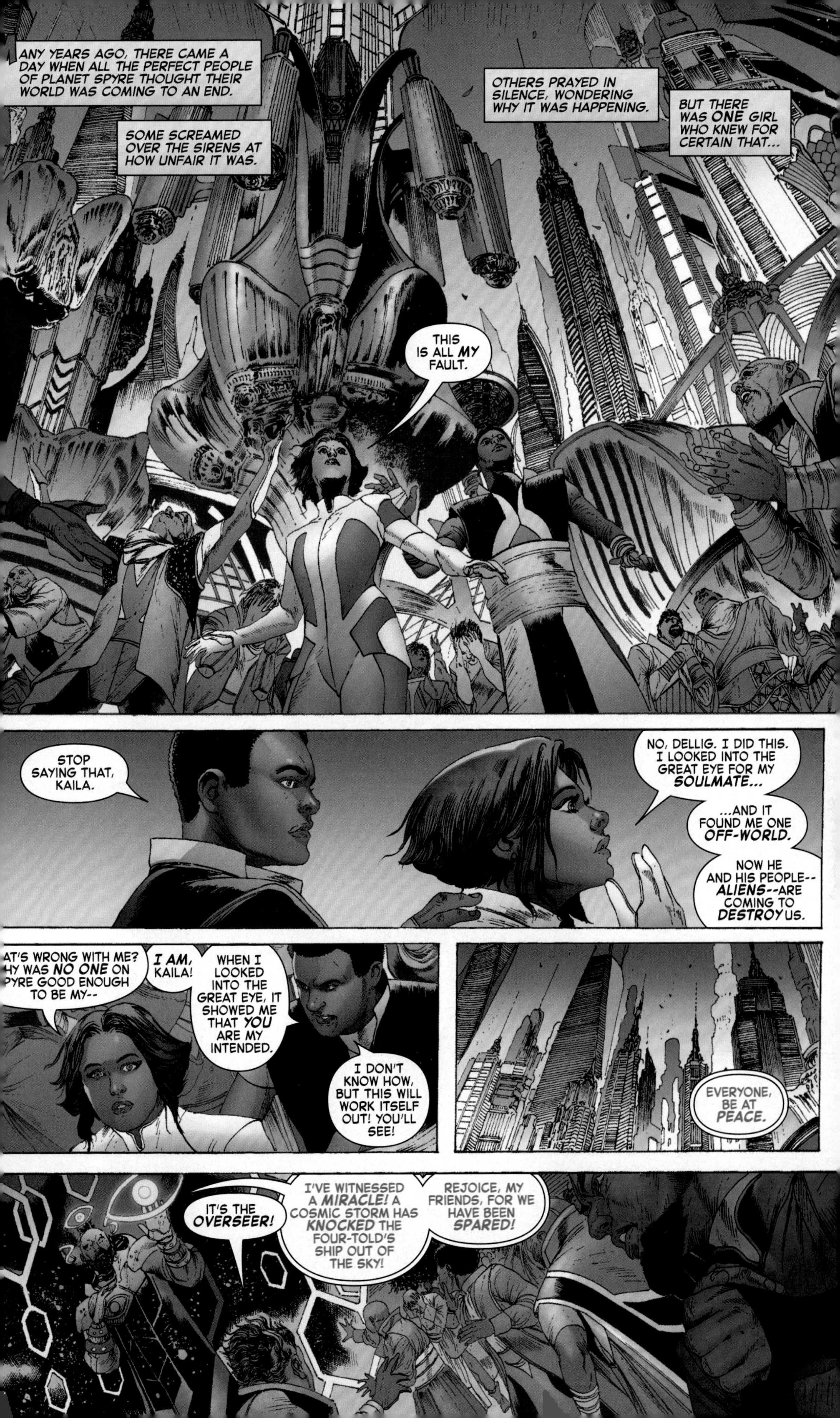
ANY YEARS AGO, THERE CAME A DAY WHEN ALL THE PERFECT PEOPLE OF PLANET SPYRE THOUGHT THEIR WORLD WAS COMING TO AN END.
SOME SCREAMED OVER THE SIRENS AT HOW UNFAIR IT WAS.
OTHERS PRAYED IN SILENCE, WONDERING WHY IT WAS HAPPENING.
BUT THERE WAS ONE GIRL WHO KNEW FOR CERTAIN THAT...
THIS IS ALL MY FAULT.
STOP SAYING THAT, KAILA.
NO, DELLIG. I DID THIS. I LOOKED INTO THE GREAT EYE FOR MY SOULMATE...
...AND IT FOUND ME ONE OFF-WORLD.
NOW HE AND HIS PEOPLE--ALIENS--ARE COMING TO DESTROY US.
AT'S WRONG WITH ME? HY WAS NO ONE ON PYRE GOOD ENOUGH TO BE MY--
I AM, KAILA!
WHEN I LOOKED INTO THE GREAT EYE, IT SHOWED ME THAT YOU ARE MY INTENDED.
I DON'T KNOW HOW, BUT THIS WILL WORK ITSELF OUT! YOU'LL SEE!
EVERYONE, BE AT PEACE.
IT'S THE OVERSEER!
I'VE WITNESSED A MIRACLE! A COSMIC STORM HAS KNOCKED THE FOUR-TOLD'S SHIP OUT OF THE SKY!
REJOICE, MY FRIENDS, FOR WE HAVE BEEN SPARED!

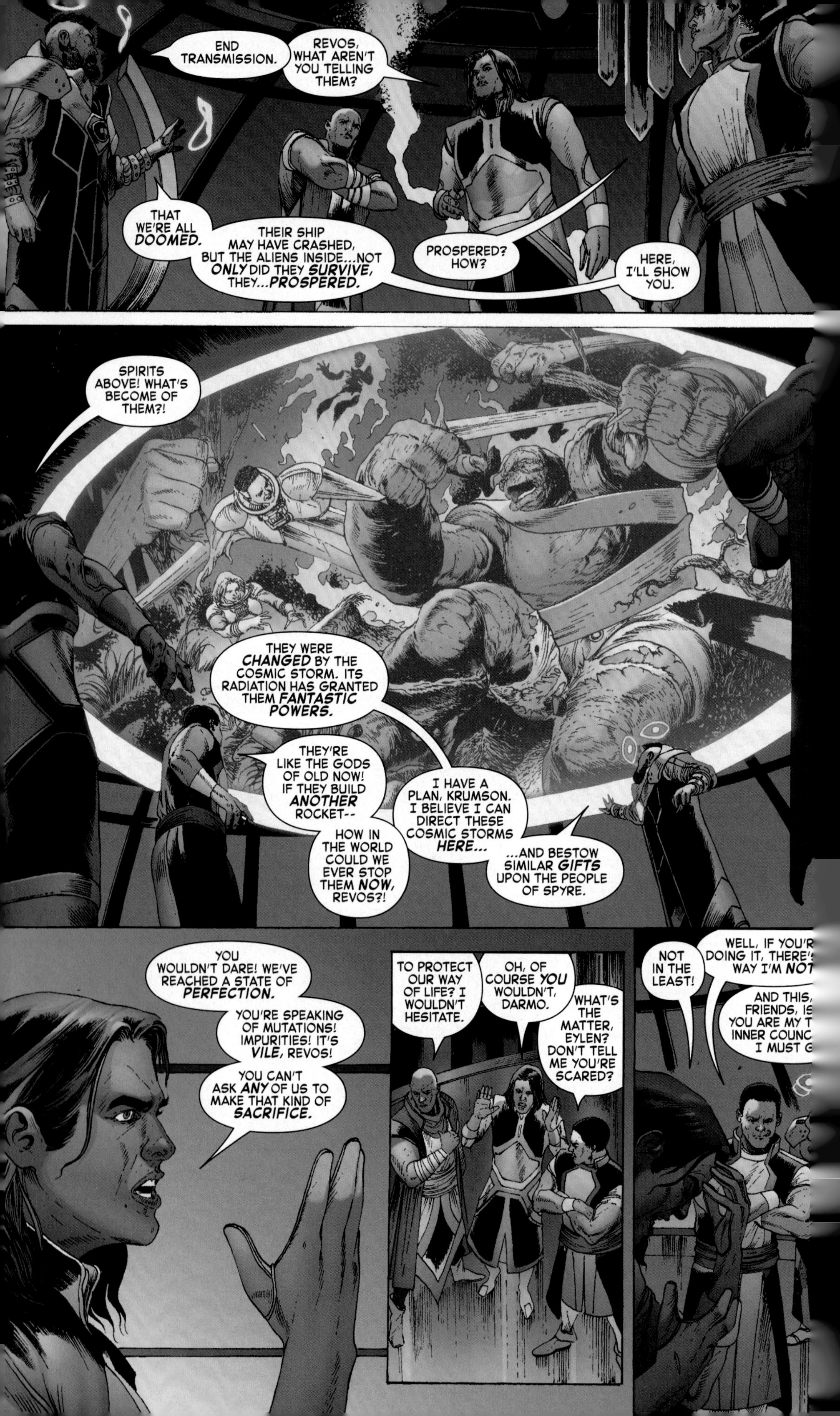

END TRANSMISSION.
REVOS, WHAT AREN'T YOU TELLING THEM?
THAT WE'RE ALL DOOMED.
THEIR SHIP MAY HAVE CRASHED, BUT THE ALIENS INSIDE...NOT ONLY DID THEY SURVIVE, THEY...PROSPERED.
PROSPERED? HOW?
HERE, I'LL SHOW YOU.
SPIRITS ABOVE! WHAT'S BECOME OF THEM?!
THEY WERE CHANGED BY THE COSMIC STORM. ITS RADIATION HAS GRANTED THEM FANTASTIC POWERS.
THEY'RE LIKE THE GODS OF OLD NOW! IF THEY BUILD ANOTHER ROCKET--
HOW IN THE WORLD COULD WE EVER STOP THEM NOW, REVOS?!
I HAVE A PLAN, KRUMSON. I BELIEVE I CAN DIRECT THESE COSMIC STORMS HERE...
...AND BESTOW SIMILAR GIFTS UPON THE PEOPLE OF SPYRE.
YOU WOULDN'T DARE! WE'VE REACHED A STATE OF PERFECTION.
YOU'RE SPEAKING OF MUTATIONS! IMPURITIES! IT'S VILE, REVOS!
YOU CAN'T ASK ANY OF US TO MAKE THAT KIND OF SACRIFICE.
TO PROTECT OUR WAY OF LIFE? I WOULDN'T HESITATE.
OH, OF COURSE YOU WOULDN'T, DARMO.
WHAT'S THE MATTER, EYLEN? DON'T TELL ME YOU'RE SCARED?
NOT IN THE LEAST!
WELL, IF YOU'R DOING IT, THERE'S WAY I'M NOT
AND THIS, FRIENDS, IS YOU ARE MY T INNER COUNC I MUST G

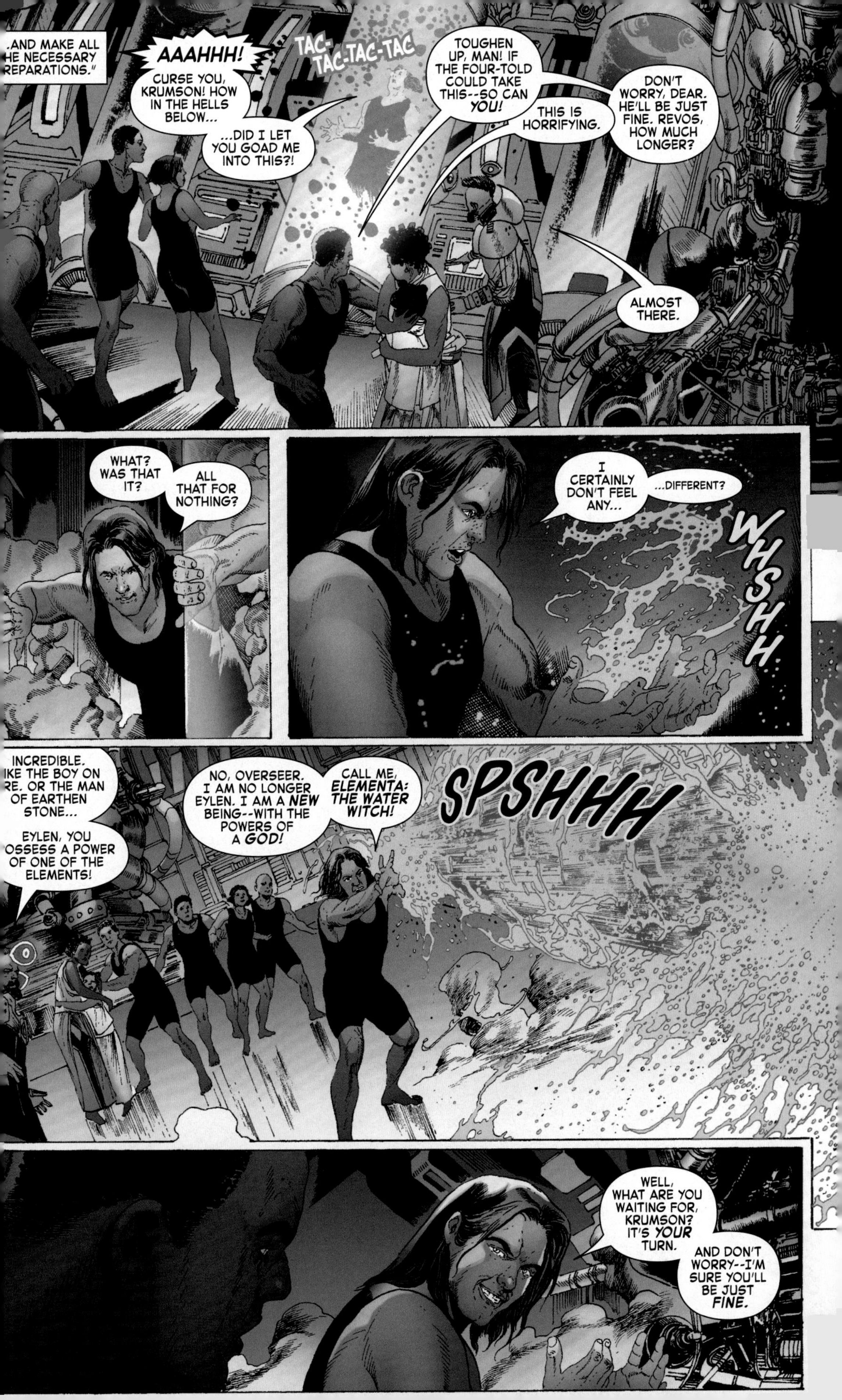
..AND MAKE ALL
HE NECESSARY
REPARATIONS."
AAAHHH!
CURSE YOU, KRUMSON! HOW IN THE HELLS BELOW...
...DID I LET YOU GOAD ME INTO THIS?!
TAC-TAC-TAC-TAC
TOUGHEN UP, MAN! IF THE FOUR-TOLD COULD TAKE THIS--SO CAN YOU!
THIS IS HORRIFYING.
DON'T WORRY, DEAR. HE'LL BE JUST FINE. REVOS, HOW MUCH LONGER?
ALMOST THERE.
WHAT? WAS THAT IT?
ALL THAT FOR NOTHING?
I CERTAINLY DON'T FEEL ANY...
...DIFFERENT?
WHSHH
INCREDIBLE. IKE THE BOY ON RE. OR THE MAN OF EARTHEN STONE...
EYLEN, YOU OSSESS A POWER OF ONE OF THE ELEMENTS!
NO, OVERSEER. I AM NO LONGER EYLEN. I AM A NEW BEING--WITH THE POWERS OF A GOD!
CALL ME, ELEMENTA: THE WATER WITCH!
SPSHHH
WELL, WHAT ARE YOU WAITING FOR, KRUMSON? IT'S YOUR TURN.
AND DON'T WORRY--I'M SURE YOU'LL BE JUST FINE.

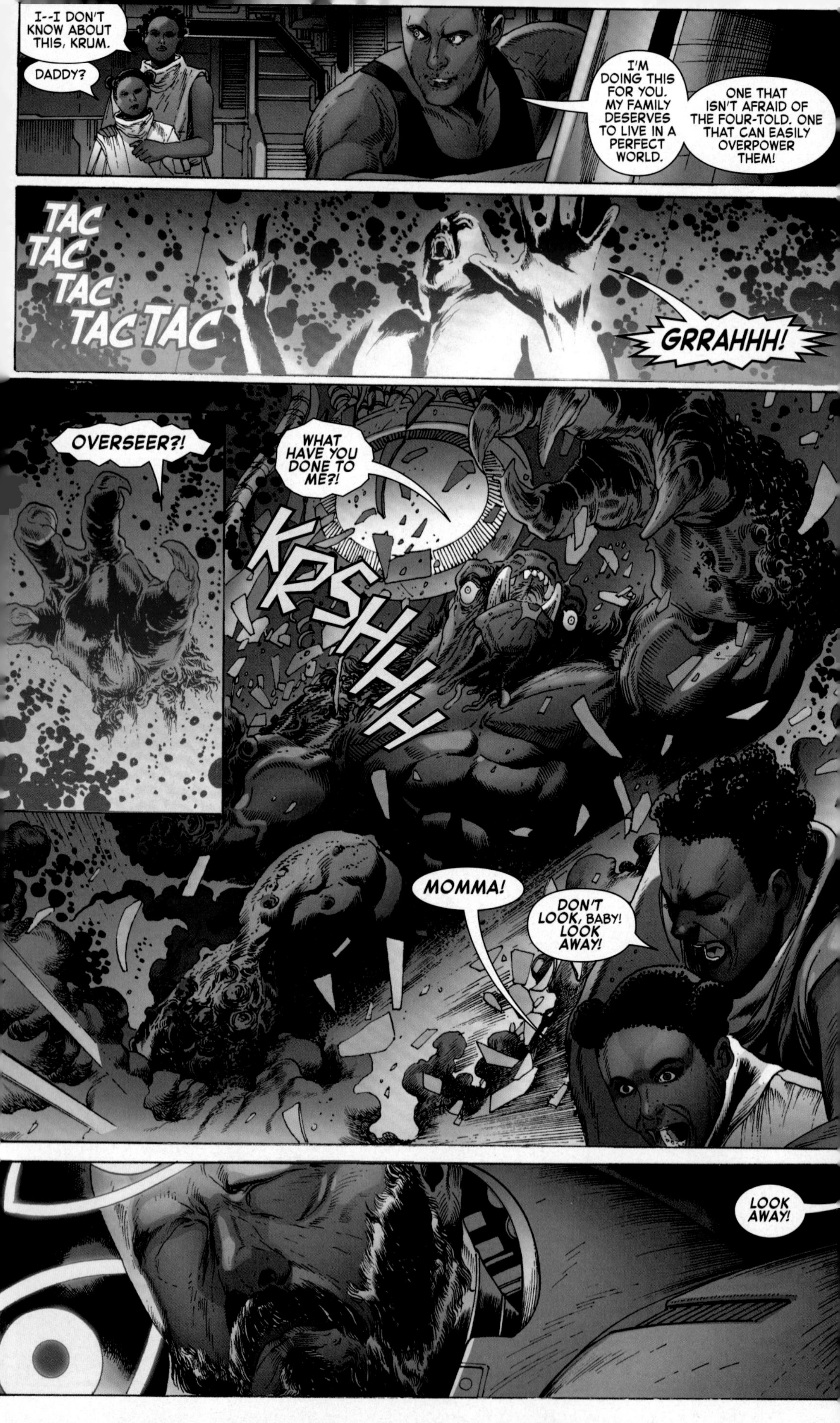
I--I DON'T KNOW ABOUT THIS, KRUM.
DADDY?
I'M DOING THIS FOR YOU. MY FAMILY DESERVES TO LIVE IN A PERFECT WORLD.
ONE THAT ISN'T AFRAID OF THE FOUR-TOLD. ONE THAT CAN EASILY OVERPOWER THEM!
TAC TAC TAC TAC TAC
GRRAHHH!
OVERSEER?!
WHAT HAVE YOU DONE TO ME?!
KRSHHHH
MOMMA!
DON'T LOOK, BABY! LOOK AWAY!
LOOK AWAY!

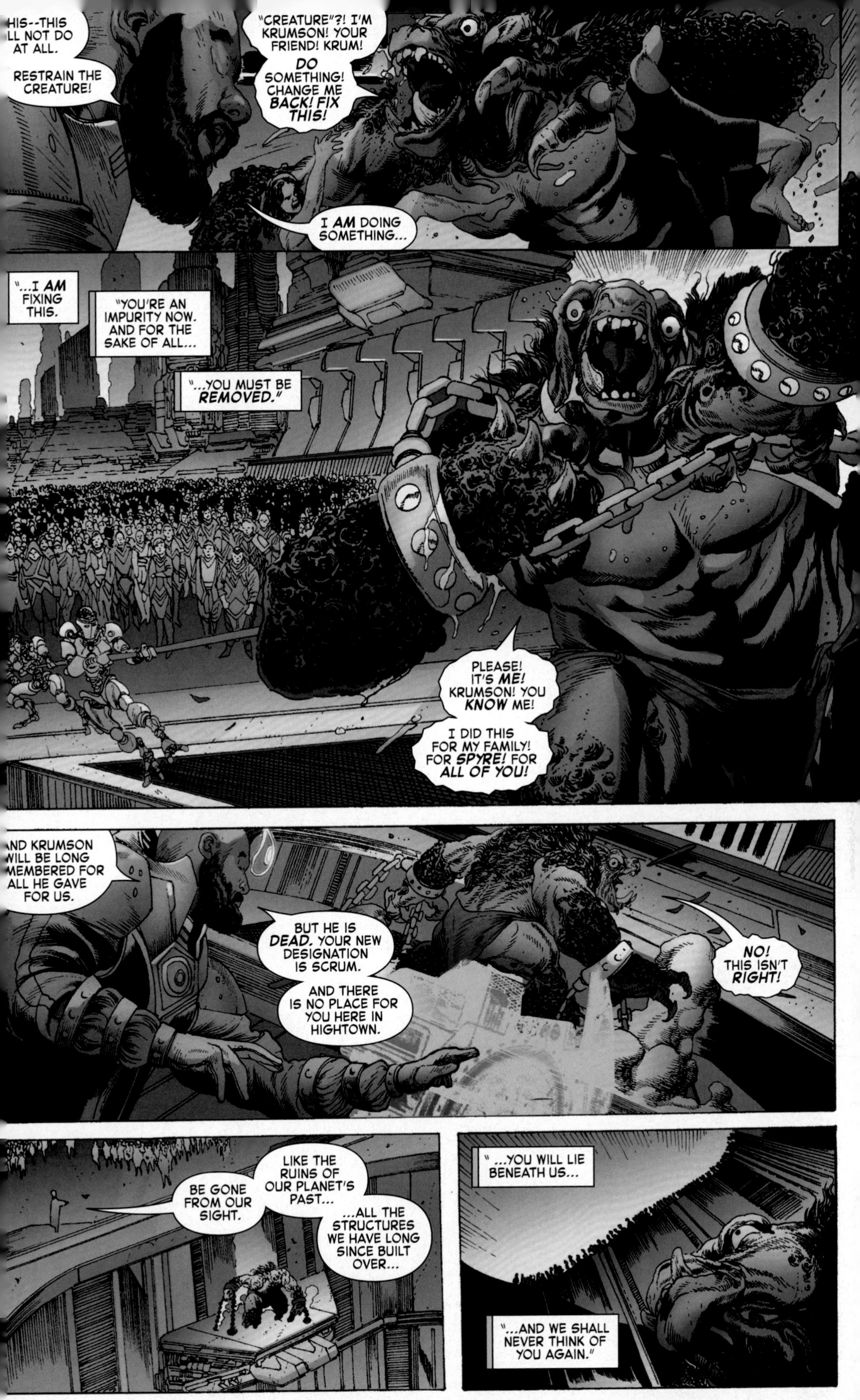
HIS--THIS
LL NOT DO
AT ALL.
RESTRAIN THE
CREATURE!
"CREATURE"?! I'M
KRUMSON! YOUR
FRIEND! KRUM!
DO
SOMETHING!
CHANGE ME
BACK! FIX
THIS!
I AM DOING
SOMETHING...
"...I AM
FIXING
THIS.
"YOU'RE AN
IMPURITY NOW.
AND FOR THE
SAKE OF ALL...
"...YOU MUST BE
REMOVED."
PLEASE!
IT'S ME!
KRUMSON! YOU
KNOW ME!
I DID THIS
FOR MY FAMILY!
FOR SPYRE! FOR
ALL OF YOU!
AND KRUMSON
WILL BE LONG
MEMBERED FOR
ALL HE GAVE
FOR US.
BUT HE IS
DEAD. YOUR NEW
DESIGNATION
IS SCRUM.
AND THERE
IS NO PLACE FOR
YOU HERE IN
HIGHTOWN.
NO!
THIS ISN'T
RIGHT!
BE GONE
FROM OUR
SIGHT.
LIKE THE
RUINS OF
OUR PLANET'S
PAST...
...ALL THE
STRUCTURES
WE HAVE LONG
SINCE BUILT
OVER...
"...YOU WILL LIE
BENEATH US...
"...AND WE SHALL
NEVER THINK OF
YOU AGAIN."

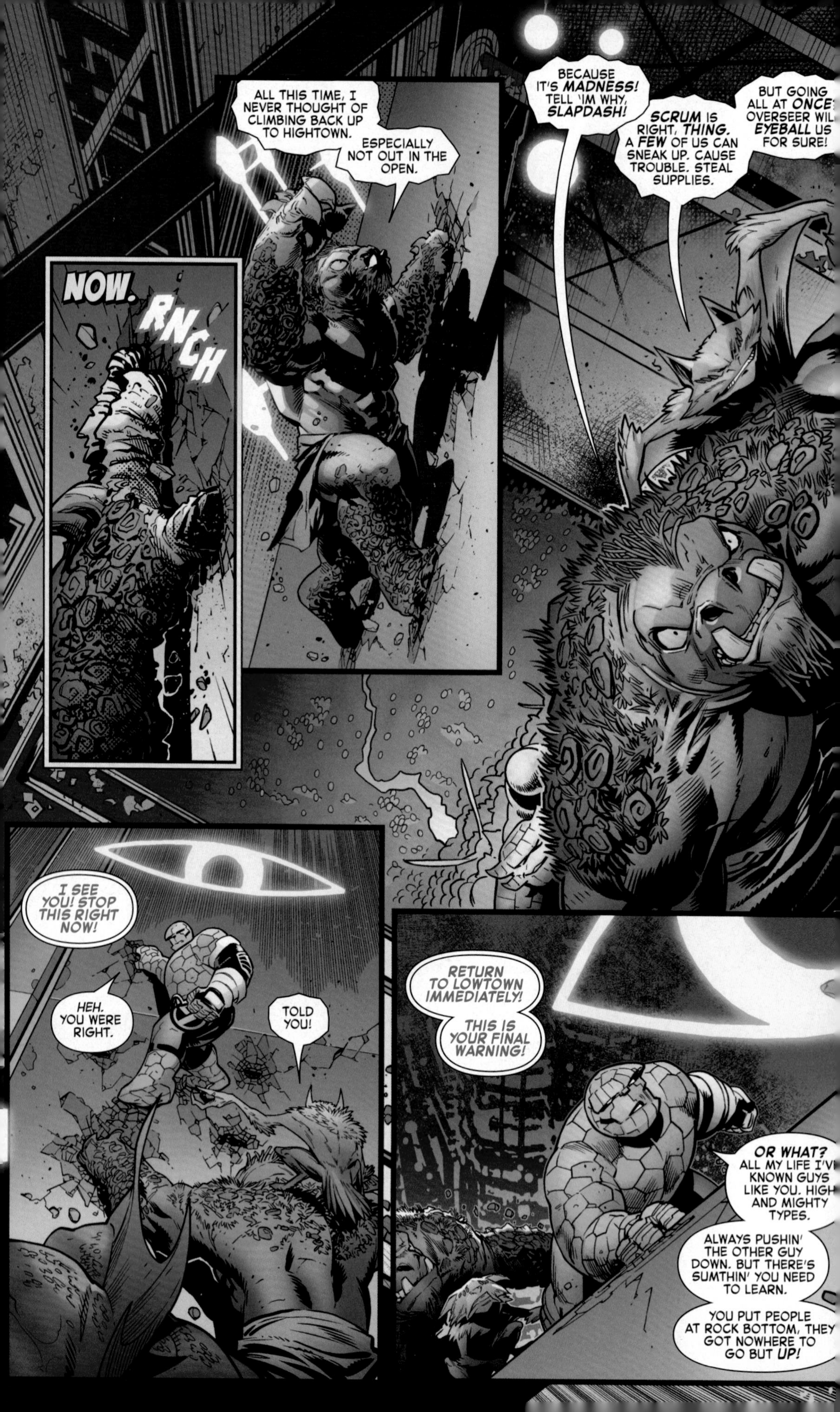
NOW.
RNCH
ALL THIS TIME, I NEVER THOUGHT OF CLIMBING BACK UP TO HIGHTOWN.
ESPECIALLY NOT OUT IN THE OPEN.
BECAUSE IT'S MADNESS! TELL 'IM WHY, SLAPDASH!
SCRUM IS RIGHT, THING. A FEW OF US CAN SNEAK UP. CAUSE TROUBLE. STEAL SUPPLIES.
BUT GOING ALL AT ONCE: OVERSEER WIL EYEBALL US FOR SURE!
I SEE YOU! STOP THIS RIGHT NOW!
HEH. YOU WERE RIGHT.
TOLD YOU!
RETURN TO LOWTOWN IMMEDIATELY!
THIS IS YOUR FINAL WARNING!
OR WHAT? ALL MY LIFE I'V KNOWN GUYS LIKE YOU. HIGH AND MIGHTY TYPES.
ALWAYS PUSHIN' THE OTHER GUY DOWN. BUT THERE'S SUMTHIN' YOU NEED TO LEARN.
YOU PUT PEOPLE AT ROCK BOTTOM, THEY GOT NOWHERE TO GO BUT UP!

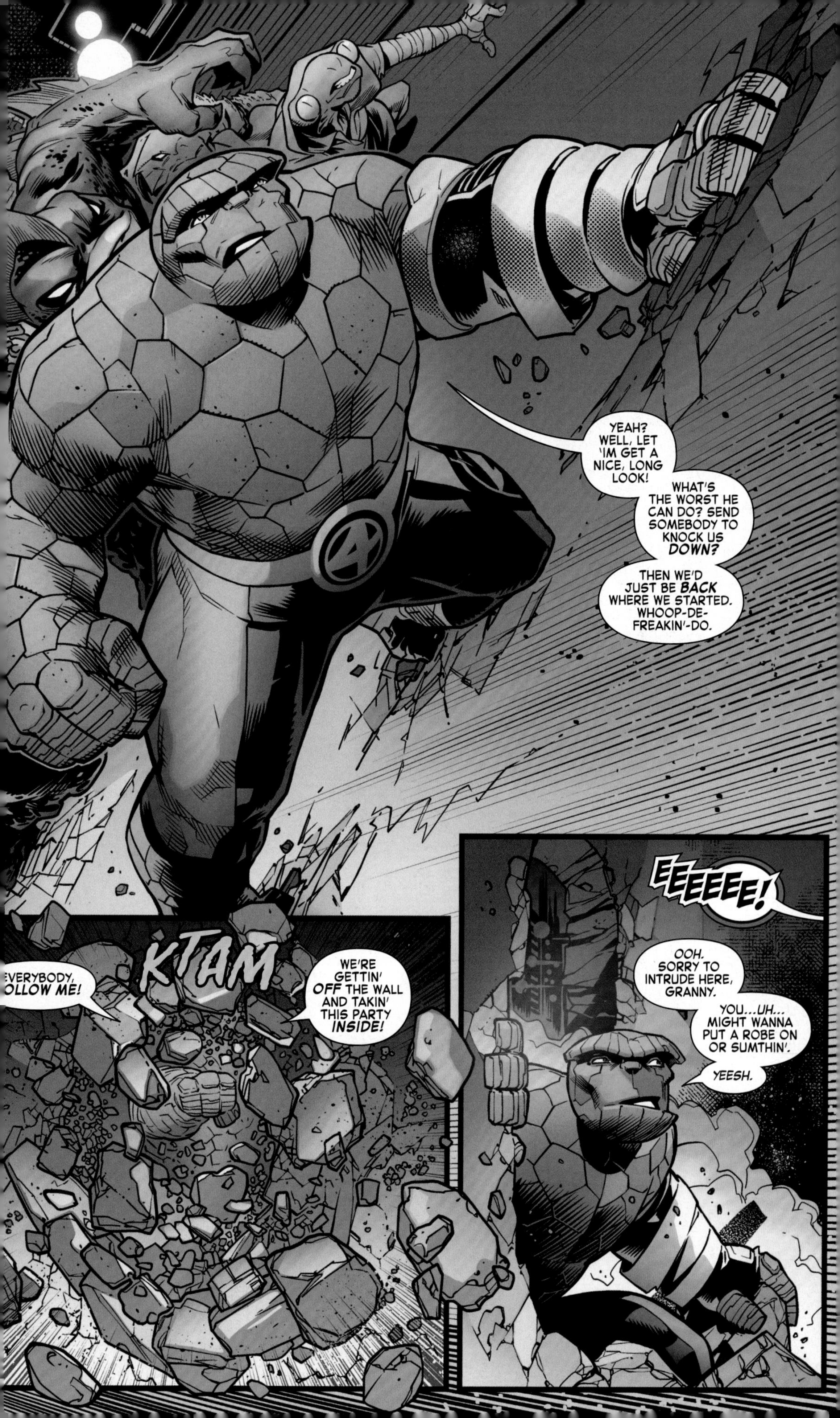
YEAH? WELL, LET 'IM GET A NICE, LONG LOOK!
WHAT'S THE WORST HE CAN DO? SEND SOMEBODY TO KNOCK US DOWN?
THEN WE'D JUST BE BACK WHERE WE STARTED. WHOOP-DE-FREAKIN'-DO.
KTAM
EVERYBODY, OLLOW ME!
WE'RE GETTIN' OFF THE WALL AND TAKIN' THIS PARTY INSIDE!
EEEEEEE!
OOH. SORRY TO INTRUDE HERE, GRANNY.
YOU...UH... MIGHT WANNA PUT A ROBE ON OR SUMTHIN'.
YEESH.

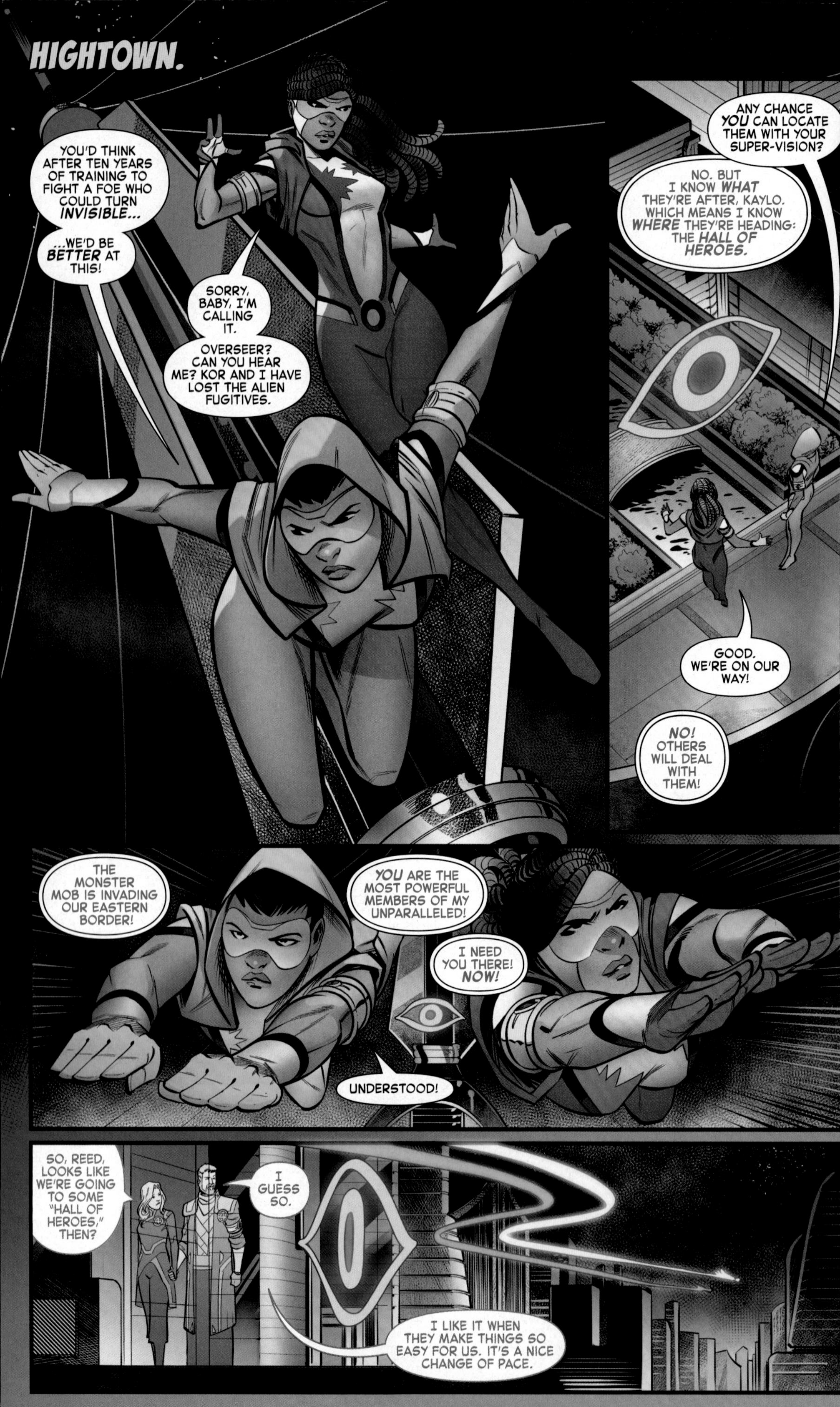
HIGHTOWN.
YOU'D THINK AFTER TEN YEARS OF TRAINING TO FIGHT A FOE WHO COULD TURN INVISIBLE...
...WE'D BE BETTER AT THIS!
SORRY, BABY, I'M CALLING IT.
OVERSEER? CAN YOU HEAR ME? KOR AND I HAVE LOST THE ALIEN FUGITIVES.
ANY CHANCE YOU CAN LOCATE THEM WITH YOUR SUPER-VISION?
NO. BUT I KNOW WHAT THEY'RE AFTER, KAYLO. WHICH MEANS I KNOW WHERE THEY'RE HEADING: THE HALL OF HEROES.
GOOD. WE'RE ON OUR WAY!
NO! OTHERS WILL DEAL WITH THEM!
THE MONSTER MOB IS INVADING OUR EASTERN BORDER!
YOU ARE THE MOST POWERFUL MEMBERS OF MY UNPARALLELED!
I NEED YOU THERE! NOW!
UNDERSTOOD!
SO, REED, LOOKS LIKE WE'RE GOING TO SOME "HALL OF HEROES," THEN?
I GUESS SO.
I LIKE IT WHEN THEY MAKE THINGS SO EASY FOR US. IT'S A NICE CHANGE OF PACE.

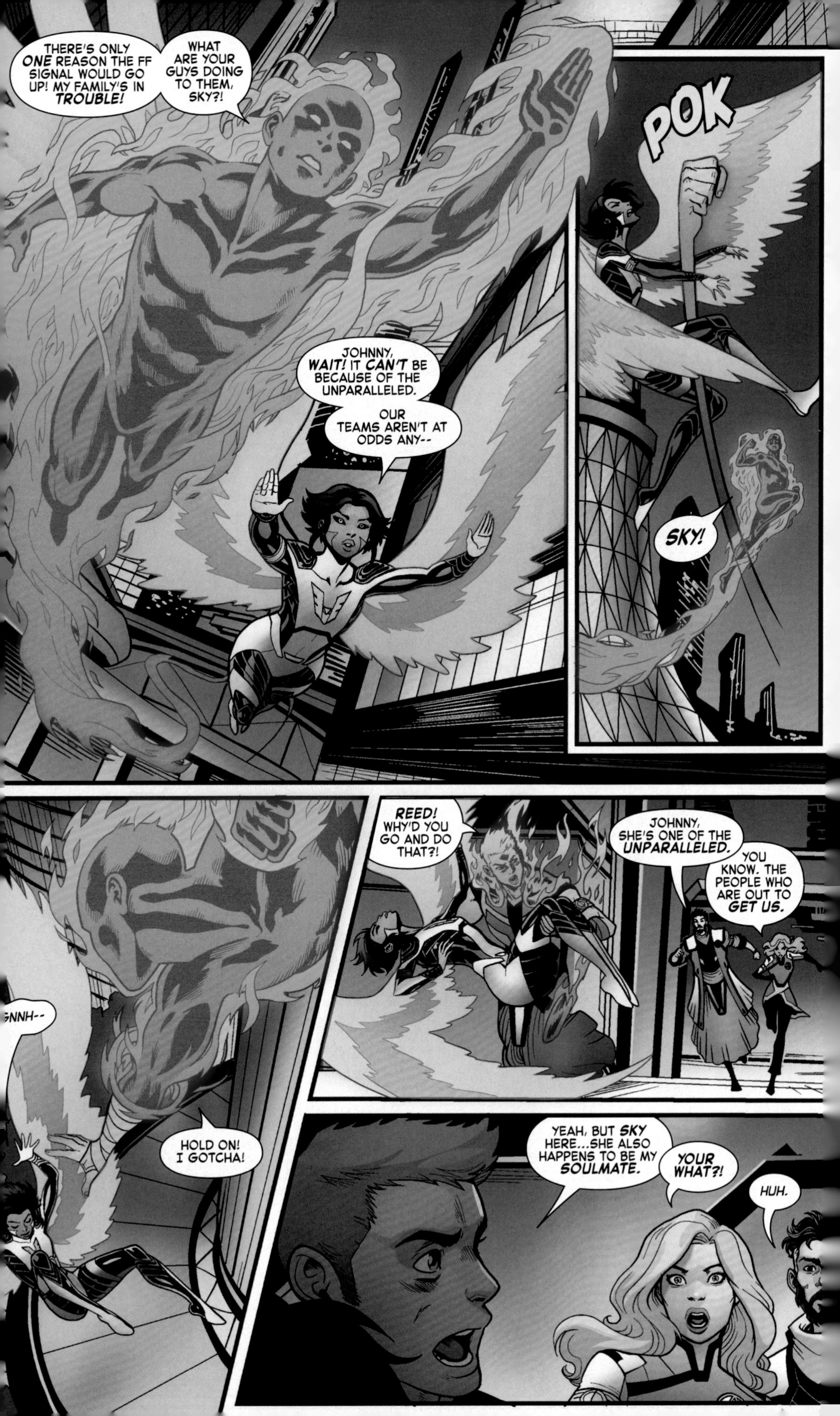
THERE'S ONLY ONE REASON THE FF SIGNAL WOULD GO UP! MY FAMILY'S IN TROUBLE!
WHAT ARE YOUR GUYS DOING TO THEM, SKY?!
JOHNNY, WAIT! IT CAN'T BE BECAUSE OF THE UNPARALLELED.
OUR TEAMS AREN'T AT ODDS ANY--
POK
SKY!
GNNH--
HOLD ON! I GOTCHA!
REED! WHY'D YOU GO AND DO THAT?!
JOHNNY, SHE'S ONE OF THE UNPARALLELED.
YOU KNOW. THE PEOPLE WHO ARE OUT TO GET US.
YEAH, BUT SKY HERE...SHE ALSO HAPPENS TO BE MY SOULMATE.
YOUR WHAT?!
HUH.

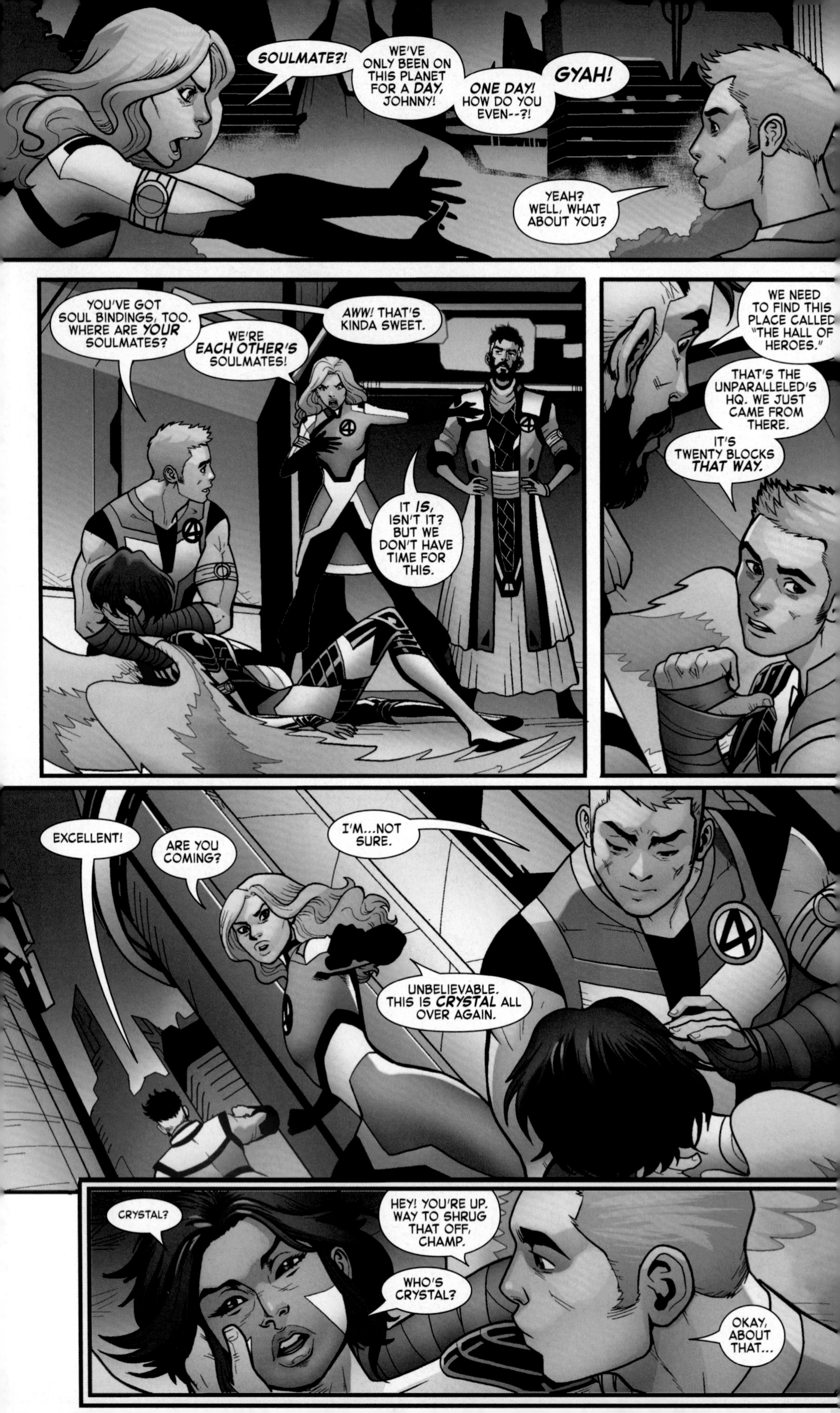
SOULMATE?!
WE'VE ONLY BEEN ON THIS PLANET FOR A DAY, JOHNNY!
ONE DAY! HOW DO YOU EVEN--?!
GYAH!
YEAH? WELL, WHAT ABOUT YOU?
YOU'VE GOT SOUL BINDINGS, TOO. WHERE ARE YOUR SOULMATES?
WE'RE EACH OTHER'S SOULMATES!
AWW! THAT'S KINDA SWEET.
IT IS, ISN'T IT? BUT WE DON'T HAVE TIME FOR THIS.
WE NEED TO FIND THIS PLACE CALLED "THE HALL OF HEROES."
THAT'S THE UNPARALLELED'S HQ. WE JUST CAME FROM THERE.
IT'S TWENTY BLOCKS THAT WAY.
EXCELLENT!
ARE YOU COMING?
I'M...NOT SURE.
UNBELIEVABLE. THIS IS CRYSTAL ALL OVER AGAIN.
CRYSTAL?
HEY! YOU'RE UP. WAY TO SHRUG THAT OFF, CHAMP.
WHO'S CRYSTAL?
OKAY, ABOUT THAT...

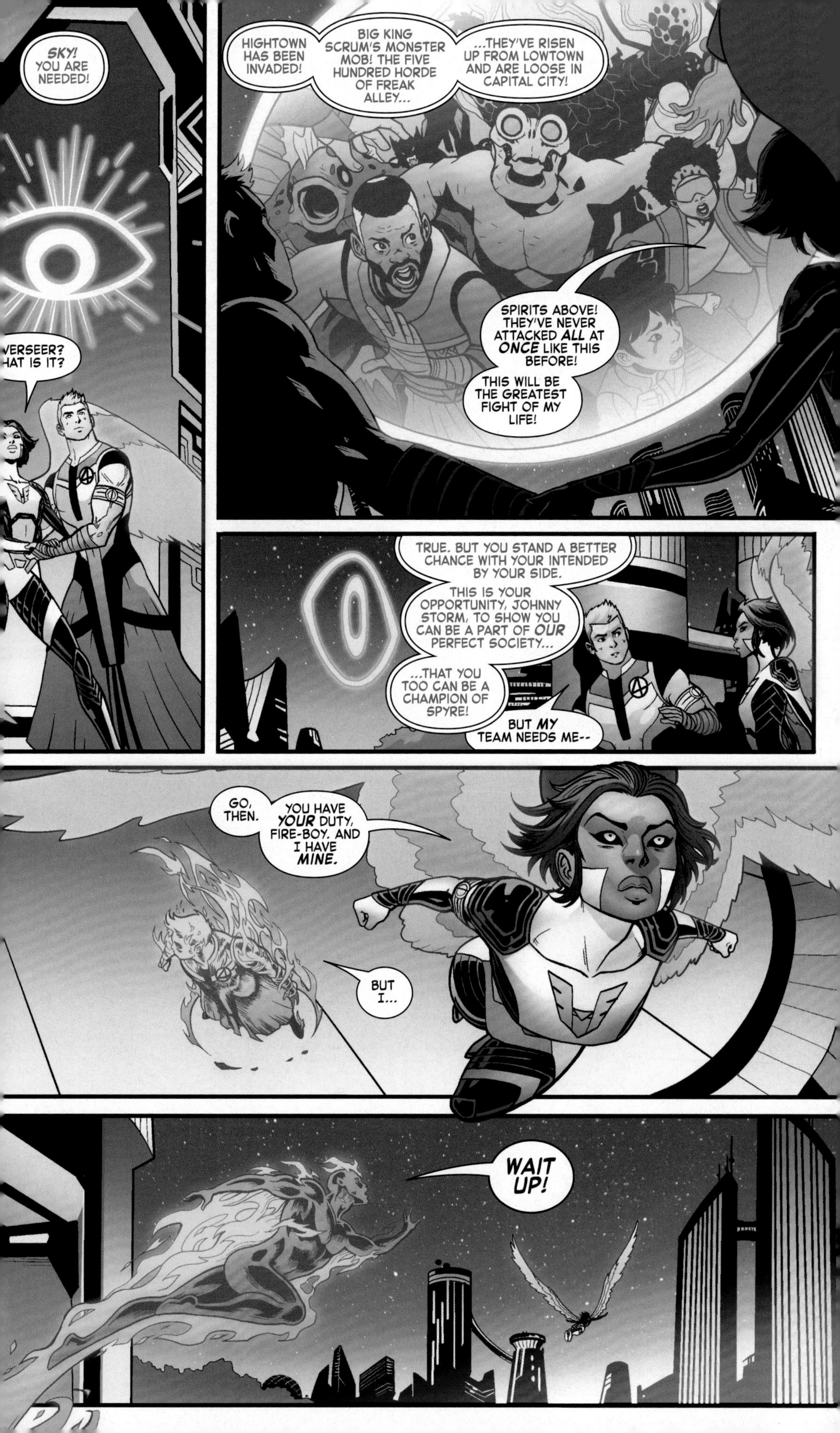
SKY! YOU ARE NEEDED!
HIGHTOWN HAS BEEN INVADED!
BIG KING SCRUM'S MONSTER MOB! THE FIVE HUNDRED HORDE OF FREAK ALLEY...
...THEY'VE RISEN UP FROM LOWTOWN AND ARE LOOSE IN CAPITAL CITY!
VERSEER? HAT IS IT?
SPIRITS ABOVE! THEY'VE NEVER ATTACKED ALL AT ONCE LIKE THIS BEFORE!
THIS WILL BE THE GREATEST FIGHT OF MY LIFE!
TRUE. BUT YOU STAND A BETTER CHANCE WITH YOUR INTENDED BY YOUR SIDE.
THIS IS YOUR OPPORTUNITY, JOHNNY STORM, TO SHOW YOU CAN BE A PART OF OUR PERFECT SOCIETY...
...THAT YOU TOO CAN BE A CHAMPION OF SPYRE!
BUT MY TEAM NEEDS ME--
GO, THEN.
YOU HAVE YOUR DUTY, FIRE-BOY. AND I HAVE MINE.
BUT I...
WAIT UP!

WELL, HERE WE ARE, GRIMM! ALL THE FREAKS...UP TOP WITH THE ELITE. WHAT'D I TELL YOU? THEY CAN'T EVEN *LOOK* AT US.

TO BE FAIR, IT COULD BE THE *SMELL*.

UGH! YES! WHY'D WE HAVE TO GO THROUGH THE *SEWERS?* DISGUSTING!

HEY, I USED TO DO IT ALL THE *TIME* BACK IN THE DAY.

ALL 'CAUSE I THOUGHT I WUZ IN A WORLD THAT WASN'T MADE FER GUYS LIKE ME.

CONSIDER THAT BATH A *KINDNESS.* THE LAST YOU SHALL RECEIVE FROM *THE UNPARALLELED!*

YOU KNOW THE *RULES*, FELLAS. THERE'S A *PLACE* FOR EVERYONE ON SPYRE.

AND YOURS *ISN'T* UP HERE.

WHAT RULES?! ALL 'A MY CREW WUZ *BORN* HERE!

C'MON GUYS, I IT'S TIME EXERCIS SOME 'A *RIGHT*

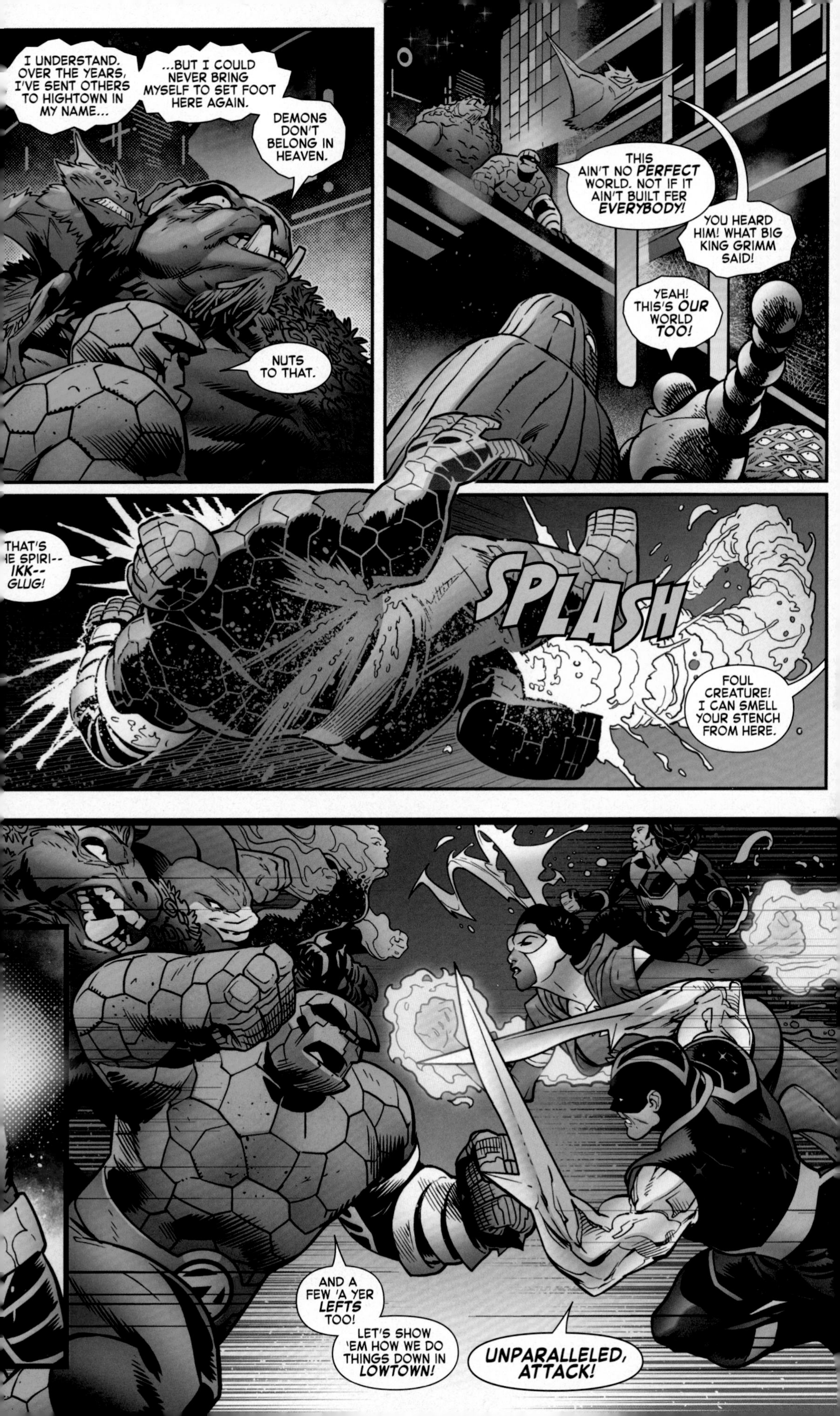

I UNDERSTAND. OVER THE YEARS, I'VE SENT OTHERS TO HIGHTOWN IN MY NAME...
...BUT I COULD NEVER BRING MYSELF TO SET FOOT HERE AGAIN.
DEMONS DON'T BELONG IN HEAVEN.
NUTS TO THAT.
THIS AIN'T NO PERFECT WORLD. NOT IF IT AIN'T BUILT FER EVERYBODY!
YOU HEARD HIM! WHAT BIG KING GRIMM SAID!
YEAH! THIS'S OUR WORLD TOO!
THAT'S
E SPIRI--
IKK--
GLUG!
SPLASH
FOUL CREATURE! I CAN SMELL YOUR STENCH FROM HERE.
AND A FEW 'A YER LEFTS TOO!
LET'S SHOW 'EM HOW WE DO THINGS DOWN IN LOWTOWN!
UNPARALLELED, ATTACK!

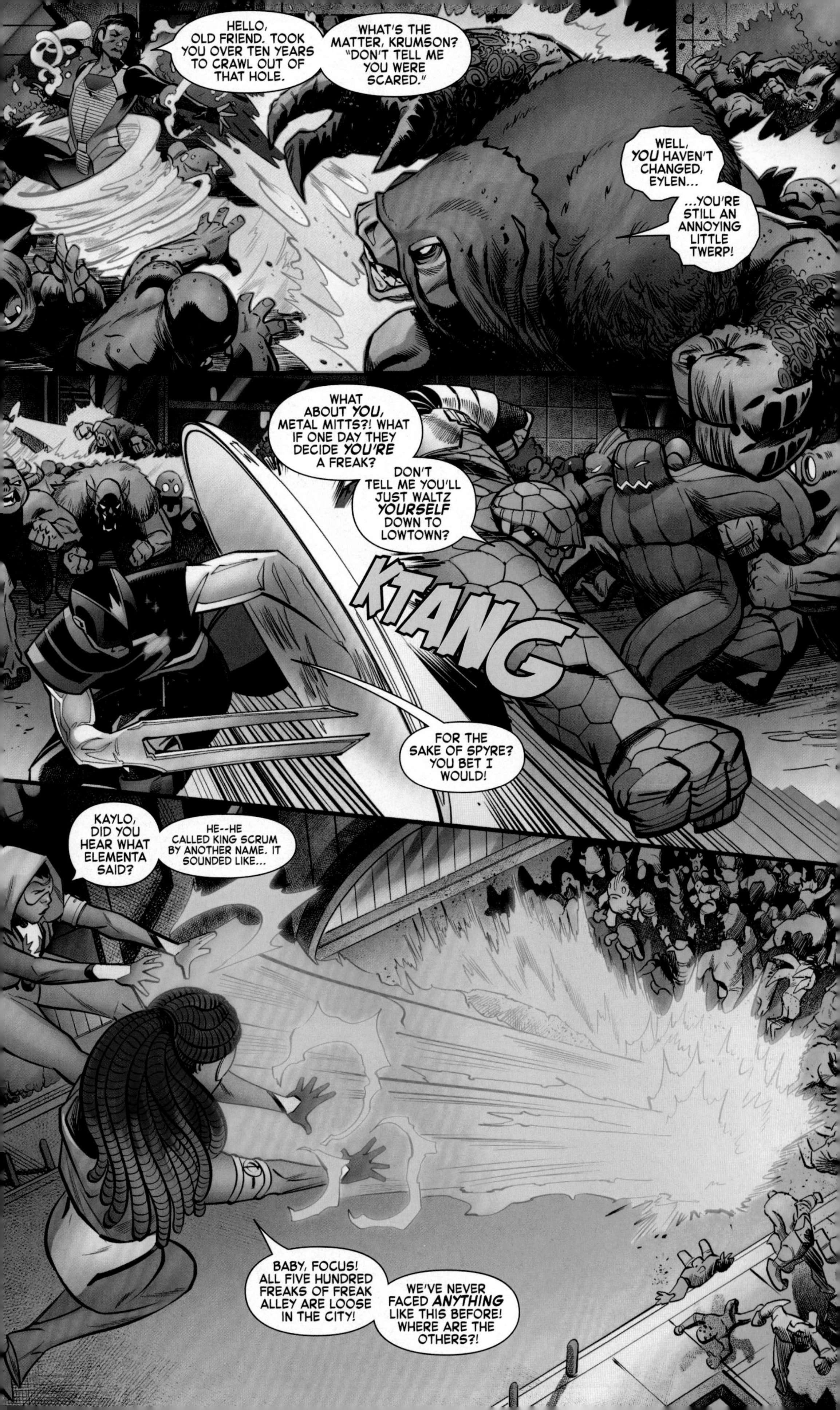
HELLO, OLD FRIEND. TOOK YOU OVER TEN YEARS TO CRAWL OUT OF THAT HOLE.
WHAT'S THE MATTER, KRUMSON? "DON'T TELL ME YOU WERE SCARED."
WELL, YOU HAVEN'T CHANGED, EYLEN...
...YOU'RE STILL AN ANNOYING LITTLE TWERP!
WHAT ABOUT YOU, METAL MITTS?! WHAT IF ONE DAY THEY DECIDE YOU'RE A FREAK?
DON'T TELL ME YOU'LL JUST WALTZ YOURSELF DOWN TO LOWTOWN?
KTANG
FOR THE SAKE OF SPYRE? YOU BET I WOULD!
KAYLO, DID YOU HEAR WHAT ELEMENTA SAID?
HE--HE CALLED KING SCRUM BY ANOTHER NAME. IT SOUNDED LIKE...
BABY, FOCUS! ALL FIVE HUNDRED FREAKS OF FREAK ALLEY ARE LOOSE IN THE CITY!
WE'VE NEVER FACED ANYTHING LIKE THIS BEFORE! WHERE ARE THE OTHERS?!

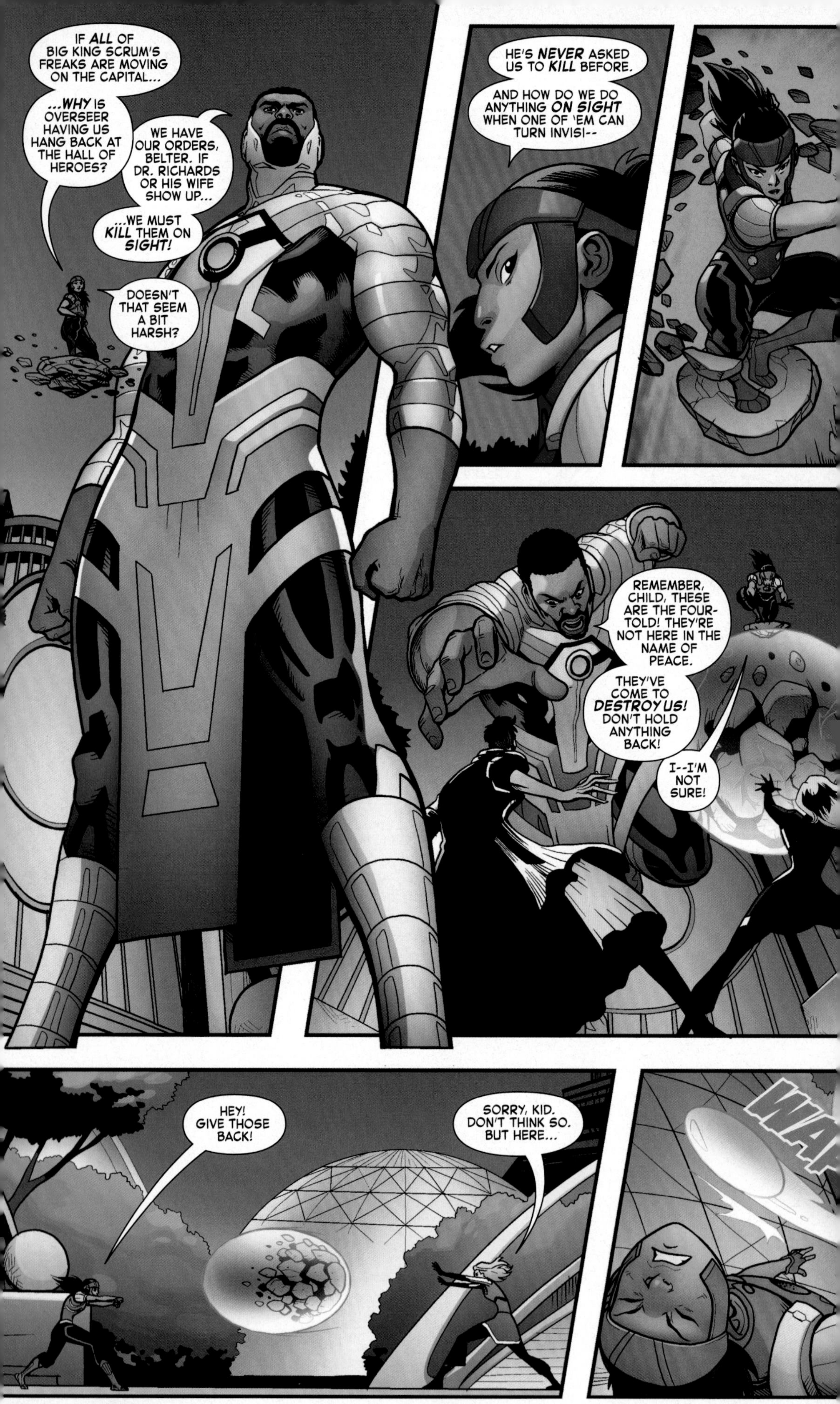

IF ALL OF BIG KING SCRUM'S FREAKS ARE MOVING ON THE CAPITAL...
...WHY IS OVERSEER HAVING US HANG BACK AT THE HALL OF HEROES?
WE HAVE OUR ORDERS, BELTER. IF DR. RICHARDS OR HIS WIFE SHOW UP...
...WE MUST KILL THEM ON SIGHT!
DOESN'T THAT SEEM A BIT HARSH?
HE'S NEVER ASKED US TO KILL BEFORE.
AND HOW DO WE DO ANYTHING ON SIGHT WHEN ONE OF 'EM CAN TURN INVISI--
REMEMBER, CHILD, THESE ARE THE FOUR-TOLD! THEY'RE NOT HERE IN THE NAME OF PEACE.
THEY'VE COME TO DESTROY US! DON'T HOLD ANYTHING BACK!
I--I'M NOT SURE!
HEY! GIVE THOSE BACK!
SORRY, KID. DON'T THINK SO. BUT HERE...

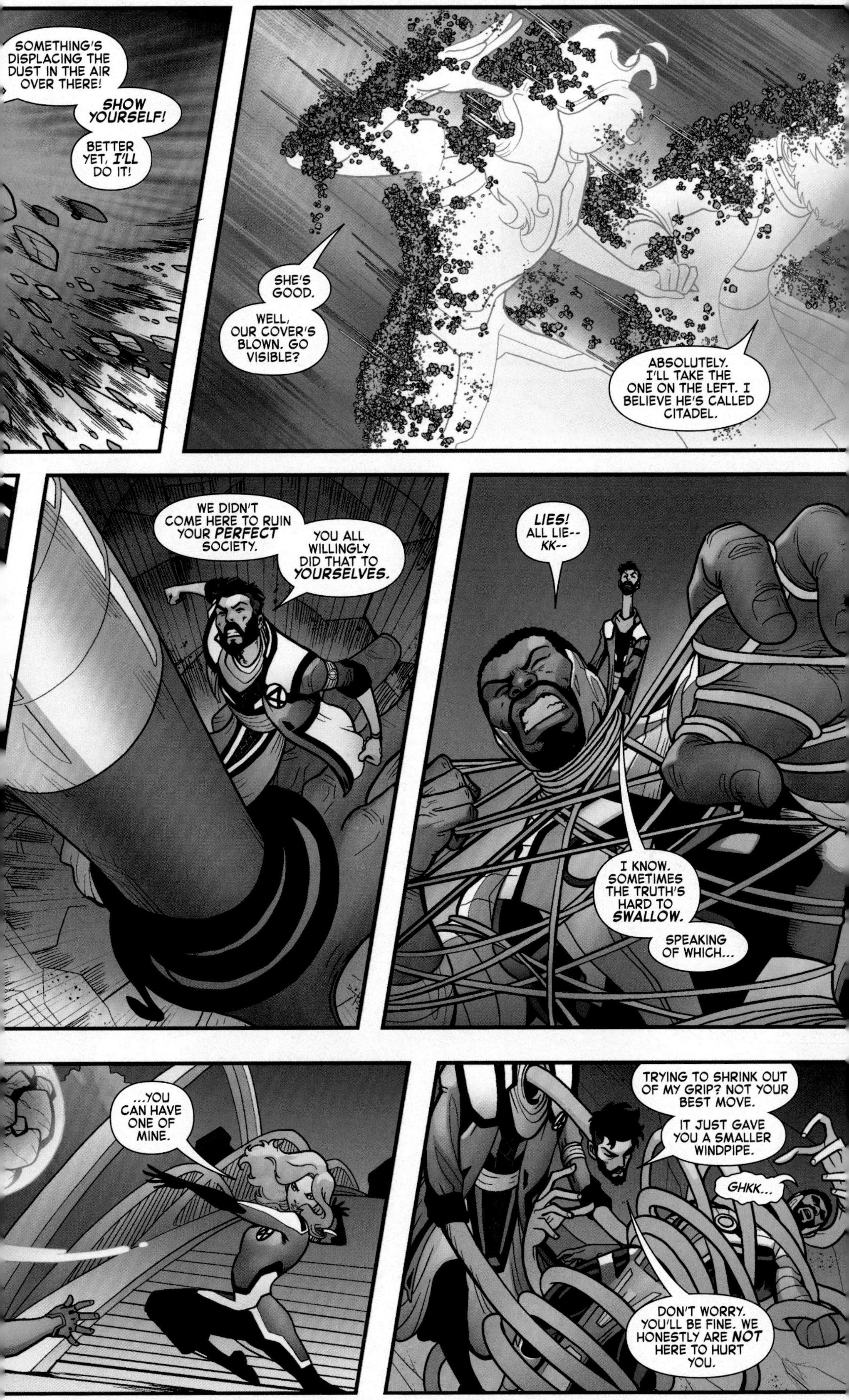

SOMETHING'S DISPLACING THE DUST IN THE AIR OVER THERE!
SHOW YOURSELF!
BETTER YET, I'LL DO IT!
SHE'S GOOD.
WELL, OUR COVER'S BLOWN. GO VISIBLE?
ABSOLUTELY. I'LL TAKE THE ONE ON THE LEFT. I BELIEVE HE'S CALLED CITADEL.
WE DIDN'T COME HERE TO RUIN YOUR PERFECT SOCIETY.
YOU ALL WILLINGLY DID THAT TO YOURSELVES.
LIES! ALL LIE-- KK--
I KNOW. SOMETIMES THE TRUTH'S HARD TO SWALLOW.
SPEAKING OF WHICH...
...YOU CAN HAVE ONE OF MINE.
TRYING TO SHRINK OUT OF MY GRIP? NOT YOUR BEST MOVE.
IT JUST GAVE YOU A SMALLER WINDPIPE.
GHKK...
DON'T WORRY. YOU'LL BE FINE. WE HONESTLY ARE NOT HERE TO HURT YOU.

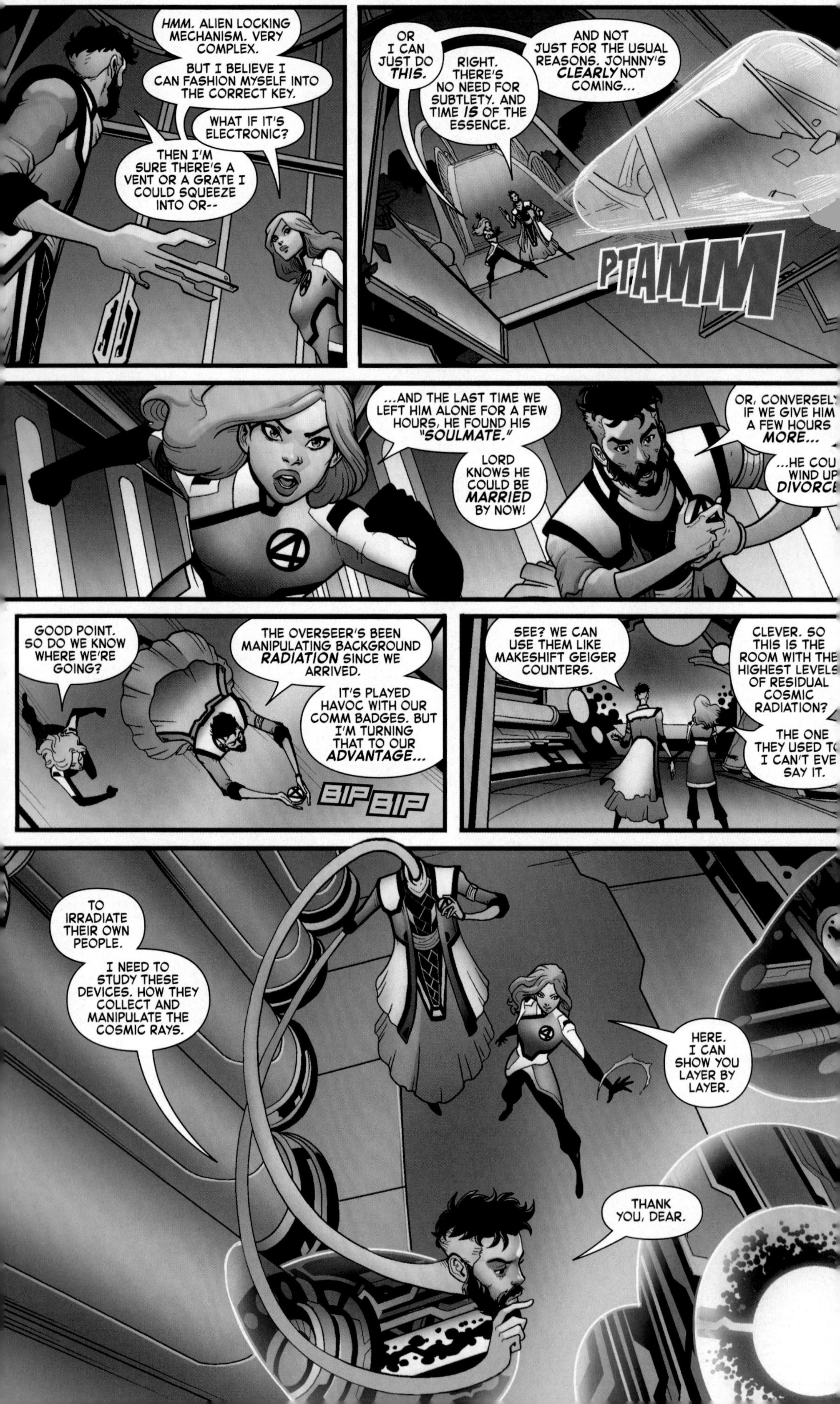
HMM. ALIEN LOCKING MECHANISM. VERY COMPLEX.
BUT I BELIEVE I CAN FASHION MYSELF INTO THE CORRECT KEY.
WHAT IF IT'S ELECTRONIC?
THEN I'M SURE THERE'S A VENT OR A GRATE I COULD SQUEEZE INTO OR--
OR I CAN JUST DO THIS.
RIGHT. THERE'S NO NEED FOR SUBTLETY. AND TIME IS OF THE ESSENCE.
AND NOT JUST FOR THE USUAL REASONS. JOHNNY'S CLEARLY NOT COMING...
PTAMM
...AND THE LAST TIME WE LEFT HIM ALONE FOR A FEW HOURS, HE FOUND HIS "SOULMATE."
LORD KNOWS HE COULD BE MARRIED BY NOW!
OR, CONVERSEL IF WE GIVE HIM A FEW HOURS MORE...
...HE COU WIND UP DIVORCE
GOOD POINT. SO DO WE KNOW WHERE WE'RE GOING?
THE OVERSEER'S BEEN MANIPULATING BACKGROUND RADIATION SINCE WE ARRIVED.
IT'S PLAYED HAVOC WITH OUR COMM BADGES. BUT I'M TURNING THAT TO OUR ADVANTAGE...
BIP BIP
SEE? WE CAN USE THEM LIKE MAKESHIFT GEIGER COUNTERS.
CLEVER. SO THIS IS THE ROOM WITH THE HIGHEST LEVELS OF RESIDUAL COSMIC RADIATION?
THE ONE THEY USED TO I CAN'T EVE SAY IT.
TO IRRADIATE THEIR OWN PEOPLE.
I NEED TO STUDY THESE DEVICES. HOW THEY COLLECT AND MANIPULATE THE COSMIC RAYS.
HERE. I CAN SHOW YOU LAYER BY LAYER.
THANK YOU, DEAR.

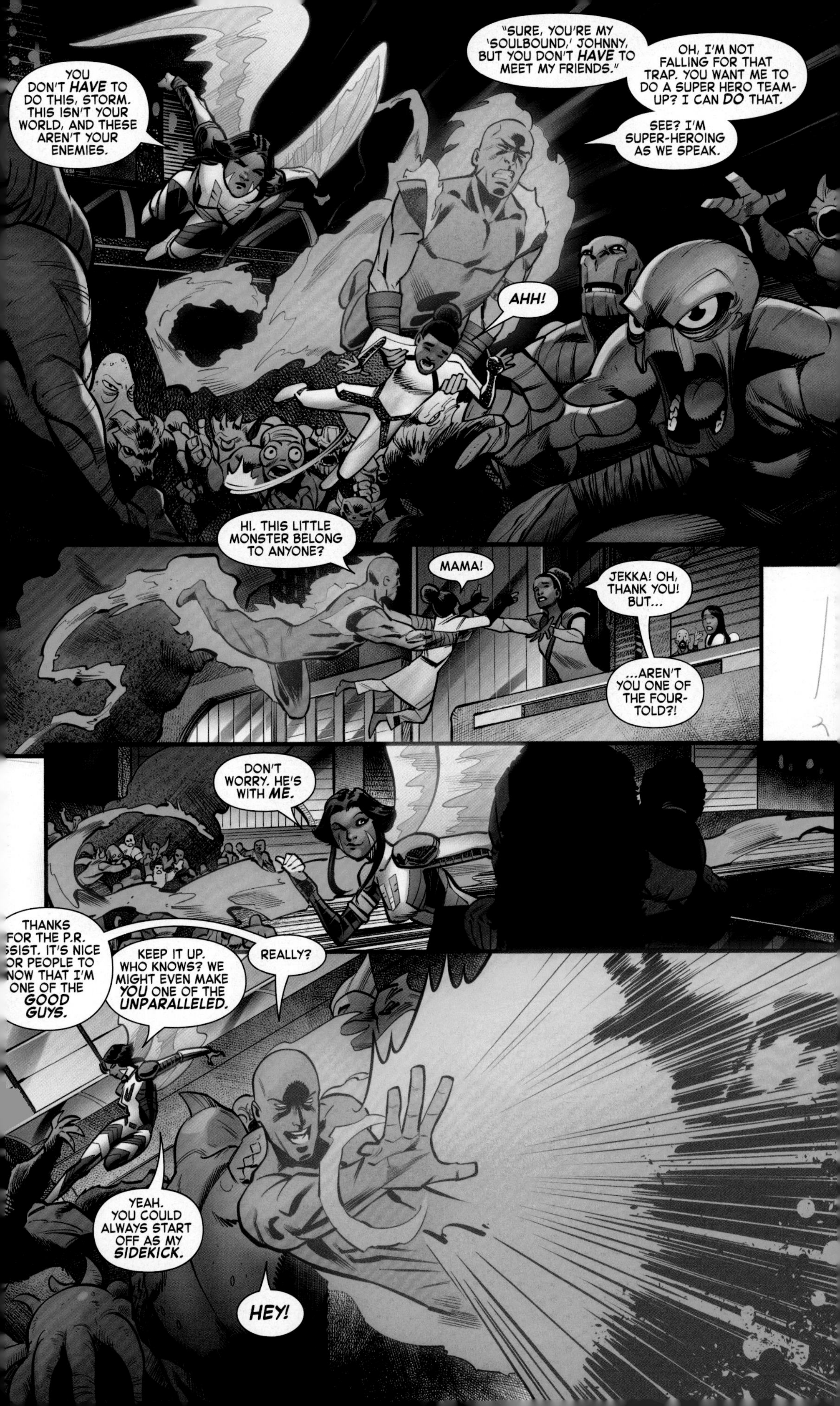

YOU DON'T *HAVE* TO DO THIS, STORM. THIS ISN'T YOUR WORLD, AND THESE AREN'T YOUR ENEMIES.
"SURE, YOU'RE MY 'SOULBOUND,' JOHNNY, BUT YOU DON'T *HAVE* TO MEET MY FRIENDS."
OH, I'M NOT FALLING FOR THAT TRAP. YOU WANT ME TO DO A SUPER HERO TEAM-UP? I CAN *DO* THAT.
SEE? I'M SUPER-HEROING AS WE SPEAK.
AHH!
HI. THIS LITTLE MONSTER BELONG TO ANYONE?
MAMA!
JEKKA! OH, THANK YOU! BUT...
...AREN'T YOU ONE OF THE FOUR-TOLD?!
DON'T WORRY. HE'S WITH *ME.*
THANKS FOR THE P.R. SSIST. IT'S NICE OR PEOPLE TO NOW THAT I'M ONE OF THE *GOOD GUYS.*
KEEP IT UP. WHO KNOWS? WE MIGHT EVEN MAKE *YOU* ONE OF THE *UNPARALLELED.*
REALLY?
YEAH. YOU COULD ALWAYS START OFF AS MY *SIDEKICK.*
HEY!

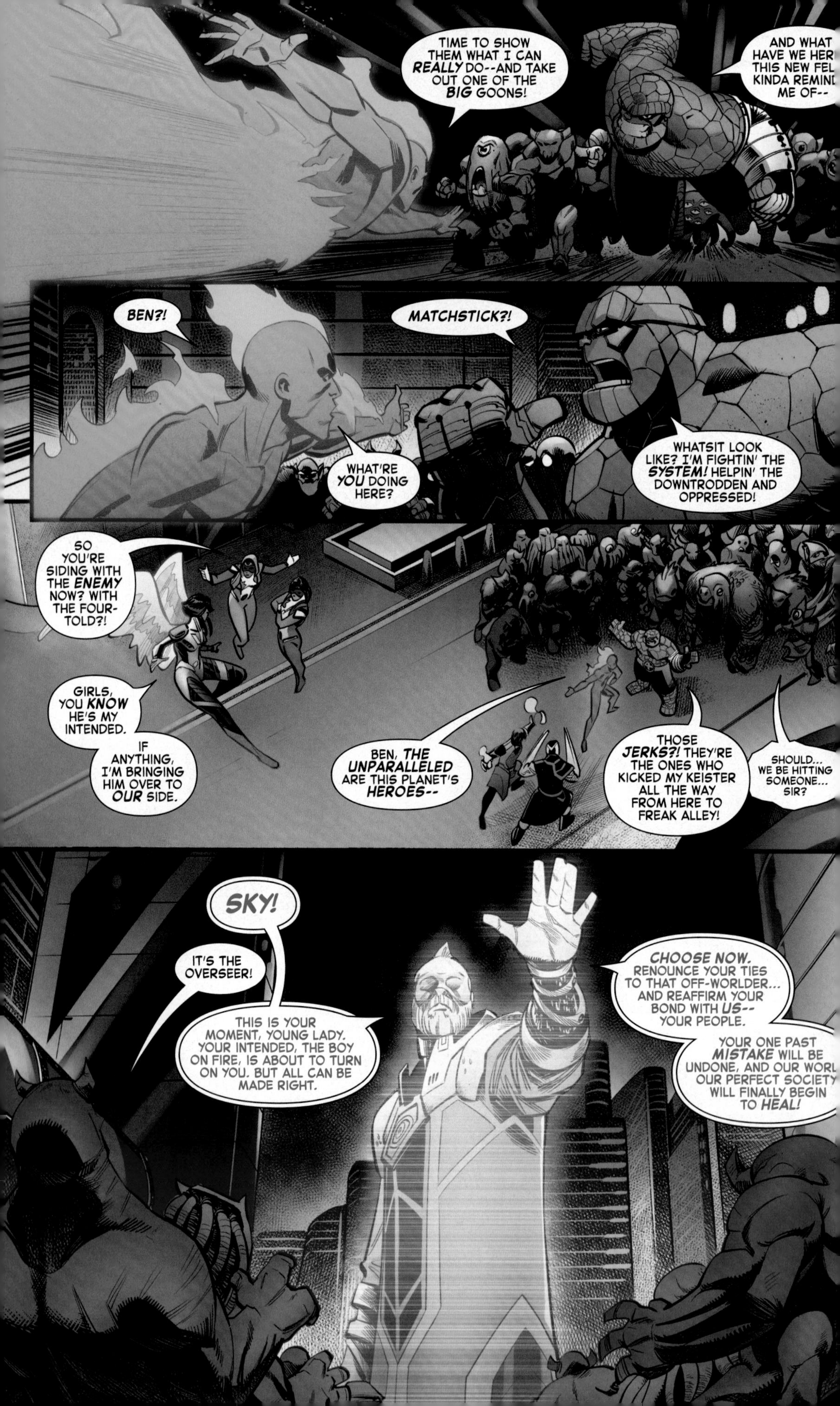

TIME TO SHOW THEM WHAT I CAN REALLY DO--AND TAKE OUT ONE OF THE BIG GOONS!
AND WHAT HAVE WE HER THIS NEW FEL KINDA REMIND ME OF--
BEN?!
MATCHSTICK?!
WHAT'RE YOU DOING HERE?
WHATSIT LOOK LIKE? I'M FIGHTIN' THE SYSTEM! HELPIN' THE DOWNTRODDEN AND OPPRESSED!
SO YOU'RE SIDING WITH THE ENEMY NOW? WITH THE FOUR-TOLD?!
GIRLS, YOU KNOW HE'S MY INTENDED.
IF ANYTHING, I'M BRINGING HIM OVER TO OUR SIDE.
BEN, THE UNPARALLELED ARE THIS PLANET'S HEROES--
THOSE JERKS?! THEY'RE THE ONES WHO KICKED MY KEISTER ALL THE WAY FROM HERE TO FREAK ALLEY!
SHOULD... WE BE HITTING SOMEONE... SIR?
SKY!
IT'S THE OVERSEER!
THIS IS YOUR MOMENT, YOUNG LADY. YOUR INTENDED, THE BOY ON FIRE, IS ABOUT TO TURN ON YOU. BUT ALL CAN BE MADE RIGHT.
CHOOSE NOW. RENOUNCE YOUR TIES TO THAT OFF-WORLDER... AND REAFFIRM YOUR BOND WITH US-- YOUR PEOPLE.
YOUR ONE PAST MISTAKE WILL BE UNDONE, AND OUR WORL OUR PERFECT SOCIETY WILL FINALLY BEGIN TO HEAL!

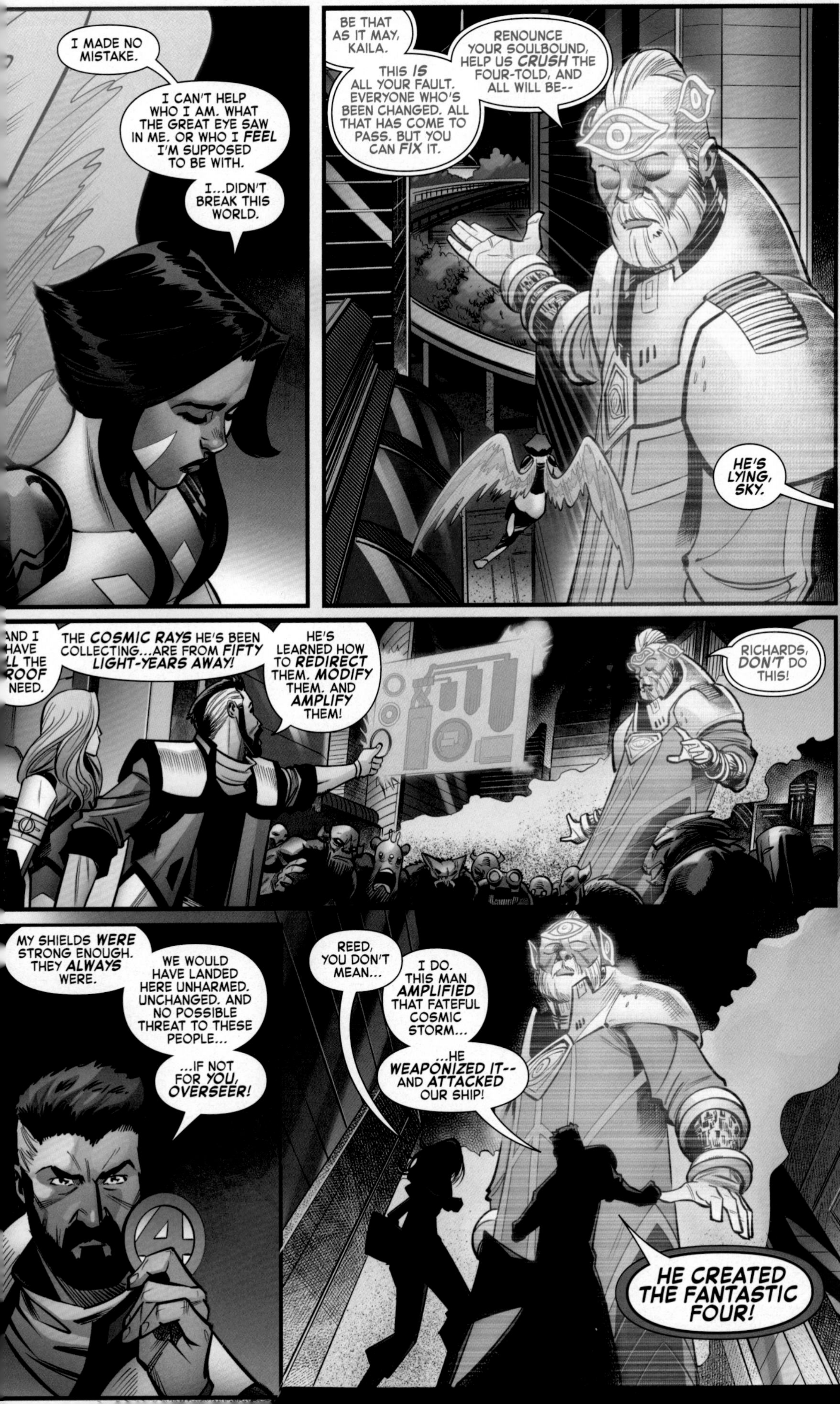
I MADE NO MISTAKE.
I CAN'T HELP WHO I AM. WHAT THE GREAT EYE SAW IN ME. OR WHO I FEEL I'M SUPPOSED TO BE WITH.
I...DIDN'T BREAK THIS WORLD.
BE THAT AS IT MAY, KAILA.
THIS IS ALL YOUR FAULT. EVERYONE WHO'S BEEN CHANGED. ALL THAT HAS COME TO PASS. BUT YOU CAN FIX IT.
RENOUNCE YOUR SOULBOUND, HELP US CRUSH THE FOUR-TOLD, AND ALL WILL BE--
HE'S LYING, SKY.
AND I HAVE ALL THE PROOF NEED.
THE COSMIC RAYS HE'S BEEN COLLECTING...ARE FROM FIFTY LIGHT-YEARS AWAY!
HE'S LEARNED HOW TO REDIRECT THEM. MODIFY THEM. AND AMPLIFY THEM!
RICHARDS, DON'T DO THIS!
MY SHIELDS WERE STRONG ENOUGH. THEY ALWAYS WERE.
WE WOULD HAVE LANDED HERE UNHARMED. UNCHANGED. AND NO POSSIBLE THREAT TO THESE PEOPLE...
...IF NOT FOR YOU, OVERSEER!
REED, YOU DON'T MEAN...
I DO. THIS MAN AMPLIFIED THAT FATEFUL COSMIC STORM...
...HE WEAPONIZED IT-- AND ATTACKED OUR SHIP!
HE CREATED THE FANTASTIC FOUR!

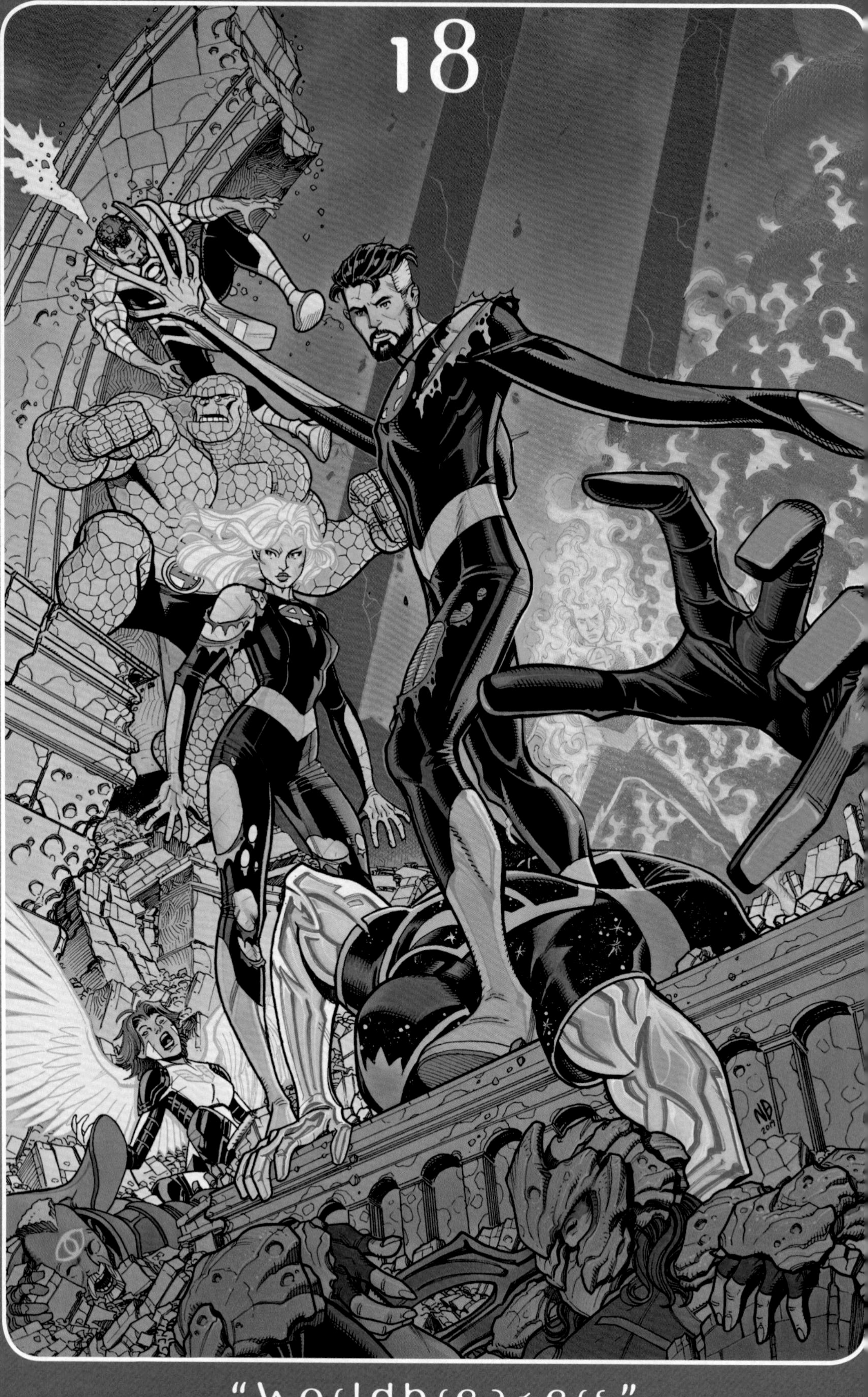
18

"Worldbreakers"

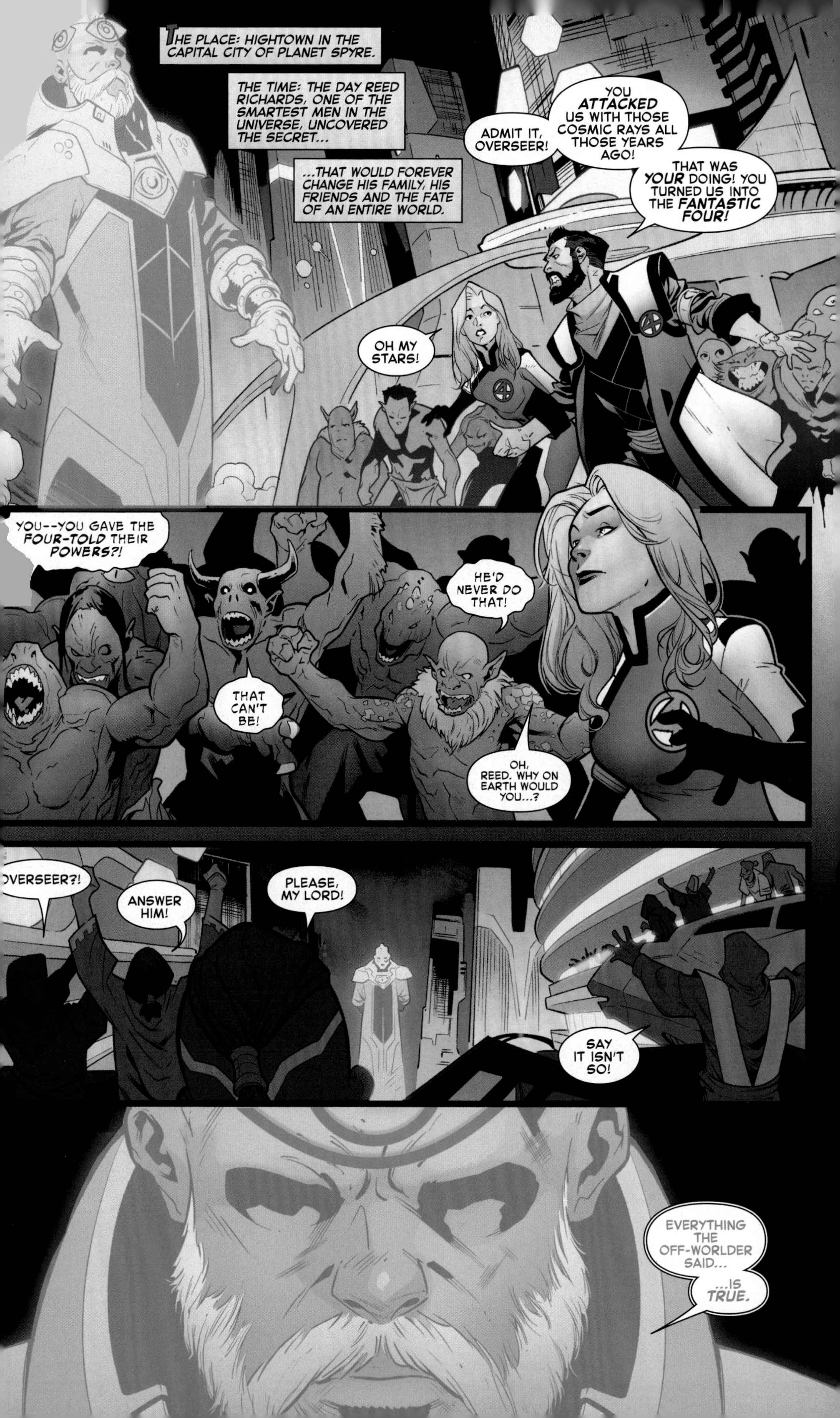
THE PLACE: HIGHTOWN IN THE CAPITAL CITY OF PLANET SPYRE.
THE TIME: THE DAY REED RICHARDS, ONE OF THE SMARTEST MEN IN THE UNIVERSE, UNCOVERED THE SECRET...
...THAT WOULD FOREVER CHANGE HIS FAMILY, HIS FRIENDS AND THE FATE OF AN ENTIRE WORLD.
ADMIT IT, OVERSEER!
YOU ATTACKED US WITH THOSE COSMIC RAYS ALL THOSE YEARS AGO!
THAT WAS YOUR DOING! YOU TURNED US INTO THE FANTASTIC FOUR!
OH MY STARS!
YOU--YOU GAVE THE FOUR-TOLD THEIR POWERS?!
HE'D NEVER DO THAT!
THAT CAN'T BE!
OH, REED. WHY ON EARTH WOULD YOU...?
OVERSEER?!
ANSWER HIM!
PLEASE, MY LORD!
SAY IT ISN'T SO!
EVERYTHING THE OFF-WORLDER SAID...
...IS TRUE.

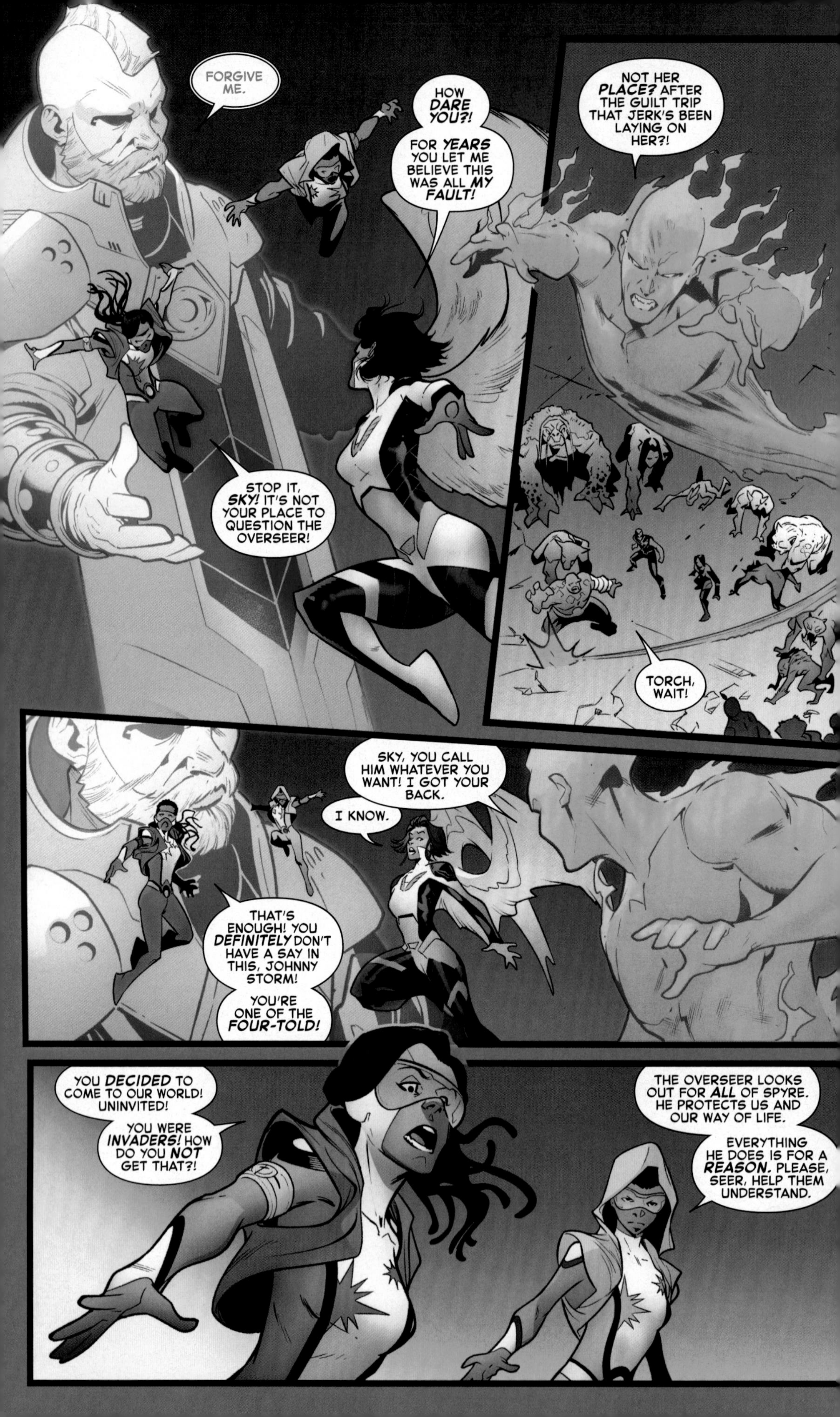
FORGIVE ME.
HOW DARE YOU?!
FOR YEARS YOU LET ME BELIEVE THIS WAS ALL MY FAULT!
NOT HER PLACE? AFTER THE GUILT TRIP THAT JERK'S BEEN LAYING ON HER?!
STOP IT, SKY! IT'S NOT YOUR PLACE TO QUESTION THE OVERSEER!
TORCH, WAIT!
SKY, YOU CALL HIM WHATEVER YOU WANT! I GOT YOUR BACK.
I KNOW.
THAT'S ENOUGH! YOU DEFINITELY DON'T HAVE A SAY IN THIS, JOHNNY STORM!
YOU'RE ONE OF THE FOUR-TOLD!
YOU DECIDED TO COME TO OUR WORLD! UNINVITED!
YOU WERE INVADERS! HOW DO YOU NOT GET THAT?!
THE OVERSEER LOOKS OUT FOR ALL OF SPYRE. HE PROTECTS US AND OUR WAY OF LIFE.
EVERYTHING HE DOES IS FOR A REASON. PLEASE, SEER, HELP THEM UNDERSTAND.

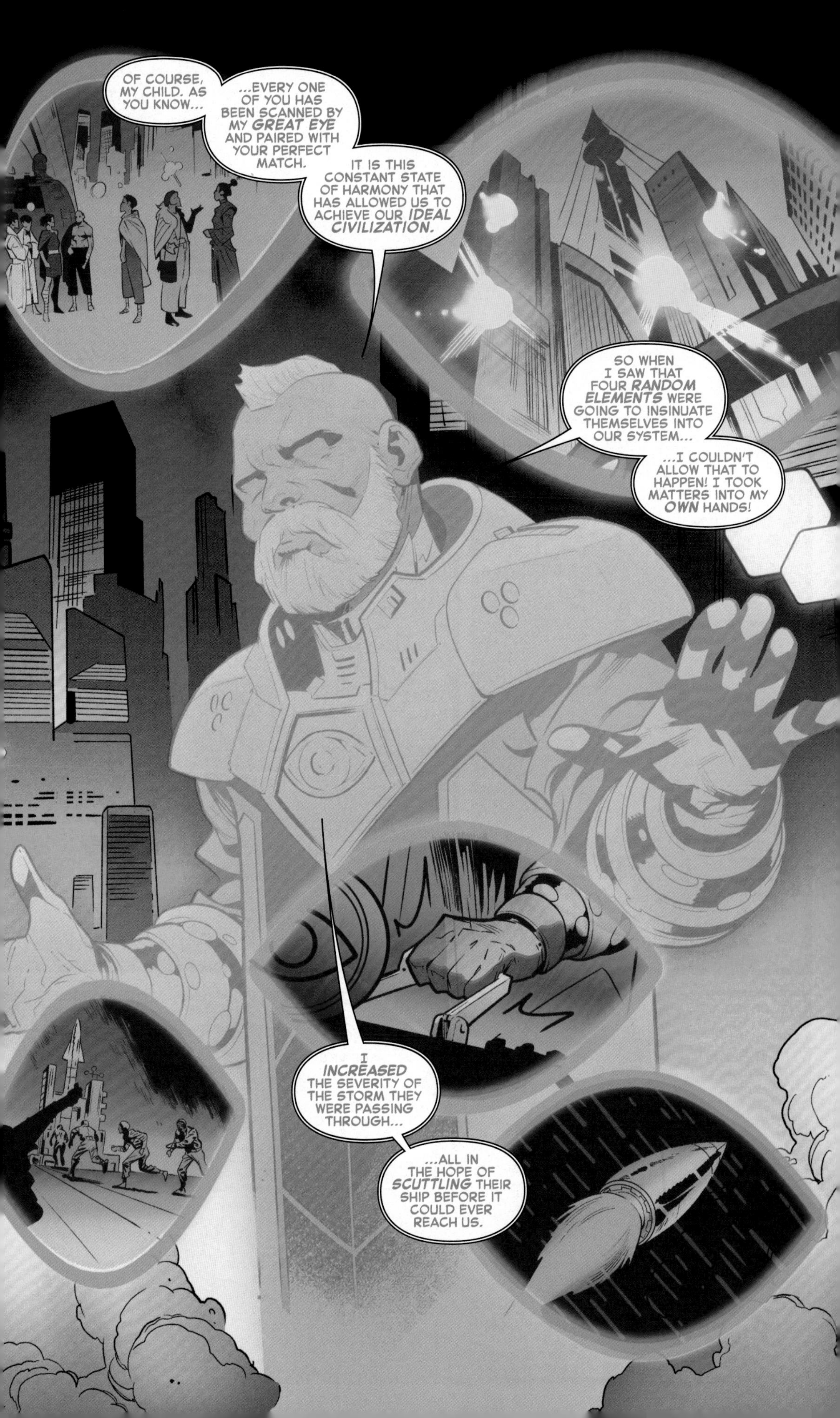
OF COURSE, MY CHILD. AS YOU KNOW...
...EVERY ONE OF YOU HAS BEEN SCANNED BY MY GREAT EYE AND PAIRED WITH YOUR PERFECT MATCH.
IT IS THIS CONSTANT STATE OF HARMONY THAT HAS ALLOWED US TO ACHIEVE OUR IDEAL CIVILIZATION.
SO WHEN I SAW THAT FOUR RANDOM ELEMENTS WERE GOING TO INSINUATE THEMSELVES INTO OUR SYSTEM...
...I COULDN'T ALLOW THAT TO HAPPEN! I TOOK MATTERS INTO MY OWN HANDS!
I INCREASED THE SEVERITY OF THE STORM THEY WERE PASSING THROUGH...
...ALL IN THE HOPE OF SCUTTLING THEIR SHIP BEFORE IT COULD EVER REACH US.

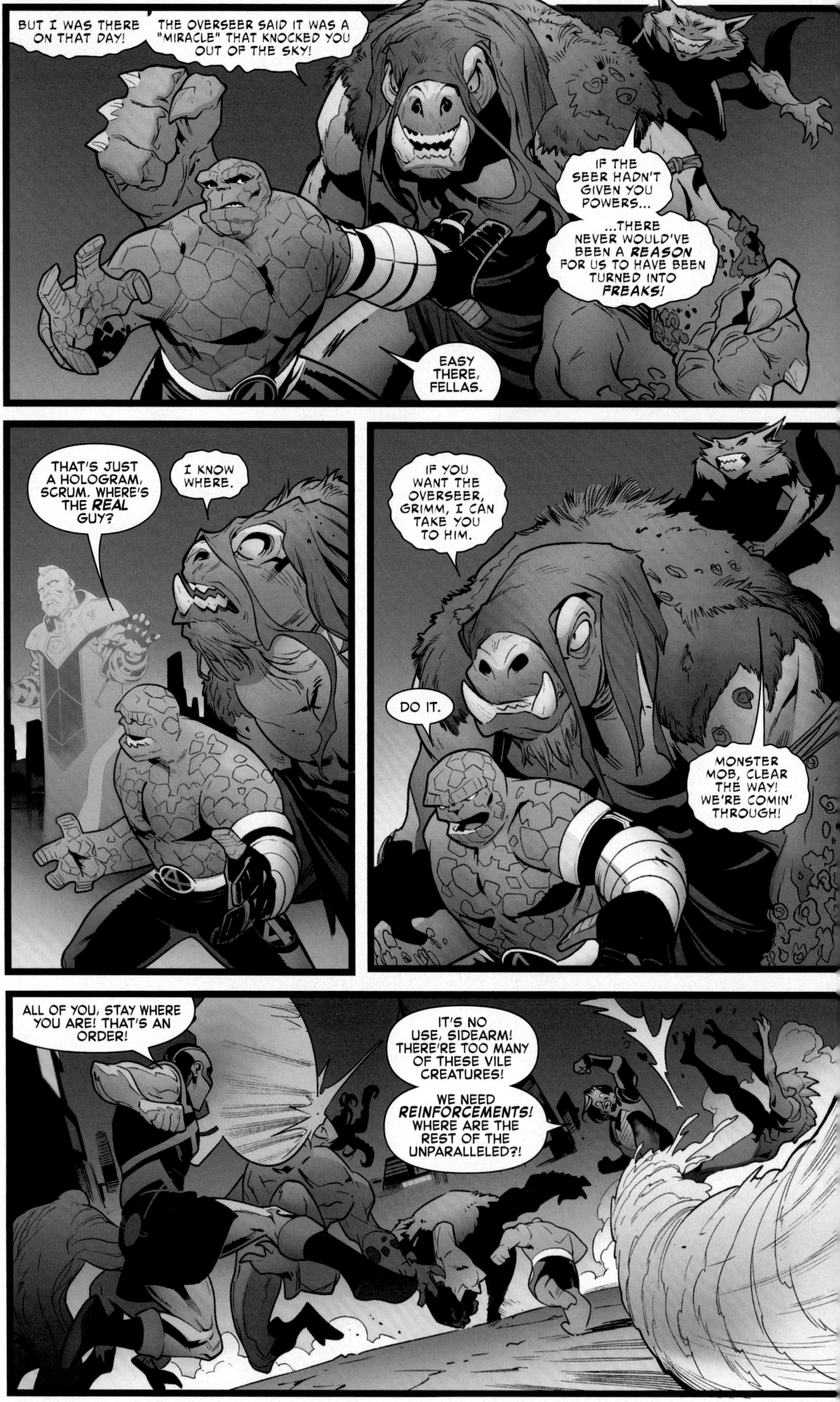

BUT I WAS THERE ON THAT DAY!
THE OVERSEER SAID IT WAS A "MIRACLE" THAT KNOCKED YOU OUT OF THE SKY!
IF THE SEER HADN'T GIVEN YOU POWERS...
...THERE NEVER WOULD'VE BEEN A REASON FOR US TO HAVE BEEN TURNED INTO FREAKS!
EASY THERE, FELLAS.
THAT'S JUST A HOLOGRAM, SCRUM. WHERE'S THE REAL GUY?
I KNOW WHERE.
IF YOU WANT THE OVERSEER, GRIMM, I CAN TAKE YOU TO HIM.
DO IT.
MONSTER MOB, CLEAR THE WAY! WE'RE COMIN' THROUGH!
ALL OF YOU, STAY WHERE YOU ARE! THAT'S AN ORDER!
IT'S NO USE, SIDEARM! THERE'RE TOO MANY OF THESE VILE CREATURES!
WE NEED REINFORCEMENTS! WHERE ARE THE REST OF THE UNPARALLELED?!

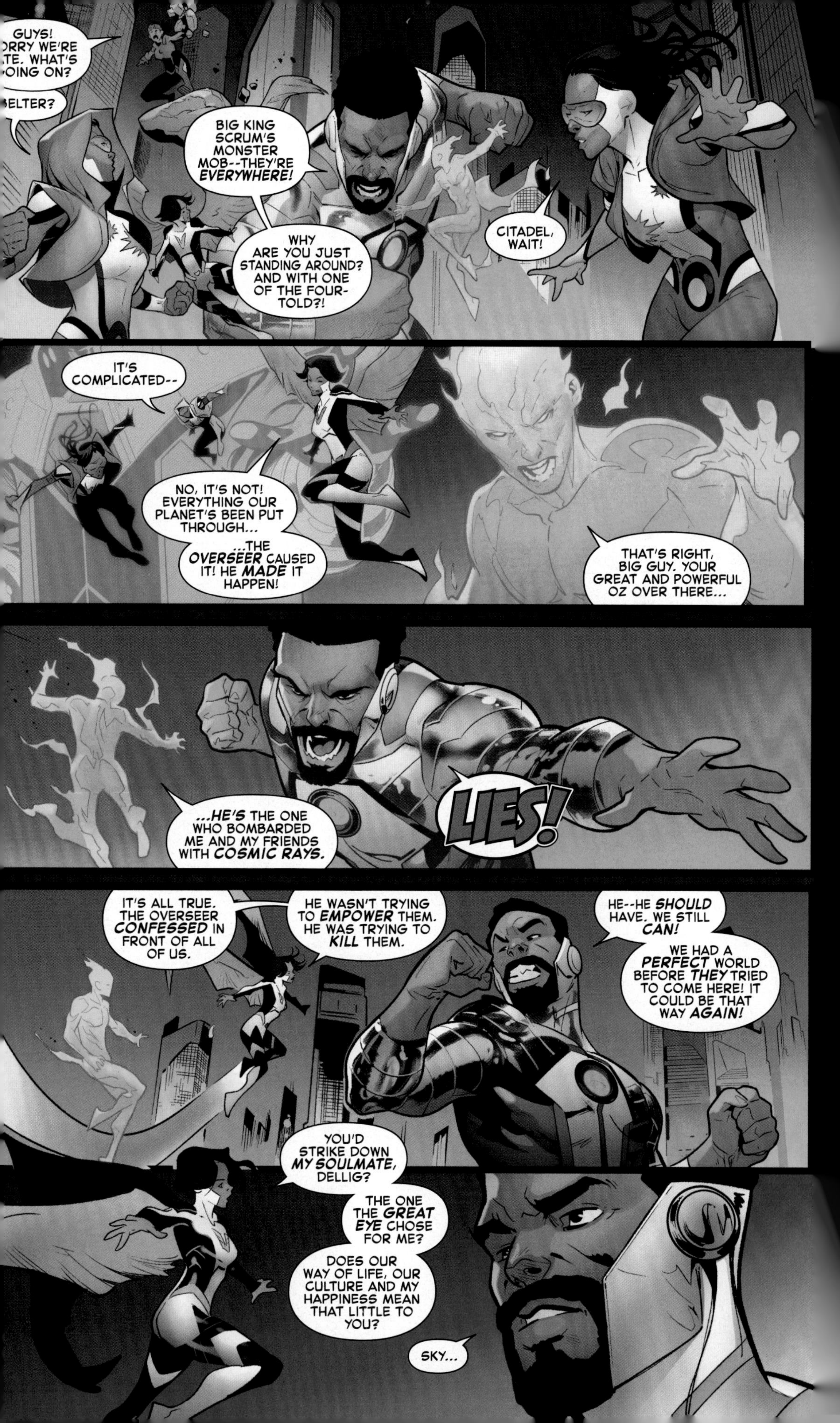
GUYS! ORRY WE'RE TE. WHAT'S OING ON?
ELTER?
BIG KING SCRUM'S MONSTER MOB--THEY'RE EVERYWHERE!
WHY ARE YOU JUST STANDING AROUND? AND WITH ONE OF THE FOUR-TOLD?!
CITADEL, WAIT!
IT'S COMPLICATED--
NO, IT'S NOT! EVERYTHING OUR PLANET'S BEEN PUT THROUGH...
...THE OVERSEER CAUSED IT! HE MADE IT HAPPEN!
THAT'S RIGHT, BIG GUY. YOUR GREAT AND POWERFUL OZ OVER THERE...
...HE'S THE ONE WHO BOMBARDED ME AND MY FRIENDS WITH COSMIC RAYS.
LIES!
IT'S ALL TRUE. THE OVERSEER CONFESSED IN FRONT OF ALL OF US.
HE WASN'T TRYING TO EMPOWER THEM. HE WAS TRYING TO KILL THEM.
HE--HE SHOULD HAVE. WE STILL CAN!
WE HAD A PERFECT WORLD BEFORE THEY TRIED TO COME HERE! IT COULD BE THAT WAY AGAIN!
YOU'D STRIKE DOWN MY SOULMATE, DELLIG?
THE ONE THE GREAT EYE CHOSE FOR ME?
DOES OUR WAY OF LIFE, OUR CULTURE AND MY HAPPINESS MEAN THAT LITTLE TO YOU?
SKY...

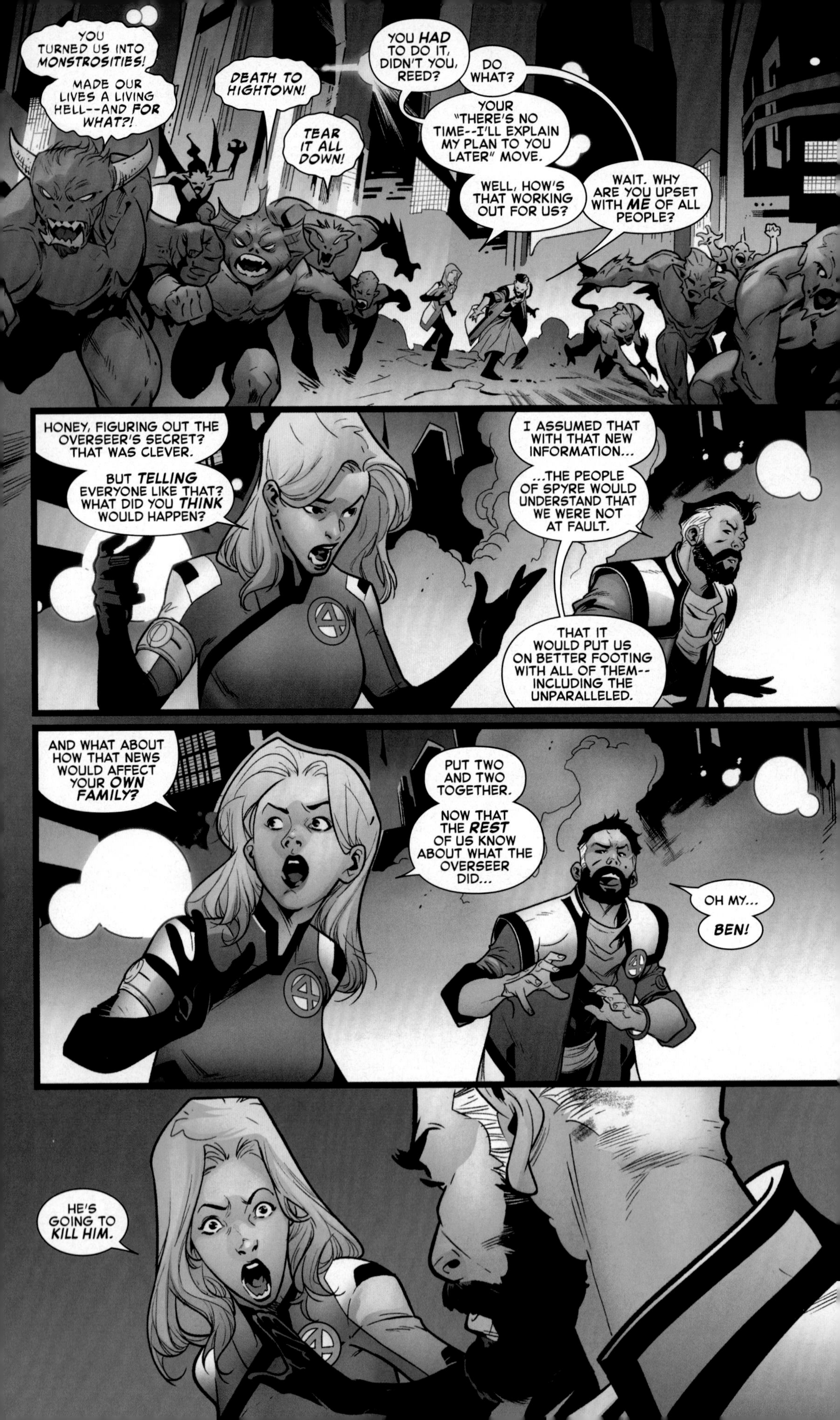

YOU TURNED US INTO MONSTROSITIES!
MADE OUR LIVES A LIVING HELL--AND FOR WHAT?!
DEATH TO HIGHTOWN!
TEAR IT ALL DOWN!
YOU HAD TO DO IT, DIDN'T YOU, REED?
DO WHAT?
YOUR "THERE'S NO TIME--I'LL EXPLAIN MY PLAN TO YOU LATER" MOVE.
WELL, HOW'S THAT WORKING OUT FOR US?
WAIT. WHY ARE YOU UPSET WITH ME OF ALL PEOPLE?
HONEY, FIGURING OUT THE OVERSEER'S SECRET? THAT WAS CLEVER.
BUT TELLING EVERYONE LIKE THAT? WHAT DID YOU THINK WOULD HAPPEN?
I ASSUMED THAT WITH THAT NEW INFORMATION...
...THE PEOPLE OF SPYRE WOULD UNDERSTAND THAT WE WERE NOT AT FAULT.
THAT IT WOULD PUT US ON BETTER FOOTING WITH ALL OF THEM--INCLUDING THE UNPARALLELED.
AND WHAT ABOUT HOW THAT NEWS WOULD AFFECT YOUR OWN FAMILY?
PUT TWO AND TWO TOGETHER.
NOW THAT THE REST OF US KNOW ABOUT WHAT THE OVERSEER DID...
OH MY...
BEN!
HE'S GOING TO KILL HIM.

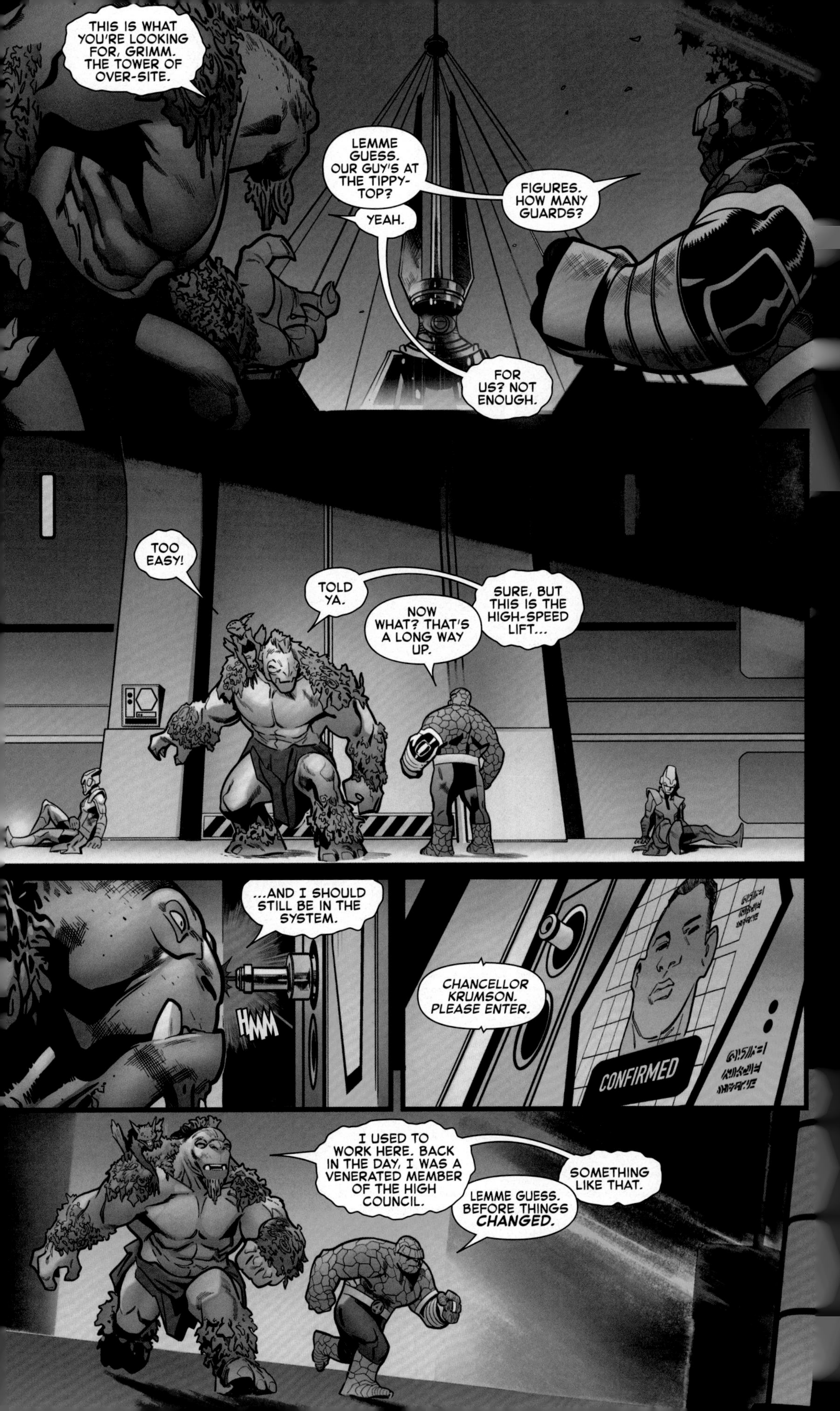
THIS IS WHAT YOU'RE LOOKING FOR, GRIMM. THE TOWER OF OVER-SITE.
LEMME GUESS. OUR GUY'S AT THE TIPPY-TOP?
YEAH.
FIGURES. HOW MANY GUARDS?
FOR US? NOT ENOUGH.
TOO EASY!
TOLD YA.
SURE, BUT THIS IS THE HIGH-SPEED LIFT...
NOW WHAT? THAT'S A LONG WAY UP.
...AND I SHOULD STILL BE IN THE SYSTEM.
HMM
CHANCELLOR KRUMSON. PLEASE ENTER.
CONFIRMED
I USED TO WORK HERE. BACK IN THE DAY, I WAS A VENERATED MEMBER OF THE HIGH COUNCIL.
LEMME GUESS. BEFORE THINGS CHANGED.
SOMETHING LIKE THAT.

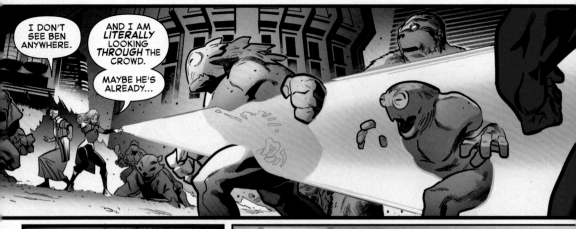

I DON'T SEE BEN ANYWHERE.

AND I AM *LITERALLY* LOOKING *THROUGH* THE CROWD.

MAYBE HE'S ALREADY...

"...ON HIS WAY *UP?*"

SUZIE?

OH NO.

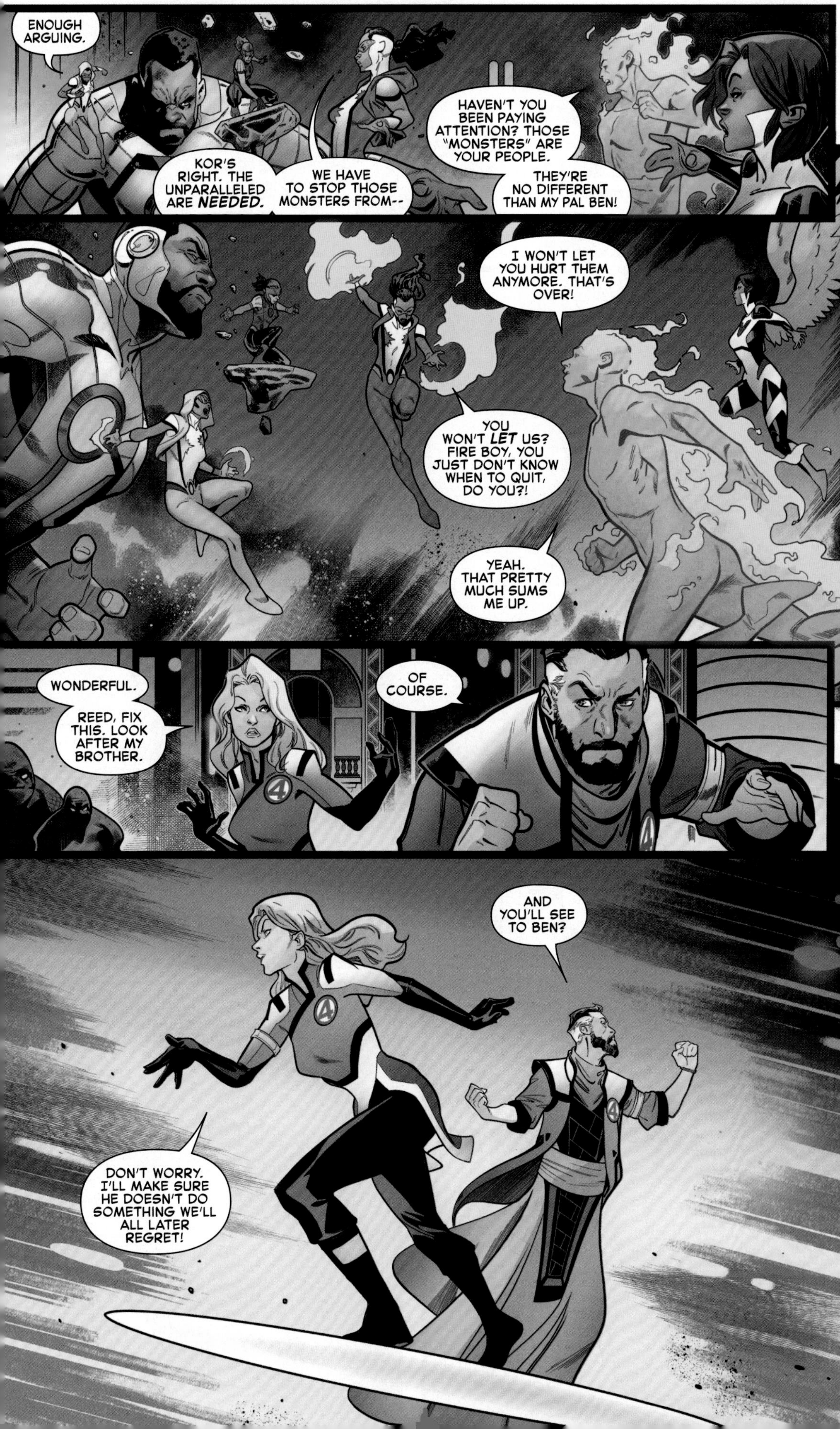
ENOUGH ARGUING.
KOR'S RIGHT. THE UNPARALLELED ARE **NEEDED.**
WE HAVE TO STOP THOSE MONSTERS FROM--
HAVEN'T YOU BEEN PAYING ATTENTION? THOSE "MONSTERS" ARE YOUR PEOPLE.
THEY'RE NO DIFFERENT THAN MY PAL BEN!
I WON'T LET YOU HURT THEM ANYMORE. THAT'S OVER!
YOU WON'T **LET** US? FIRE BOY, YOU JUST DON'T KNOW WHEN TO QUIT, DO YOU?!
YEAH. THAT PRETTY MUCH SUMS ME UP.
WONDERFUL.
REED, FIX THIS. LOOK AFTER MY BROTHER.
OF COURSE.
AND YOU'LL SEE TO BEN?
DON'T WORRY. I'LL MAKE SURE HE DOESN'T DO SOMETHING WE'LL ALL LATER REGRET!

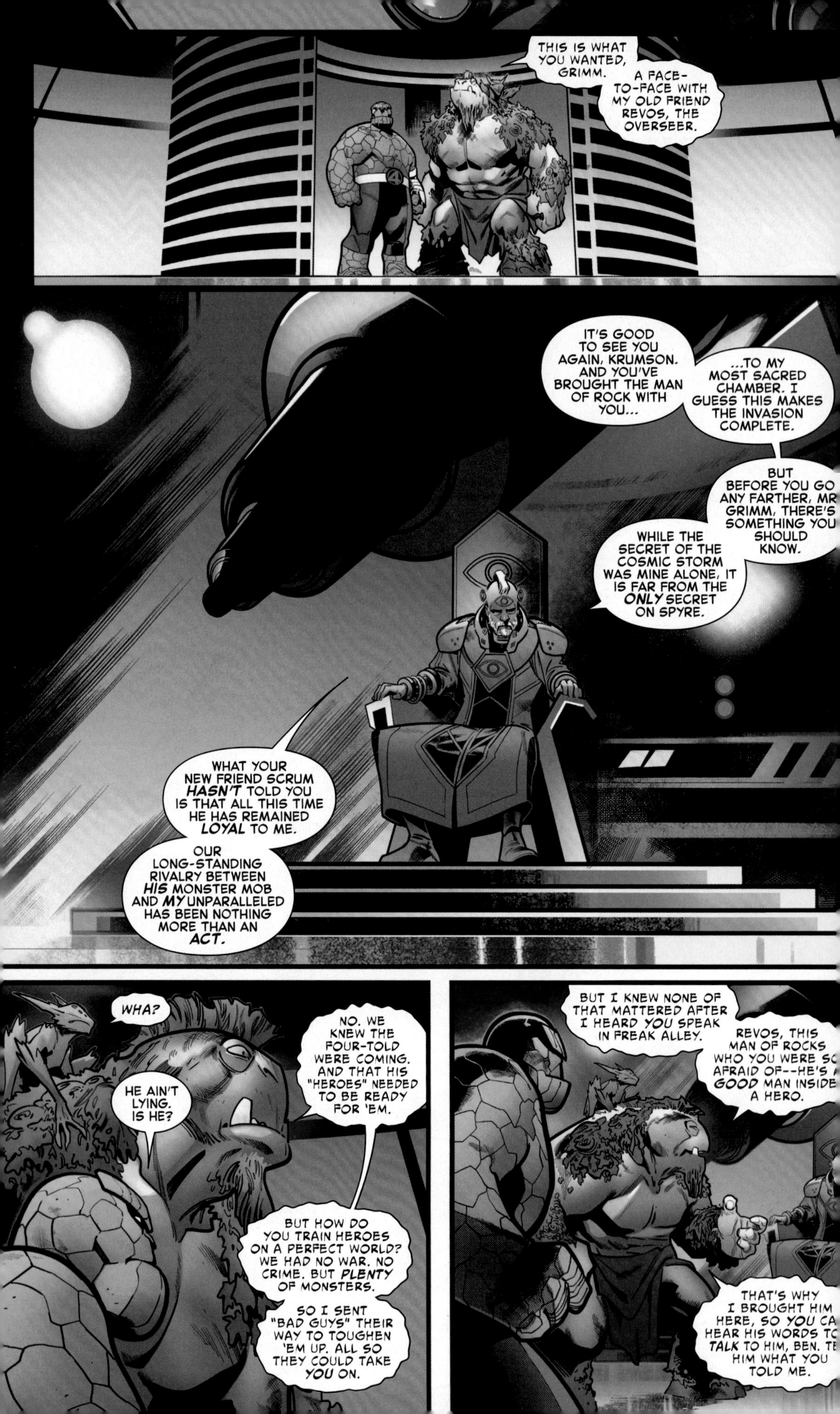
THIS IS WHAT YOU WANTED, GRIMM.
A FACE-TO-FACE WITH MY OLD FRIEND REVOS, THE OVERSEER.
IT'S GOOD TO SEE YOU AGAIN, KRUMSON. AND YOU'VE BROUGHT THE MAN OF ROCK WITH YOU...
...TO MY MOST SACRED CHAMBER. I GUESS THIS MAKES THE INVASION COMPLETE.
BUT BEFORE YOU GO ANY FARTHER, MR GRIMM, THERE'S SOMETHING YOU SHOULD KNOW.
WHILE THE SECRET OF THE COSMIC STORM WAS MINE ALONE, IT IS FAR FROM THE *ONLY* SECRET ON SPYRE.
WHAT YOUR NEW FRIEND SCRUM *HASN'T* TOLD YOU IS THAT ALL THIS TIME HE HAS REMAINED *LOYAL* TO ME.
OUR LONG-STANDING RIVALRY BETWEEN *HIS* MONSTER MOB AND *MY* UNPARALLELED HAS BEEN NOTHING MORE THAN AN *ACT*.
WHA?
HE AIN'T LYING. IS HE?
NO. WE KNEW THE FOUR-TOLD WERE COMING. AND THAT HIS "HEROES" NEEDED TO BE READY FOR 'EM.
BUT HOW DO YOU TRAIN HEROES ON A PERFECT WORLD? WE HAD NO WAR. NO CRIME. BUT *PLENTY* OF MONSTERS.
SO I SENT "BAD GUYS" THEIR WAY TO TOUGHEN 'EM UP. ALL SO THEY COULD TAKE *YOU* ON.
BUT I KNEW NONE OF THAT MATTERED AFTER I HEARD *YOU* SPEAK IN FREAK ALLEY.
REVOS, THIS MAN OF ROCKS WHO YOU WERE SO AFRAID OF--HE'S A *GOOD* MAN INSIDE A HERO.
THAT'S WHY I BROUGHT HIM HERE, SO *YOU* CAN HEAR HIS WORDS TO *TALK* TO HIM, BEN. TELL HIM WHAT YOU TOLD ME.

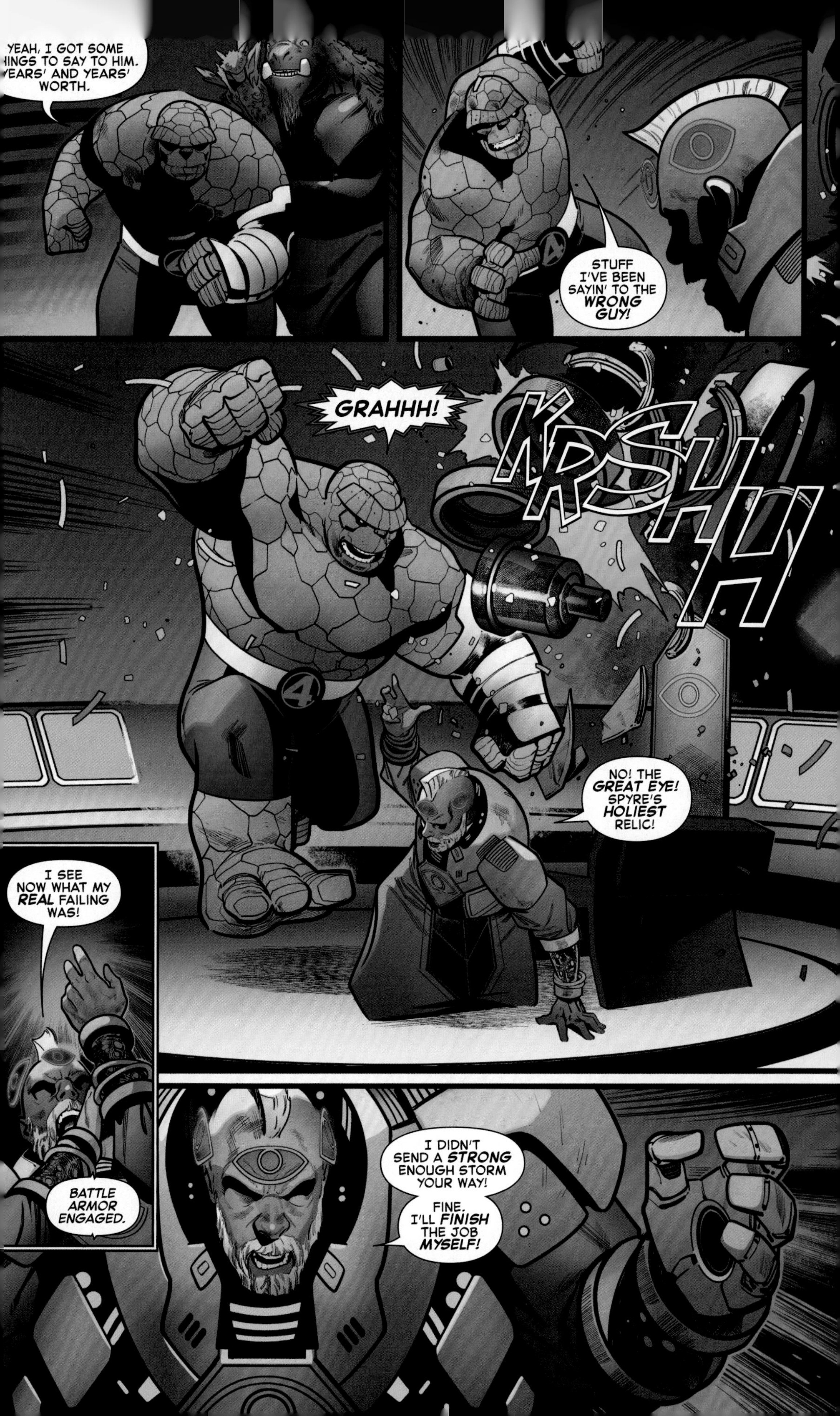
YEAH, I GOT SOME
HINGS TO SAY TO HIM.
YEARS' AND YEARS'
WORTH.
STUFF I'VE BEEN SAYIN' TO THE WRONG GUY!
GRAHHH!
KRSHHH
NO! THE GREAT EYE! SPYRE'S HOLIEST RELIC!
I SEE NOW WHAT MY REAL FAILING WAS!
BATTLE ARMOR ENGAGED.
I DIDN'T SEND A STRONG ENOUGH STORM YOUR WAY!
FINE. I'LL FINISH THE JOB MYSELF!

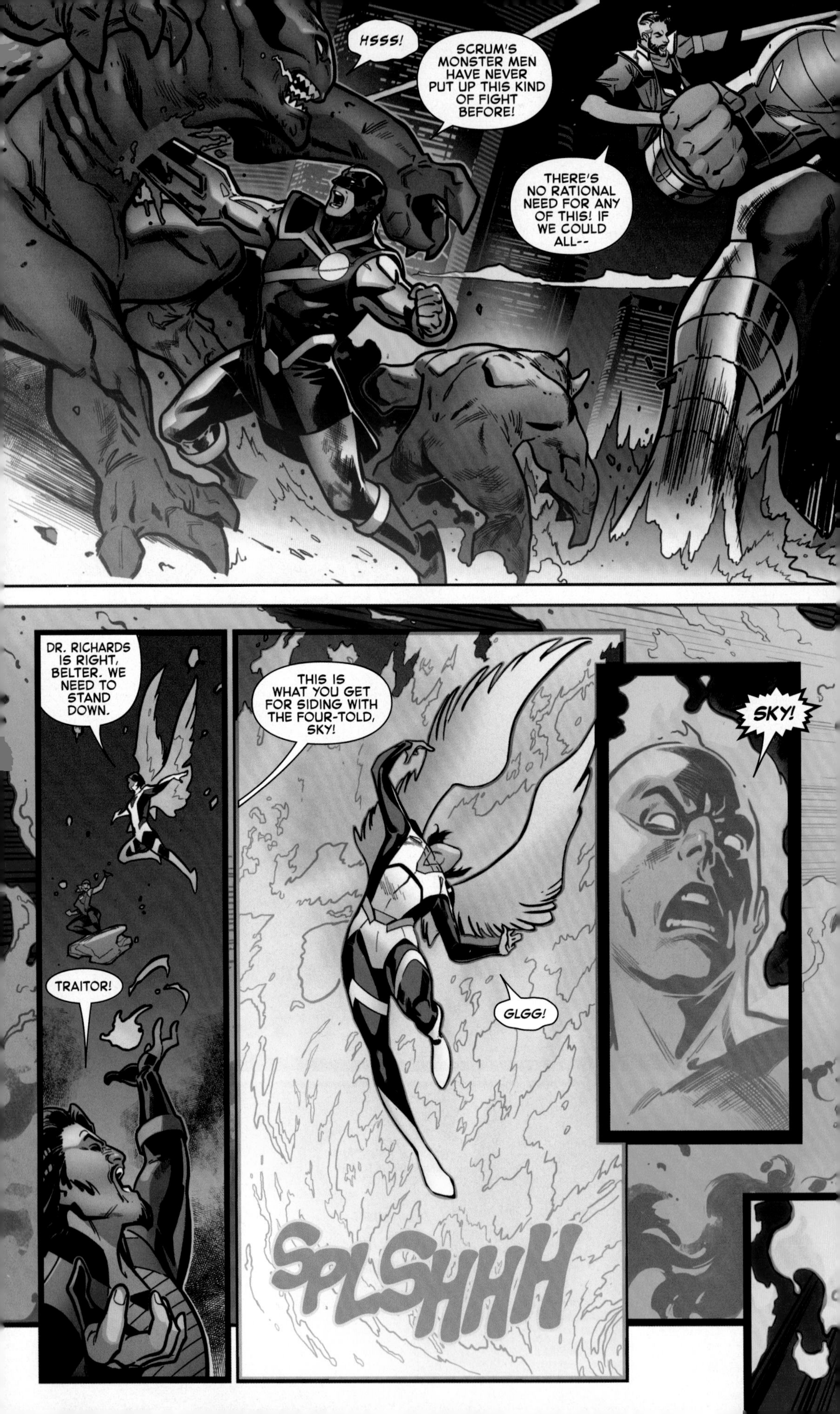
HSSS!
SCRUM'S MONSTER MEN HAVE NEVER PUT UP THIS KIND OF FIGHT BEFORE!
THERE'S NO RATIONAL NEED FOR ANY OF THIS! IF WE COULD ALL--
DR. RICHARDS IS RIGHT, BELTER. WE NEED TO STAND DOWN.
TRAITOR!
THIS IS WHAT YOU GET FOR SIDING WITH THE FOUR-TOLD, SKY!
GLGG!
SPLSHHH
SKY!

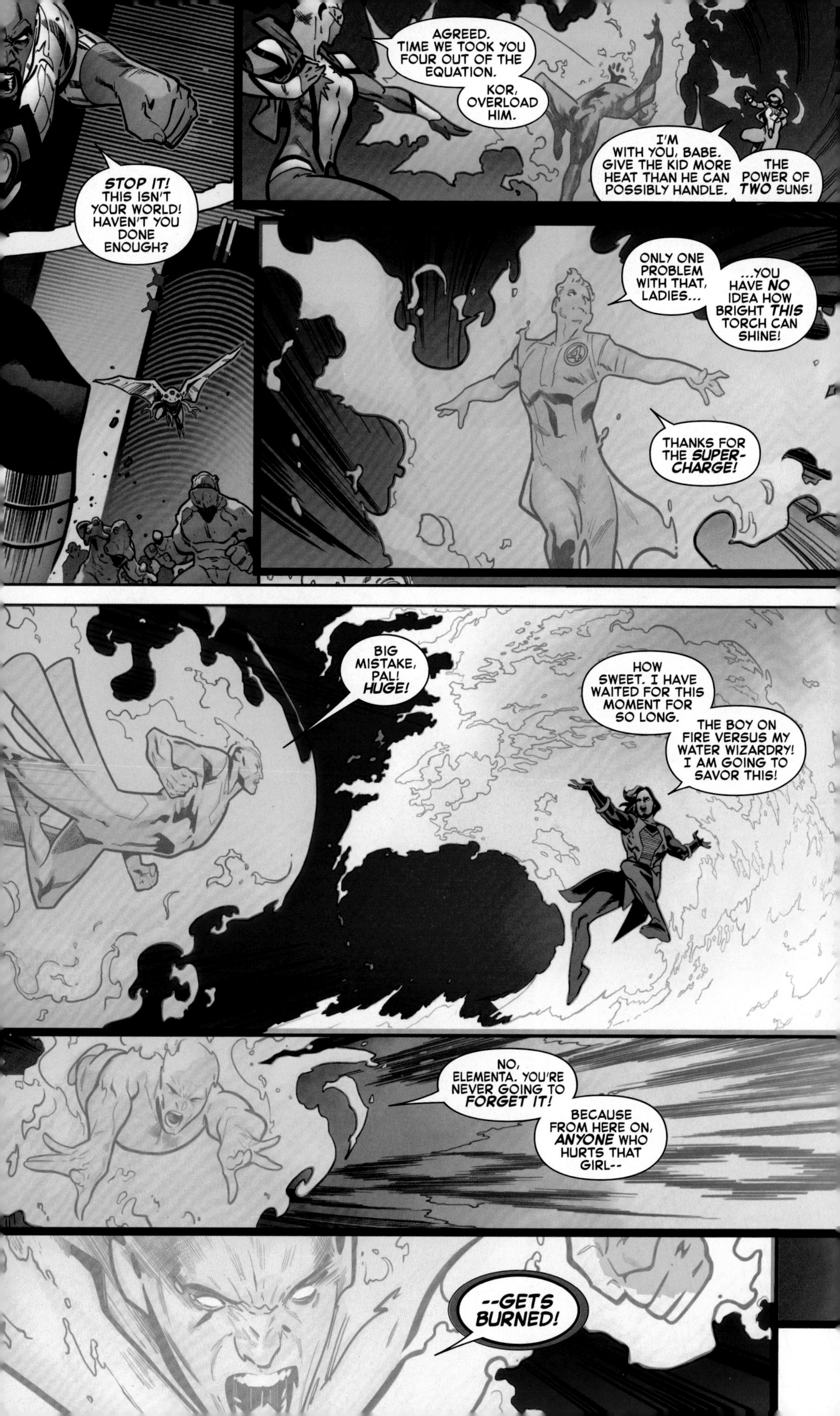
AGREED. TIME WE TOOK YOU FOUR OUT OF THE EQUATION.
KOR, OVERLOAD HIM.
I'M WITH YOU, BABE. GIVE THE KID MORE HEAT THAN HE CAN POSSIBLY HANDLE.
THE POWER OF TWO SUNS!
STOP IT! THIS ISN'T YOUR WORLD! HAVEN'T YOU DONE ENOUGH?
ONLY ONE PROBLEM WITH THAT, LADIES...
...YOU HAVE NO IDEA HOW BRIGHT THIS TORCH CAN SHINE!
THANKS FOR THE SUPER-CHARGE!
BIG MISTAKE, PAL! HUGE!
HOW SWEET. I HAVE WAITED FOR THIS MOMENT FOR SO LONG.
THE BOY ON FIRE VERSUS MY WATER WIZARDRY! I AM GOING TO SAVOR THIS!
NO, ELEMENTA. YOU'RE NEVER GOING TO FORGET IT!
BECAUSE FROM HERE ON, ANYONE WHO HURTS THAT GIRL--
--GETS BURNED!

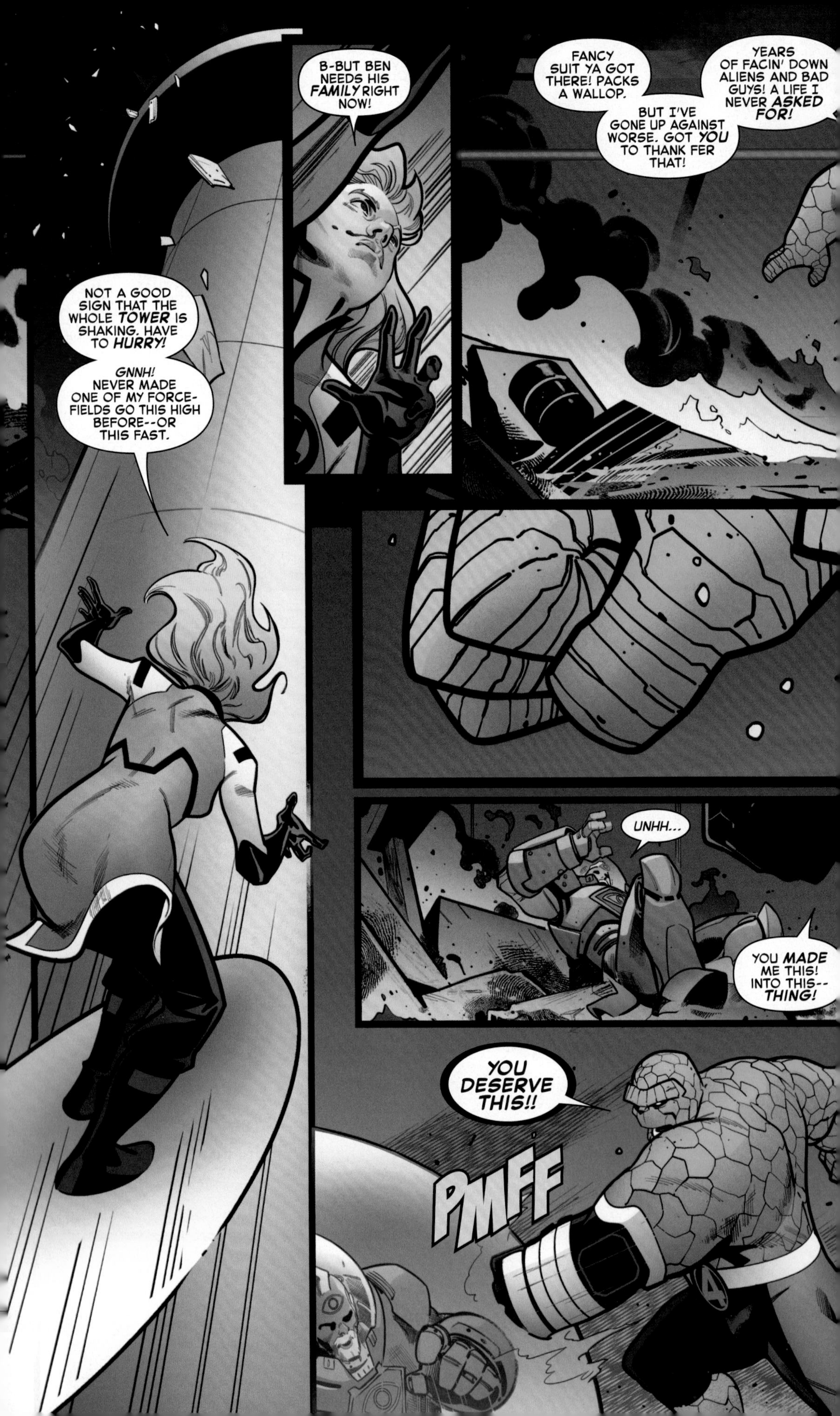
NOT A GOOD SIGN THAT THE WHOLE TOWER IS SHAKING. HAVE TO HURRY!
GNNH! NEVER MADE ONE OF MY FORCE-FIELDS GO THIS HIGH BEFORE--OR THIS FAST.
B-BUT BEN NEEDS HIS FAMILY RIGHT NOW!
FANCY SUIT YA GOT THERE! PACKS A WALLOP.
BUT I'VE GONE UP AGAINST WORSE. GOT YOU TO THANK FER THAT!
YEARS OF FACIN' DOWN ALIENS AND BAD GUYS! A LIFE I NEVER ASKED FOR!
UNHH...
YOU MADE ME THIS! INTO THIS--THING!
YOU DESERVE THIS!!
PMFF

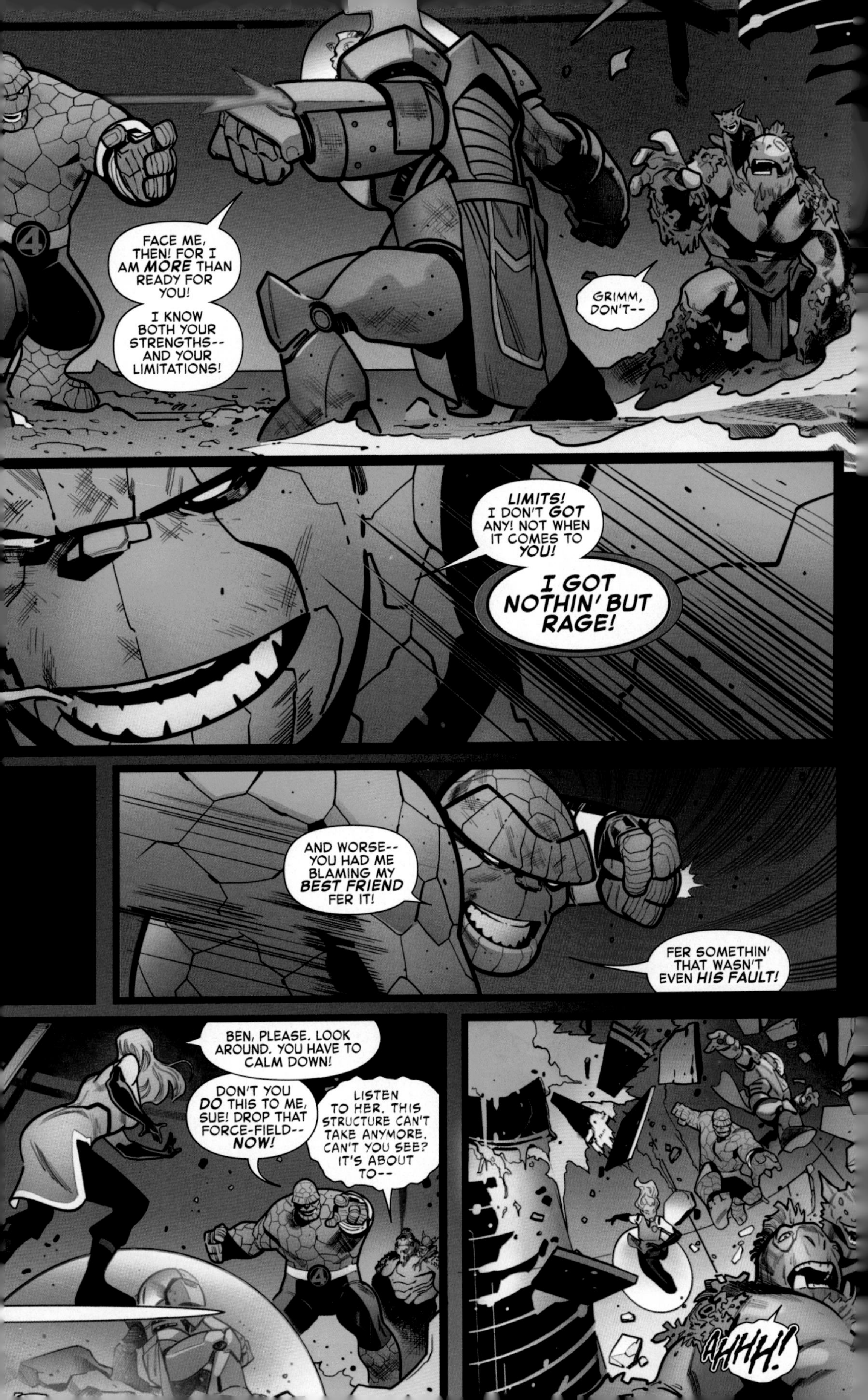

FACE ME, THEN! FOR I AM MORE THAN READY FOR YOU!
I KNOW BOTH YOUR STRENGTHS-- AND YOUR LIMITATIONS!
GRIMM, DON'T--
LIMITS! I DON'T GOT ANY! NOT WHEN IT COMES TO YOU!
I GOT NOTHIN' BUT RAGE!
AND WORSE-- YOU HAD ME BLAMING MY BEST FRIEND FER IT!
FER SOMETHIN' THAT WASN'T EVEN HIS FAULT!
BEN, PLEASE. LOOK AROUND. YOU HAVE TO CALM DOWN!
DON'T YOU DO THIS TO ME, SUE! DROP THAT FORCE-FIELD-- NOW!
LISTEN TO HER. THIS STRUCTURE CAN'T TAKE ANYMORE. CAN'T YOU SEE? IT'S ABOUT TO--
AHHH!

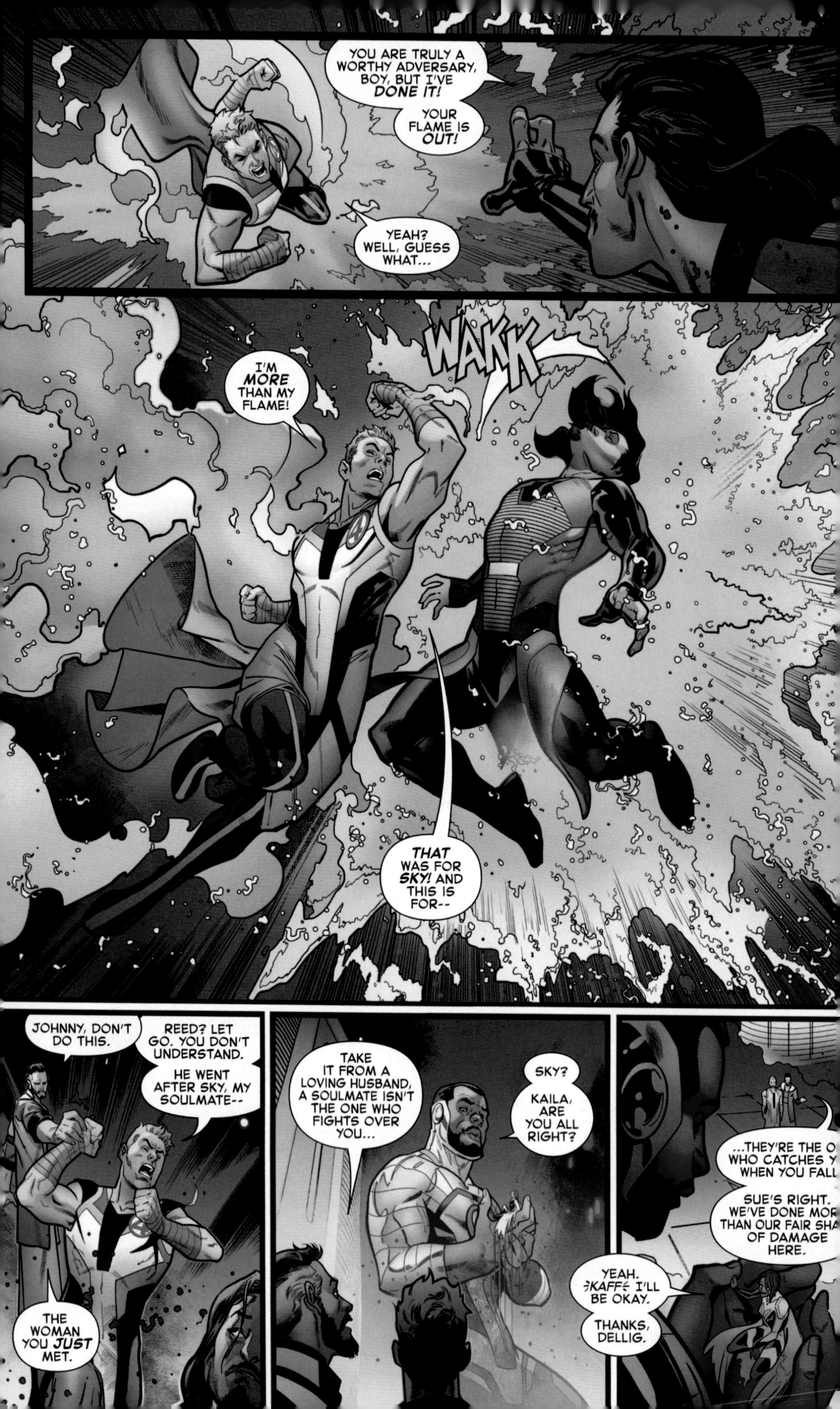
YOU ARE TRULY A WORTHY ADVERSARY, BOY, BUT I'VE DONE IT!
YOUR FLAME IS OUT!
YEAH? WELL, GUESS WHAT...
WAKK
I'M MORE THAN MY FLAME!
THAT WAS FOR SKY! AND THIS IS FOR--
JOHNNY, DON'T DO THIS.
REED? LET GO. YOU DON'T UNDERSTAND.
HE WENT AFTER SKY, MY SOULMATE--
THE WOMAN YOU JUST MET.
TAKE IT FROM A LOVING HUSBAND, A SOULMATE ISN'T THE ONE WHO FIGHTS OVER YOU...
SKY?
KAILA, ARE YOU ALL RIGHT?
...THEY'RE THE O WHO CATCHES Y WHEN YOU FALL
SUE'S RIGHT. WE'VE DONE MOR THAN OUR FAIR SHA OF DAMAGE HERE.
YEAH. *KAFF* I'LL BE OKAY.
THANKS, DELLIG.

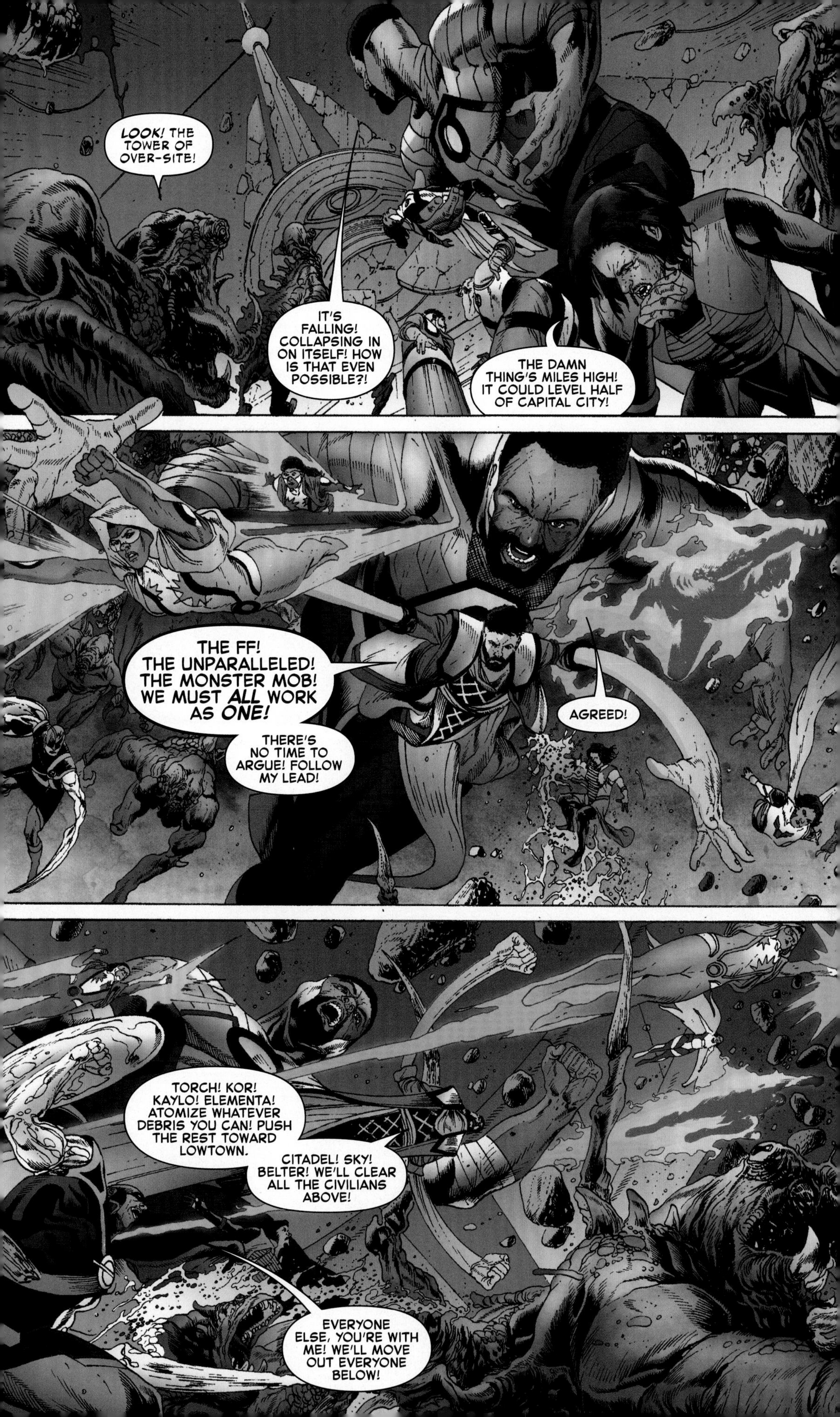
LOOK! THE TOWER OF OVER-SITE!
IT'S FALLING! COLLAPSING IN ON ITSELF! HOW IS THAT EVEN POSSIBLE?!
THE DAMN THING'S MILES HIGH! IT COULD LEVEL HALF OF CAPITAL CITY!
THE FF! THE UNPARALLELED! THE MONSTER MOB! WE MUST ALL WORK AS ONE!
THERE'S NO TIME TO ARGUE! FOLLOW MY LEAD!
AGREED!
TORCH! KOR! KAYLO! ELEMENTA! ATOMIZE WHATEVER DEBRIS YOU CAN! PUSH THE REST TOWARD LOWTOWN.
CITADEL! SKY! BELTER! WE'LL CLEAR ALL THE CIVILIANS ABOVE!
EVERYONE ELSE, YOU'RE WITH ME! WE'LL MOVE OUT EVERYONE BELOW!

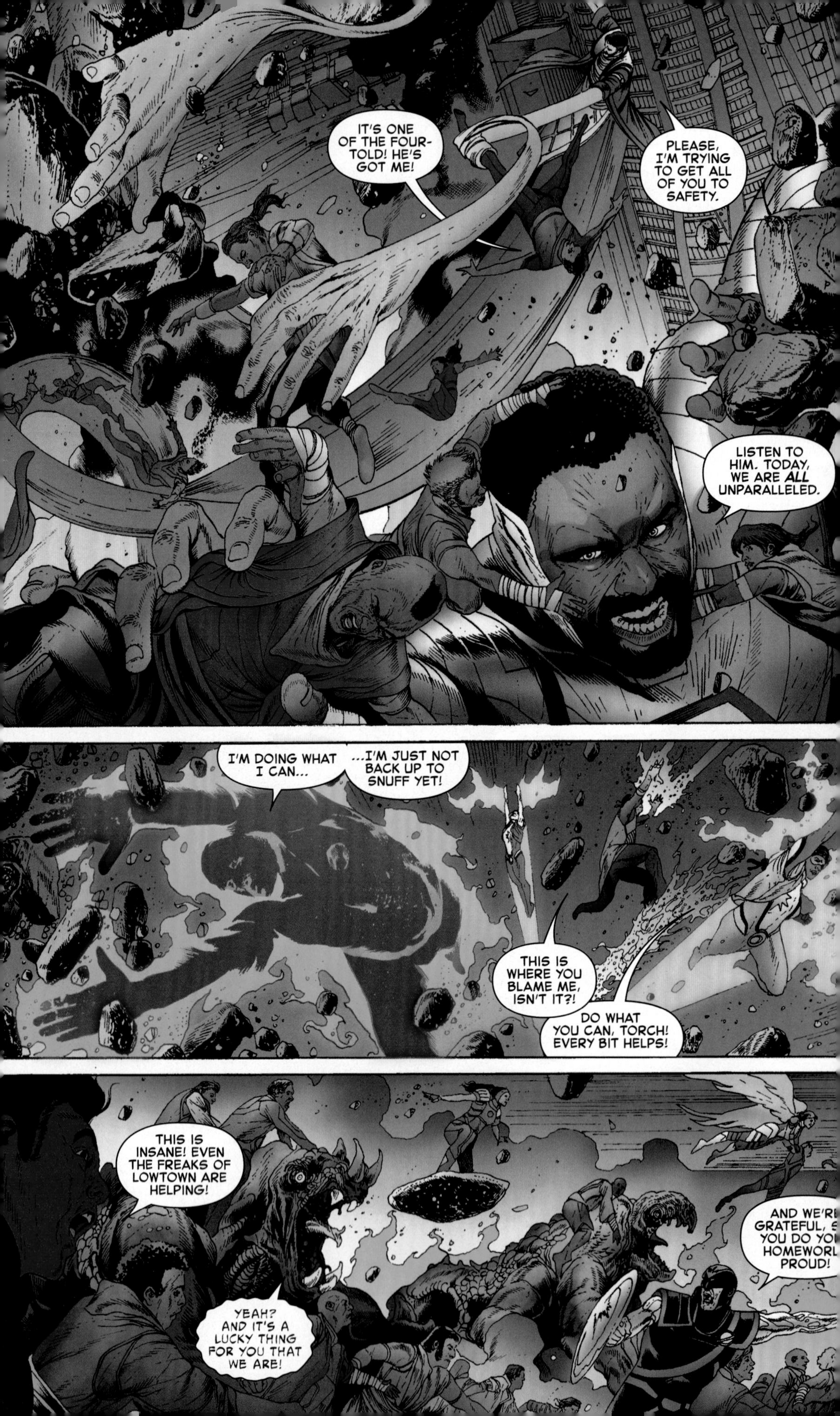
IT'S ONE OF THE FOUR-TOLD! HE'S GOT ME!
PLEASE, I'M TRYING TO GET ALL OF YOU TO SAFETY.
LISTEN TO HIM. TODAY, WE ARE *ALL* UNPARALLELED.
I'M DOING WHAT I CAN...
...I'M JUST NOT BACK UP TO SNUFF YET!
THIS IS WHERE YOU BLAME ME, ISN'T IT?!
DO WHAT YOU CAN, TORCH! EVERY BIT HELPS!
THIS IS INSANE! EVEN THE FREAKS OF LOWTOWN ARE HELPING!
YEAH? AND IT'S A LUCKY THING FOR YOU THAT WE ARE!
AND WE'R GRATEFUL, S YOU DO YO HOMEWORL PROUD!

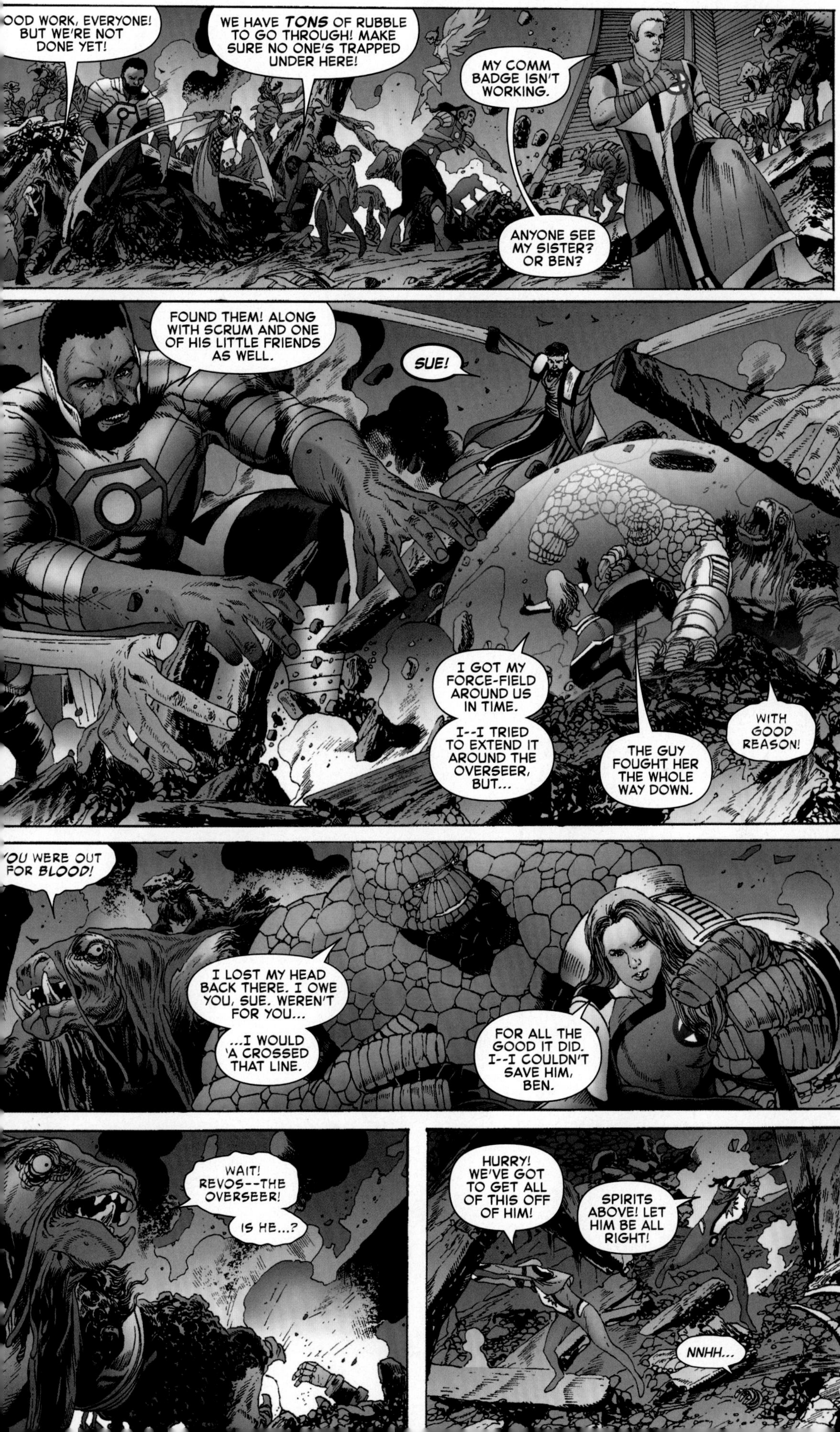
OOD WORK, EVERYONE! BUT WE'RE NOT DONE YET!
WE HAVE TONS OF RUBBLE TO GO THROUGH! MAKE SURE NO ONE'S TRAPPED UNDER HERE!
MY COMM BADGE ISN'T WORKING.
ANYONE SEE MY SISTER? OR BEN?
FOUND THEM! ALONG WITH SCRUM AND ONE OF HIS LITTLE FRIENDS AS WELL.
SUE!
I GOT MY FORCE-FIELD AROUND US IN TIME.
I--I TRIED TO EXTEND IT AROUND THE OVERSEER, BUT...
THE GUY FOUGHT HER THE WHOLE WAY DOWN.
WITH GOOD REASON!
OU WERE OUT FOR BLOOD!
I LOST MY HEAD BACK THERE. I OWE YOU, SUE. WEREN'T FOR YOU...
...I WOULD 'A CROSSED THAT LINE.
FOR ALL THE GOOD IT DID. I--I COULDN'T SAVE HIM, BEN.
WAIT! REVOS--THE OVERSEER!
IS HE...?
HURRY! WE'VE GOT TO GET ALL OF THIS OFF OF HIM!
SPIRITS ABOVE! LET HIM BE ALL RIGHT!
NNHH...

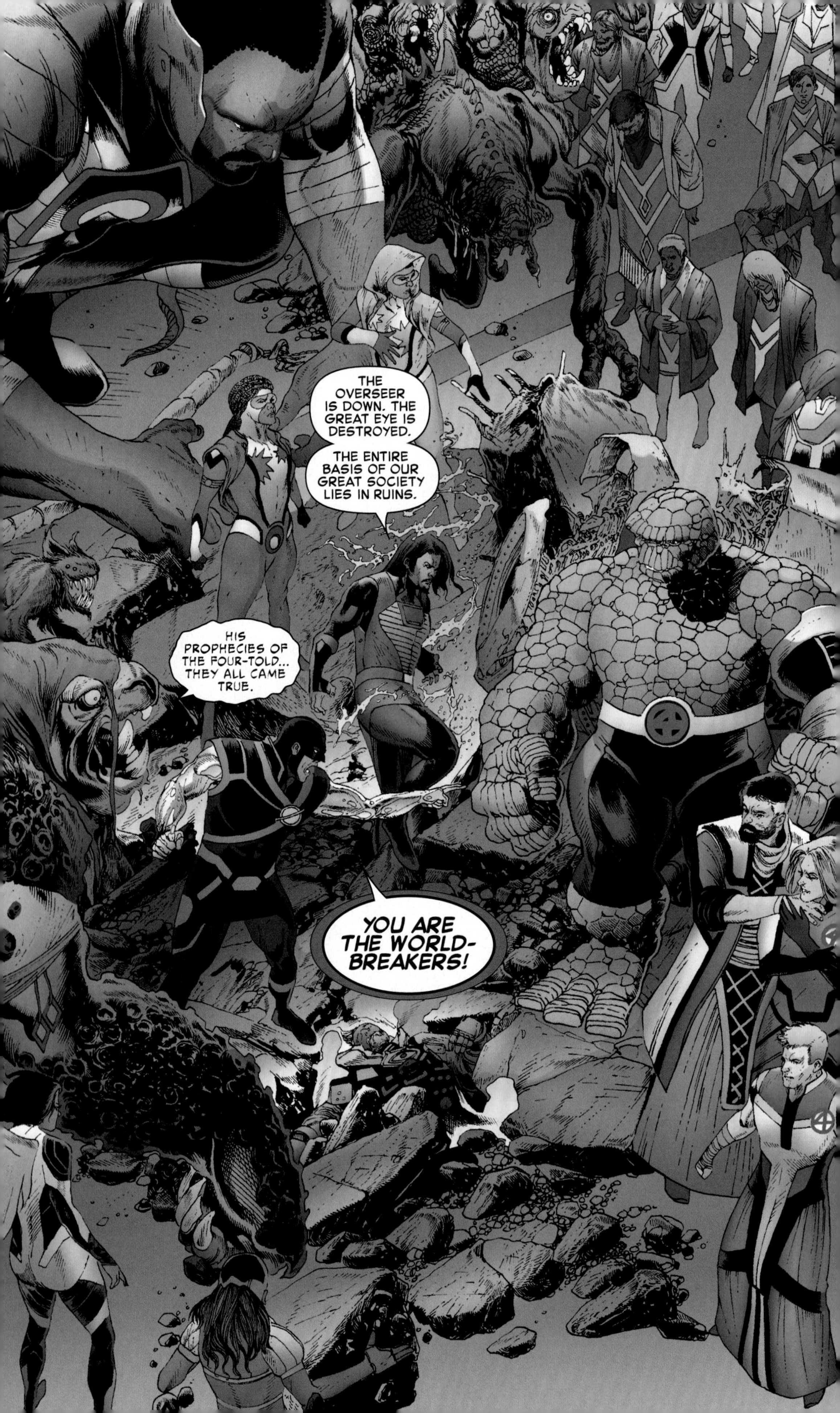
THE OVERSEER IS DOWN. THE GREAT EYE IS DESTROYED.
THE ENTIRE BASIS OF OUR GREAT SOCIETY LIES IN RUINS.
HIS PROPHECIES OF THE FOUR-TOLD... THEY ALL CAME TRUE.
YOU ARE THE WORLD-BREAKERS!

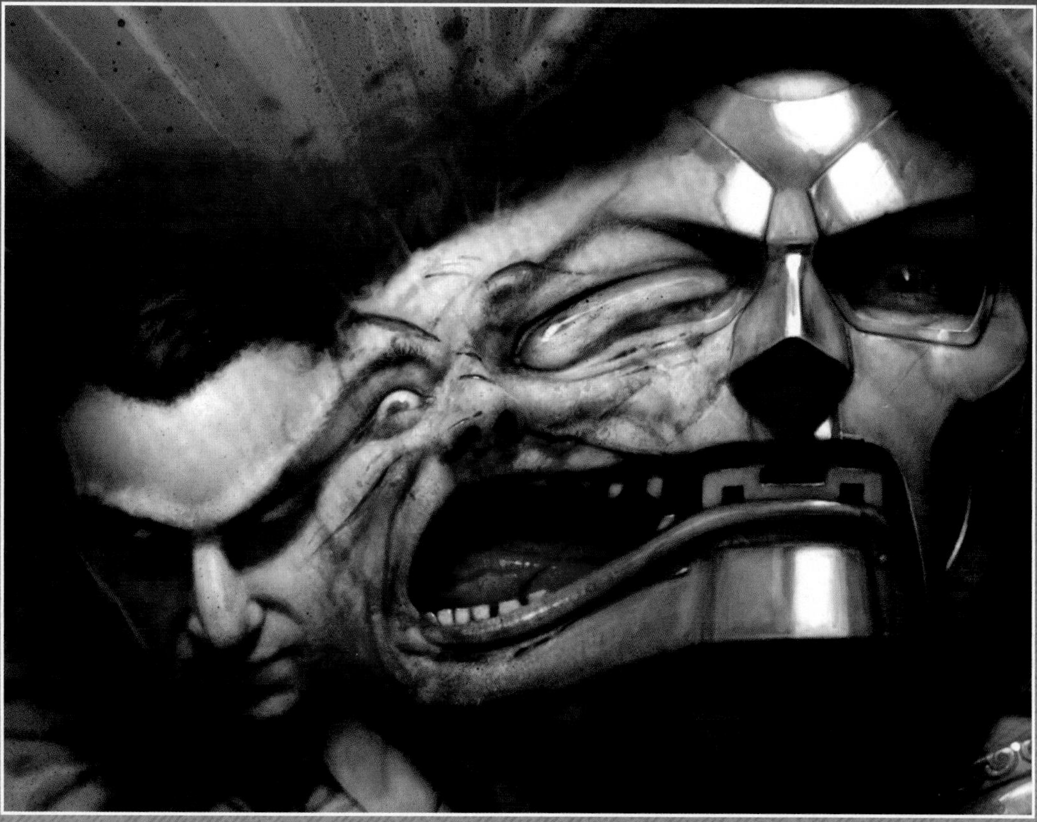

#14 Immortal variant by
Ryan Brown

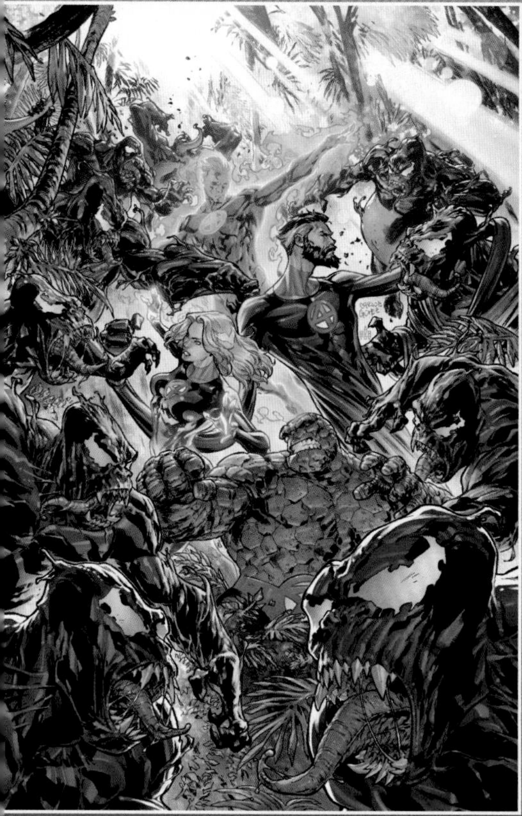

#17 Venom Island variant by
Carlos Gómez & **Jesus Aburtov**

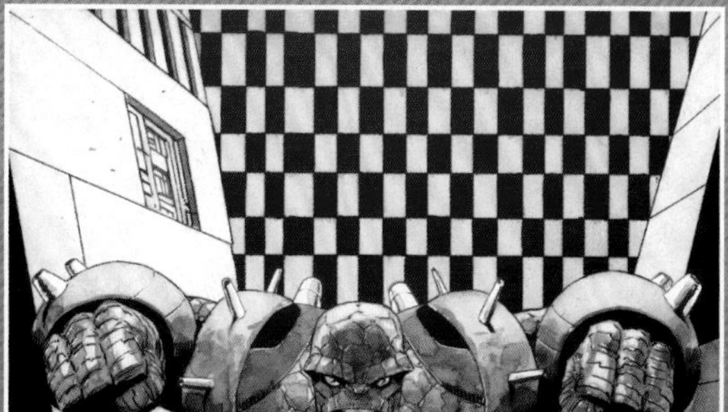

#17 2020 variant by
Khoi Pham & **Morry Hollowell**

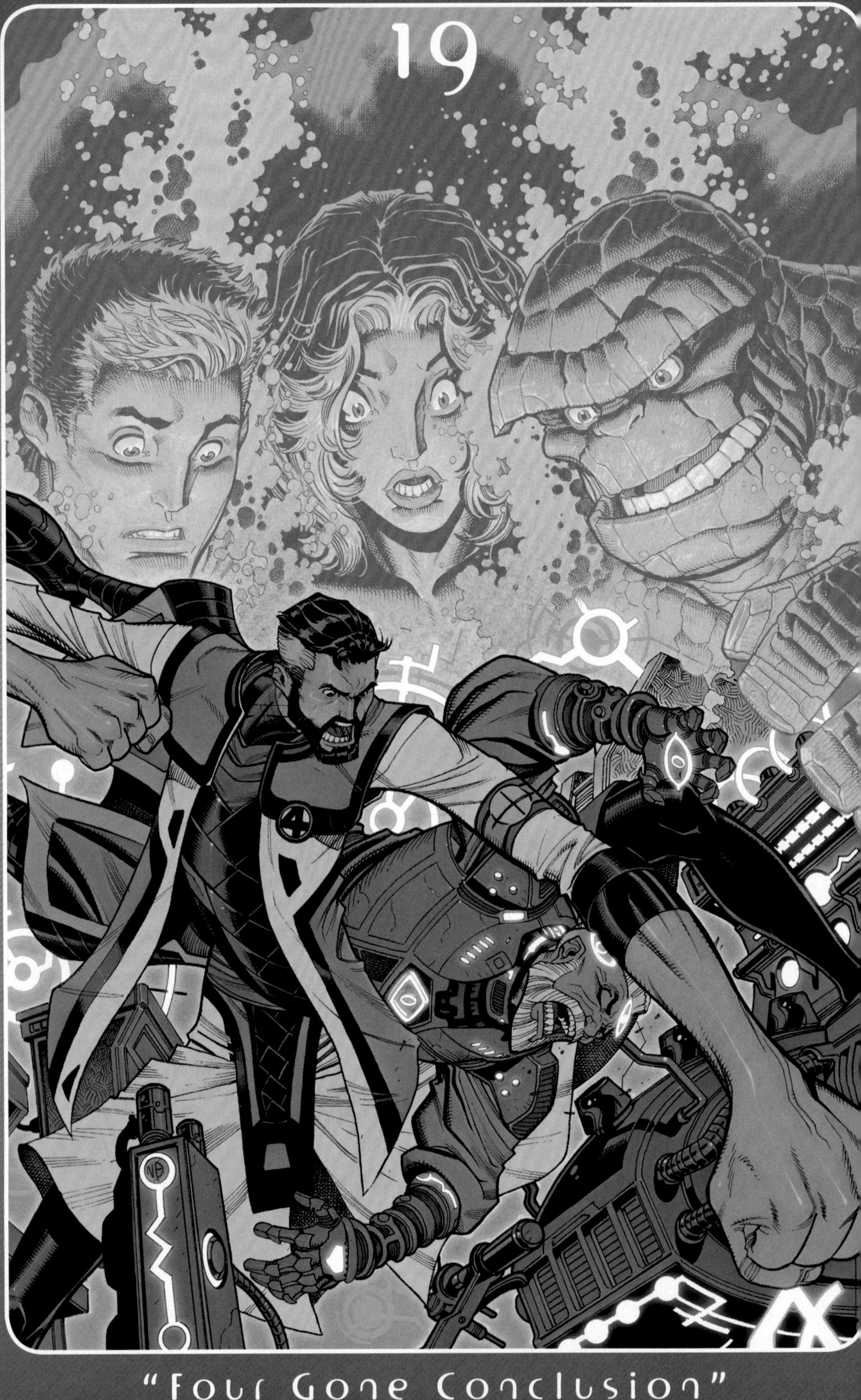
19

"Four Gone Conclusion"

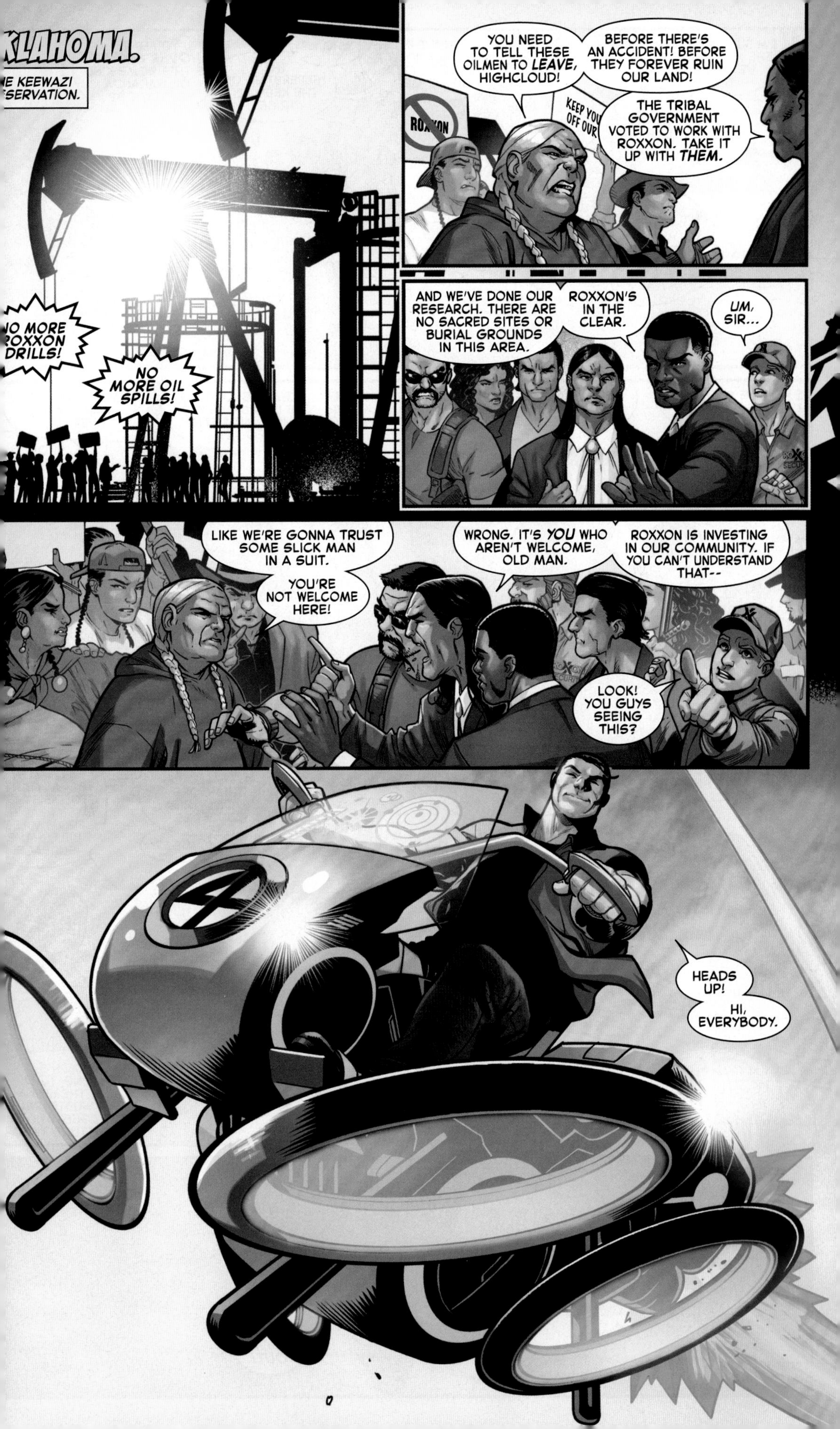
KLAHOMA.
E KEEWAZI
SERVATION.
NO MORE
ROXXON
DRILLS!
NO
MORE OIL
SPILLS!
ROXXON
KEEP YOU
OFF OUR
YOU NEED TO TELL THESE OILMEN TO LEAVE, HIGHCLOUD!
BEFORE THERE'S AN ACCIDENT! BEFORE THEY FOREVER RUIN OUR LAND!
THE TRIBAL GOVERNMENT VOTED TO WORK WITH ROXXON. TAKE IT UP WITH THEM.
AND WE'VE DONE OUR RESEARCH. THERE ARE NO SACRED SITES OR BURIAL GROUNDS IN THIS AREA.
ROXXON'S IN THE CLEAR.
UM, SIR...
LIKE WE'RE GONNA TRUST SOME SLICK MAN IN A SUIT.
YOU'RE NOT WELCOME HERE!
WRONG. IT'S YOU WHO AREN'T WELCOME, OLD MAN.
ROXXON IS INVESTING IN OUR COMMUNITY. IF YOU CAN'T UNDERSTAND THAT--
LOOK! YOU GUYS SEEING THIS?
HEADS UP!
HI, EVERYBODY.

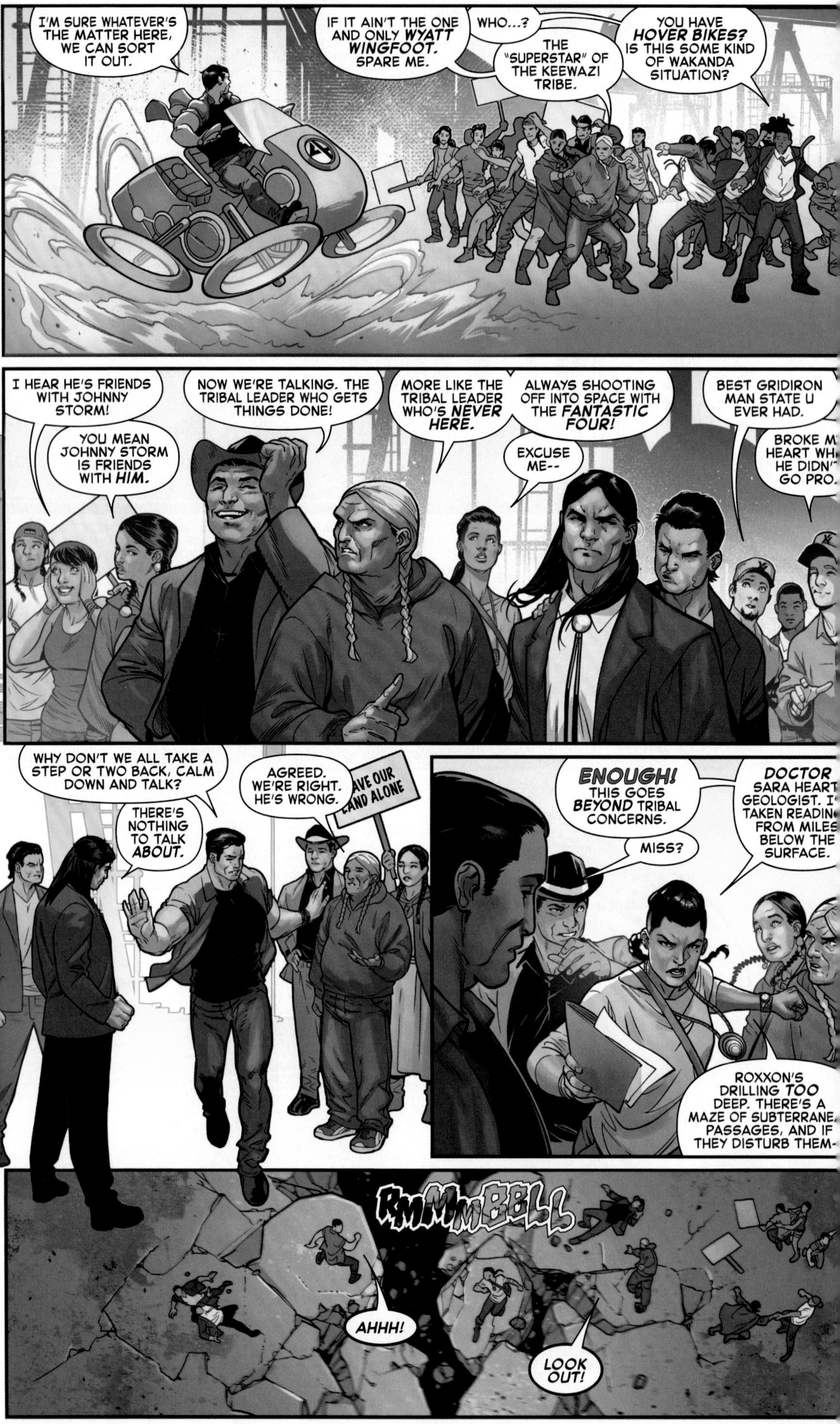

I'M SURE WHATEVER'S THE MATTER HERE, WE CAN SORT IT OUT.
IF IT AIN'T THE ONE AND ONLY WYATT WINGFOOT. SPARE ME.
WHO...?
THE "SUPERSTAR" OF THE KEEWAZI TRIBE.
YOU HAVE HOVER BIKES? IS THIS SOME KIND OF WAKANDA SITUATION?
I HEAR HE'S FRIENDS WITH JOHNNY STORM!
YOU MEAN JOHNNY STORM IS FRIENDS WITH HIM.
NOW WE'RE TALKING. THE TRIBAL LEADER WHO GETS THINGS DONE!
MORE LIKE THE TRIBAL LEADER WHO'S NEVER HERE.
ALWAYS SHOOTING OFF INTO SPACE WITH THE FANTASTIC FOUR!
EXCUSE ME--
BEST GRIDIRON MAN STATE U EVER HAD.
WHY DON'T WE ALL TAKE A STEP OR TWO BACK, CALM DOWN AND TALK?
THERE'S NOTHING TO TALK ABOUT.
AGREED. WE'RE RIGHT. HE'S WRONG.
LAND ALONE
ENOUGH! THIS GOES BEYOND TRIBAL CONCERNS.
MISS?
ROXXON'S DRILLING TOO DEEP. THERE'S A
PASSAGES, AND IF THEY DISTURB THEM-
RMMMMBBLL
AHHH!
LOOK OUT!

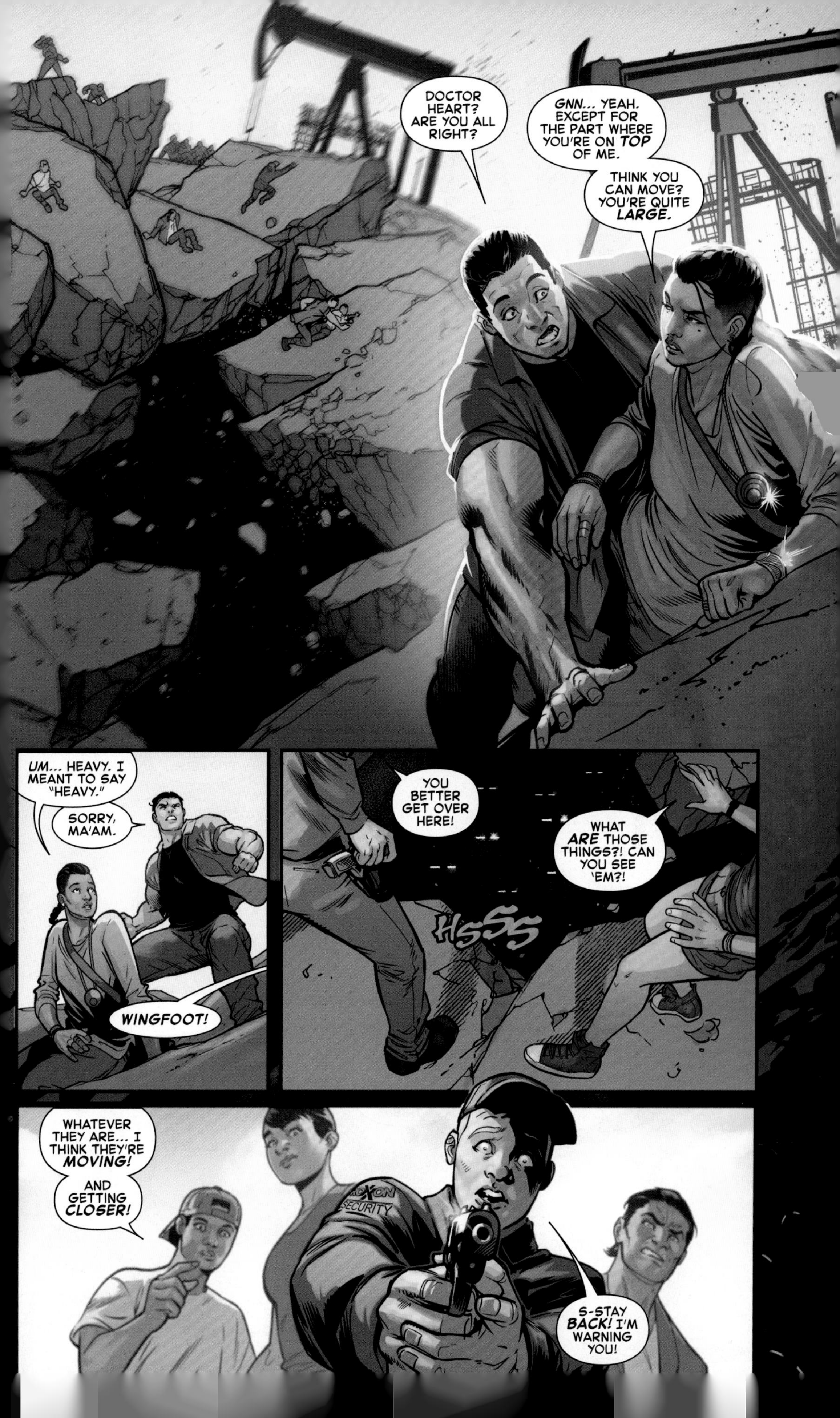
DOCTOR HEART? ARE YOU ALL RIGHT?
GNN... YEAH. EXCEPT FOR THE PART WHERE YOU'RE ON TOP OF ME.
THINK YOU CAN MOVE? YOU'RE QUITE LARGE.
UM... HEAVY. I MEANT TO SAY "HEAVY."
SORRY, MA'AM.
WINGFOOT!
YOU BETTER GET OVER HERE!
WHAT ARE THOSE THINGS?! CAN YOU SEE 'EM?!
HSSS
WHATEVER THEY ARE... I THINK THEY'RE MOVING!
AND GETTING CLOSER!
ROXXON SECURITY
S-STAY BACK! I'M WARNING YOU!

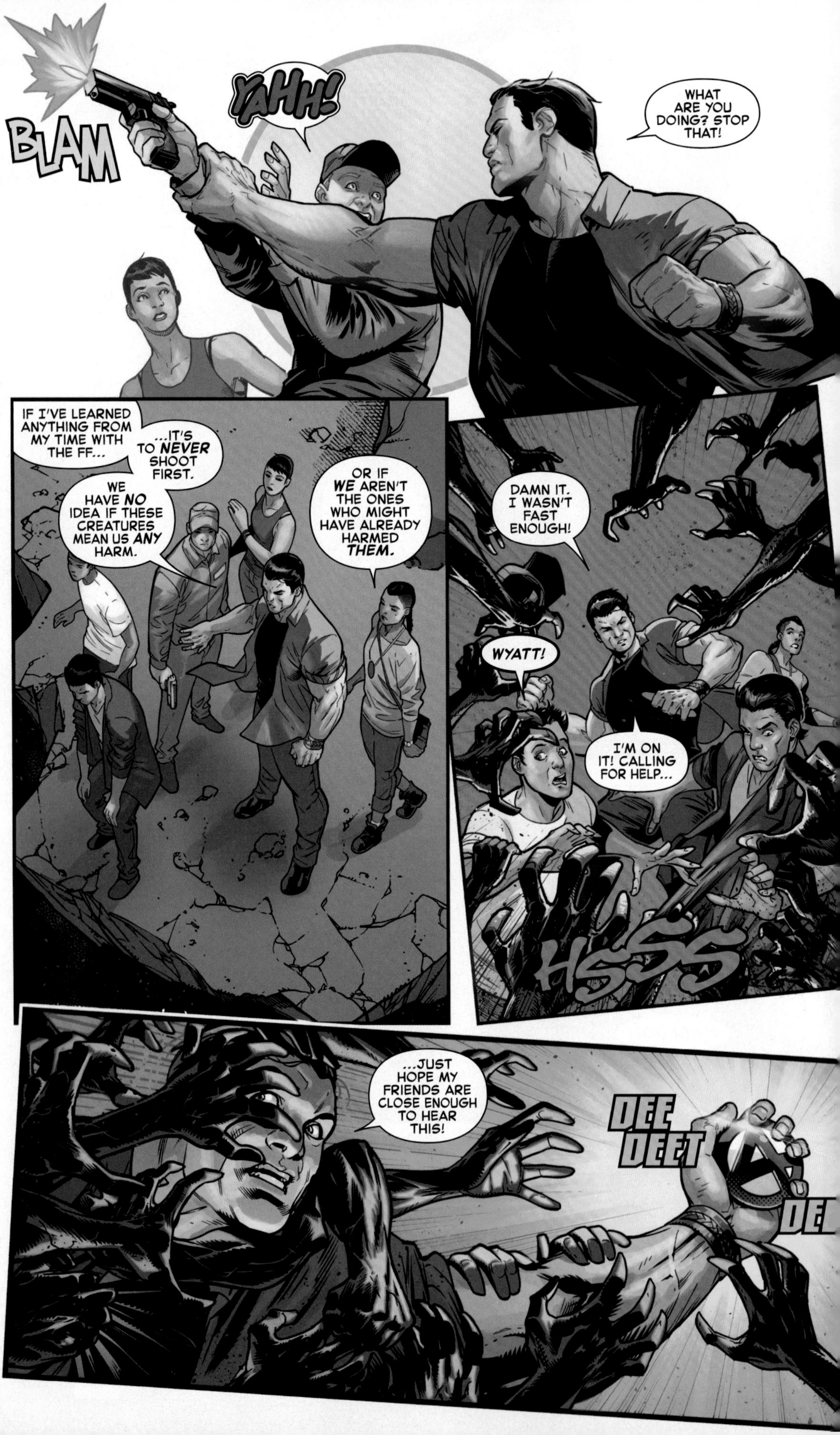
BLAM
YAHH!
WHAT ARE YOU DOING? STOP THAT!
IF I'VE LEARNED ANYTHING FROM MY TIME WITH THE FF...
...IT'S TO NEVER SHOOT FIRST.
WE HAVE NO IDEA IF THESE CREATURES MEAN US ANY HARM.
OR IF WE AREN'T THE ONES WHO MIGHT HAVE ALREADY HARMED THEM.
DAMN IT. I WASN'T FAST ENOUGH!
WYATT!
I'M ON IT! CALLING FOR HELP...
HSSS
...JUST HOPE MY FRIENDS ARE CLOSE ENOUGH TO HEAR THIS!
DEE DEET
DE

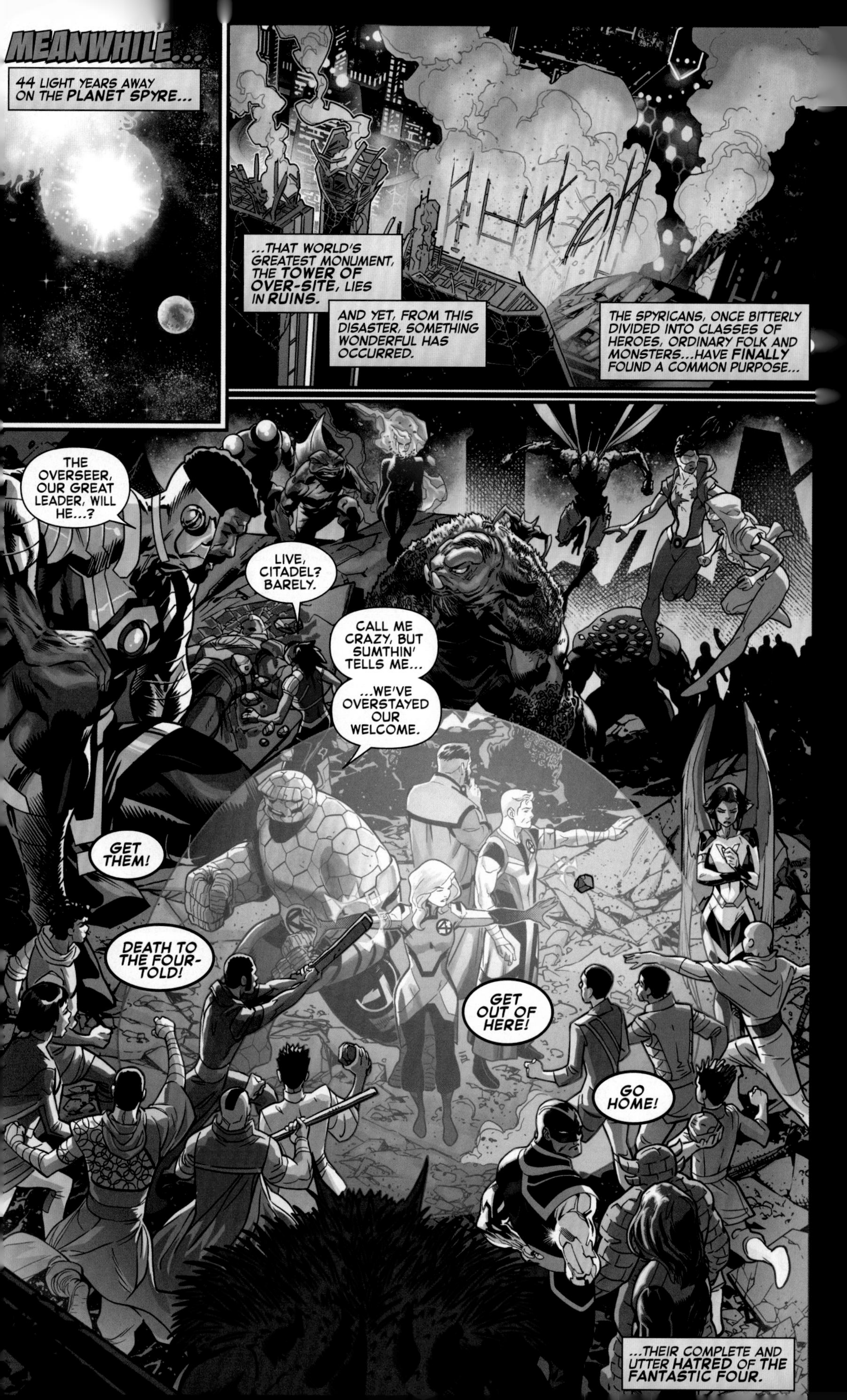
MEANWHILE...
44 LIGHT YEARS AWAY ON THE PLANET SPYRE...
...THAT WORLD'S GREATEST MONUMENT, THE TOWER OF OVER-SITE, LIES IN RUINS.
AND YET, FROM THIS DISASTER, SOMETHING WONDERFUL HAS OCCURRED.
THE SPYRICANS, ONCE BITTERLY DIVIDED INTO CLASSES OF HEROES, ORDINARY FOLK AND MONSTERS...HAVE FINALLY FOUND A COMMON PURPOSE...
THE OVERSEER, OUR GREAT LEADER, WILL HE...?
LIVE, CITADEL? BARELY.
CALL ME CRAZY, BUT SUMTHIN' TELLS ME...
...WE'VE OVERSTAYED OUR WELCOME.
GET THEM!
DEATH TO THE FOUR-TOLD!
GET OUT OF HERE!
GO HOME!
...THEIR COMPLETE AND UTTER HATRED OF THE FANTASTIC FOUR.

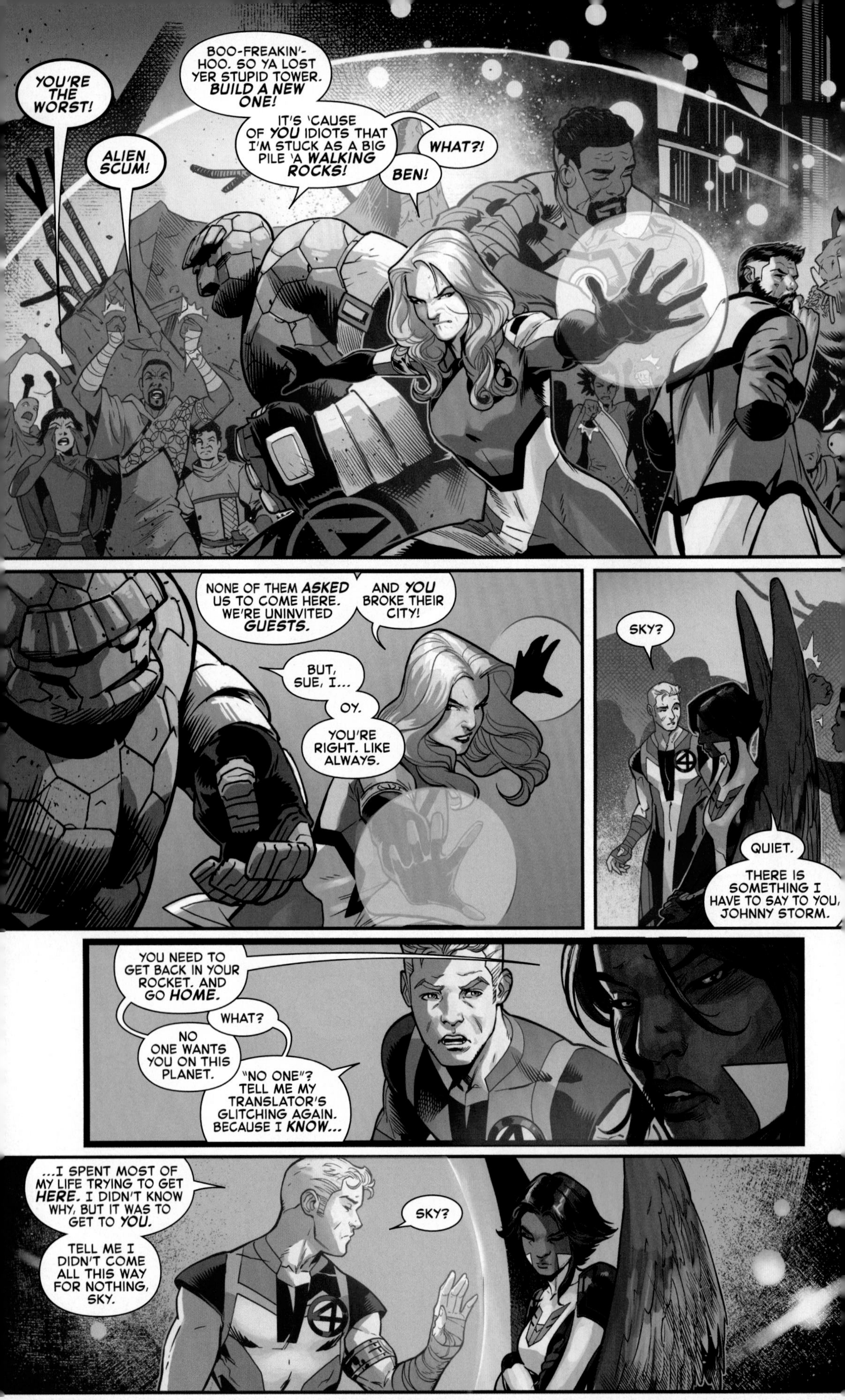
YOU'RE THE WORST!
ALIEN SCUM!
BOO-FREAKIN'-HOO. SO YA LOST YER STUPID TOWER. BUILD A NEW ONE!
IT'S 'CAUSE OF YOU IDIOTS THAT I'M STUCK AS A BIG PILE 'A WALKING ROCKS!
WHAT?!
BEN!
NONE OF THEM ASKED US TO COME HERE. WE'RE UNINVITED GUESTS.
AND YOU BROKE THEIR CITY!
BUT, SUE, I...
OY.
YOU'RE RIGHT. LIKE ALWAYS.
SKY?
QUIET.
THERE IS SOMETHING I HAVE TO SAY TO YOU, JOHNNY STORM.
YOU NEED TO GET BACK IN YOUR ROCKET. AND GO HOME.
WHAT?
NO ONE WANTS YOU ON THIS PLANET.
"NO ONE"? TELL ME MY TRANSLATOR'S GLITCHING AGAIN. BECAUSE I KNOW...
...I SPENT MOST OF MY LIFE TRYING TO GET HERE. I DIDN'T KNOW WHY, BUT IT WAS TO GET TO YOU.
TELL ME I DIDN'T COME ALL THIS WAY FOR NOTHING, SKY.
SKY?

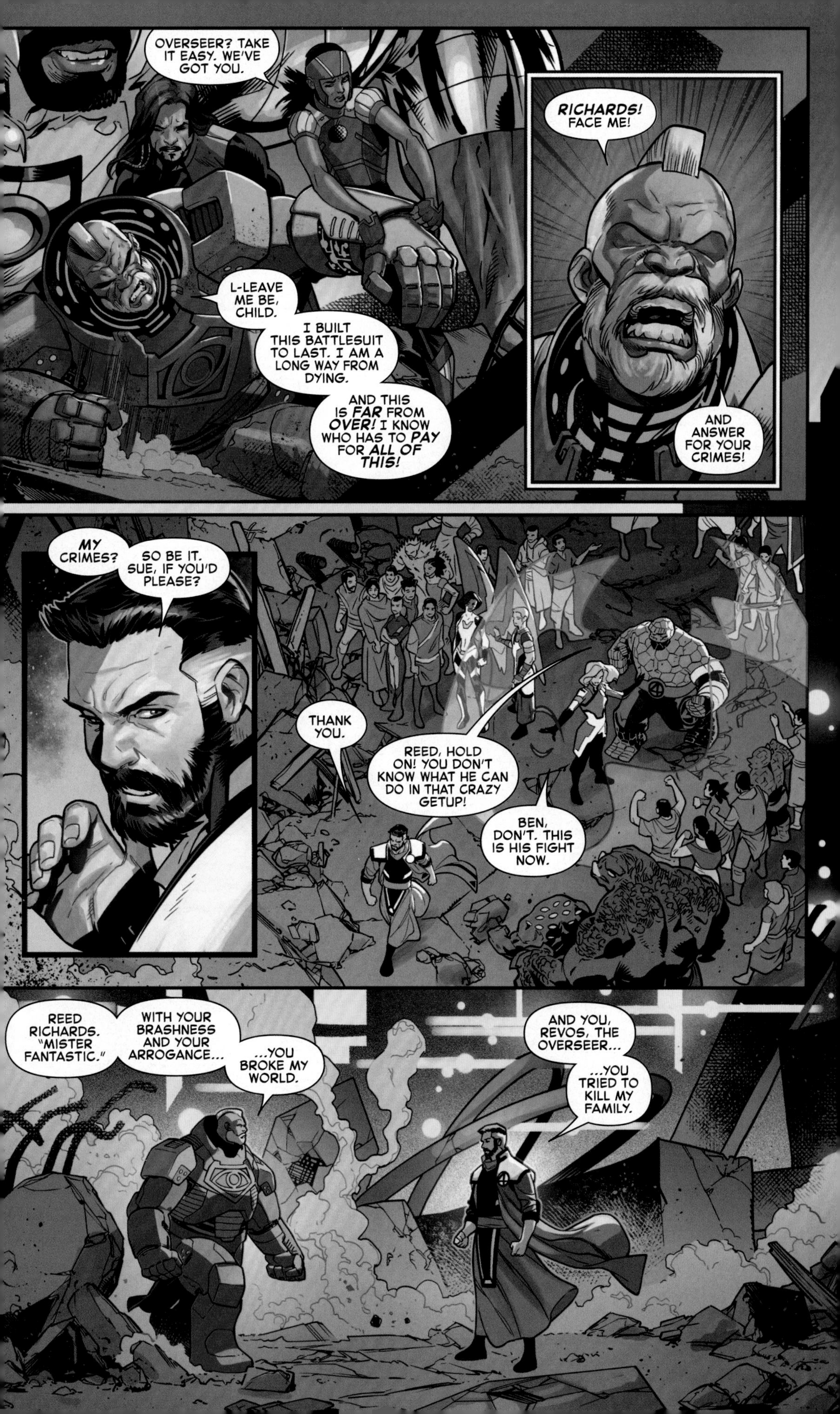
OVERSEER? TAKE IT EASY. WE'VE GOT YOU.
L-LEAVE ME BE, CHILD.
I BUILT THIS BATTLESUIT TO LAST. I AM A LONG WAY FROM DYING.
AND THIS IS FAR FROM OVER! I KNOW WHO HAS TO PAY FOR ALL OF THIS!
RICHARDS! FACE ME!
AND ANSWER FOR YOUR CRIMES!
MY CRIMES?
SO BE IT. SUE, IF YOU'D PLEASE?
THANK YOU.
REED, HOLD ON! YOU DON'T KNOW WHAT HE CAN DO IN THAT CRAZY GETUP!
BEN, DON'T. THIS IS HIS FIGHT NOW.
REED RICHARDS. "MISTER FANTASTIC."
WITH YOUR BRASHNESS AND YOUR ARROGANCE...
...YOU BROKE MY WORLD.
AND YOU, REVOS, THE OVERSEER...
...YOU TRIED TO KILL MY FAMILY.

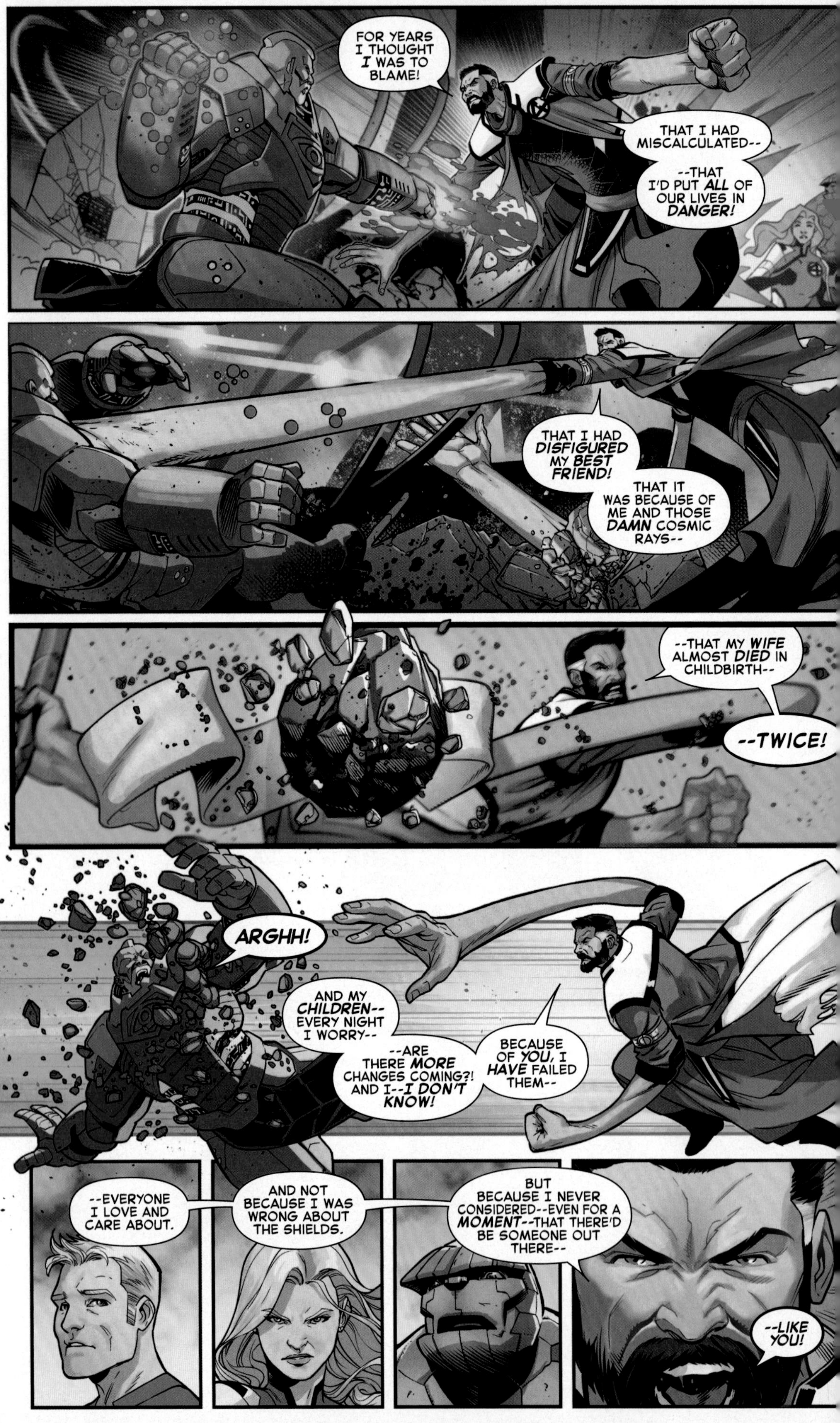
FOR YEARS I THOUGHT I WAS TO BLAME!
THAT I HAD MISCALCULATED--
--THAT I'D PUT ALL OF OUR LIVES IN DANGER!
THAT I HAD DISFIGURED MY BEST FRIEND!
THAT IT WAS BECAUSE OF ME AND THOSE DAMN COSMIC RAYS--
--THAT MY WIFE ALMOST DIED IN CHILDBIRTH--
--TWICE!
ARGHH!
AND MY CHILDREN-- EVERY NIGHT I WORRY--
--ARE THERE MORE CHANGES COMING?! AND I--I DON'T KNOW!
BECAUSE OF YOU, I HAVE FAILED THEM--
--EVERYONE I LOVE AND CARE ABOUT.
AND NOT BECAUSE I WAS WRONG ABOUT THE SHIELDS.
BUT BECAUSE I NEVER CONSIDERED--EVEN FOR A MOMENT--THAT THERE'D BE SOMEONE OUT THERE--
--LIKE YOU!

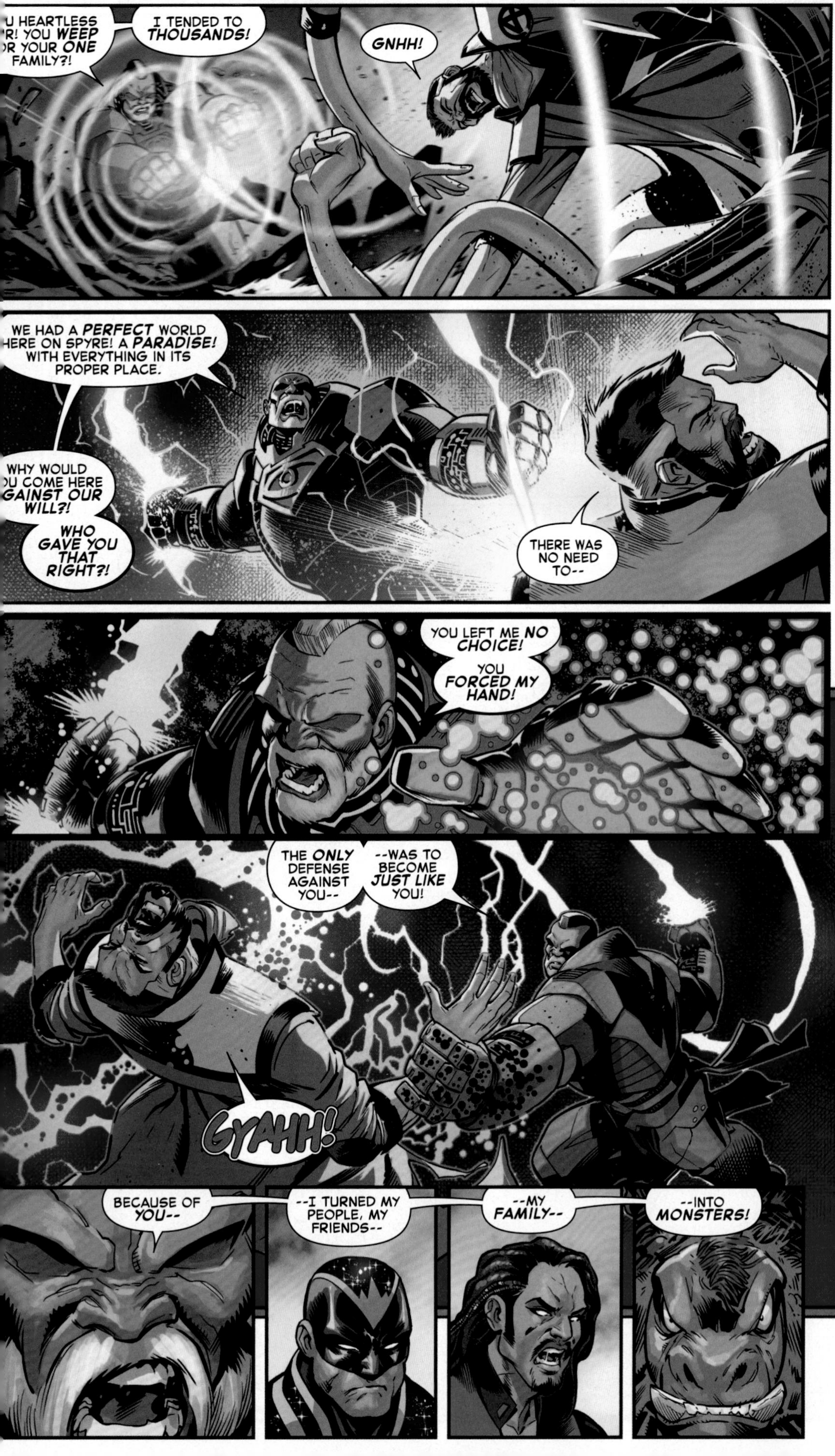
U HEARTLESS R! YOU WEEP OR YOUR ONE FAMILY?!
I TENDED TO THOUSANDS!
GNHH!
WE HAD A PERFECT WORLD HERE ON SPYRE! A PARADISE! WITH EVERYTHING IN ITS PROPER PLACE.
WHY WOULD OU COME HERE GAINST OUR WILL?!
WHO GAVE YOU THAT RIGHT?!
THERE WAS NO NEED TO--
YOU LEFT ME NO CHOICE!
YOU FORCED MY HAND!
THE ONLY DEFENSE AGAINST YOU--
--WAS TO BECOME JUST LIKE YOU!
GYAHH!
BECAUSE OF YOU--
--I TURNED MY PEOPLE, MY FRIENDS--
--MY FAMILY--
--INTO MONSTERS!

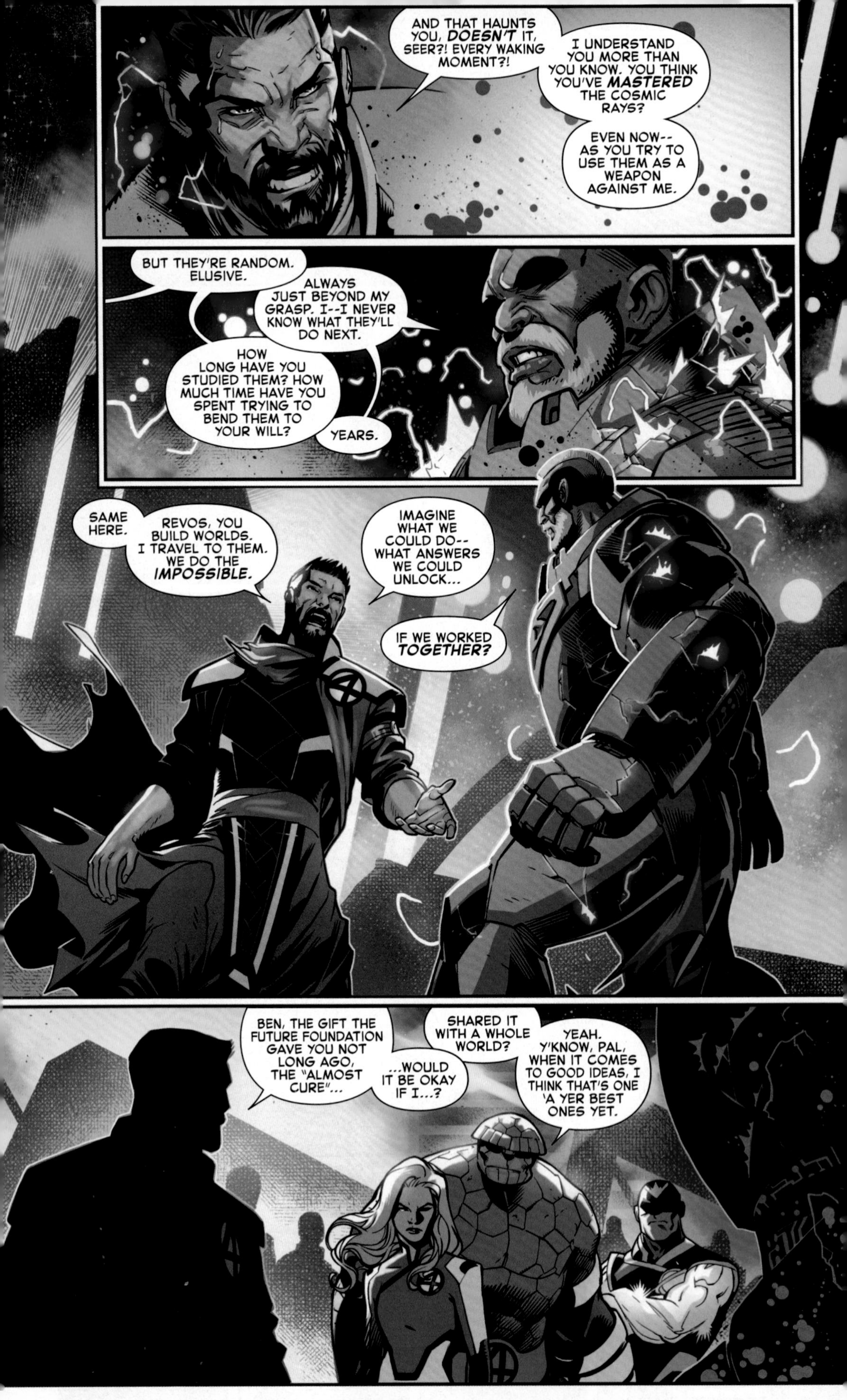

AND THAT HAUNTS YOU, *DOESN'T* IT, SEER?! EVERY WAKING MOMENT?!
I UNDERSTAND YOU MORE THAN YOU KNOW. YOU THINK YOU'VE *MASTERED* THE COSMIC RAYS?
EVEN NOW-- AS YOU TRY TO USE THEM AS A WEAPON AGAINST ME.
BUT THEY'RE RANDOM. ELUSIVE.
ALWAYS JUST BEYOND MY GRASP. I--I NEVER KNOW WHAT THEY'LL DO NEXT.
HOW LONG HAVE YOU STUDIED THEM? HOW MUCH TIME HAVE YOU SPENT TRYING TO BEND THEM TO YOUR WILL?
YEARS.
SAME HERE.
REVOS, YOU BUILD WORLDS. I TRAVEL TO THEM. WE DO THE *IMPOSSIBLE.*
IMAGINE WHAT WE COULD DO-- WHAT ANSWERS WE COULD UNLOCK...
IF WE WORKED *TOGETHER?*
BEN, THE GIFT THE FUTURE FOUNDATION GAVE YOU NOT LONG AGO, THE "ALMOST CURE"...
...WOULD IT BE OKAY IF I...?
SHARED IT WITH A WHOLE WORLD?
YEAH. Y'KNOW, PAL, WHEN IT COMES TO GOOD IDEAS, I THINK THAT'S ONE 'A YER BEST ONES YET.

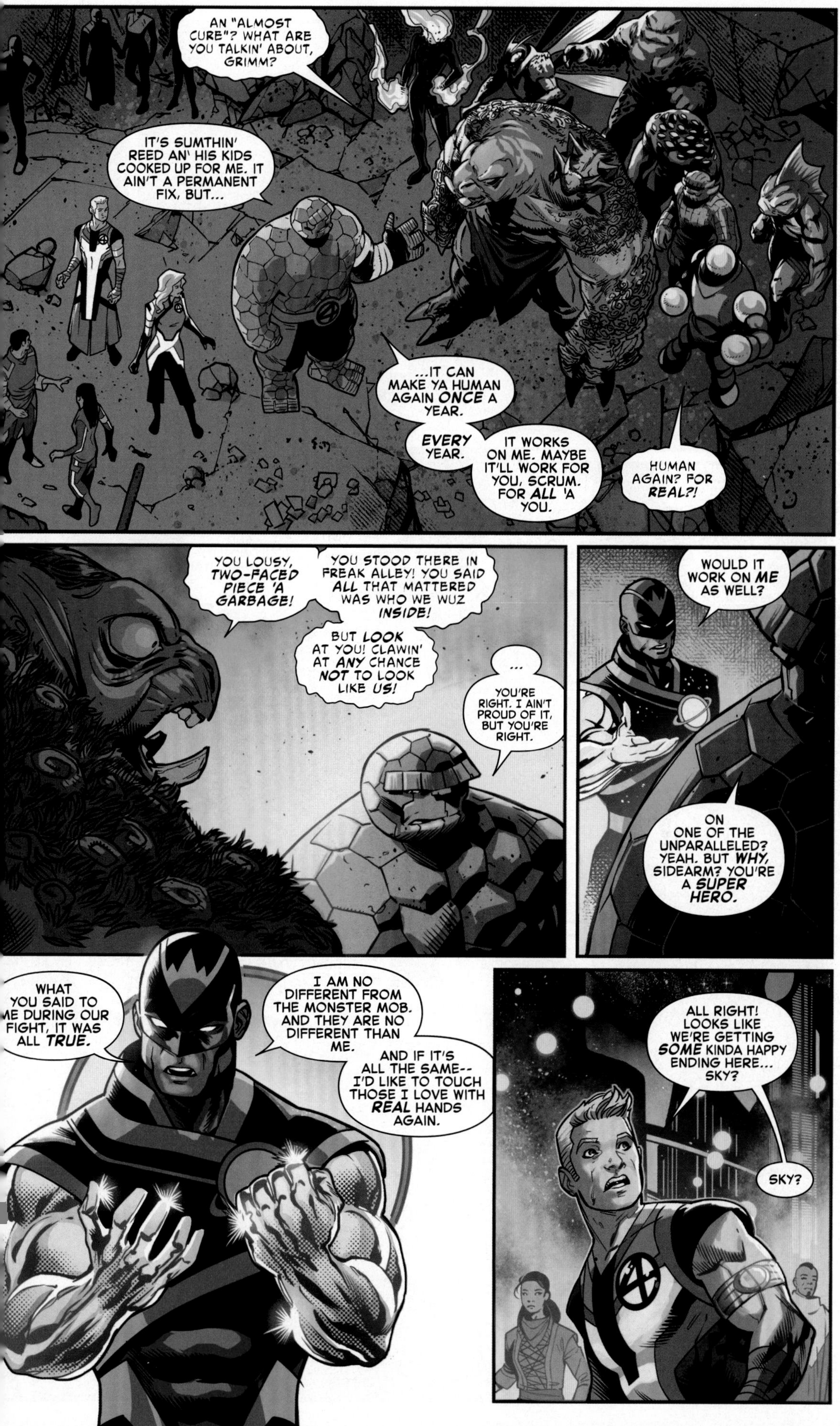
AN "ALMOST CURE"? WHAT ARE YOU TALKIN' ABOUT, GRIMM?
IT'S SUMTHIN' REED AN' HIS KIDS COOKED UP FOR ME. IT AIN'T A PERMANENT FIX, BUT...
...IT CAN MAKE YA HUMAN AGAIN ONCE A YEAR.
EVERY YEAR.
IT WORKS ON ME. MAYBE IT'LL WORK FOR YOU, SCRUM. FOR ALL 'A YOU.
HUMAN AGAIN? FOR REAL?!
YOU LOUSY, TWO-FACED PIECE 'A GARBAGE!
YOU STOOD THERE IN FREAK ALLEY! YOU SAID ALL THAT MATTERED WAS WHO WE WUZ INSIDE!
BUT LOOK AT YOU! CLAWIN' AT ANY CHANCE NOT TO LOOK LIKE US!
...
YOU'RE RIGHT. I AIN'T PROUD OF IT, BUT YOU'RE RIGHT.
WOULD IT WORK ON ME AS WELL?
ON ONE OF THE UNPARALLELED? YEAH. BUT WHY, SIDEARM? YOU'RE A SUPER HERO.
WHAT YOU SAID TO ME DURING OUR FIGHT, IT WAS ALL TRUE.
I AM NO DIFFERENT FROM THE MONSTER MOB. AND THEY ARE NO DIFFERENT THAN ME.
AND IF IT'S ALL THE SAME-- I'D LIKE TO TOUCH THOSE I LOVE WITH REAL HANDS AGAIN.
ALL RIGHT! LOOKS LIKE WE'RE GETTING SOME KINDA HAPPY ENDING HERE... SKY?
SKY?

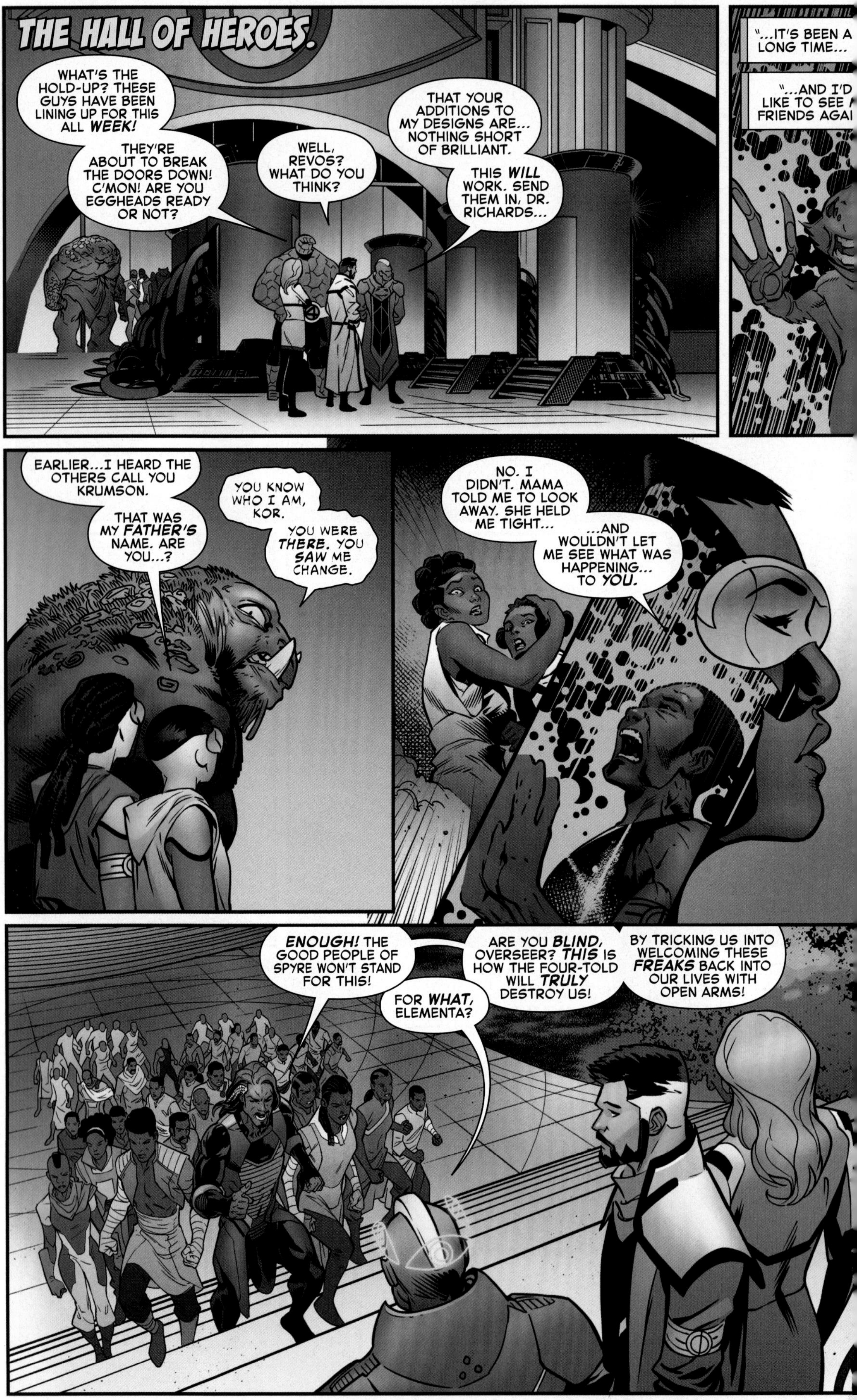
THE HALL OF HEROES.
WHAT'S THE HOLD-UP? THESE GUYS HAVE BEEN LINING UP FOR THIS ALL WEEK!
THEY'RE ABOUT TO BREAK THE DOORS DOWN! C'MON! ARE YOU EGGHEADS READY OR NOT?
WELL, REVOS? WHAT DO YOU THINK?
THAT YOUR ADDITIONS TO MY DESIGNS ARE... NOTHING SHORT OF BRILLIANT.
THIS WILL WORK. SEND THEM IN, DR. RICHARDS...
"...IT'S BEEN A LONG TIME...
"...AND I'D LIKE TO SEE FRIENDS AGAI
EARLIER...I HEARD THE OTHERS CALL YOU KRUMSON.
THAT WAS MY FATHER'S NAME. ARE YOU...?
YOU KNOW WHO I AM, KOR.
YOU WERE THERE. YOU SAW ME CHANGE.
NO. I DIDN'T. MAMA TOLD ME TO LOOK AWAY. SHE HELD ME TIGHT...
...AND WOULDN'T LET ME SEE WHAT WAS HAPPENING... TO YOU.
ENOUGH! THE GOOD PEOPLE OF SPYRE WON'T STAND FOR THIS!
FOR WHAT, ELEMENTA?
ARE YOU BLIND, OVERSEER? THIS IS HOW THE FOUR-TOLD WILL TRULY DESTROY US!
BY TRICKING US INTO WELCOMING THESE FREAKS BACK INTO OUR LIVES WITH OPEN ARMS!

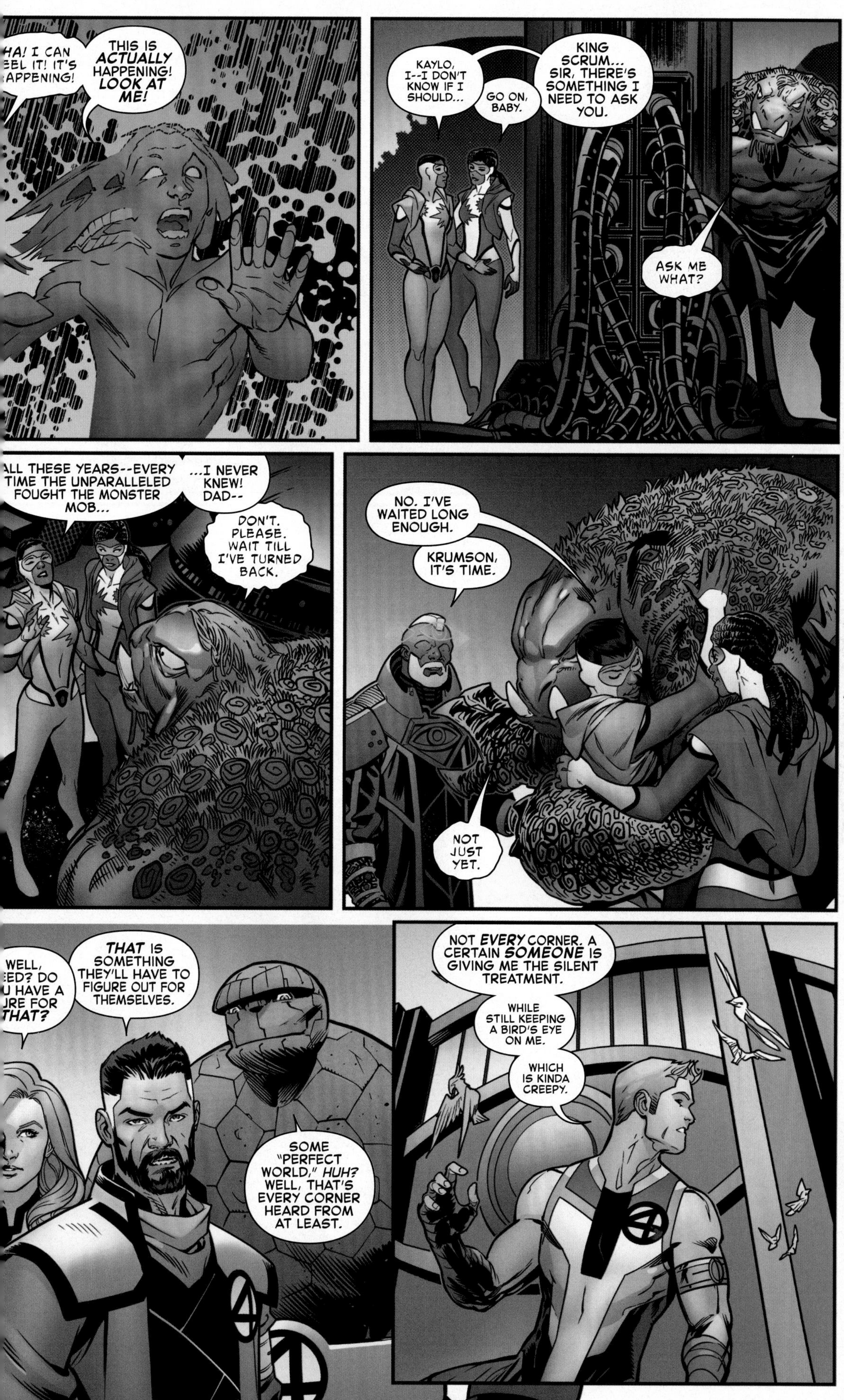
HA! I CAN EEL IT! IT'S APPENING!
THIS IS ACTUALLY HAPPENING! LOOK AT ME!
KAYLO, I--I DON'T KNOW IF I SHOULD...
GO ON, BABY.
KING SCRUM... SIR, THERE'S SOMETHING I NEED TO ASK YOU.
ASK ME WHAT?
ALL THESE YEARS--EVERY TIME THE UNPARALLELED FOUGHT THE MONSTER MOB...
...I NEVER KNEW! DAD--
DON'T. PLEASE. WAIT TILL I'VE TURNED BACK.
NO. I'VE WAITED LONG ENOUGH.
KRUMSON, IT'S TIME.
NOT JUST YET.
WELL, EED? DO U HAVE A URE FOR THAT?
THAT IS SOMETHING THEY'LL HAVE TO FIGURE OUT FOR THEMSELVES.
SOME "PERFECT WORLD," HUH? WELL, THAT'S EVERY CORNER HEARD FROM AT LEAST.
NOT EVERY CORNER. A CERTAIN SOMEONE IS GIVING ME THE SILENT TREATMENT.
WHILE STILL KEEPING A BIRD'S EYE ON ME.
WHICH IS KINDA CREEPY.

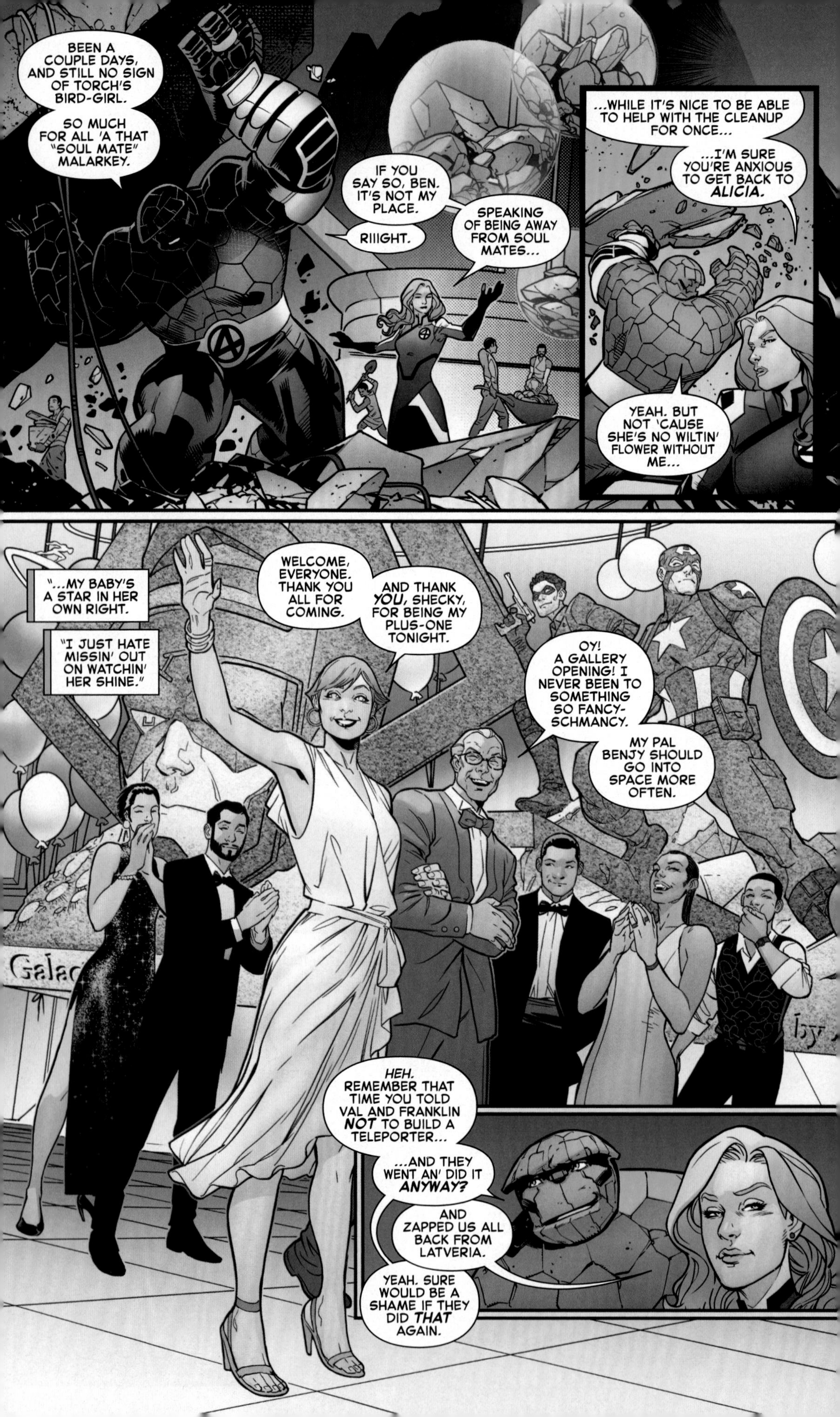

BEEN A COUPLE DAYS, AND STILL NO SIGN OF TORCH'S BIRD-GIRL.
SO MUCH FOR ALL 'A THAT "SOUL MATE" MALARKEY.
IF YOU SAY SO, BEN. IT'S NOT MY PLACE.
RIIIGHT.
SPEAKING OF BEING AWAY FROM SOUL MATES...
...WHILE IT'S NICE TO BE ABLE TO HELP WITH THE CLEANUP FOR ONCE...
...I'M SURE YOU'RE ANXIOUS TO GET BACK TO ALICIA.
YEAH. BUT NOT 'CAUSE SHE'S NO WILTIN' FLOWER WITHOUT ME...
"...MY BABY'S A STAR IN HER OWN RIGHT.
"I JUST HATE MISSIN' OUT ON WATCHIN' HER SHINE."
WELCOME, EVERYONE. THANK YOU ALL FOR COMING.
AND THANK YOU, SHECKY, FOR BEING MY PLUS-ONE TONIGHT.
OY! A GALLERY OPENING! I NEVER BEEN TO SOMETHING SO FANCY-SCHMANCY.
MY PAL BENJY SHOULD GO INTO SPACE MORE OFTEN.
Galac
by
HEH. REMEMBER THAT TIME YOU TOLD VAL AND FRANKLIN NOT TO BUILD A TELEPORTER...
...AND THEY WENT AN' DID IT ANYWAY?
AND ZAPPED US ALL BACK FROM LATVERIA.
YEAH. SURE WOULD BE A SHAME IF THEY DID THAT AGAIN.

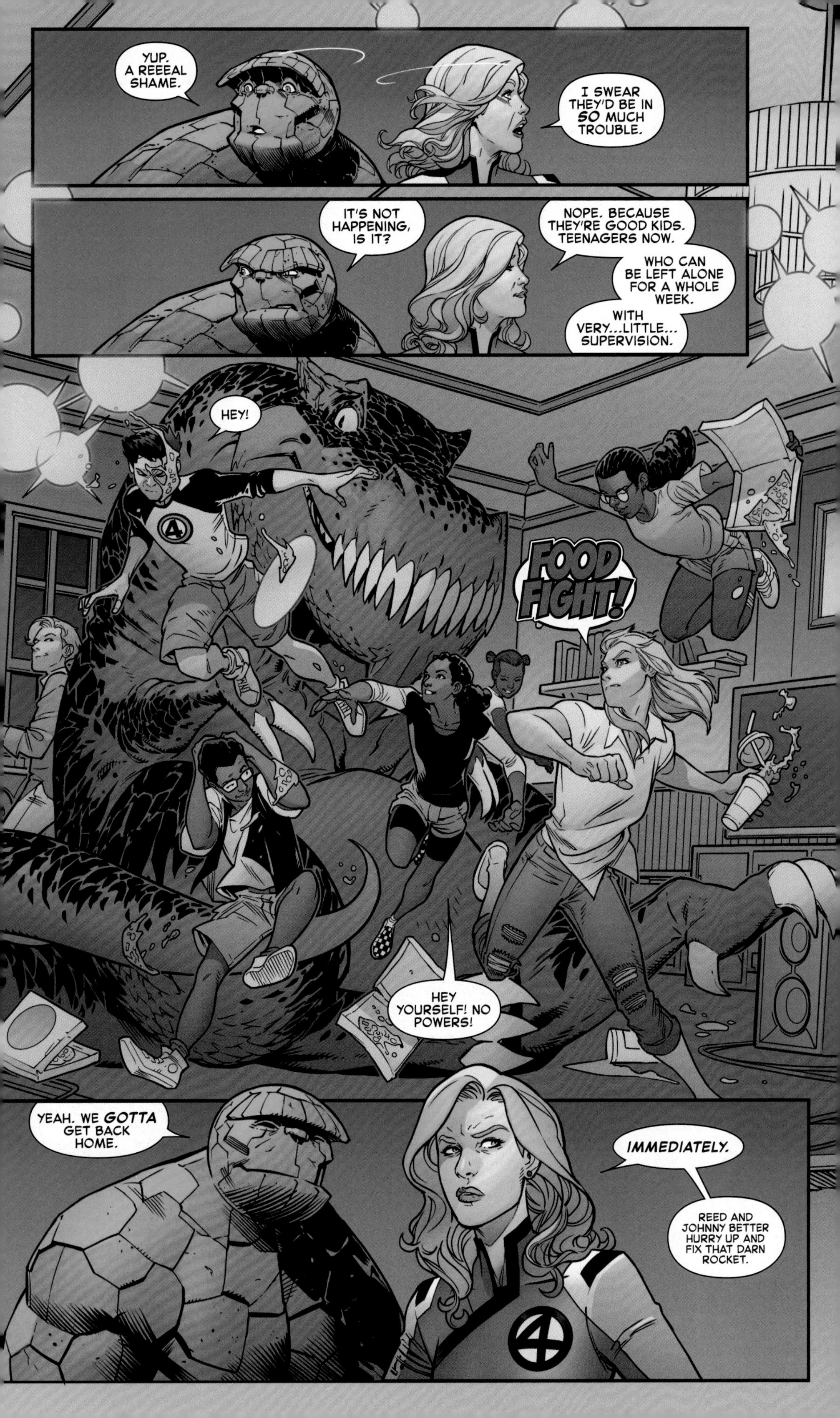
YUP. A REEEAL SHAME.
I SWEAR THEY'D BE IN SO MUCH TROUBLE.
IT'S NOT HAPPENING, IS IT?
NOPE. BECAUSE THEY'RE GOOD KIDS. TEENAGERS NOW.
WHO CAN BE LEFT ALONE FOR A WHOLE WEEK.
WITH VERY...LITTLE... SUPERVISION.
HEY!
FOOD FIGHT!
HEY YOURSELF! NO POWERS!
YEAH. WE GOTTA GET BACK HOME.
IMMEDIATELY.
REED AND JOHNNY BETTER HURRY UP AND FIX THAT DARN ROCKET.

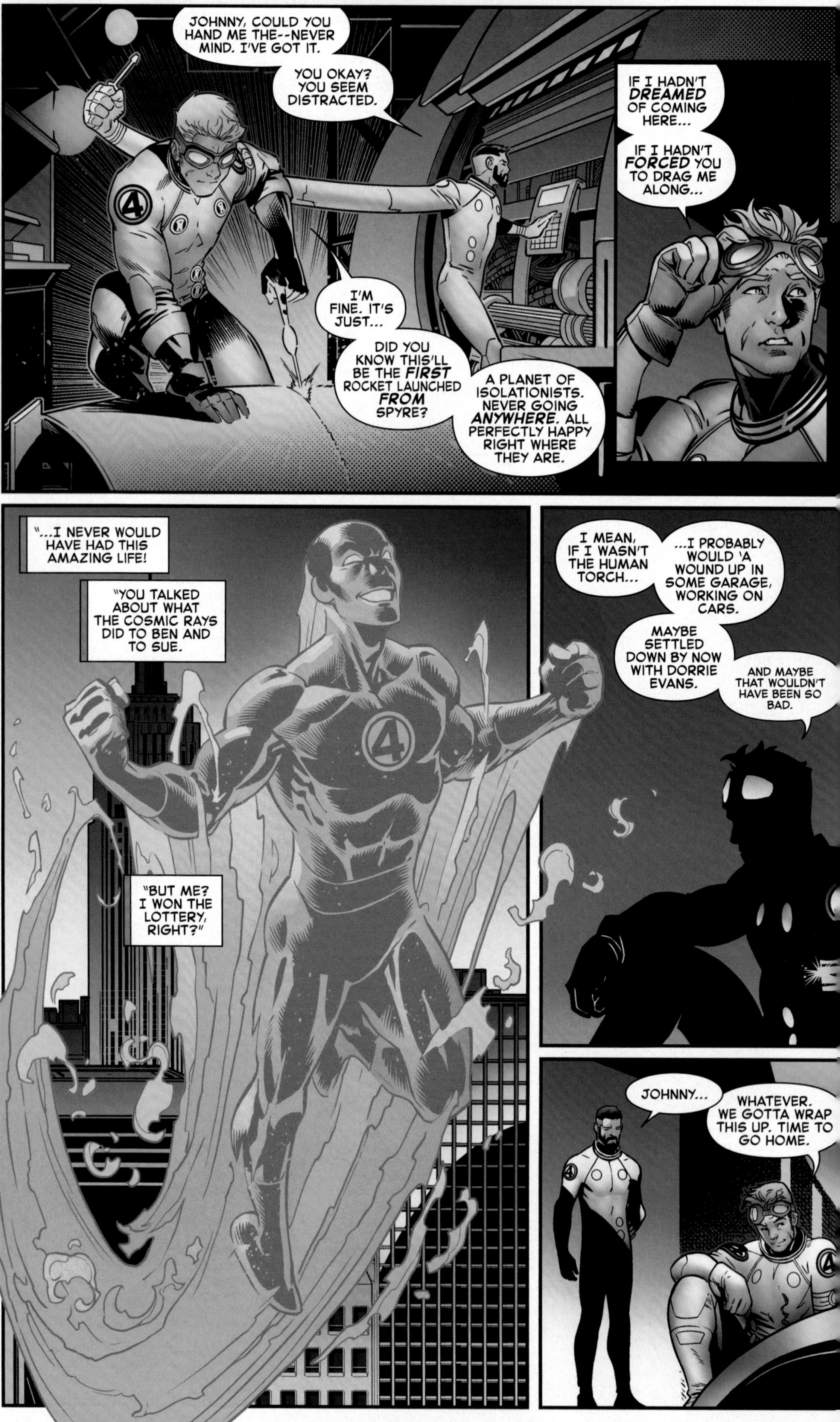

JOHNNY, COULD YOU HAND ME THE--NEVER MIND. I'VE GOT IT.
YOU OKAY? YOU SEEM DISTRACTED.
I'M FINE. IT'S JUST...
DID YOU KNOW THIS'LL BE THE FIRST ROCKET LAUNCHED FROM SPYRE?
A PLANET OF ISOLATIONISTS. NEVER GOING ANYWHERE. ALL PERFECTLY HAPPY RIGHT WHERE THEY ARE.
IF I HADN'T DREAMED OF COMING HERE...
IF I HADN'T FORCED YOU TO DRAG ME ALONG...
"...I NEVER WOULD HAVE HAD THIS AMAZING LIFE!
"YOU TALKED ABOUT WHAT THE COSMIC RAYS DID TO BEN AND TO SUE.
"BUT ME? I WON THE LOTTERY, RIGHT?"
I MEAN, IF I WASN'T THE HUMAN TORCH...
...I PROBABLY WOULD 'A WOUND UP IN SOME GARAGE, WORKING ON CARS.
MAYBE SETTLED DOWN BY NOW WITH DORRIE EVANS.
AND MAYBE THAT WOULDN'T HAVE BEEN SO BAD.
JOHNNY...
WHATEVER. WE GOTTA WRAP THIS UP. TIME TO GO HOME.

FAREWELL, DOCTOR RICHARDS. I KNOW THIS SOUNDS ODD, BUT...

...I DO HOPE WE'LL MEET AGAIN. THERE IS SO MUCH WE CAN LEARN FROM EACH OTHER.

AGREED. ESPECIALLY WHEN IT COMES TO THESE "SOUL BINDINGS."

I GUESS THIS PROVES IT THEN, DEAR. I'M YOURS AND YOU'RE MINE.

AND THERE AREN'T ANY...FEMALE ARCHAEOLOGISTS IN THE MIX.

HEH. WHO AM I TO ARGUE WITH SCIENCE?

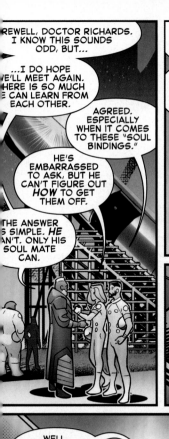

HE'S EMBARRASSED TO ASK, BUT HE CAN'T FIGURE OUT *HOW* TO GET THEM OFF.

THE ANSWER IS SIMPLE. *HE* CAN'T. ONLY HIS SOUL MATE CAN.

HEY, BEN, HOW'D YOU AVOID GETTING ONE OF THESE SLAPPED ON YOU?

HOW *COULD* THEY, JUNIOR?

WHEN YOURS TRULY IS ALREADY SPOKEN FOR?

WELL, WHADDAYA KNOW. HERE COMES *YOUR* BALL AND CHAIN NOW.

KNOCK IT OFF.

KID, YOU REMEMBER WHAT I TOLD YOU A WHILE BACK? ABOUT THE NEXT TIME YOU GOT A CHANCE LIKE THIS...

YOU SAID I SHOULD DIVE RIGHT IN AND "NOT WAIT FOR STRONGER SHIELDING."

YEAH. WELL, NEVER LISTEN TO ME. I'M AN IDIOT.

JOHNNY, I...

YOU WANT ME TO TAKE OFF *YOUR* INTERSTELLAR FRIENDSHIP BRACELET BEFORE WE SCOOT?

I GET IT.

NO. YOU DON'T.

HUH?

YOU CAN KEEP YOURS, TOO.

WHAT? NO! TAKE IT OFF.

I REFUSE. NOW, ABOUT THIS ROCKET SHIP OF YOURS...

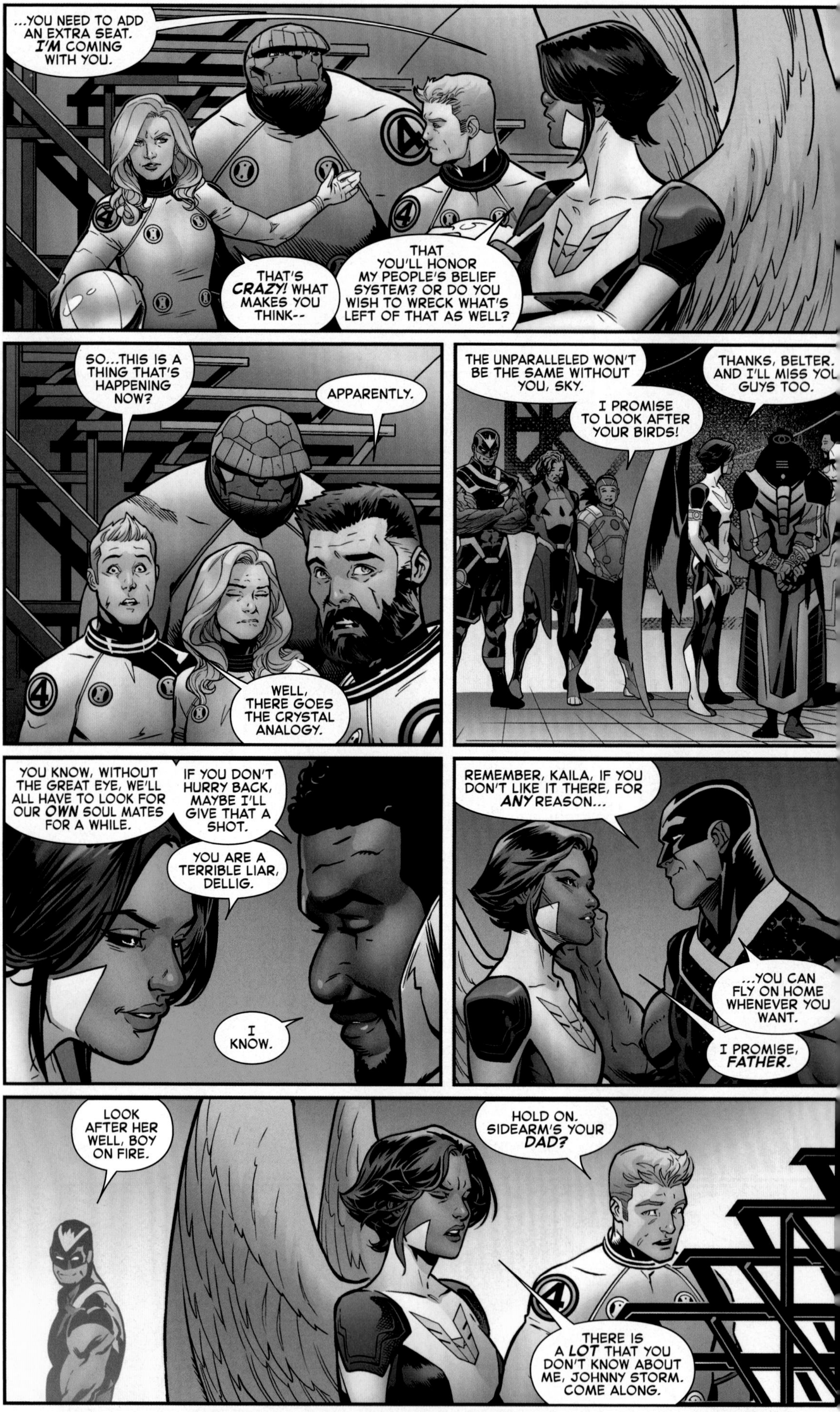

...YOU NEED TO ADD AN EXTRA SEAT. I'M COMING WITH YOU.
THAT'S CRAZY! WHAT MAKES YOU THINK--
THAT YOU'LL HONOR MY PEOPLE'S BELIEF SYSTEM? OR DO YOU WISH TO WRECK WHAT'S LEFT OF THAT AS WELL?
SO...THIS IS A THING THAT'S HAPPENING NOW?
APPARENTLY.
WELL, THERE GOES THE CRYSTAL ANALOGY.
THE UNPARALLELED WON'T BE THE SAME WITHOUT YOU, SKY.
I PROMISE TO LOOK AFTER YOUR BIRDS!
THANKS, BELTER. AND I'LL MISS YOU GUYS TOO.
YOU KNOW, WITHOUT THE GREAT EYE, WE'LL ALL HAVE TO LOOK FOR OUR OWN SOUL MATES FOR A WHILE.
IF YOU DON'T HURRY BACK, MAYBE I'LL GIVE THAT A SHOT.
YOU ARE A TERRIBLE LIAR, DELLIG.
I KNOW.
REMEMBER, KAILA, IF YOU DON'T LIKE IT THERE, FOR ANY REASON...
...YOU CAN FLY ON HOME WHENEVER YOU WANT.
I PROMISE, FATHER.
LOOK AFTER HER WELL, BOY ON FIRE.
HOLD ON. SIDEARM'S YOUR DAD?
THERE IS A LOT THAT YOU DON'T KNOW ABOUT ME, JOHNNY STORM. COME ALONG.

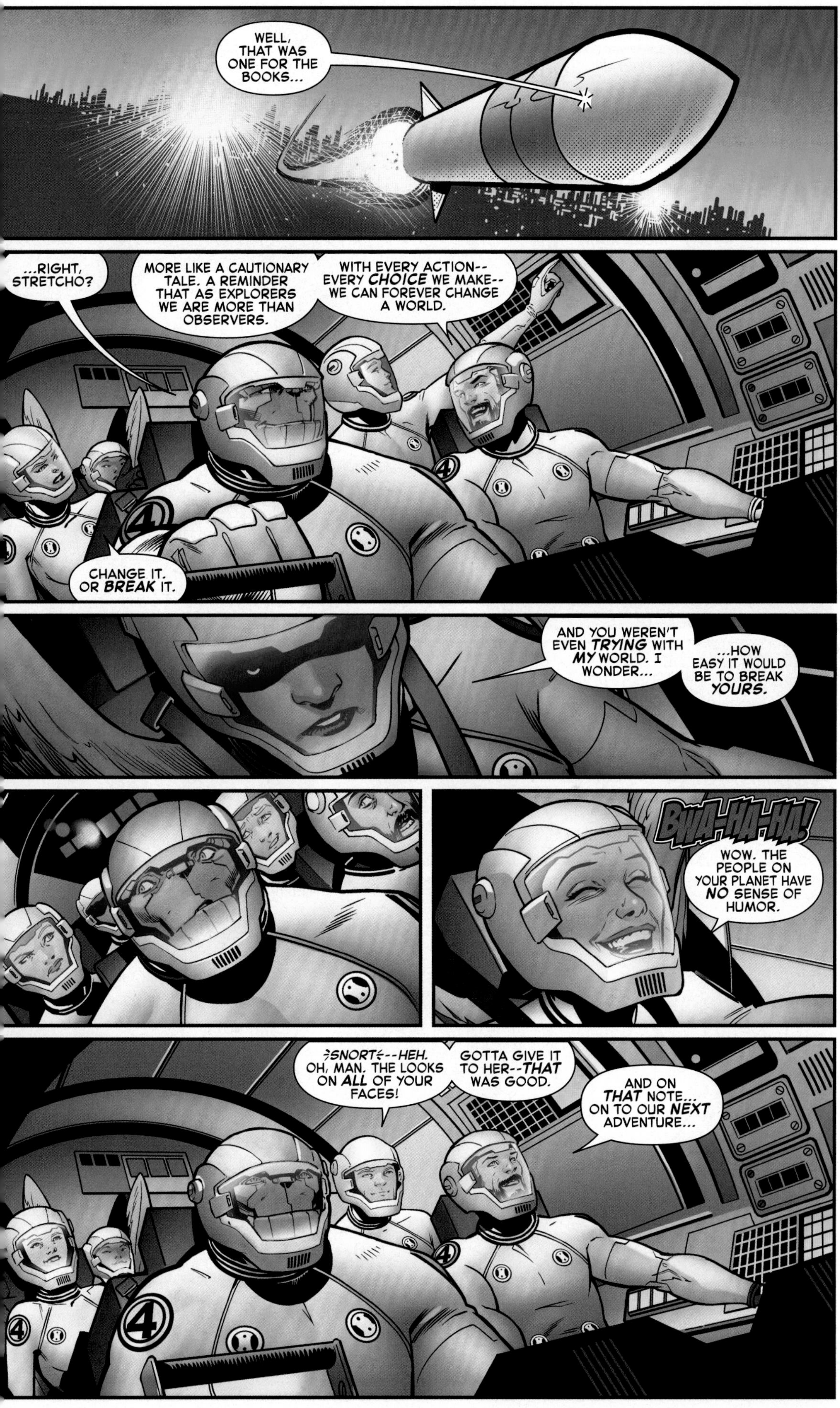
WELL, THAT WAS ONE FOR THE BOOKS...
...RIGHT, STRETCHO?
MORE LIKE A CAUTIONARY TALE. A REMINDER THAT AS EXPLORERS WE ARE MORE THAN OBSERVERS.
WITH EVERY ACTION-- EVERY CHOICE WE MAKE-- WE CAN FOREVER CHANGE A WORLD.
CHANGE IT. OR BREAK IT.
AND YOU WEREN'T EVEN TRYING WITH MY WORLD. I WONDER...
...HOW EASY IT WOULD BE TO BREAK YOURS.
BWA-HA-HA!
WOW. THE PEOPLE ON YOUR PLANET HAVE NO SENSE OF HUMOR.
SNORT--HEH. OH, MAN. THE LOOKS ON ALL OF YOUR FACES!
GOTTA GIVE IT TO HER--THAT WAS GOOD.
AND ON THAT NOTE... ON TO OUR NEXT ADVENTURE...

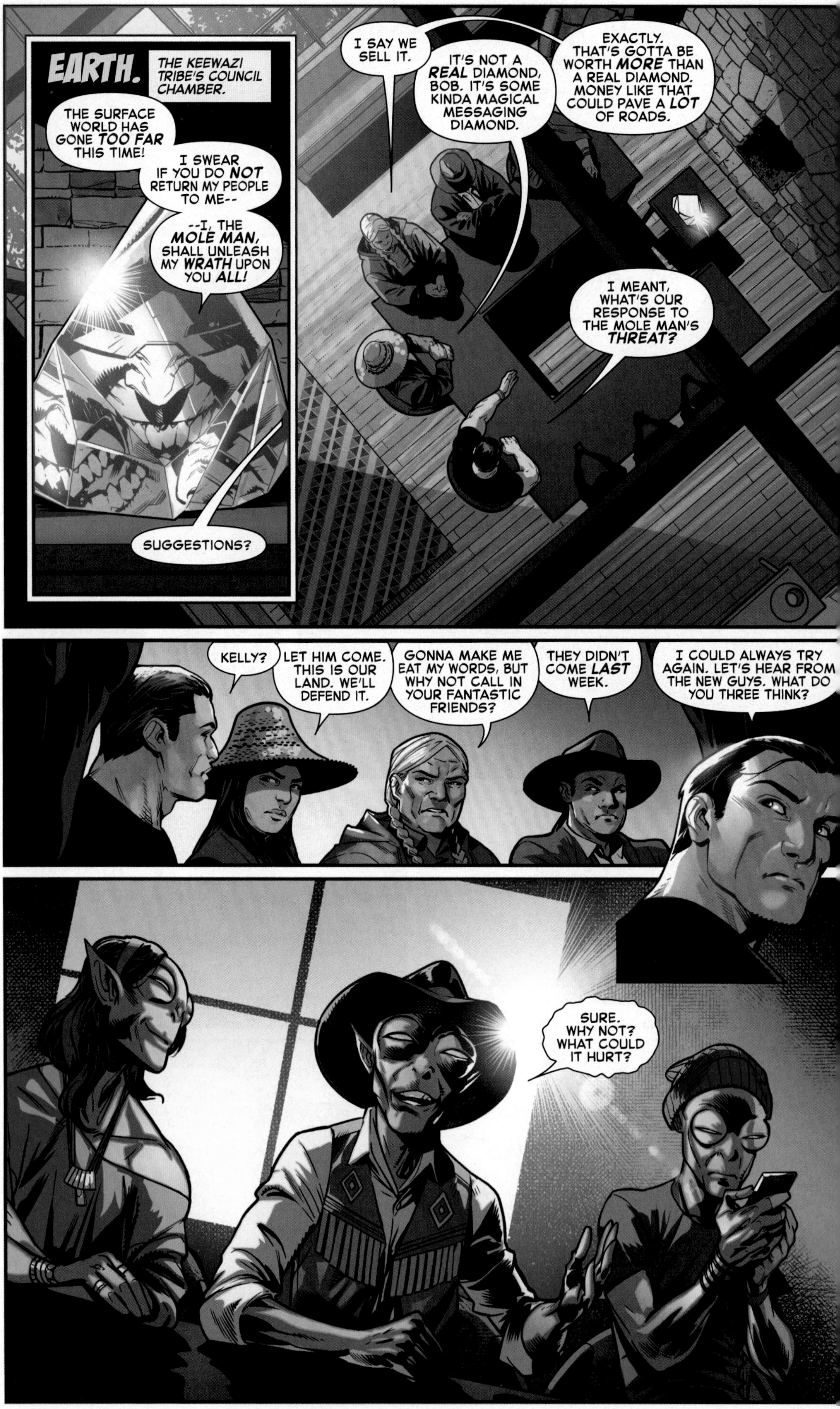
EARTH.
THE KEEWAZI TRIBE'S COUNCIL CHAMBER.
THE SURFACE WORLD HAS GONE TOO FAR THIS TIME!
I SWEAR IF YOU DO NOT RETURN MY PEOPLE TO ME--
--I, THE MOLE MAN, SHALL UNLEASH MY WRATH UPON YOU ALL!
SUGGESTIONS?
I SAY WE SELL IT.
IT'S NOT A REAL DIAMOND, BOB. IT'S SOME KINDA MAGICAL MESSAGING DIAMOND.
EXACTLY. THAT'S GOTTA BE WORTH MORE THAN A REAL DIAMOND. MONEY LIKE THAT COULD PAVE A LOT OF ROADS.
I MEANT, WHAT'S OUR RESPONSE TO THE MOLE MAN'S THREAT?
KELLY?
LET HIM COME. THIS IS OUR LAND. WE'LL DEFEND IT.
GONNA MAKE ME EAT MY WORDS, BUT WHY NOT CALL IN YOUR FANTASTIC FRIENDS?
THEY DIDN'T COME LAST WEEK.
I COULD ALWAYS TRY AGAIN. LET'S HEAR FROM THE NEW GUYS. WHAT DO YOU THREE THINK?
SURE. WHY NOT? WHAT COULD IT HURT?

20

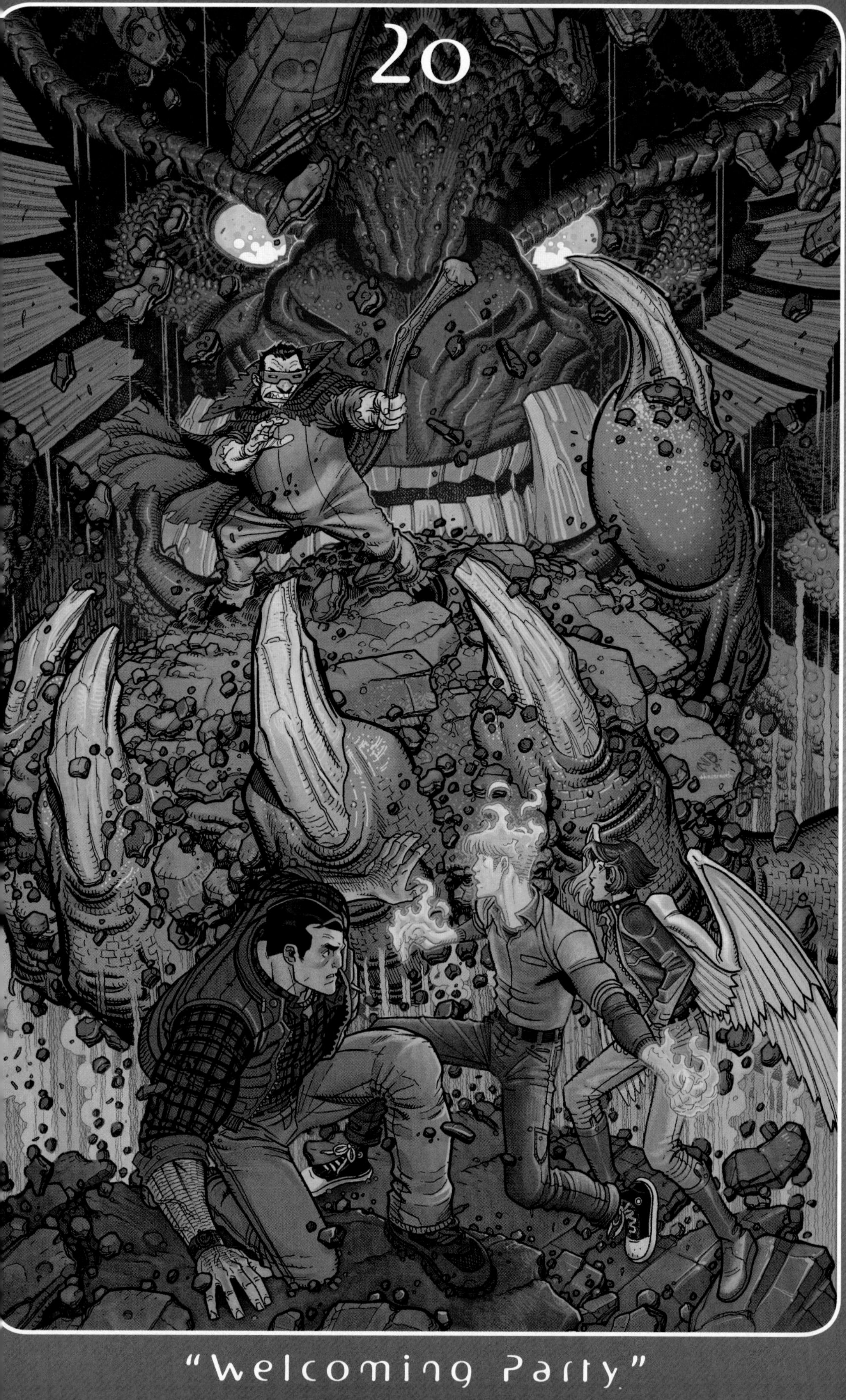

"Welcoming Party"

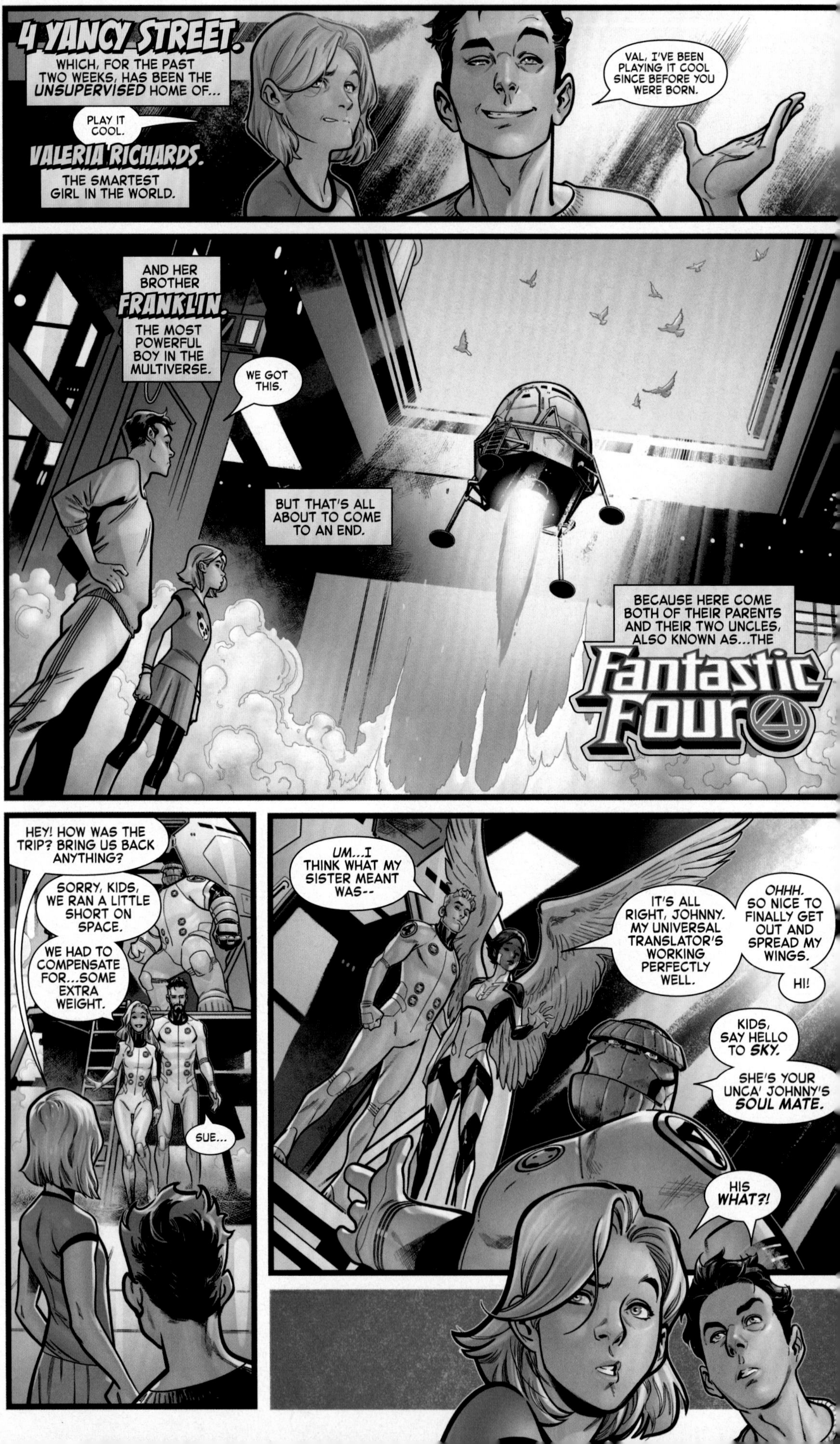
4 YANCY STREET.
WHICH, FOR THE PAST TWO WEEKS, HAS BEEN THE UNSUPERVISED HOME OF...
PLAY IT COOL.
VALERIA RICHARDS.
THE SMARTEST GIRL IN THE WORLD.
VAL, I'VE BEEN PLAYING IT COOL SINCE BEFORE YOU WERE BORN.
AND HER BROTHER
FRANKLIN.
THE MOST POWERFUL BOY IN THE MULTIVERSE.
WE GOT THIS.
BUT THAT'S ALL ABOUT TO COME TO AN END.
BECAUSE HERE COME BOTH OF THEIR PARENTS AND THEIR TWO UNCLES, ALSO KNOWN AS...THE
Fantastic Four
HEY! HOW WAS THE TRIP? BRING US BACK ANYTHING?
SORRY, KIDS, WE RAN A LITTLE SHORT ON SPACE.
WE HAD TO COMPENSATE FOR...SOME EXTRA WEIGHT.
SUE...
UM...I THINK WHAT MY SISTER MEANT WAS--
IT'S ALL RIGHT, JOHNNY. MY UNIVERSAL TRANSLATOR'S WORKING PERFECTLY WELL.
OHHH. SO NICE TO FINALLY GET OUT AND SPREAD MY WINGS.
HI!
KIDS, SAY HELLO TO SKY.
SHE'S YOUR UNCA' JOHNNY'S SOUL MATE.
HIS WHAT?!

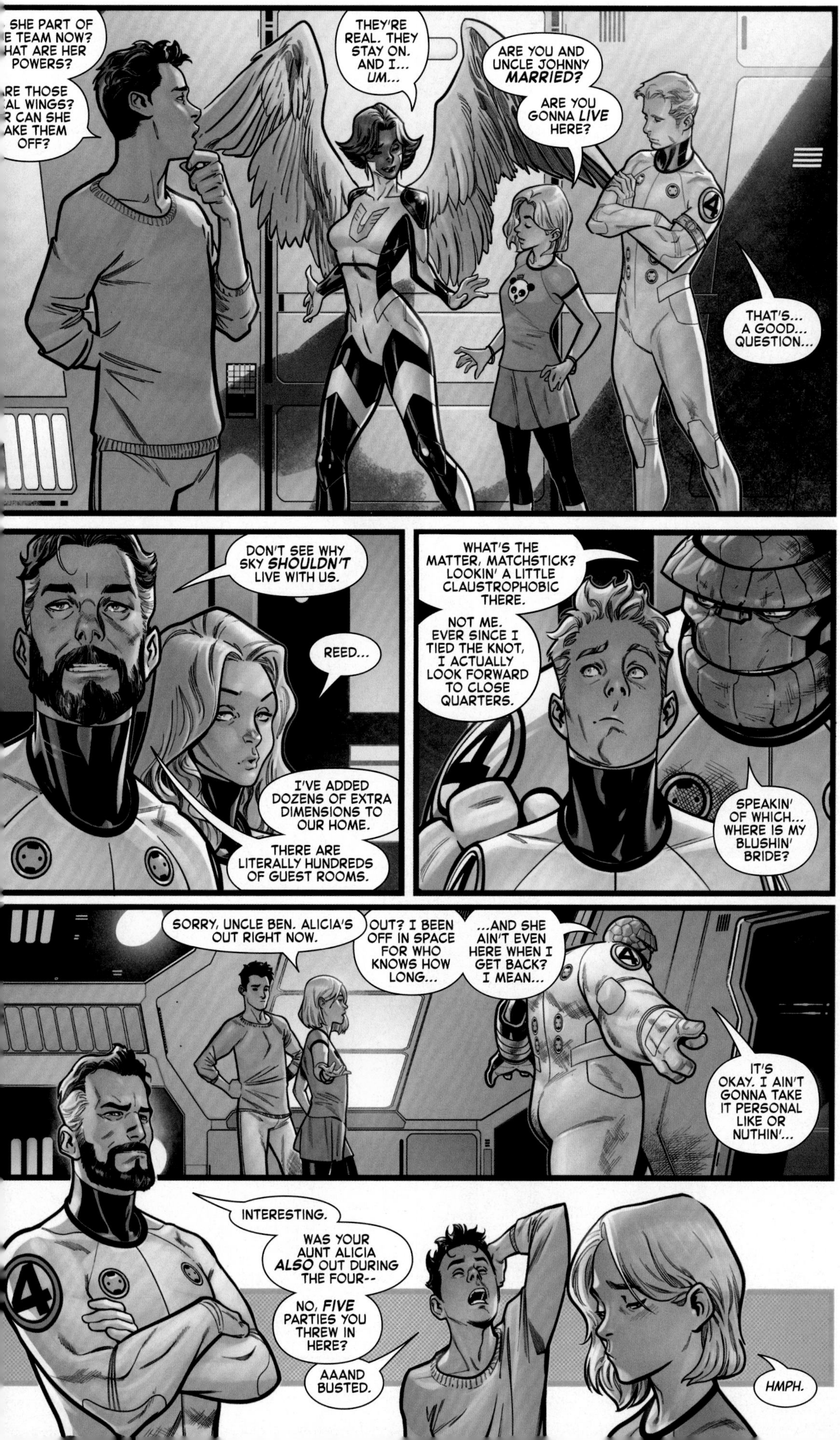
SHE PART OF
E TEAM NOW?
HAT ARE HER
POWERS?
RE THOSE
AL WINGS?
R CAN SHE
AKE THEM
OFF?
THEY'RE REAL. THEY STAY ON. AND I... UM...
ARE YOU AND UNCLE JOHNNY MARRIED?
ARE YOU GONNA LIVE HERE?
THAT'S... A GOOD... QUESTION...
DON'T SEE WHY SKY SHOULDN'T LIVE WITH US.
REED...
I'VE ADDED DOZENS OF EXTRA DIMENSIONS TO OUR HOME.
THERE ARE LITERALLY HUNDREDS OF GUEST ROOMS.
WHAT'S THE MATTER, MATCHSTICK? LOOKIN' A LITTLE CLAUSTROPHOBIC THERE.
NOT ME. EVER SINCE I TIED THE KNOT, I ACTUALLY LOOK FORWARD TO CLOSE QUARTERS.
SPEAKIN' OF WHICH... WHERE IS MY BLUSHIN' BRIDE?
SORRY, UNCLE BEN. ALICIA'S OUT RIGHT NOW.
OUT? I BEEN OFF IN SPACE FOR WHO KNOWS HOW LONG...
...AND SHE AIN'T EVEN HERE WHEN I GET BACK? I MEAN...
IT'S OKAY. I AIN'T GONNA TAKE IT PERSONAL LIKE OR NUTHIN'...
INTERESTING.
WAS YOUR AUNT ALICIA ALSO OUT DURING THE FOUR--
NO, FIVE PARTIES YOU THREW IN HERE?
AAAND BUSTED.
HMPH.

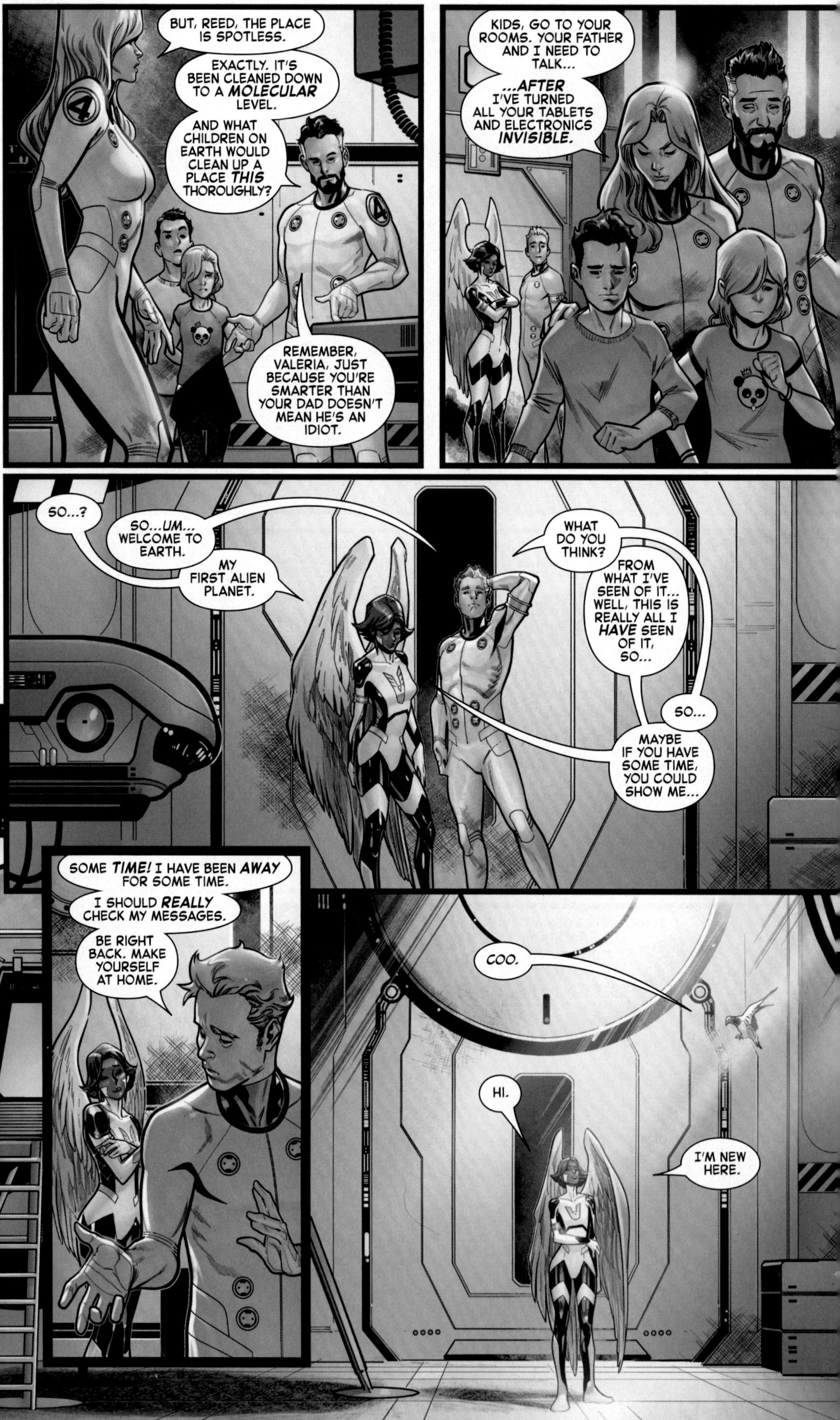
BUT, REED, THE PLACE IS SPOTLESS.
EXACTLY. IT'S BEEN CLEANED DOWN TO A ***MOLECULAR*** LEVEL.
AND WHAT CHILDREN ON EARTH WOULD CLEAN UP A PLACE ***THIS*** THOROUGHLY?
REMEMBER, VALERIA, JUST BECAUSE YOU'RE SMARTER THAN YOUR DAD DOESN'T MEAN HE'S AN IDIOT.
KIDS, GO TO YOUR ROOMS. YOUR FATHER AND I NEED TO TALK...
...AFTER I'VE TURNED ALL YOUR TABLETS AND ELECTRONICS ***INVISIBLE.***
SO...?
SO...UM... WELCOME TO EARTH.
MY FIRST ALIEN PLANET.
WHAT DO YOU THINK?
FROM WHAT I'VE SEEN OF IT... WELL, THIS IS REALLY ALL I ***HAVE*** SEEN OF IT, SO...
SO...
MAYBE IF YOU HAVE SOME TIME, YOU COULD SHOW ME...
SOME ***TIME!*** I HAVE BEEN ***AWAY*** FOR SOME TIME.
I SHOULD ***REALLY*** CHECK MY MESSAGES.
BE RIGHT BACK. MAKE YOURSELF AT HOME.
COO.
HI.
I'M NEW HERE.

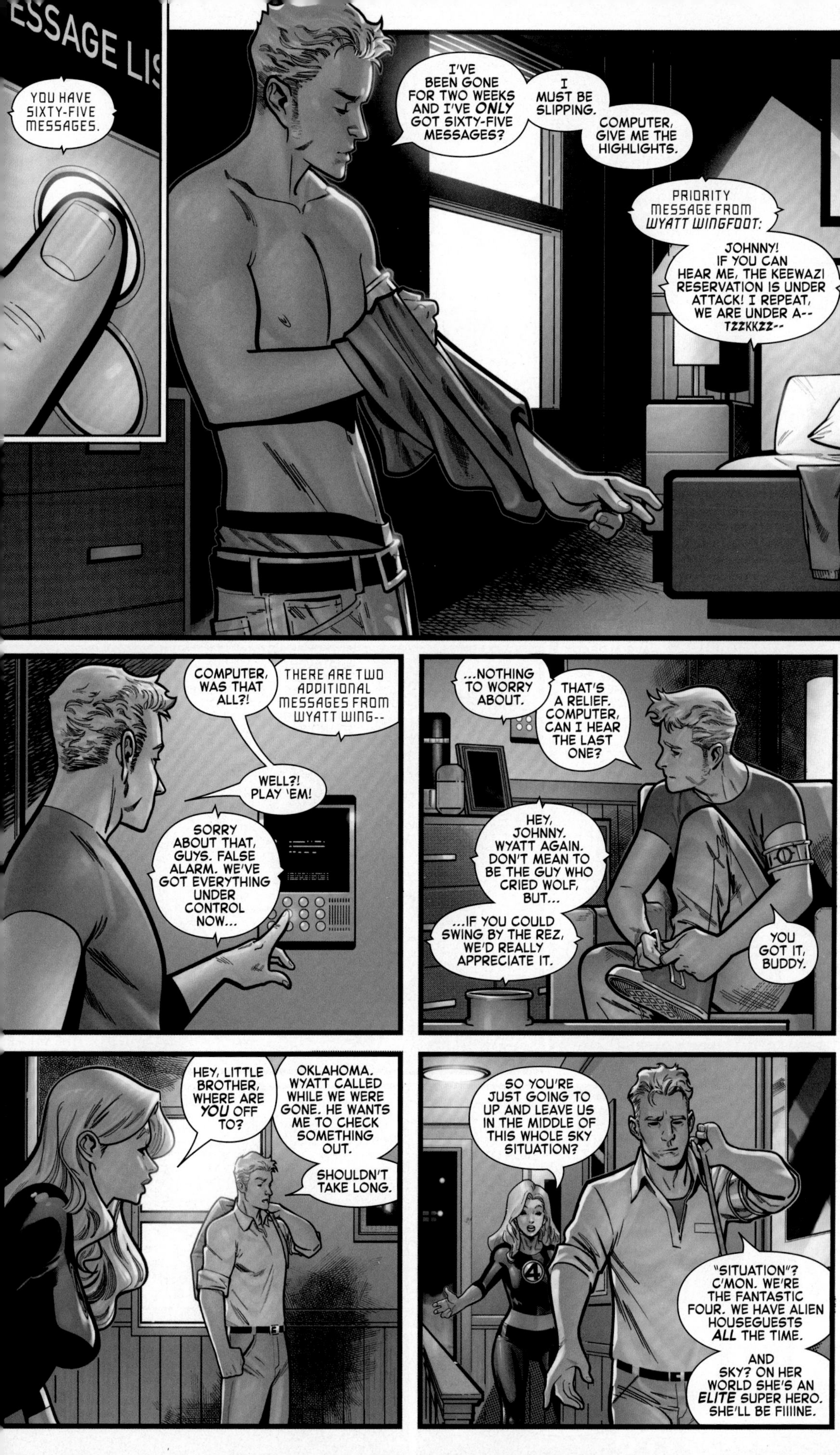
ESSAGE LIS
YOU HAVE SIXTY-FIVE MESSAGES.
I'VE BEEN GONE FOR TWO WEEKS AND I'VE ONLY GOT SIXTY-FIVE MESSAGES?
I MUST BE SLIPPING.
COMPUTER, GIVE ME THE HIGHLIGHTS.
PRIORITY MESSAGE FROM WYATT WINGFOOT:
JOHNNY! IF YOU CAN HEAR ME, THE KEEWAZI RESERVATION IS UNDER ATTACK! I REPEAT, WE ARE UNDER A-- TZZKKZZ--
COMPUTER, WAS THAT ALL?!
THERE ARE TWO ADDITIONAL MESSAGES FROM WYATT WING--
WELL?! PLAY 'EM!
SORRY ABOUT THAT, GUYS. FALSE ALARM. WE'VE GOT EVERYTHING UNDER CONTROL NOW...
...NOTHING TO WORRY ABOUT.
THAT'S A RELIEF. COMPUTER, CAN I HEAR THE LAST ONE?
HEY, JOHNNY. WYATT AGAIN. DON'T MEAN TO BE THE GUY WHO CRIED WOLF, BUT...
...IF YOU COULD SWING BY THE REZ, WE'D REALLY APPRECIATE IT.
YOU GOT IT, BUDDY.
HEY, LITTLE BROTHER, WHERE ARE YOU OFF TO?
OKLAHOMA. WYATT CALLED WHILE WE WERE GONE. HE WANTS ME TO CHECK SOMETHING OUT.
SHOULDN'T TAKE LONG.
SO YOU'RE JUST GOING TO UP AND LEAVE US IN THE MIDDLE OF THIS WHOLE SKY SITUATION?
"SITUATION"? C'MON. WE'RE THE FANTASTIC FOUR. WE HAVE ALIEN HOUSEGUESTS ALL THE TIME.
AND SKY? ON HER WORLD SHE'S AN ELITE SUPER HERO. SHE'LL BE FIIIINE.

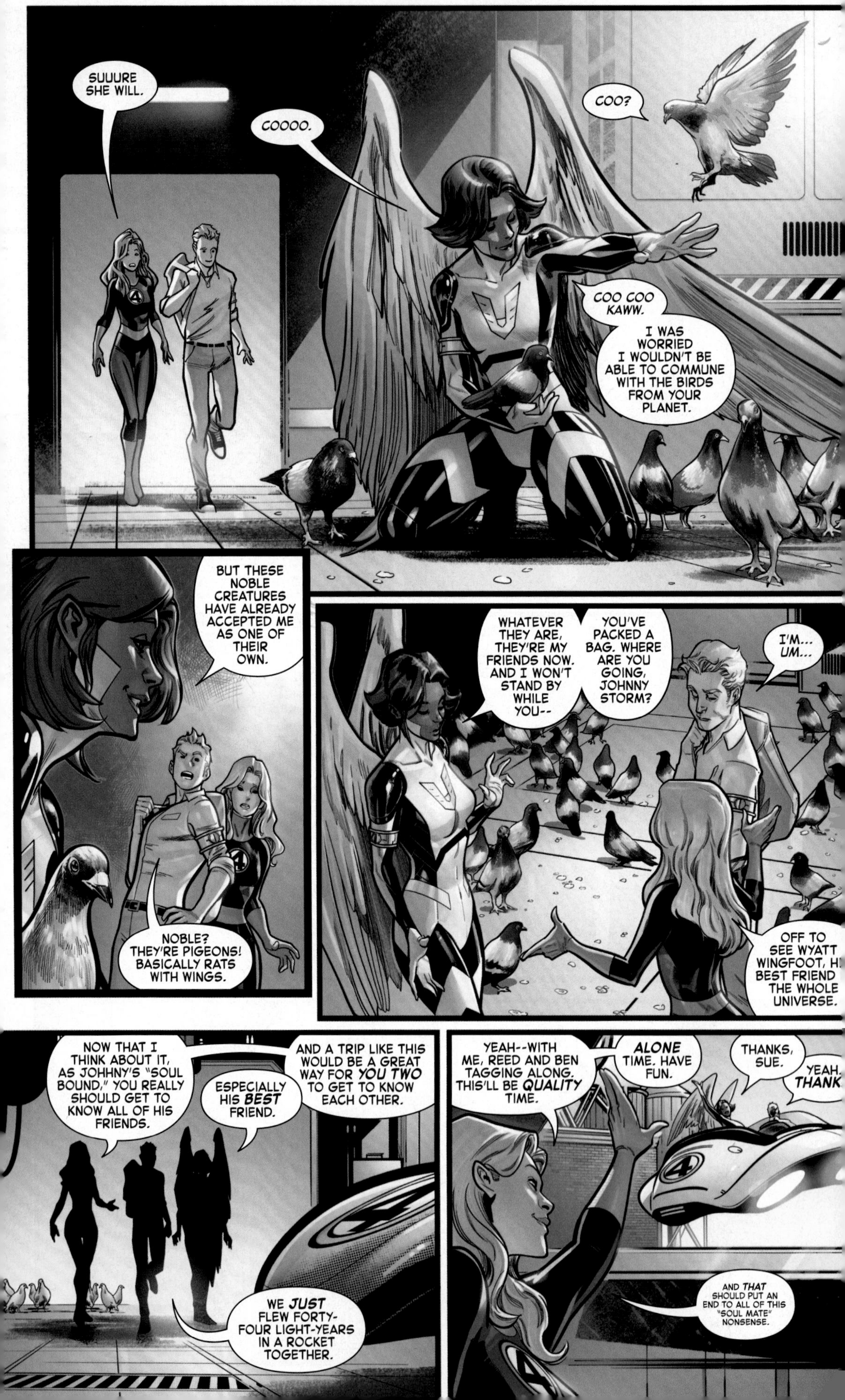
SUUURE SHE WILL.
COOOO.
COO?
COO COO KAWW.
I WAS WORRIED I WOULDN'T BE ABLE TO COMMUNE WITH THE BIRDS FROM YOUR PLANET.
BUT THESE NOBLE CREATURES HAVE ALREADY ACCEPTED ME AS ONE OF THEIR OWN.
NOBLE? THEY'RE PIGEONS! BASICALLY RATS WITH WINGS.
WHATEVER THEY ARE, THEY'RE MY FRIENDS NOW. AND I WON'T STAND BY WHILE YOU--
YOU'VE PACKED A BAG. WHERE ARE YOU GOING, JOHNNY STORM?
I'M... UM...
OFF TO SEE WYATT WINGFOOT, H BEST FRIEND THE WHOLE UNIVERSE.
NOW THAT I THINK ABOUT IT, AS JOHHNY'S "SOUL BOUND," YOU REALLY SHOULD GET TO KNOW ALL OF HIS FRIENDS.
ESPECIALLY HIS BEST FRIEND.
AND A TRIP LIKE THIS WOULD BE A GREAT WAY FOR YOU TWO TO GET TO KNOW EACH OTHER.
WE JUST FLEW FORTY-FOUR LIGHT-YEARS IN A ROCKET TOGETHER.
YEAH--WITH ME, REED AND BEN TAGGING ALONG. THIS'LL BE QUALITY TIME.
ALONE TIME. HAVE FUN.
THANKS, SUE.
YEAH, THANK
AND THAT SHOULD PUT AN END TO ALL OF THIS "SOUL MATE" NONSENSE.

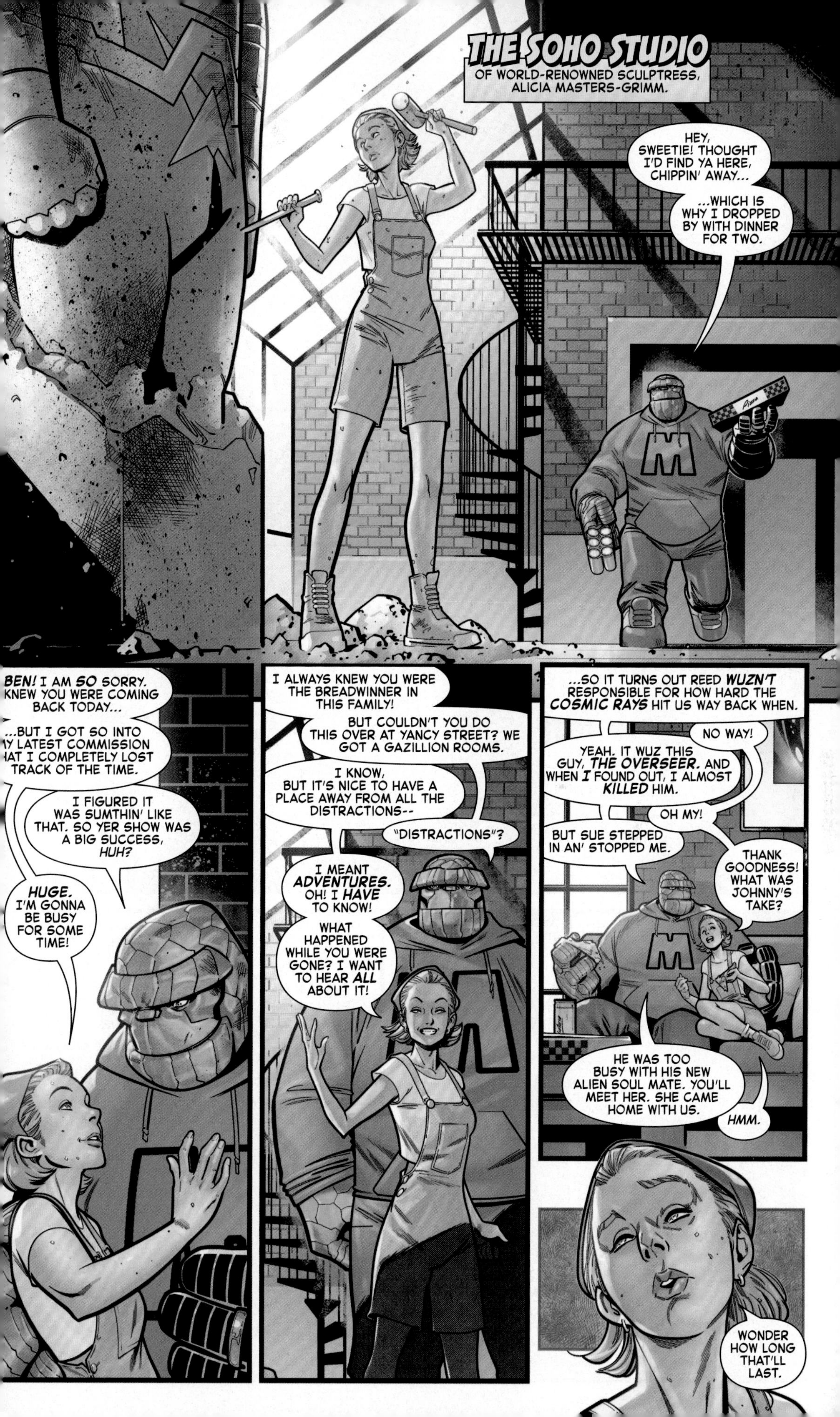
THE SOHO STUDIO
OF WORLD-RENOWNED SCULPTRESS, ALICIA MASTERS-GRIMM.
HEY, SWEETIE! THOUGHT I'D FIND YA HERE, CHIPPIN' AWAY...
...WHICH IS WHY I DROPPED BY WITH DINNER FOR TWO.
BEN! I AM SO SORRY. KNEW YOU WERE COMING BACK TODAY...
...BUT I GOT SO INTO Y LATEST COMMISSION AT I COMPLETELY LOST TRACK OF THE TIME.
I FIGURED IT WAS SUMTHIN' LIKE THAT. SO YER SHOW WAS A BIG SUCCESS, HUH?
HUGE. I'M GONNA BE BUSY FOR SOME TIME!
I ALWAYS KNEW YOU WERE THE BREADWINNER IN THIS FAMILY!
BUT COULDN'T YOU DO THIS OVER AT YANCY STREET? WE GOT A GAZILLION ROOMS.
I KNOW, BUT IT'S NICE TO HAVE A PLACE AWAY FROM ALL THE DISTRACTIONS--
"DISTRACTIONS"?
I MEANT ADVENTURES. OH! I HAVE TO KNOW!
WHAT HAPPENED WHILE YOU WERE GONE? I WANT TO HEAR ALL ABOUT IT!
...SO IT TURNS OUT REED WUZN'T RESPONSIBLE FOR HOW HARD THE COSMIC RAYS HIT US WAY BACK WHEN.
NO WAY!
YEAH. IT WUZ THIS GUY, THE OVERSEER. AND WHEN I FOUND OUT, I ALMOST KILLED HIM.
OH MY!
BUT SUE STEPPED IN AN' STOPPED ME.
THANK GOODNESS! WHAT WAS JOHNNY'S TAKE?
HE WAS TOO BUSY WITH HIS NEW ALIEN SOUL MATE. YOU'LL MEET HER. SHE CAME HOME WITH US.
HMM.
WONDER HOW LONG THAT'LL LAST.

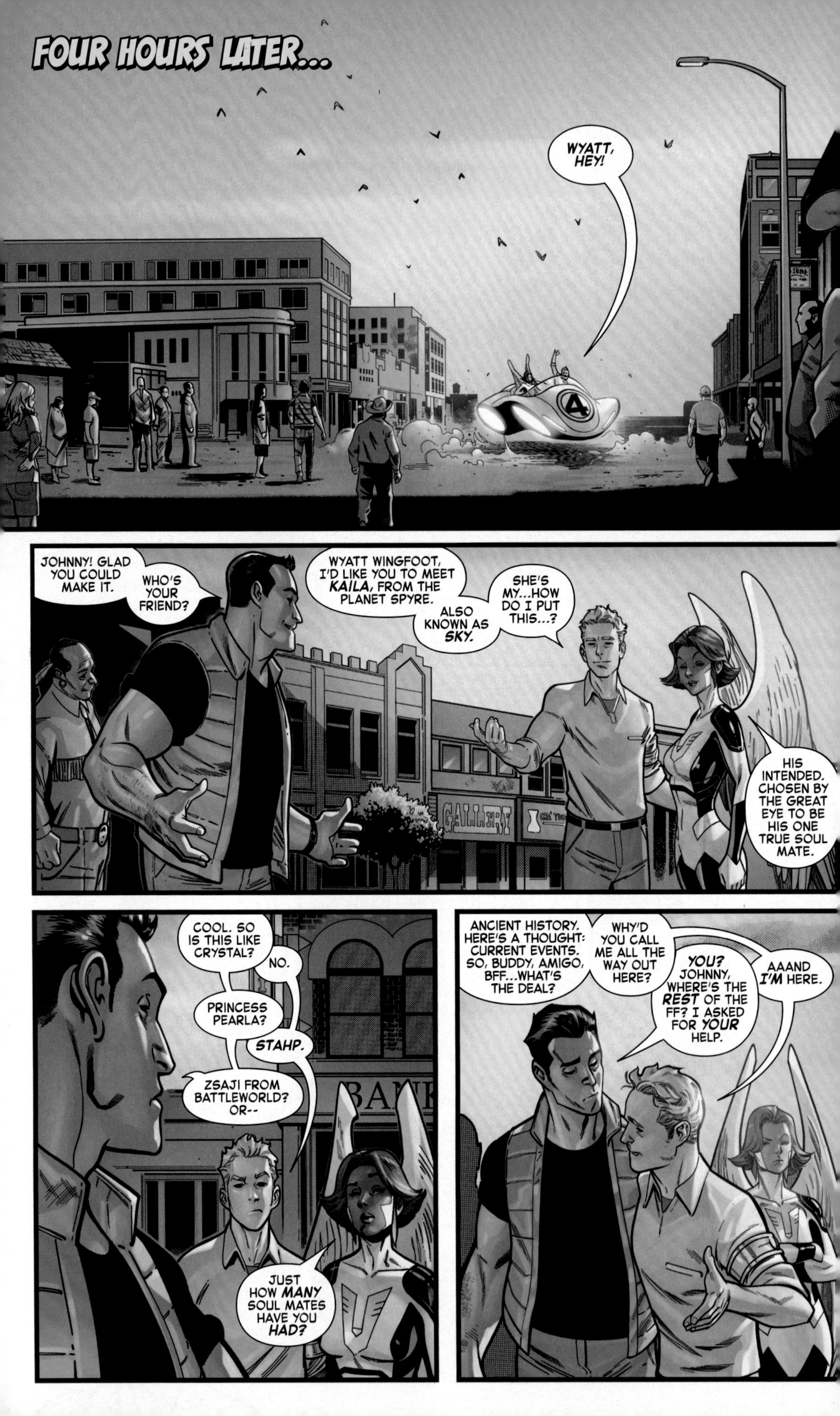
FOUR HOURS LATER...
WYATT, HEY!
JOHNNY! GLAD YOU COULD MAKE IT.
WHO'S YOUR FRIEND?
WYATT WINGFOOT, I'D LIKE YOU TO MEET KAILA, FROM THE PLANET SPYRE.
ALSO KNOWN AS SKY.
SHE'S MY...HOW DO I PUT THIS...?
HIS INTENDED. CHOSEN BY THE GREAT EYE TO BE HIS ONE TRUE SOUL MATE.
GALLERY
COOL. SO IS THIS LIKE CRYSTAL?
NO.
PRINCESS PEARLA?
STAHP.
ZSAJI FROM BATTLEWORLD? OR--
JUST HOW MANY SOUL MATES HAVE YOU HAD?
ANCIENT HISTORY. HERE'S A THOUGHT: CURRENT EVENTS. SO, BUDDY, AMIGO, BFF...WHAT'S THE DEAL?
WHY'D YOU CALL ME ALL THE WAY OUT HERE?
YOU? JOHNNY, WHERE'S THE REST OF THE FF? I ASKED FOR YOUR HELP.
AAAND I'M HERE.

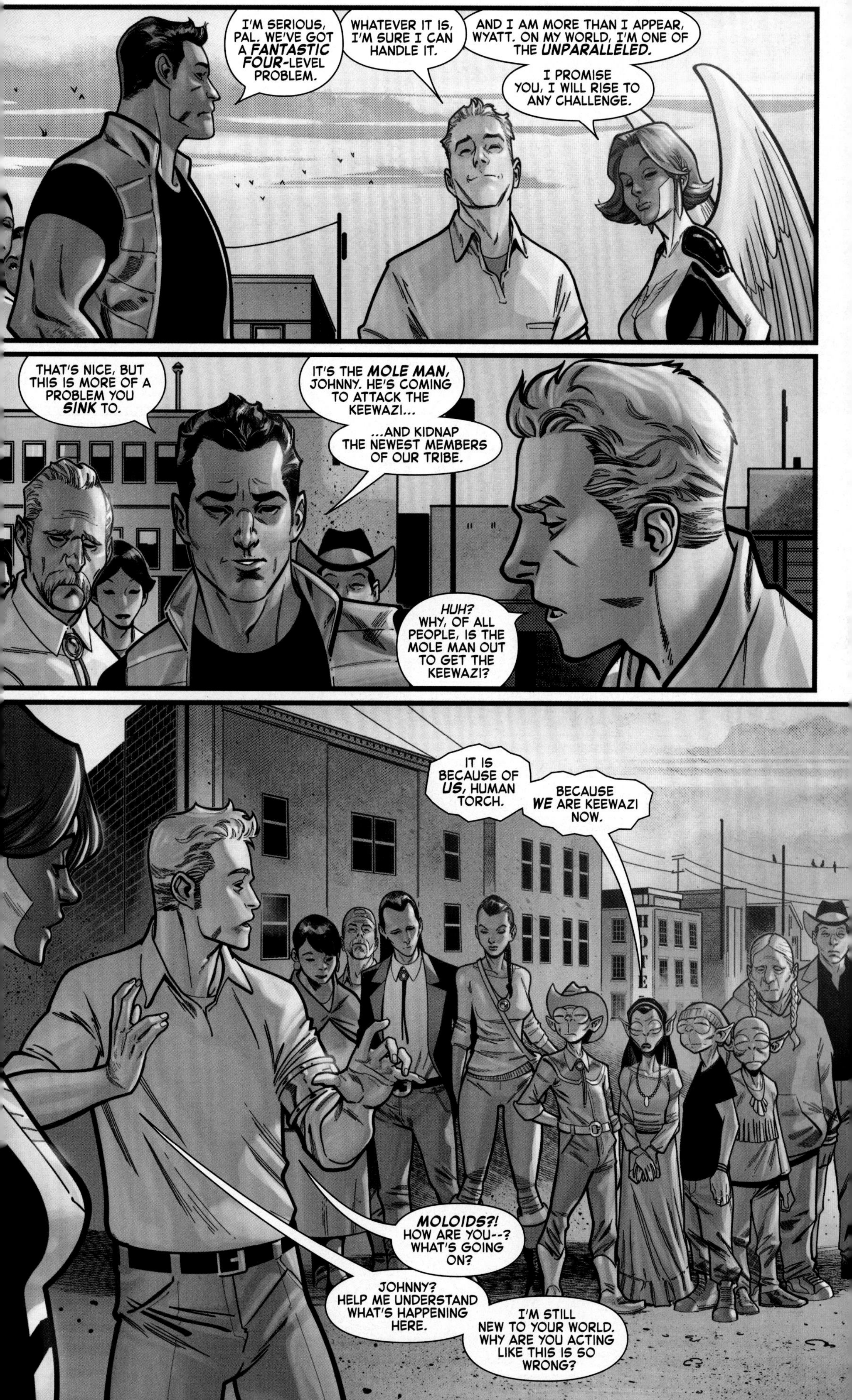
I'M SERIOUS, PAL. WE'VE GOT A FANTASTIC FOUR-LEVEL PROBLEM.
WHATEVER IT IS, I'M SURE I CAN HANDLE IT.
AND I AM MORE THAN I APPEAR, WYATT. ON MY WORLD, I'M ONE OF THE UNPARALLELED.
I PROMISE YOU, I WILL RISE TO ANY CHALLENGE.
THAT'S NICE, BUT THIS IS MORE OF A PROBLEM YOU SINK TO.
IT'S THE MOLE MAN, JOHNNY. HE'S COMING TO ATTACK THE KEEWAZI...
...AND KIDNAP THE NEWEST MEMBERS OF OUR TRIBE.
HUH? WHY, OF ALL PEOPLE, IS THE MOLE MAN OUT TO GET THE KEEWAZI?
IT IS BECAUSE OF US, HUMAN TORCH.
BECAUSE WE ARE KEEWAZI NOW.
MOLOIDS?! HOW ARE YOU--? WHAT'S GOING ON?
JOHNNY? HELP ME UNDERSTAND WHAT'S HAPPENING HERE.
I'M STILL NEW TO YOUR WORLD. WHY ARE YOU ACTING LIKE THIS IS SO WRONG?

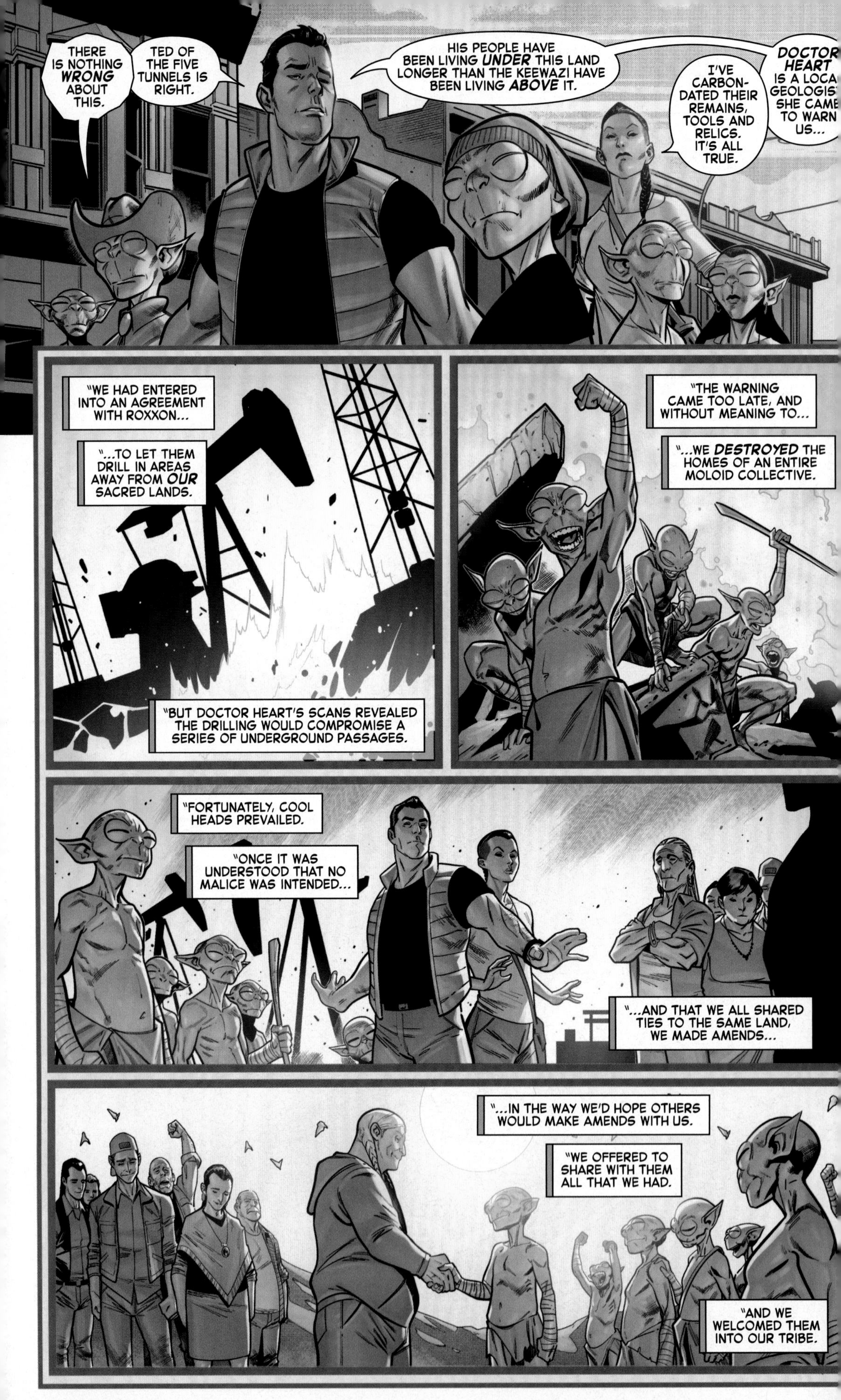
THERE IS NOTHING WRONG ABOUT THIS.
TED OF THE FIVE TUNNELS IS RIGHT.
HIS PEOPLE HAVE BEEN LIVING UNDER THIS LAND LONGER THAN THE KEEWAZI HAVE BEEN LIVING ABOVE IT.
DOCTOR HEART IS A LOCA GEOLOGIS SHE CAME TO WARN US...
I'VE CARBON-DATED THEIR REMAINS, TOOLS AND RELICS. IT'S ALL TRUE.
"WE HAD ENTERED INTO AN AGREEMENT WITH ROXXON...
"...TO LET THEM DRILL IN AREAS AWAY FROM OUR SACRED LANDS.
"BUT DOCTOR HEART'S SCANS REVEALED THE DRILLING WOULD COMPROMISE A SERIES OF UNDERGROUND PASSAGES.
"THE WARNING CAME TOO LATE, AND WITHOUT MEANING TO...
"...WE DESTROYED THE HOMES OF AN ENTIRE MOLOID COLLECTIVE.
"FORTUNATELY, COOL HEADS PREVAILED.
"ONCE IT WAS UNDERSTOOD THAT NO MALICE WAS INTENDED...
"...AND THAT WE ALL SHARED TIES TO THE SAME LAND, WE MADE AMENDS...
"...IN THE WAY WE'D HOPE OTHERS WOULD MAKE AMENDS WITH US.
"WE OFFERED TO SHARE WITH THEM ALL THAT WE HAD.
"AND WE WELCOMED THEM INTO OUR TRIBE.

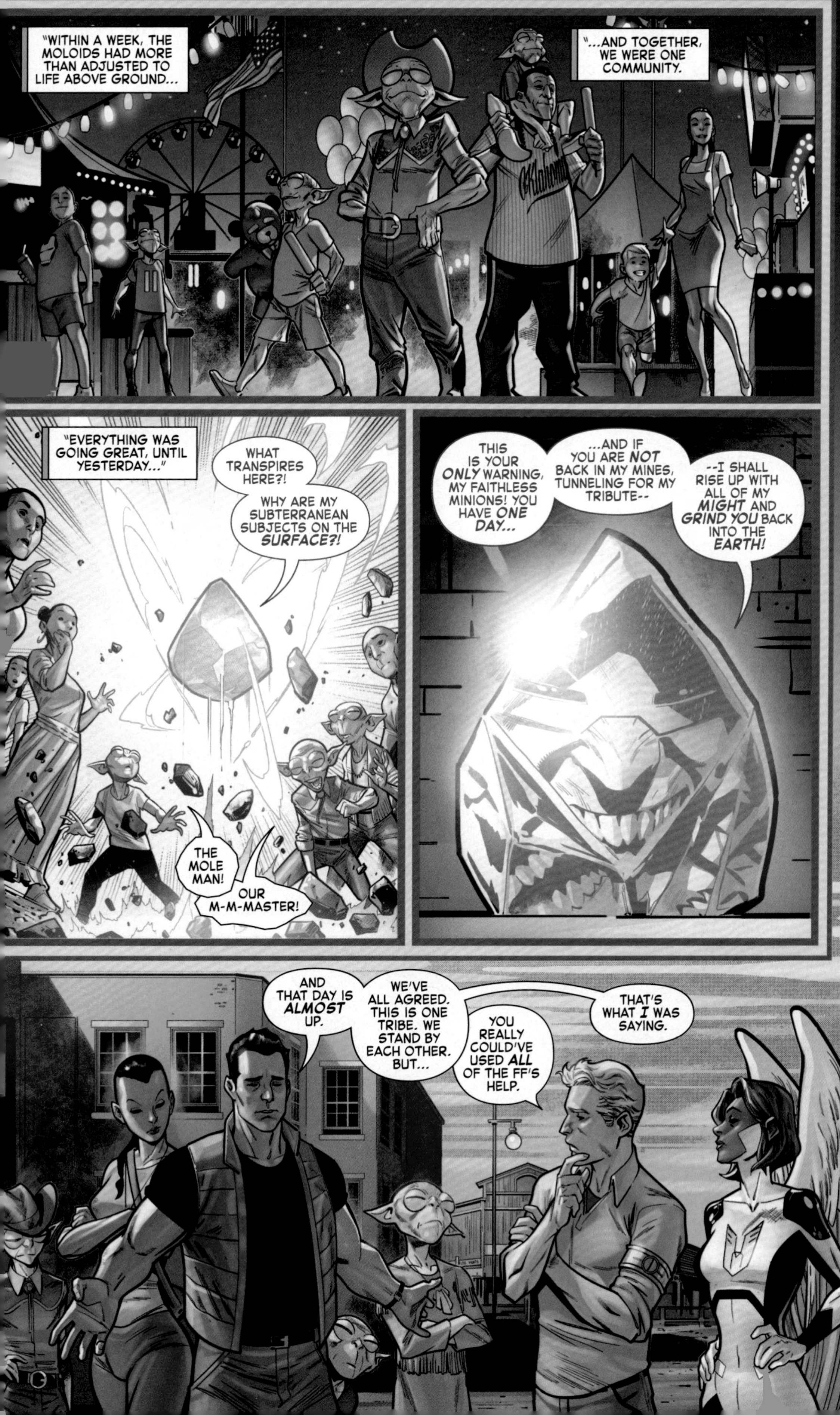
"WITHIN A WEEK, THE MOLOIDS HAD MORE THAN ADJUSTED TO LIFE ABOVE GROUND...
"...AND TOGETHER, WE WERE ONE COMMUNITY.
"EVERYTHING WAS GOING GREAT, UNTIL YESTERDAY..."
WHAT TRANSPIRES HERE?!
WHY ARE MY SUBTERRANEAN SUBJECTS ON THE SURFACE?!
THE MOLE MAN!
OUR M-M-MASTER!
THIS IS YOUR ONLY WARNING, MY FAITHLESS MINIONS! YOU HAVE ONE DAY...
...AND IF YOU ARE NOT BACK IN MY MINES, TUNNELING FOR MY TRIBUTE--
--I SHALL RISE UP WITH ALL OF MY MIGHT AND GRIND YOU BACK INTO THE EARTH!
AND THAT DAY IS ALMOST UP.
WE'VE ALL AGREED. THIS IS ONE TRIBE. WE STAND BY EACH OTHER. BUT...
YOU REALLY COULD'VE USED ALL OF THE FF'S HELP.
THAT'S WHAT I WAS SAYING.

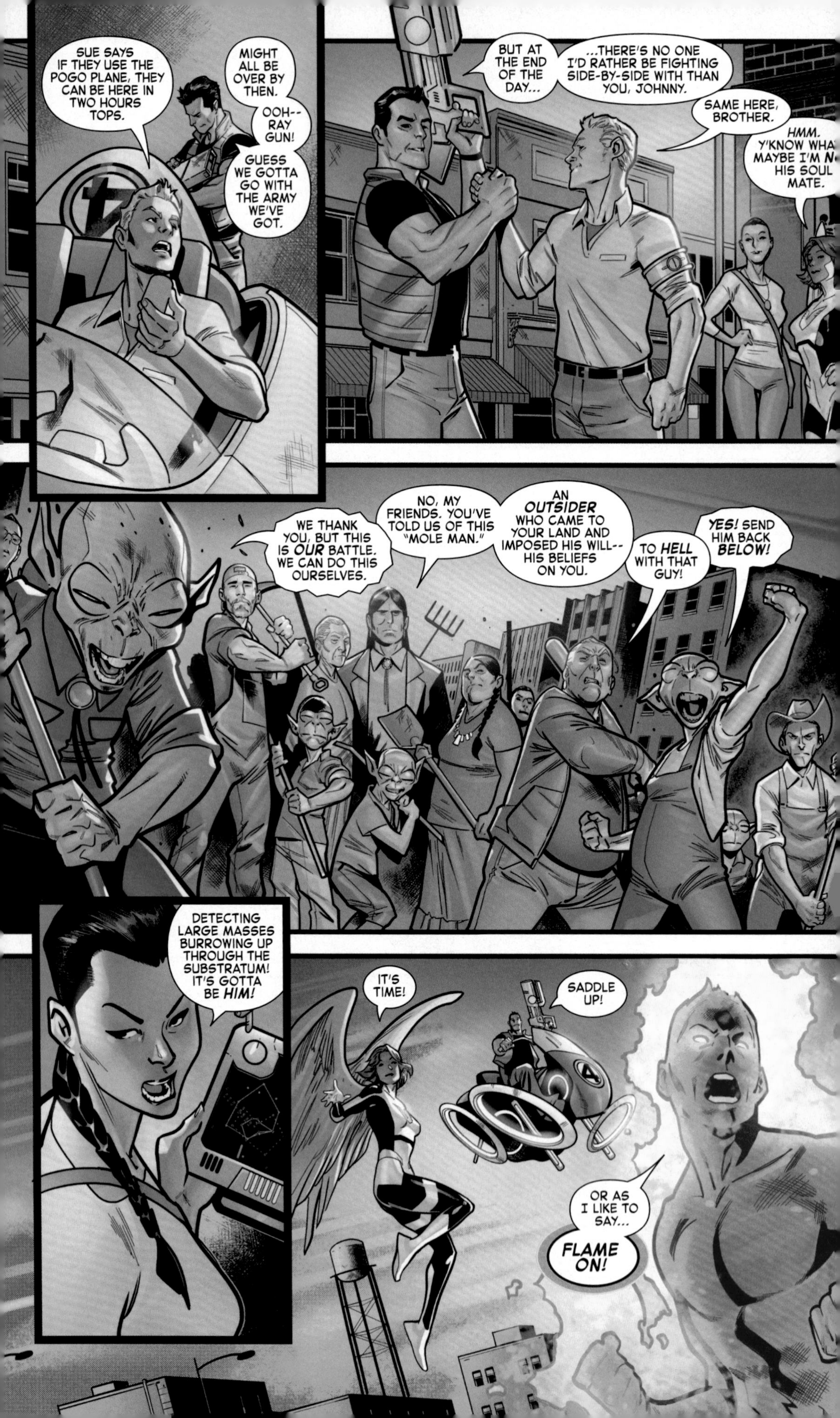
SUE SAYS IF THEY USE THE POGO PLANE, THEY CAN BE HERE IN TWO HOURS TOPS.
MIGHT ALL BE OVER BY THEN.
OOH-- RAY GUN!
GUESS WE GOTTA GO WITH THE ARMY WE'VE GOT.
BUT AT THE END OF THE DAY...
...THERE'S NO ONE I'D RATHER BE FIGHTING SIDE-BY-SIDE WITH THAN YOU, JOHNNY.
SAME HERE, BROTHER.
HMM. Y'KNOW WHA MAYBE I'M N HIS SOUL MATE.
WE THANK YOU, BUT THIS IS OUR BATTLE. WE CAN DO THIS OURSELVES.
NO, MY FRIENDS. YOU'VE TOLD US OF THIS "MOLE MAN."
AN OUTSIDER WHO CAME TO YOUR LAND AND IMPOSED HIS WILL-- HIS BELIEFS ON YOU.
TO HELL WITH THAT GUY!
YES! SEND HIM BACK BELOW!
DETECTING LARGE MASSES BURROWING UP THROUGH THE SUBSTRATUM! IT'S GOTTA BE HIM!
IT'S TIME!
SADDLE UP!
OR AS I LIKE TO SAY...
FLAME ON!

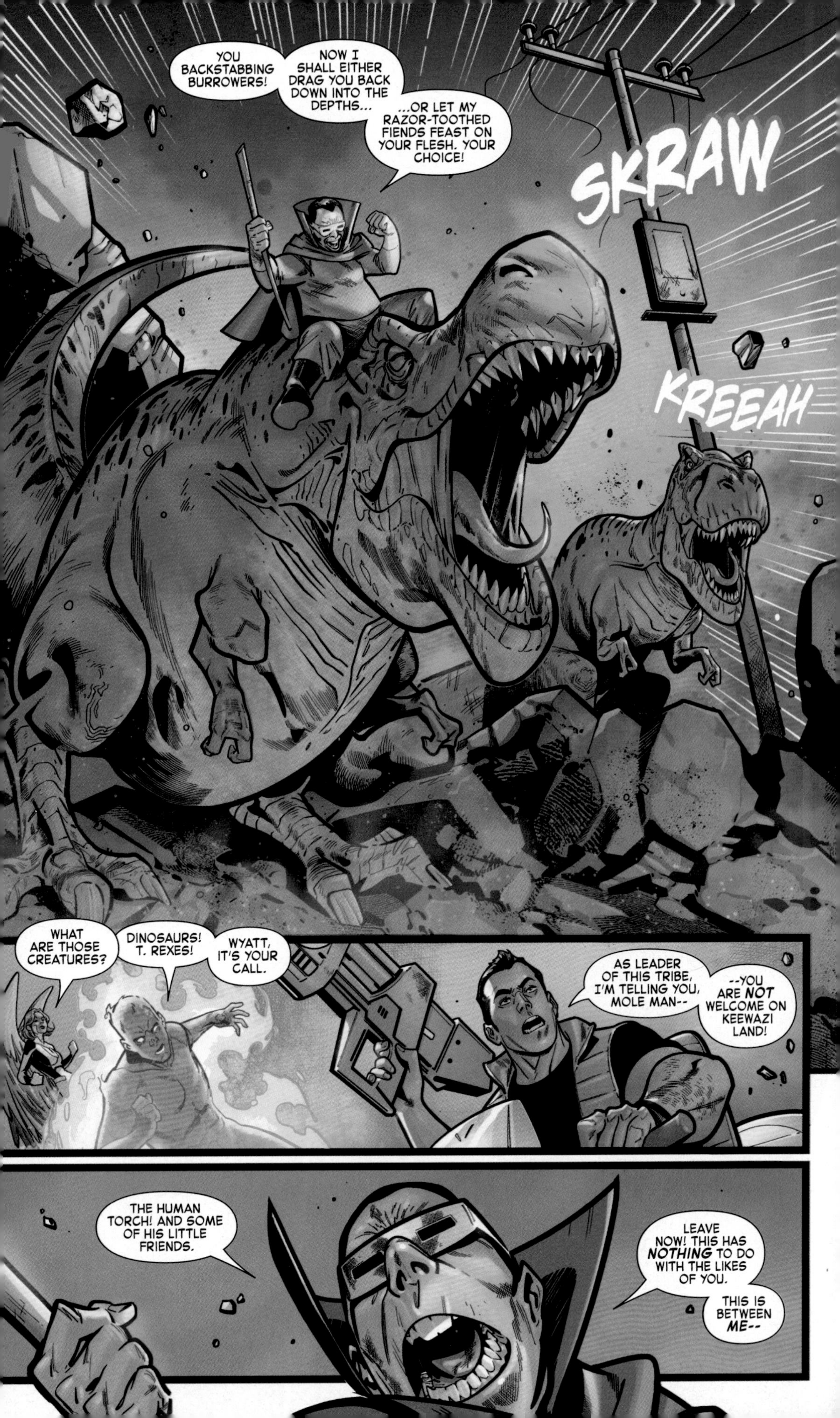
YOU BACKSTABBING BURROWERS!
NOW I SHALL EITHER DRAG YOU BACK DOWN INTO THE DEPTHS...
...OR LET MY RAZOR-TOOTHED FIENDS FEAST ON YOUR FLESH. YOUR CHOICE!
SKRAW
KREEAH
WHAT ARE THOSE CREATURES?
DINOSAURS! T. REXES!
WYATT, IT'S YOUR CALL.
AS LEADER OF THIS TRIBE, I'M TELLING YOU, MOLE MAN--
--YOU ARE NOT WELCOME ON KEEWAZI LAND!
THE HUMAN TORCH! AND SOME OF HIS LITTLE FRIENDS.
LEAVE NOW! THIS HAS NOTHING TO DO WITH THE LIKES OF YOU.
THIS IS BETWEEN ME--

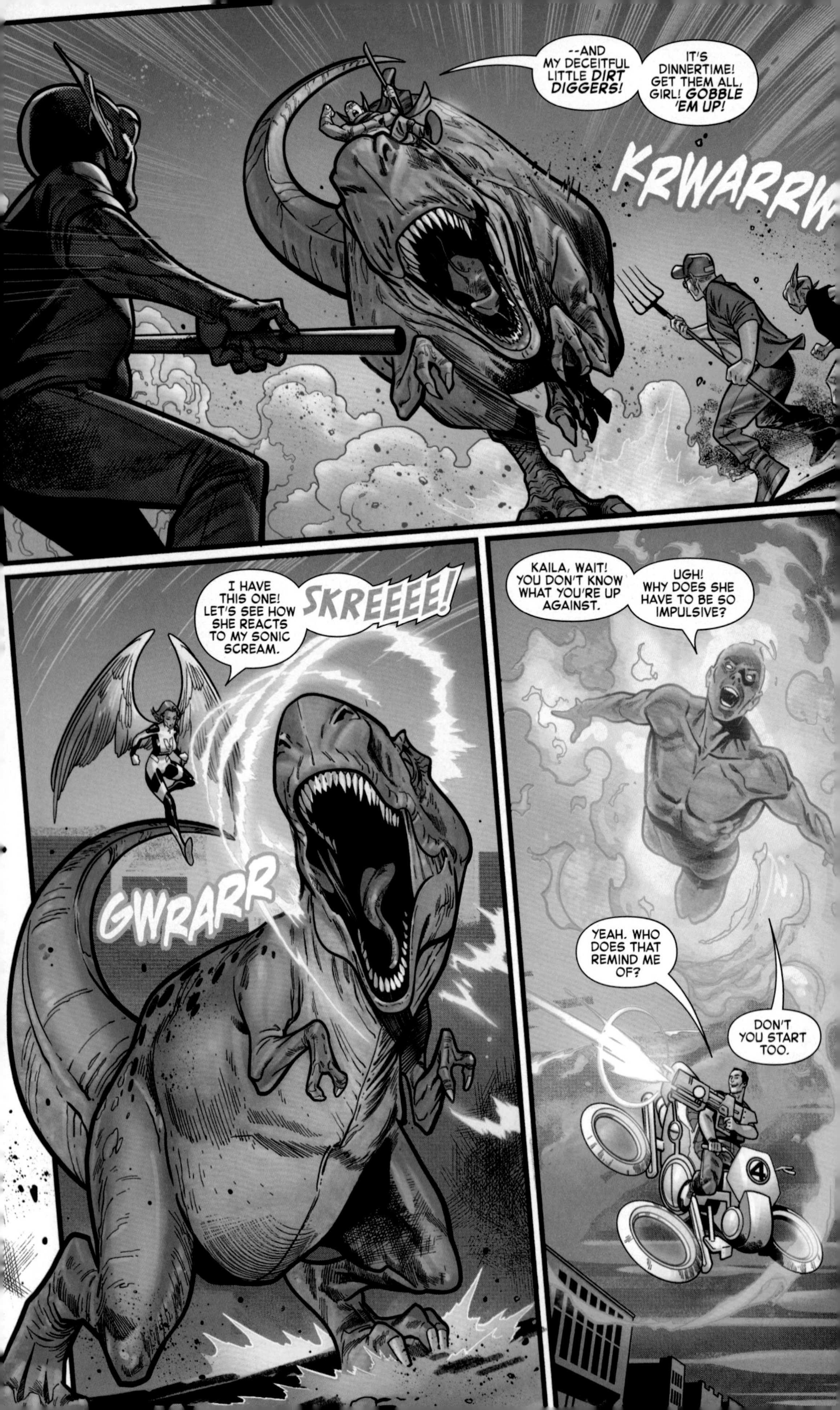
--AND MY DECEITFUL LITTLE DIRT DIGGERS!
IT'S DINNERTIME! GET THEM ALL, GIRL! GOBBLE 'EM UP!
KRWARRW
I HAVE THIS ONE! LET'S SEE HOW SHE REACTS TO MY SONIC SCREAM.
SKREEEE!
GWRARR
KAILA, WAIT! YOU DON'T KNOW WHAT YOU'RE UP AGAINST.
UGH! WHY DOES SHE HAVE TO BE SO IMPULSIVE?
YEAH. WHO DOES THAT REMIND ME OF?
DON'T YOU START TOO.

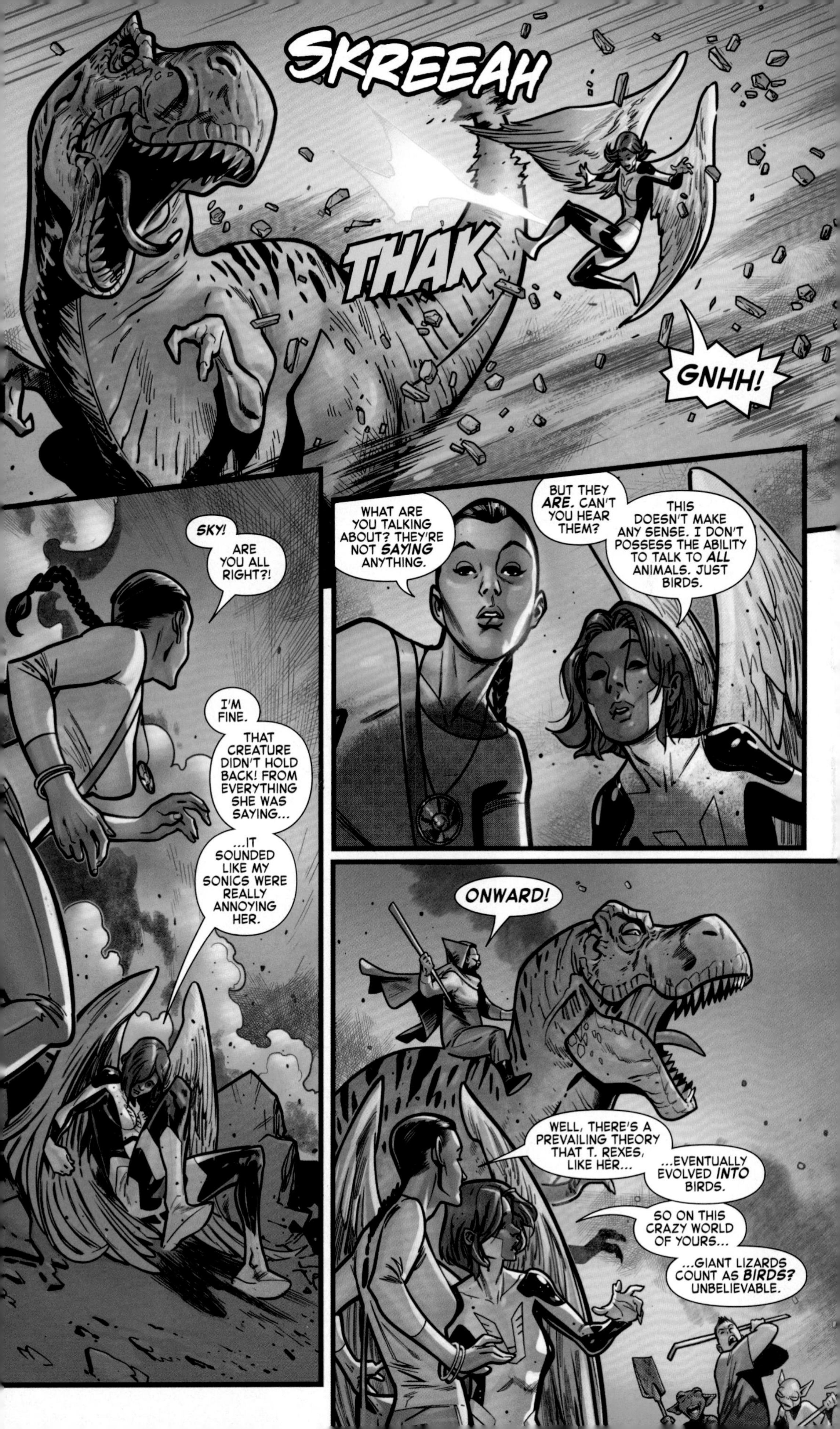

SKREEAH
THAK
GNHH!
SKY!
ARE YOU ALL RIGHT?!
I'M FINE.
THAT CREATURE DIDN'T HOLD BACK! FROM EVERYTHING SHE WAS SAYING...
...IT SOUNDED LIKE MY SONICS WERE REALLY ANNOYING HER.
WHAT ARE YOU TALKING ABOUT? THEY'RE NOT SAYING ANYTHING.
BUT THEY ARE. CAN'T YOU HEAR THEM?
THIS DOESN'T MAKE ANY SENSE. I DON'T POSSESS THE ABILITY TO TALK TO ALL ANIMALS. JUST BIRDS.
ONWARD!
WELL, THERE'S A PREVAILING THEORY THAT T. REXES, LIKE HER...
...EVENTUALLY EVOLVED INTO BIRDS.
SO ON THIS CRAZY WORLD OF YOURS...
...GIANT LIZARDS COUNT AS BIRDS? UNBELIEVABLE.

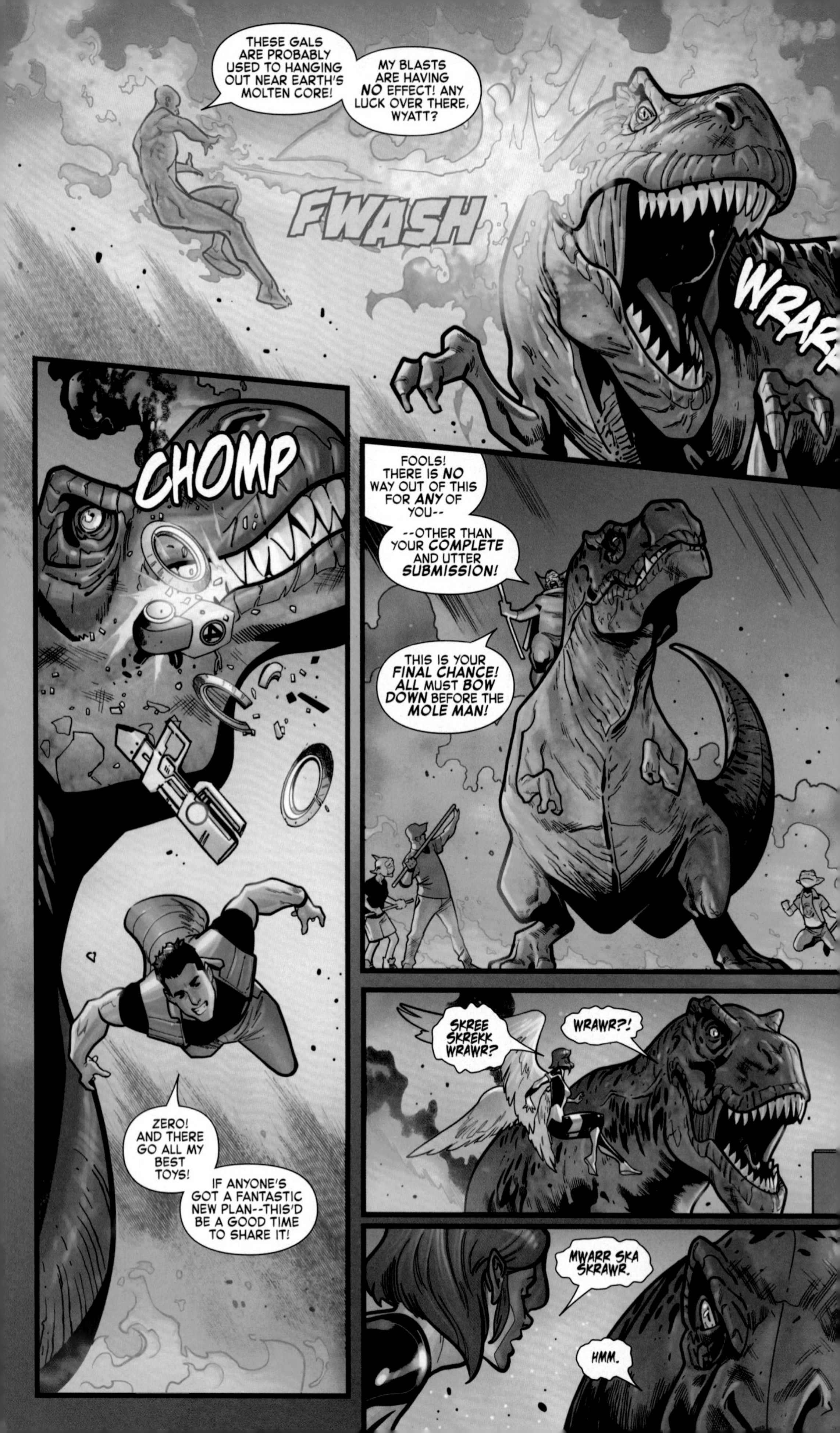

THESE GALS ARE PROBABLY USED TO HANGING OUT NEAR EARTH'S MOLTEN CORE!
MY BLASTS ARE HAVING NO EFFECT! ANY LUCK OVER THERE, WYATT?
FWASH
WRAR
CHOMP
ZERO! AND THERE GO ALL MY BEST TOYS!
IF ANYONE'S GOT A FANTASTIC NEW PLAN--THIS'D BE A GOOD TIME TO SHARE IT!
FOOLS! THERE IS NO WAY OUT OF THIS FOR ANY OF YOU--
--OTHER THAN YOUR COMPLETE AND UTTER SUBMISSION!
THIS IS YOUR FINAL CHANCE! ALL MUST BOW DOWN BEFORE THE MOLE MAN!
SKREE SKREKK WRAWR?
WRAWR?!
MWARR SKA SKRAWR.
HMM.

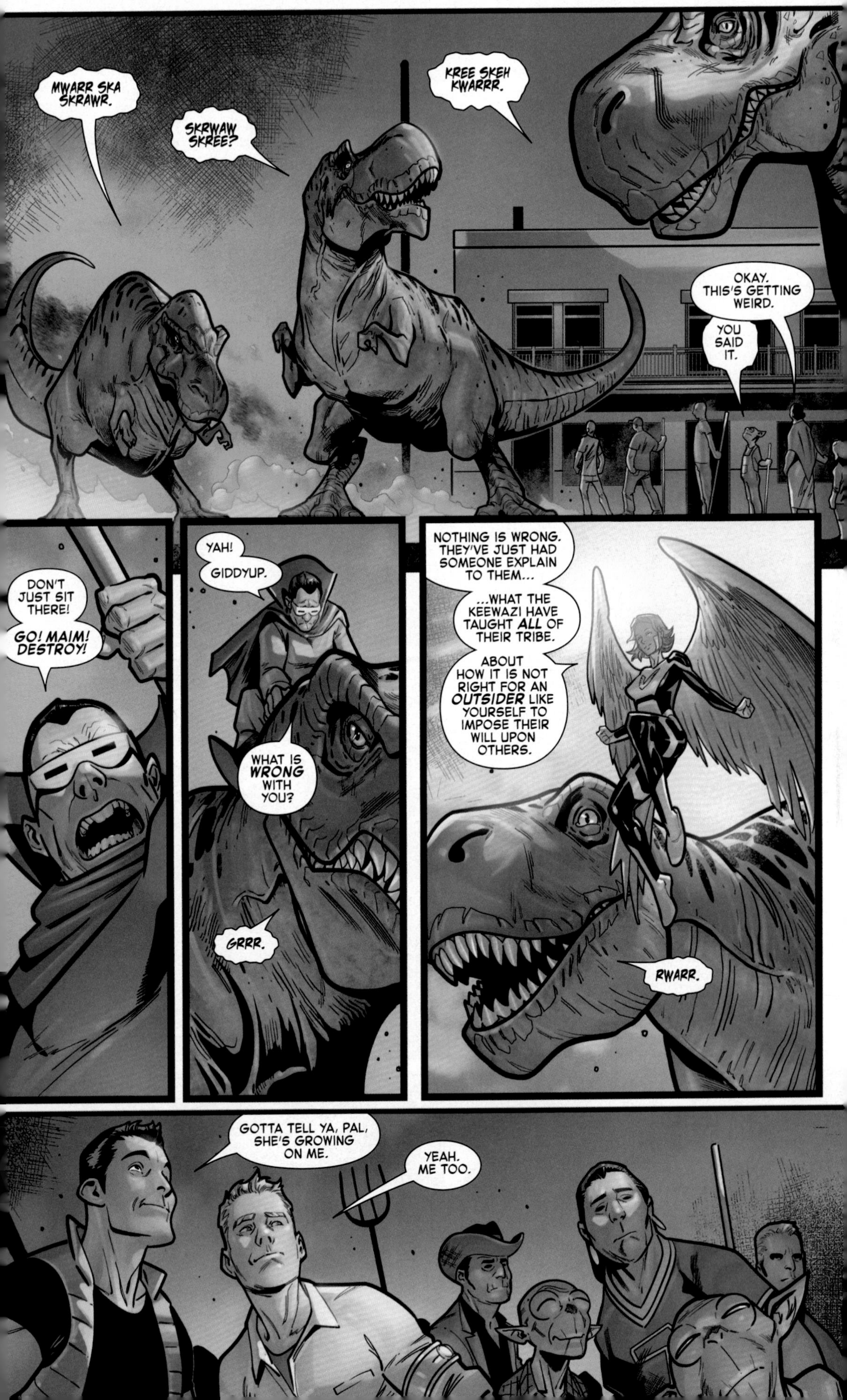
MWARR SKA SKRAWR.
SKRWAW SKREE?
KREE SKEH KWARRR.
OKAY. THIS'S GETTING WEIRD.
YOU SAID IT.
DON'T JUST SIT THERE!
GO! MAIM! DESTROY!
YAH!
GIDDYUP.
WHAT IS WRONG WITH YOU?
GRRR.
NOTHING IS WRONG. THEY'VE JUST HAD SOMEONE EXPLAIN TO THEM...
...WHAT THE KEEWAZI HAVE TAUGHT ALL OF THEIR TRIBE.
ABOUT HOW IT IS NOT RIGHT FOR AN OUTSIDER LIKE YOURSELF TO IMPOSE THEIR WILL UPON OTHERS.
RWARR.
GOTTA TELL YA, PAL, SHE'S GROWING ON ME.
YEAH. ME TOO.

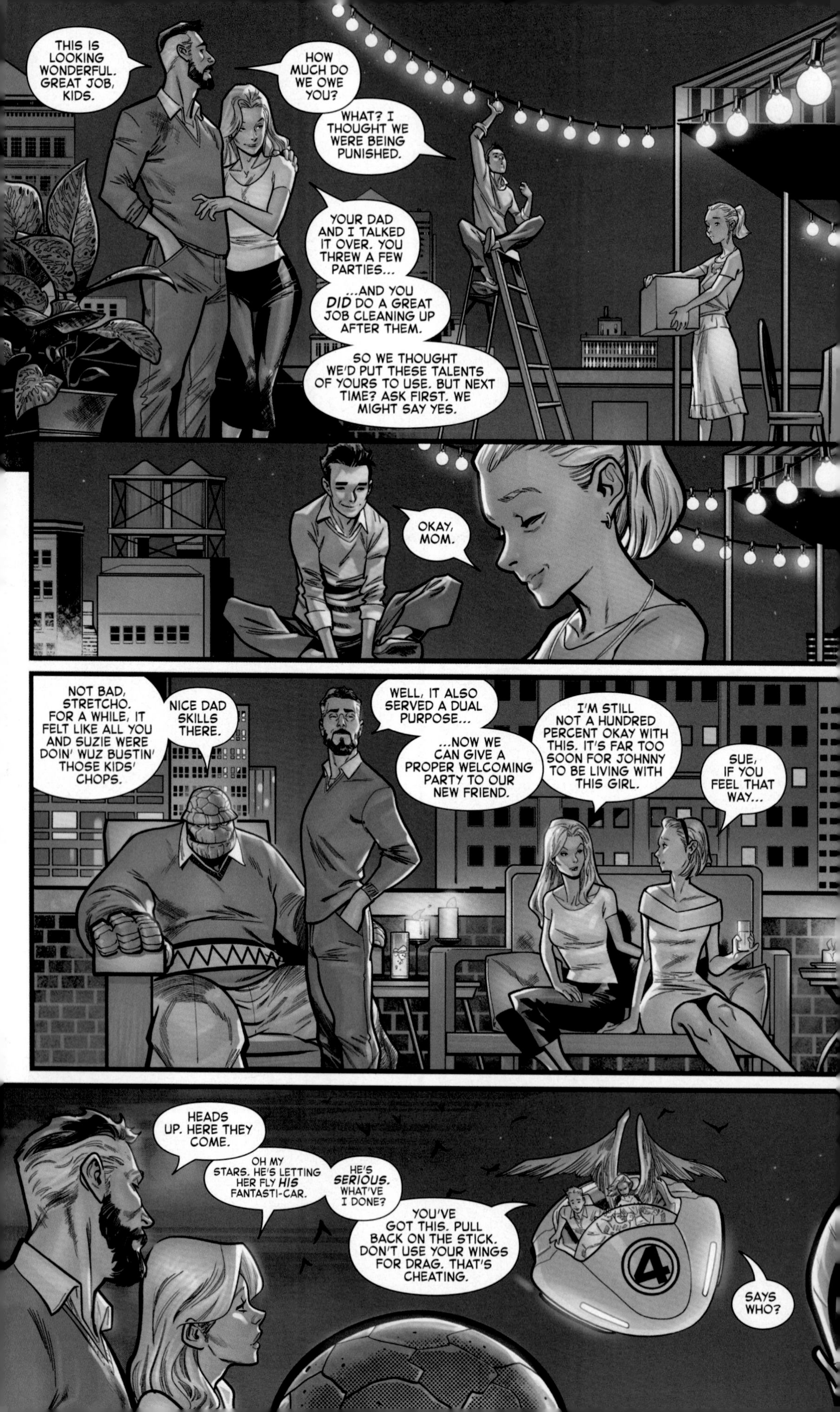
THIS IS LOOKING WONDERFUL. GREAT JOB, KIDS.
HOW MUCH DO WE OWE YOU?
WHAT? I THOUGHT WE WERE BEING PUNISHED.
YOUR DAD AND I TALKED IT OVER. YOU THREW A FEW PARTIES...
...AND YOU *DID* DO A GREAT JOB CLEANING UP AFTER THEM.
SO WE THOUGHT WE'D PUT THESE TALENTS OF YOURS TO USE. BUT NEXT TIME? ASK FIRST. WE MIGHT SAY YES.
OKAY, MOM.
NOT BAD, STRETCHO. FOR A WHILE, IT FELT LIKE ALL YOU AND SUZIE WERE DOIN' WUZ BUSTIN' THOSE KIDS' CHOPS.
NICE DAD SKILLS THERE.
WELL, IT ALSO SERVED A DUAL PURPOSE...
...NOW WE CAN GIVE A PROPER WELCOMING PARTY TO OUR NEW FRIEND.
I'M STILL NOT A HUNDRED PERCENT OKAY WITH THIS. IT'S FAR TOO SOON FOR JOHNNY TO BE LIVING WITH THIS GIRL.
SUE, IF YOU FEEL THAT WAY...
HEADS UP. HERE THEY COME.
OH MY STARS. HE'S LETTING HER FLY *HIS* FANTASTI-CAR.
HE'S *SERIOUS.* WHAT'VE I DONE?
YOU'VE GOT THIS. PULL BACK ON THE STICK. DON'T USE YOUR WINGS FOR DRAG. THAT'S CHEATING.
SAYS WHO?

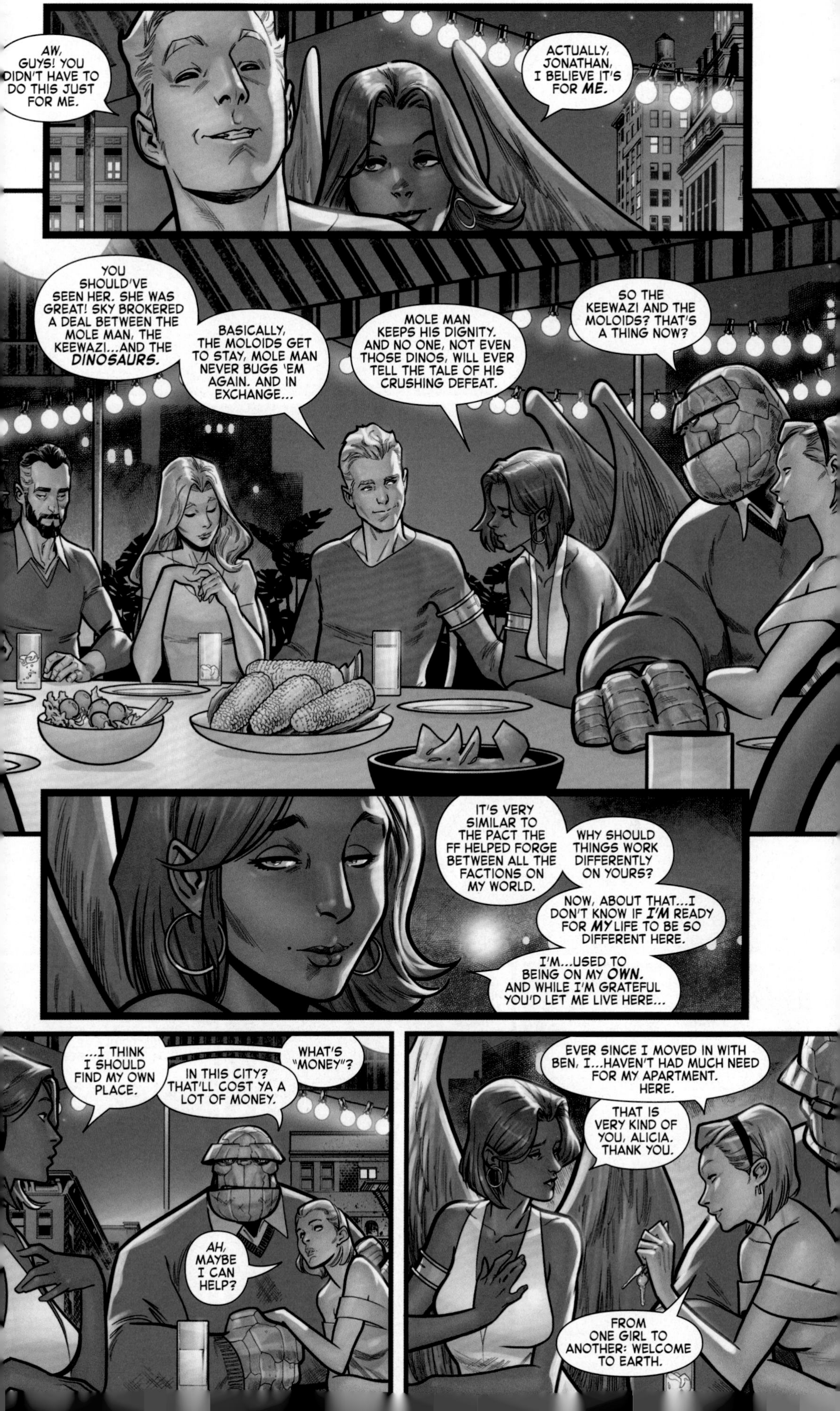
AW, GUYS! YOU DIDN'T HAVE TO DO THIS JUST FOR ME.
ACTUALLY, JONATHAN, I BELIEVE IT'S FOR ME.
YOU SHOULD'VE SEEN HER. SHE WAS GREAT! SKY BROKERED A DEAL BETWEEN THE MOLE MAN, THE KEEWAZI...AND THE DINOSAURS.
BASICALLY, THE MOLOIDS GET TO STAY, MOLE MAN NEVER BUGS 'EM AGAIN. AND IN EXCHANGE...
MOLE MAN KEEPS HIS DIGNITY. AND NO ONE, NOT EVEN THOSE DINOS, WILL EVER TELL THE TALE OF HIS CRUSHING DEFEAT.
SO THE KEEWAZI AND THE MOLOIDS? THAT'S A THING NOW?
IT'S VERY SIMILAR TO THE PACT THE FF HELPED FORGE BETWEEN ALL THE FACTIONS ON MY WORLD.
WHY SHOULD THINGS WORK DIFFERENTLY ON YOURS?
NOW, ABOUT THAT...I DON'T KNOW IF I'M READY FOR MY LIFE TO BE SO DIFFERENT HERE.
I'M...USED TO BEING ON MY OWN. AND WHILE I'M GRATEFUL YOU'D LET ME LIVE HERE...
...I THINK I SHOULD FIND MY OWN PLACE.
IN THIS CITY? THAT'LL COST YA A LOT OF MONEY.
WHAT'S "MONEY"?
AH, MAYBE I CAN HELP?
EVER SINCE I MOVED IN WITH BEN, I...HAVEN'T HAD MUCH NEED FOR MY APARTMENT. HERE.
THAT IS VERY KIND OF YOU, ALICIA. THANK YOU.
FROM ONE GIRL TO ANOTHER: WELCOME TO EARTH.

THAT'S ONE HELL OF A GAL YOU HAVE THERE, BEN.

AND THAT WAS ONE VERY GENEROUS GIFT.

SHE GETS IT FROM ME. Y'KNOW I CAN BE A LITTLE MAGNANIMOUS MYSELF SOMETIMES.

CASE IN POINT...

I GOT A GIFT FER *YOU*, PAL. ONE I'VE BEEN HOLDIN' ON TO FOR ABOUT...FIFTEEN YEARS OR SO.

A BOTTLE OF CHAMPAGNE?

THERE WERE DAYS I THOUGHT OF SMASHIN' THIS TO PIECES. AND OTHER TIMES...

...WHEN I WANTED TO HIT YOU OVER THE HEAD WITH IT. BUT TONIGHT... CONSIDER IT A PEACE OFFERIN'.

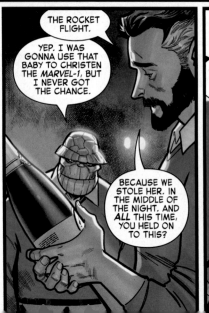

THE ROCKET FLIGHT.

YEP. I WAS GONNA USE THAT BABY TO CHRISTEN THE *MARVEL-1*, BUT I NEVER GOT THE CHANCE.

BECAUSE WE STOLE HER. IN THE MIDDLE OF THE NIGHT. AND *ALL* THIS TIME, YOU HELD ON TO THIS?

I HELD ON TO A *LOT* 'A THINGS.

YOU WERE *RIGHT* ABOUT THE SHIELDS.

FOR AGES I BLAMED YOU FOR SUMTHIN' THAT WEREN'T EVEN YOUR FAULT.

TIME TO BURY THE HATCHET-- AND TOAST THE *BEST* FRIENDSHIP I EVER HAD.

BEN, DON'T DO THIS. I'M *STILL* TO BLAME. I MAY HAVE GOTTEN THE SCIENCE *RIGHT*...

...BUT I GOT EVERYTHI ELSE WRO I NEVE CONSIDER THERE'D SO MUC *FEAR* IN T UNIVERS

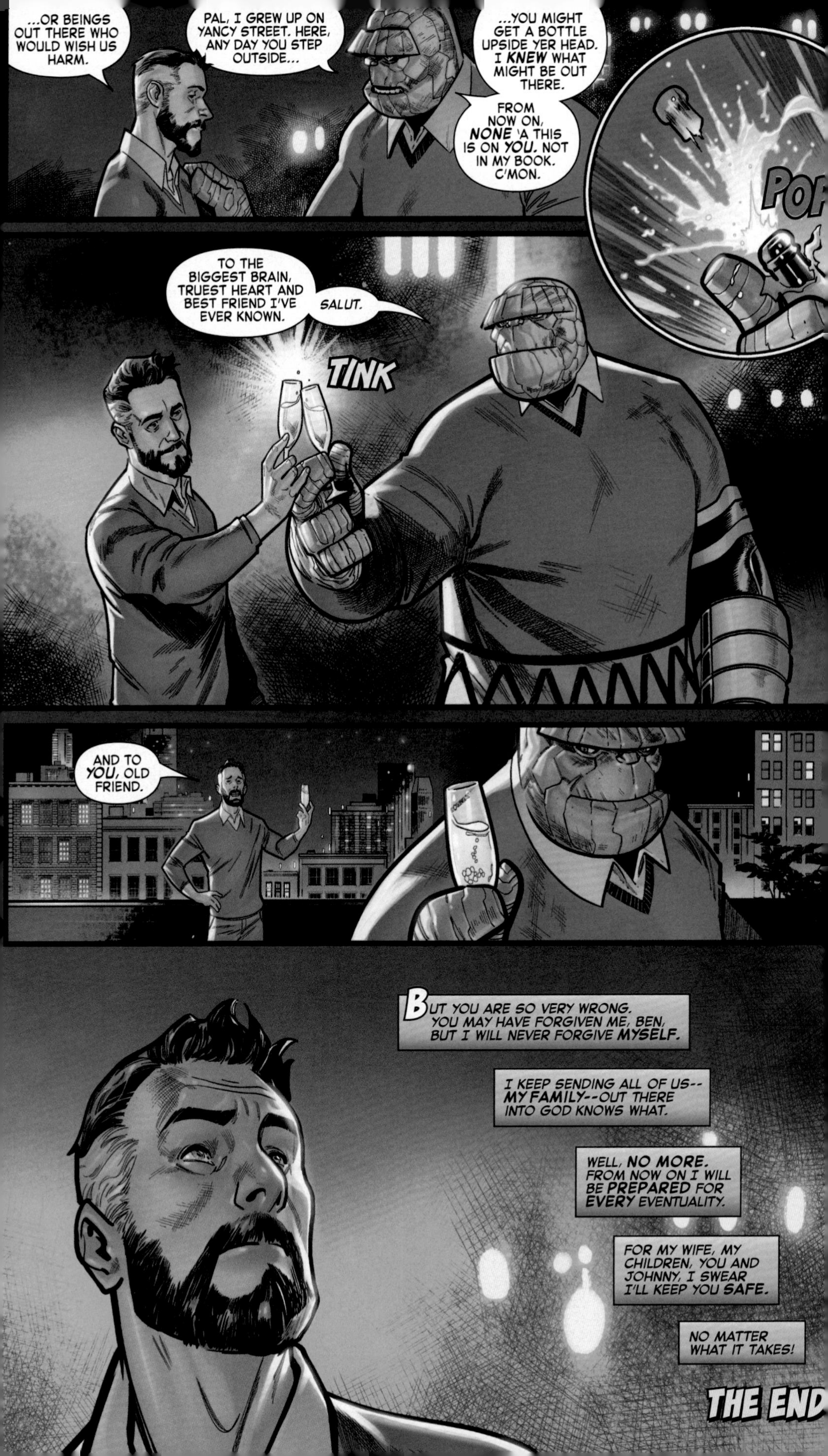

...OR BEINGS OUT THERE WHO WOULD WISH US HARM.
PAL, I GREW UP ON YANCY STREET. HERE, ANY DAY YOU STEP OUTSIDE...
...YOU MIGHT GET A BOTTLE UPSIDE YER HEAD. I KNEW WHAT MIGHT BE OUT THERE.
FROM NOW ON, NONE 'A THIS IS ON YOU. NOT IN MY BOOK. C'MON.
TO THE BIGGEST BRAIN, TRUEST HEART AND BEST FRIEND I'VE EVER KNOWN.
SALUT.
TINK
AND TO YOU, OLD FRIEND.
BUT YOU ARE SO VERY WRONG. YOU MAY HAVE FORGIVEN ME, BEN, BUT I WILL NEVER FORGIVE MYSELF.
I KEEP SENDING ALL OF US-- MY FAMILY--OUT THERE INTO GOD KNOWS WHAT.
WELL, NO MORE. FROM NOW ON I WILL BE PREPARED FOR EVERY EVENTUALITY.
FOR MY WIFE, MY CHILDREN, YOU AND JOHNNY, I SWEAR I'LL KEEP YOU SAFE.
NO MATTER WHAT IT TAKES!
THE END

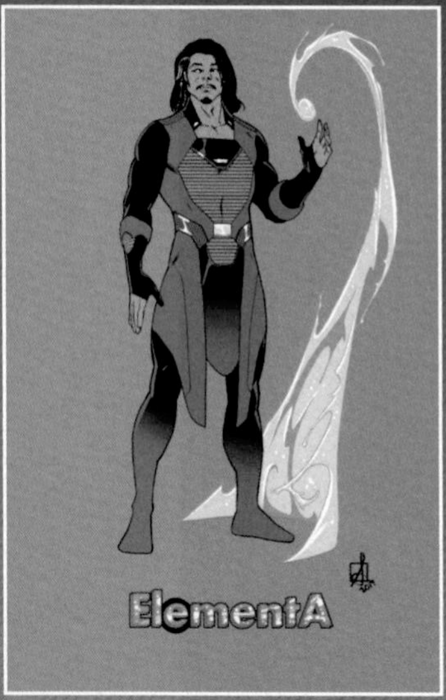
ElementA

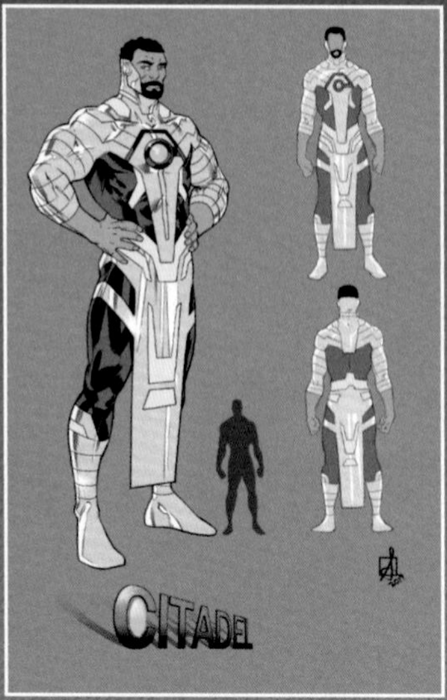
CITADEL

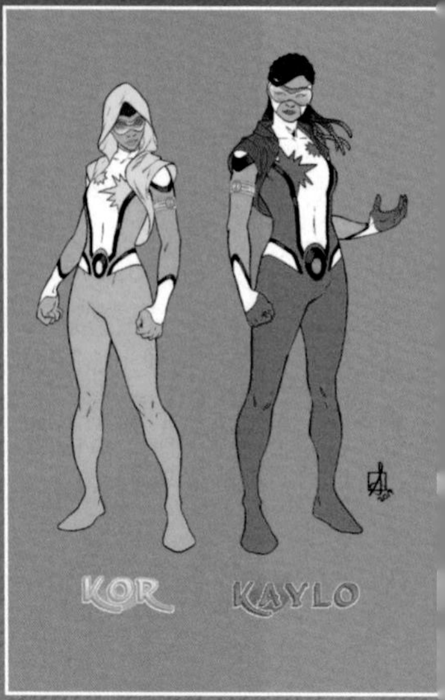
KOR
KAYLO

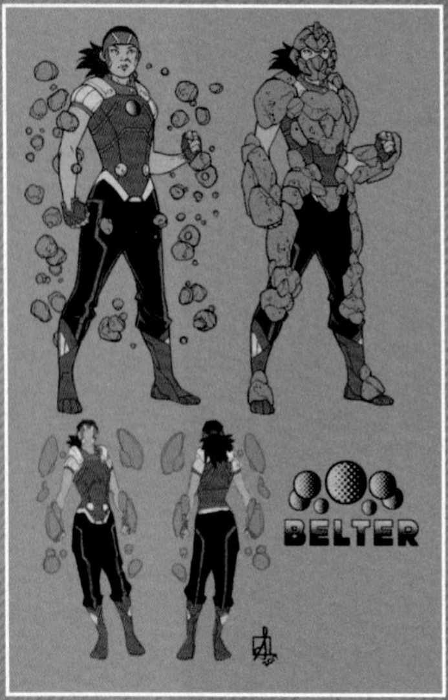
BELTER

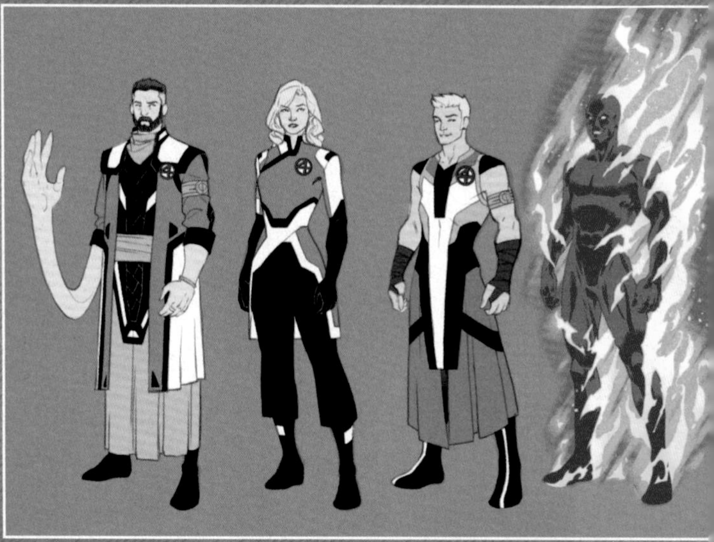

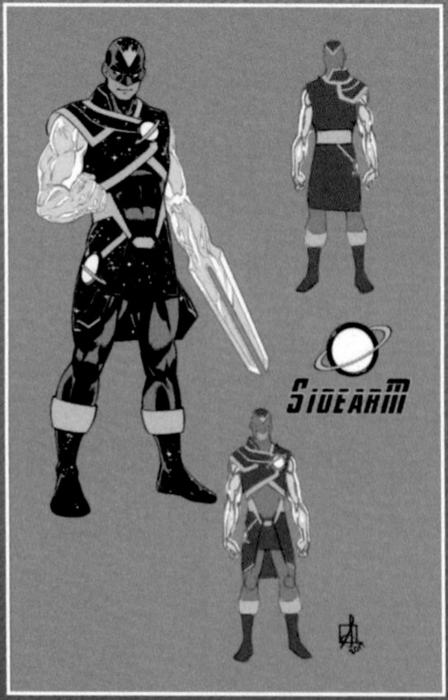
SIDEARM

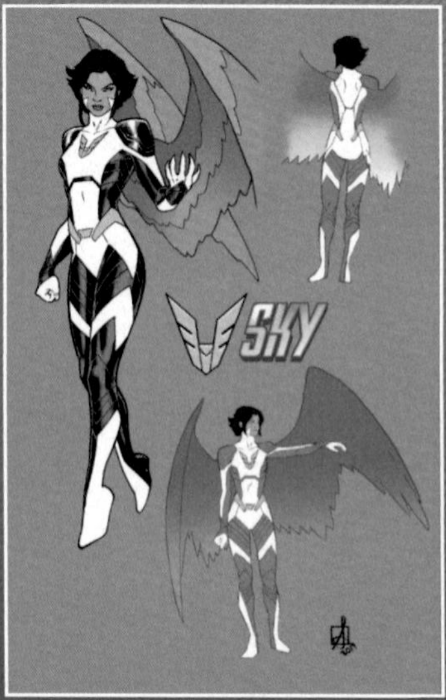
SKY

Sketches by **Sean Izaakse**

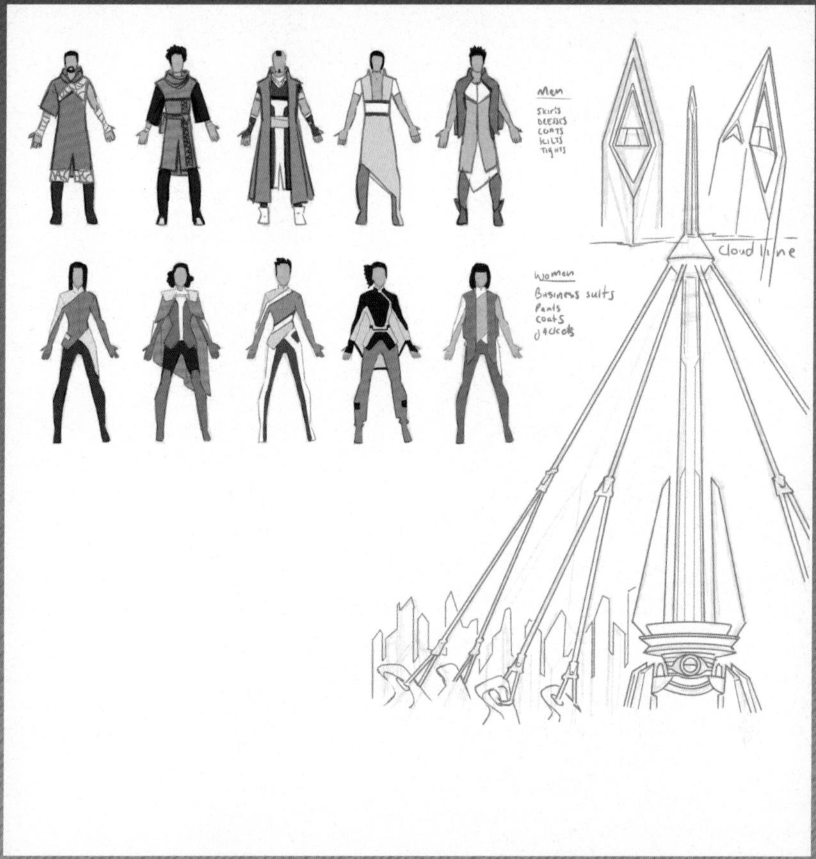
Men
Skirts
Dresses
Coats
Kilts
Tights
Women
Business suits
Pants
Coats
Jackets
Cloud line

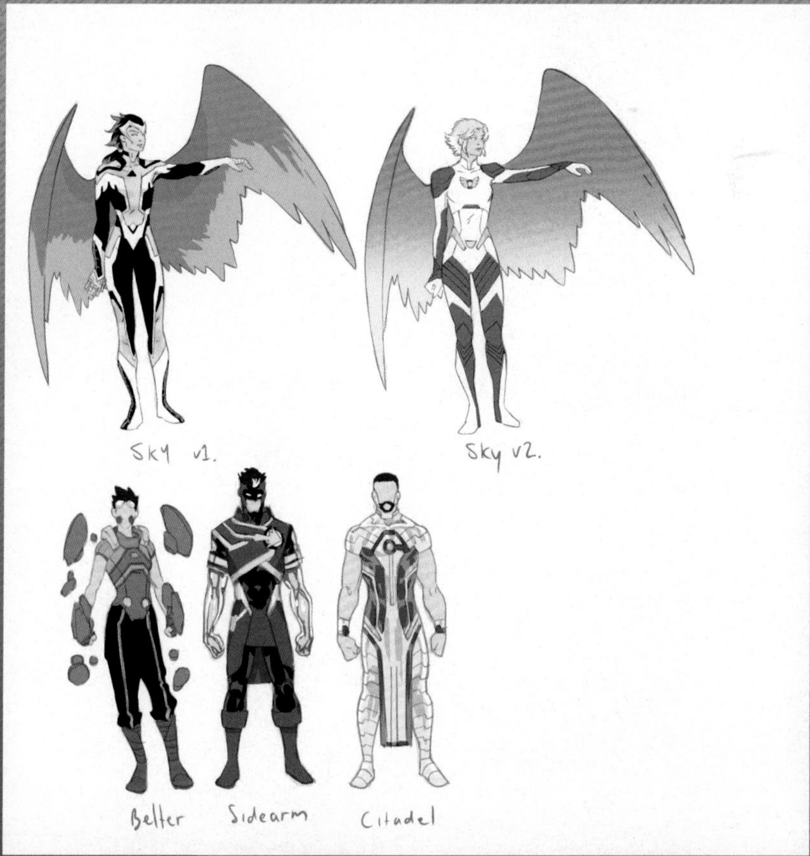
Sky v1.
Sky v2.
Belter
Sidearm
Citadel

Sketches by **Sean Izaakse**

Hi, Fantastic Fans!
If you were wondering what the FF were saying in FANTASTIC FOUR #15 while their universal translators were broken, wonder no more! Here is all of their dialogue from that issue translated back into English. Big props to those of you who built your own ciphers and code breakers to figure it all out! Clearly you guys have some serious Reed and Valeria Richards-size smarts!

PAGE 9
Panel Four
SUE (alien text): Oh my stars!
THING (alien text): Wonderful--now our ship's got its own sunroof.
REED (alien text): EVERYONE, HOLD ON!

PAGE 10
Panel One
SFX: KTAM
REED (alien text): First, THIS should stop our friend from doing more damage to our rocket!

Panel Two
KOR: Relax, Sidearm. I've got you.
SIDEARM: It's them, all right! The Four-Told of legend!
SIDEARM: The man of rocks! The one who can twist his shape--
KAYLO: Whatever they are, I doubt they can withstand the full force--of a LIVING SUN!

Panel Three
SUE (alien text): GYAHH! Force-field's holding --for now!
SUE (alien text): I don't know how long I can hold this! And THAT'S saying something.

Panel Four
BEN (alien text): Some planet. Love the way they say "hello."
JOHNNY (alien text): Yeah? Well I've got a few choice words for 'em. Two, in fact...

PAGE 11
Panel One
JOHNNY (alien text): FLAME ON!

Panel Two
SKY: It's HIM! The boy on fire.
CITADEL: The only one of the FOUR-TOLD who can fly.

Panel Three
SKY: All of you, stay back. I'll handle him.
ELEMENTA: Girl, I have WATER powers. Logically, I should--

Panel Four
SKY: NO! I have waited a LONG time for this.
SKY: He's MINE. And mine ALONE.
JOHNNY (alien text): Lady, I don't know what your deal is, but if I were you, I'd back up...
JOHNNY (alien text): ...unless you wanna get your wings SINGED.

PAGE 12
Panel One
ONLOOKER #1: Spirits above! What is it?!
ONLOOKER #2: Whatever it is, Kaylo knocked it out of the sky! That means it can't be anything GOOD.
SFX: SPSHRRCHH

Panel Two
REED (alien text): Excellent landing, Ben... given the circumstances. Sue, if you could...?
SUE (alien text): Way ahead of you, dear.
SFX: FLANG
WOMAN: There was someone inside... Look at them! They have POWERS! Like the Unparalleled!
WOMAN: Could it be...? Do you think they're...

Panel Three
BYSTANDER: It's the FOUR-TOLD!

BYSTANDER: It has to be!
SUE (alien text): What's going on? Why can't we understand them?
REED (alien text): Our universal translators aren't working.

Panel Four
THING (alien text): Peachy. So we won't have a clue as to what anybody's sayin'?

Panel Five
THING (alien text): Then again, some things ya can pick up from CONTEXT.
PERSON RUNNING AWAY: It's the monster! Made of ROCKS!
PERSON RUNNING AWAY: The legend's TRUE! The aliens will destroy us all! RUN!

PAGE 13
Panel One
BELTER: So this is IT, huh? Everything we've worked for--it's all been leading...to THIS!
BELTER: What if we SCREW UP?
CITADEL: We won't, kid. They're no different from any of the other creeps we've tangled with.
SIDEARM: That's the spirit, big guy! All that matters--
SIDEARM: --all that's EVER mattered--is fighting the GOOD FIGHT!

Panel Two
BELTER: Bit short for one of your motivational speeches, boss, but I'll take it.
THING (alien text): Hey! Cut that out! I think what we got here is a misunderstandin'.
THING (alien text): Maybe we should all just calm down and--
SIDEARM: Nice work, Belter. You know the routine. We'll keep him distracted. Citadel, you're UP!

Panel Three
SFX: FWAM
THING (alien text): UMF!

Panel Four
THING (alien text): All right, you asked for it...
THING (alien text): IT'S CLOBBERIN' TIME!
SFX: PKOWW

PAGES 14 and 15
Panel One
ELEMENTA: Overseer claims that the woman is their most powerful member.
ELEMENTA: A worthy test of MY abilities.

Panel Two
SUE (alien text): What? One of them got around me!

Panel Three
ELEMENTA: Hmm.
ELEMENTA: As if the outcome were ever in doubt.
SUE (alien text): glug

Panel Four
REED (alien text): Sue!

Panel Five
KOR: Need any help, sweetie?
KAYLO: You'd think I would...
KAYLO: ...against such a long-prophesied threat...
KAYLO: But actually? Not really. No.
REED (alien text): There are too many of them. And they're too well prepared for us...
REED (alien text): ...which raises QUITE a number of--

Panel Six
REED (JAGGED – alien text): ARHH!

Panel Seven
JOHNNY (alien text): What's wrong with me?! WHY aren't I blasting you out of the sky?!
SKY: You're holding back, aren't you? I know why.

SKY: You feel like you KNOW me.

Panel Eight
SILENT

Panel Nine
SFX: SKREE

Panel Ten
JOHNNY (alien text): Unhh...

Panel Eleven
SKY: You do.

PAGE 16
Panel One
THING (alien text): That's it!
THING (alien text): The kid gloves are OFF!

Panel Two
CITADEL: Back to the stars with you, you vile creature!
THING (alien text): YOW!
SFX: FWOK
SIDEARM: Citadel, no! You hit him too hard!
SIDEARM: He's heading OVER the BORDER WALL!
BELTER: Good! He's LOWTOWN'S problem now. That is...

Panel Three
BELTER (caption): ...if he survives the FALL.
THING (alien text): Guys? Little help here!
THING (alien text): Johnny? Suze?! REED!

Panel Four
THING (alien text): Great.
THING (alien text): Well, ain't this a revoltin' develop...

Panel Five
THING (alien text): ...mennnt!

PAGE 17
Panel One
REED (alien text): AH! There's the problem: A high level of background radiation.
REED (alien text): It's playing havoc with our universal translators.
REED (alien text): But this should--
KOR (off-panel): STOP!

Panel Two
KOR: The Overseer warned us about YOU. The super-scientist from another world--capable of ANYTHING!
KAYLO: Hands away from that device! NOW!
SUE (alien text): Hurry! I don't think I have another force-field in me!
REED (alien text): Finished.

Panel Three
REED (alien text, with the italicized words in ENGLISH): I hope *this* is *working* now. Can you *understand me?*
REED (alien text, with italicized words in ENGLISH): We're explorers. We mean you no harm. *We come in peace.*

Panel Four
REED (alien text, with italicized words in ENGLISH): *Sue, look. That did it.* They're *backing off.*
SUE (alien text, with italicized words in ENGLISH): *Really?* "We come in peace"? *Reed, this isn't* one of your old sci-fi movies.
REED (alien text, with italicized words in ENGLISH): *Trust me, dear.* Always go *with the classics.* In fact...
REED (All English now): Take me to your leader.
KOR: The aliens are speaking Spyrican now. What do we do?
KAYLO: They want an audience with the OVERSEER. I say we give them what they want. KAYLO: He'll know where to go from here.

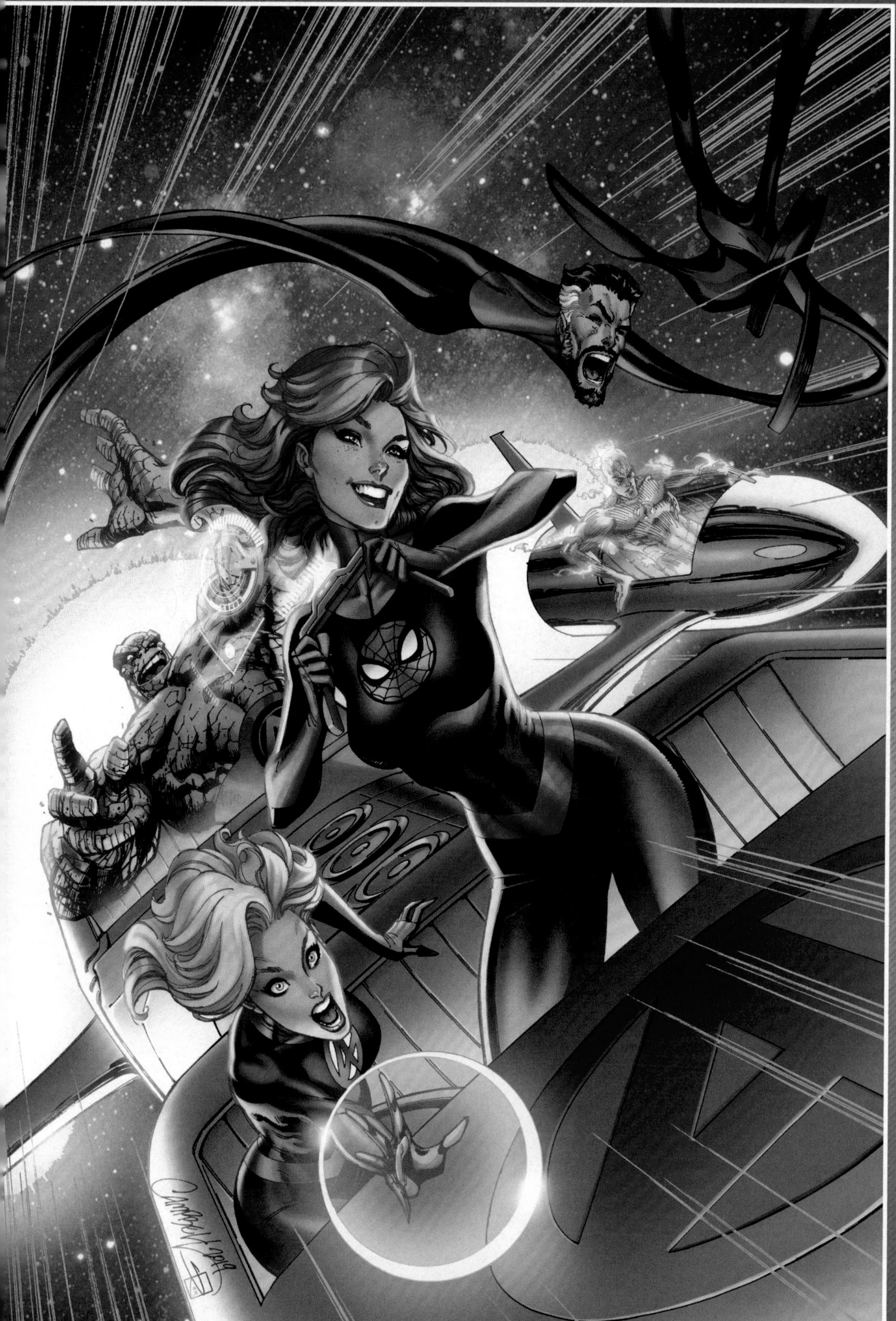

#15 Mary Jane variant by **J. Scott Campbell** & **Sabine Rich**

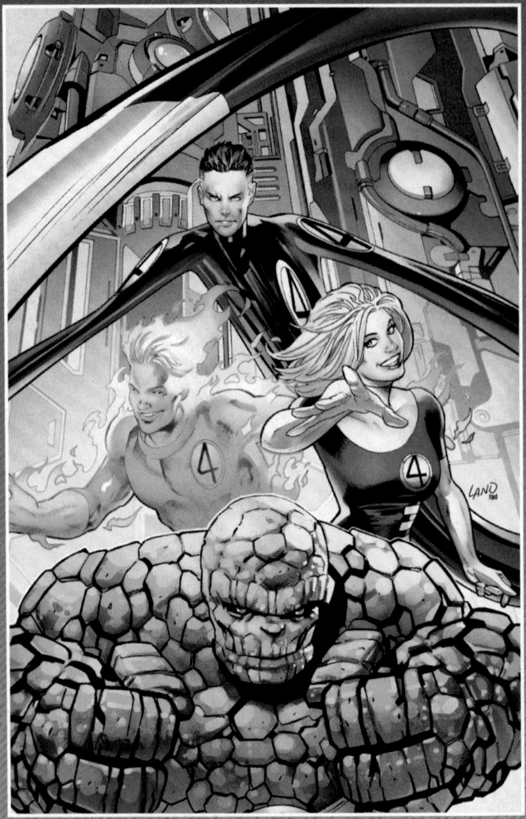

#16 2099 variant by
Greg Land & **Frank D'Armata**

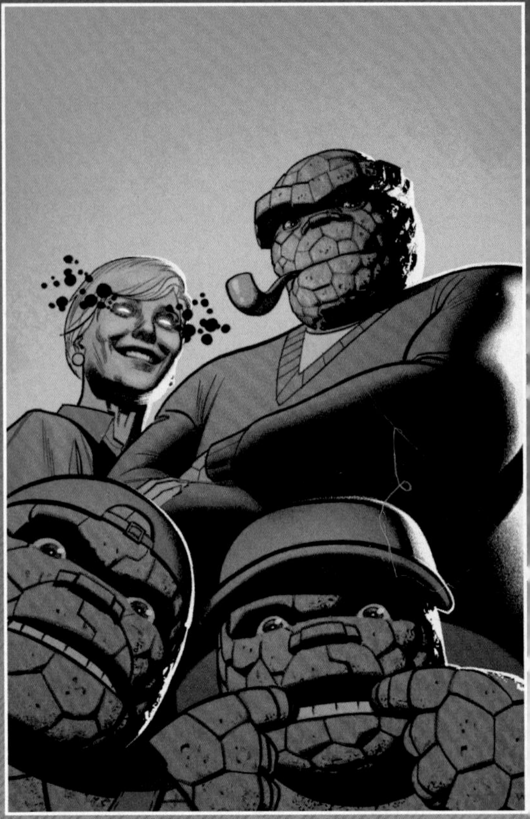

#18 Marvels X variant by
Greg Smallwood

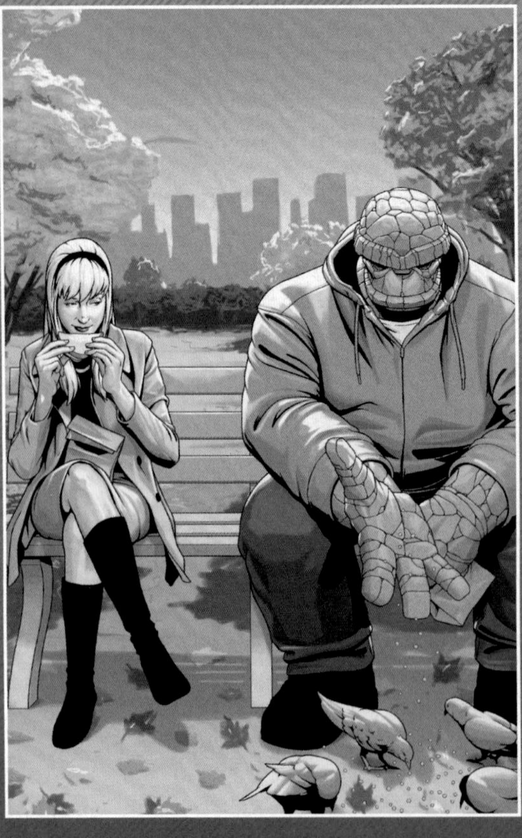

#19 Gwen Stacy variant by
John Tyler Christopher

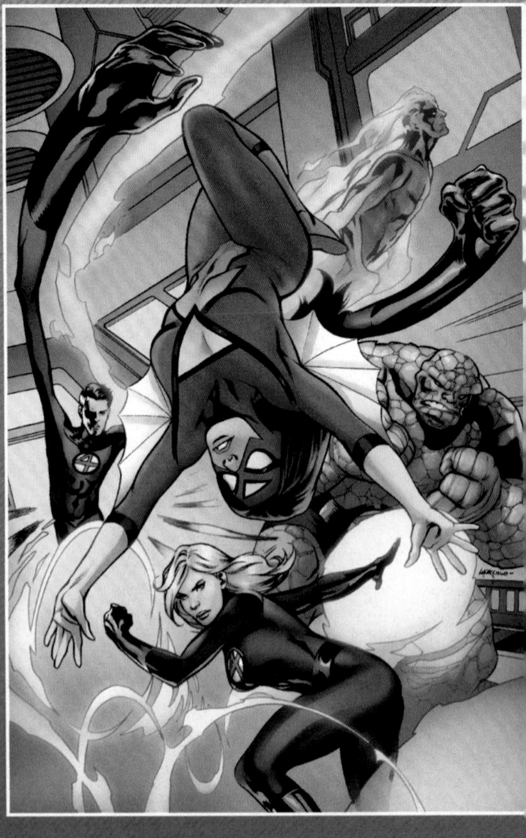

#20 Spider-Woman variant by
Ema Lupacchino & **Jason Keith**